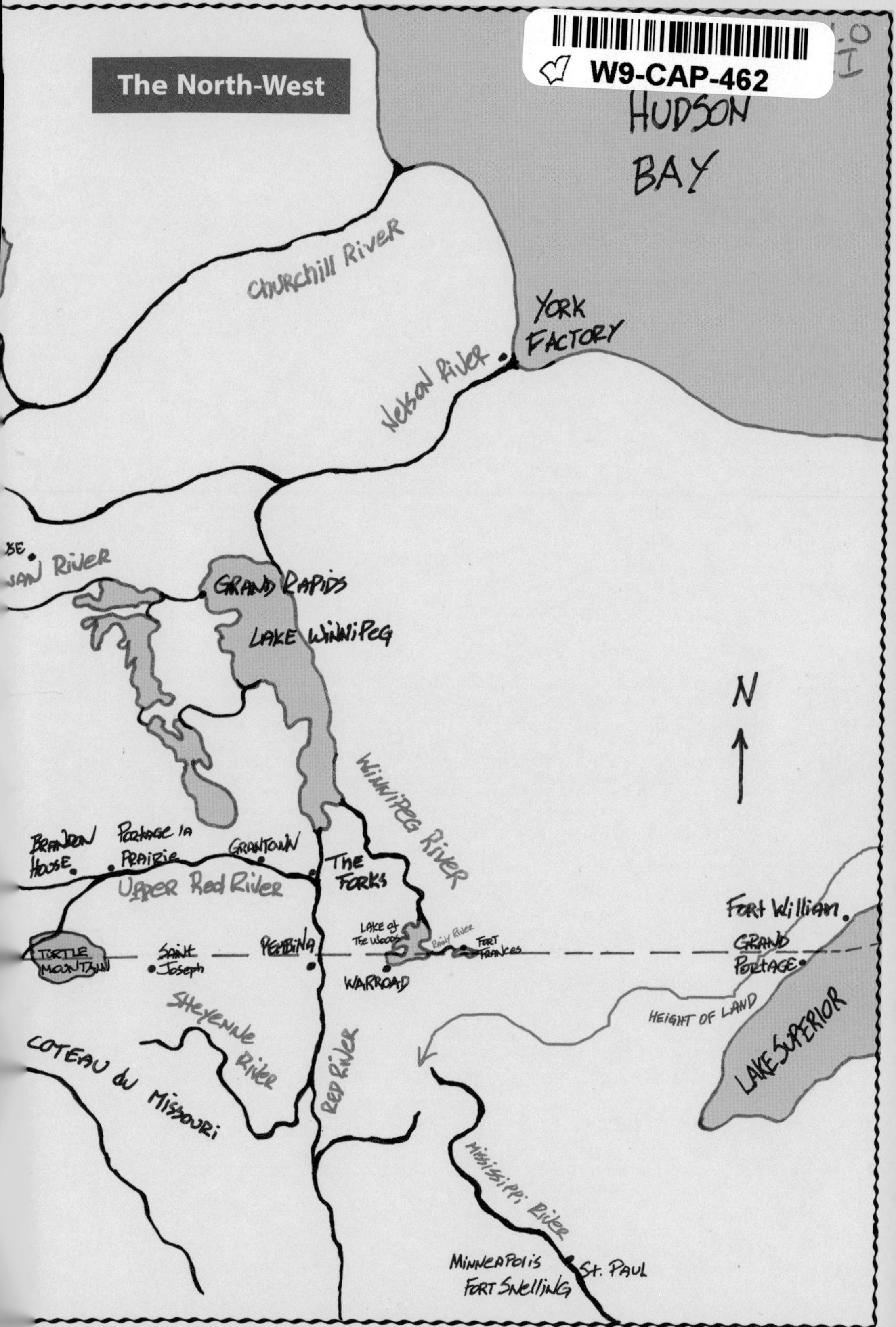

The North-West

HUDSON BAY
Churchill River
YORK FACTORY
Nelson River
SE.
WAN RIVER
GRAND RAPIDS
LAKE WINNIPEG
WINNIPEG RIVER
N
BRANDON HOUSE
Portage la PRAIRIE
GRANTOWN
THE FORKS
Upper Red River
Fort William
LAKE of The Woods
Rainy River
FORT FRANCES
TURTLE MOUNTAIN
Saint Joseph
PEMBINA
WARROAD
GRAND PORTAGE
HEIGHT OF LAND
LAKE SUPERIOR
SHEYENNE River
COTEAU du MISSOURI
RED RIVER
Mississippi River
MINNEAPOLIS
St. PAUL
FORT SNELLING

THE NORTH-WEST IS OUR MOTHER

THE NORTH-WEST IS OUR MOTHER

THE NORTH-WEST IS OUR MOTHER

THE STORY OF LOUIS RIEL'S PEOPLE, THE MÉTIS NATION

JEAN TEILLET

Patrick Crean Editions
An imprint of HarperCollins*PublishersLtd*

Published by Patrick Crean Editions, an imprint of HarperCollins Publishers Ltd

First edition

HarperCollins Publishers Ltd
Bay Adelaide Centre, East Tower
22 Adelaide Street West, 41st Floor
Toronto, Ontario, Canada
M5H 4E3

www.harpercollins.ca

All interior maps by Jean Teillet, Ed Henderson and Mike Teillet. Front endpaper map of the North-West by Jean Teillet, Ed Henderson and Mike Teillet. Back endpaper map of the Homeland of the Métis Nation courtesy of the Métis National Council.
Part-opener photographs: Library and Archives Canada, C-081767.

Library and Archives Canada Cataloguing in Publication information is available upon request.

ISBN 978-1-4434-5012-6

Printed and bound in the United States

LSC/H 9 8 7 6 5 4 3 2 1

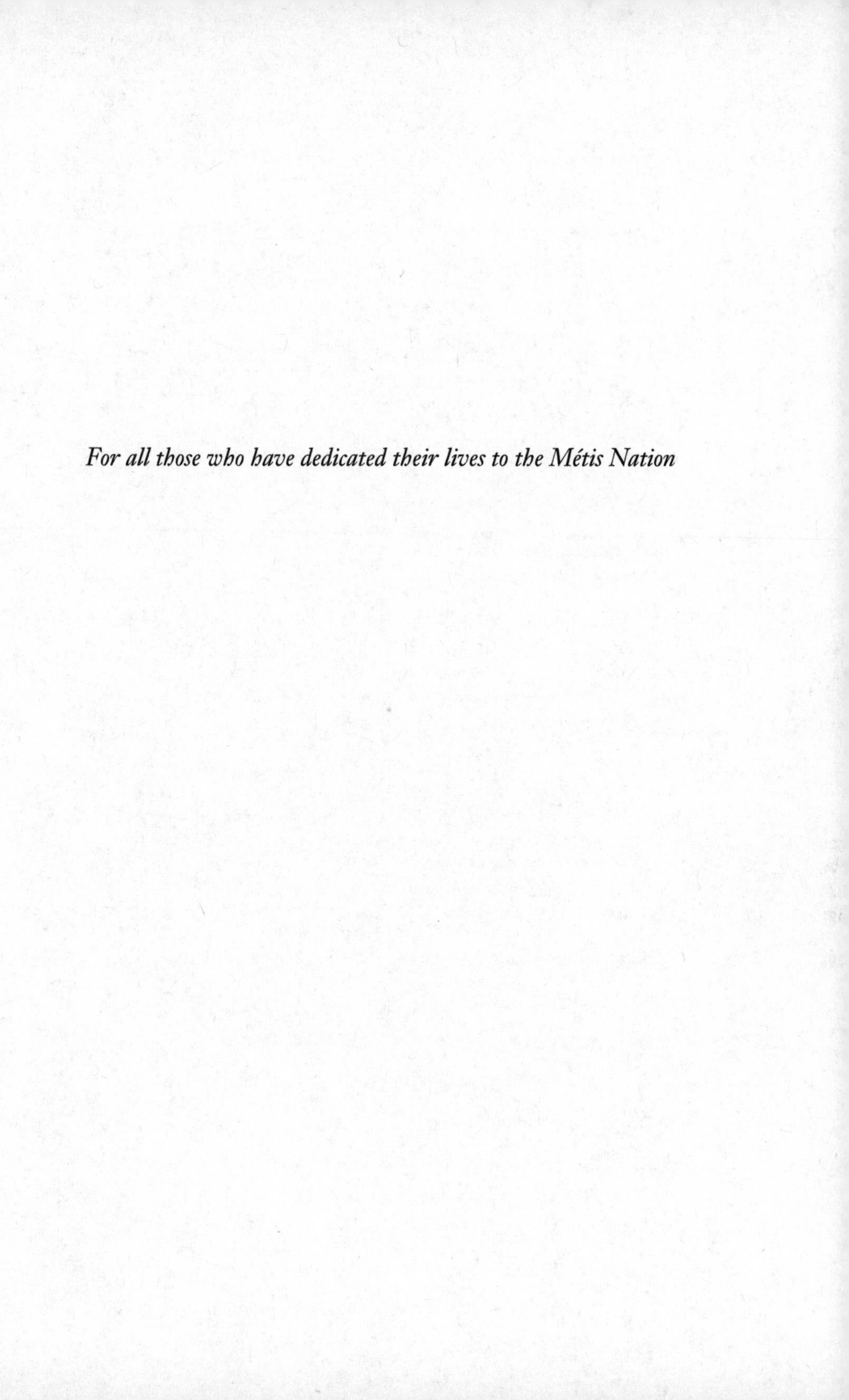

For all those who have dedicated their lives to the Métis Nation

The North-West is also my mother, it is my mother country . . .
and I am sure that my mother country will not kill me . . .
because a mother is always a mother . . .

Of all the things on earth, the motherland is the most important
and sacred to us because we inherited it from our ancestors.

—Louis Riel

Contents

List of Maps

Introduction

THE PEOPLE

This is a history of one of the Indigenous peoples of the Canadian North-West, the Métis Nation. Canadians are generally familiar with one of the Métis Nation's great leaders, Louis Riel. Most know Riel was hanged for treason; very few can articulate what Riel did that was so wrong. For some, references to the Métis raise foggy recollections from school history lessons about the voyageurs, the fur trade and the buffalo hunters. But how that history ties together with the Métis is a mystery for most. Who are the Métis anyway? Aren't they just people who have some Indian ancestry? What makes them a nation? Are they still around? The answers to all of these questions are in this book.

This narrative begins in the 1790s and follows the Métis Nation's history right up to 2018. For over two hundred years, the Métis Nation has insisted on its existence as an Indigenous people and a nation. Throughout those two centuries, the Métis Nation has fought—on the battlefield, in the courts and at the negotiation table—for recognition, protection of their lands and resources, and for their very existence. Their long battle is also central to the development of Canada, particularly in the North-West.

Despite this, confusion remains about who they are. While Louis Riel has retained a prominent place in the Canadian imagination, the low historical profile of his people remains an intriguing quirk of Canadian history. In some ways this is because the people in this history walked lightly on the land, at least in terms of their physical effect on the geography. *Lii vyeu*, their "old ones," left little physical evidence behind other than beautiful fabrics decorated with thread, quills and beads—until recently, nothing the curators of the world's museums would call "art."[1] They left monuments dedicated to their heroes, and some of their cart tracks are still visible in a few places. But with few exceptions the physical structures the old ones built have returned to the earth. Until the twentieth century theirs was an oral culture, so most of what remains are songs, dances and stories.

The Métis lived lives of constant movement, and their songs and stories reflect that mobility. Their songs are celebrations, satiric comments or laments. Their stories contain little reflection or contemplation. Most of the stories the Métis tell and retell are the stories of their own history. Today they delight in placing their direct ancestors into the old stories. They introduce themselves proudly as descendants of their famous heroes—as a Dumont, Lépine, Grant or Riel. Referencing their ancestors places them instantly in the Métis Nation's historiography. This is how the Métis Nation defines its citizens. Their stories and their motherland form the demarcation line between those who are of the Métis Nation and those who are not. Only the descendants of those who lived those stories within the geographic boundaries of their motherland are part of the historic Métis Nation.

THE PLACE

The North-West is the birthplace and motherland of the Métis Nation. The historic North-West was more of a perspective than a geographic place with fixed boundaries. The name provokes one to ask, North of what? West of where? The North-West was always the land north and west of Montreal. As the centuries passed the North-West shifted and shrank, always farther north and farther west. By the time the first generation of the Métis Nation was being born in the 1790s, the North-West began at the height of land west of Lake Superior.

In the 1790s the North-West was an endless stretch of land with delicious food, clean water and rich resources. The lakes and rivers were the highways. The furbearers in the forests and the great herds of buffalo on the Plains were gifts from the land. The parklands and boreal forest provided shelter, water, wood, fish and meat. The old ones thought of the North-West as a mother who protected them and provided for them. They called the North-West their motherland. She was a thousand miles of plenty and in her hands she held the "storehouses of the good God."[2]

THE SOURCES

In the traditional way of the Métis, I place myself into the Métis Nation's historiography and introduce myself. I come from three Métis Nation families. I am a Riel, a Poitras and a Grant. I am a great-grandniece of Louis Riel. My paternal grandmother was Sara Riel. Sara's father, my great-grandfather, was Joseph Riel, Louis Riel's younger brother. Sara's mother, my great-grandmother, was Eleanor Poitras, the granddaughter of Cuthbert Grant's sister Marguerite. I was born in Red River, as were several generations of my family. Every generation of my family has played a role in the stories and history of the Métis Nation. As one of the Métis Nation's legal warriors and in writing this story, I too am playing my part in the ongoing history of the Métis Nation.

Some of what I have written in these pages comes from my family stories. I was raised to be proud of being a Riel—very proud—and that was at a time when most Canadians viewed the Métis as dirty drunks and Riel as a treasonous madman. Some of what I know also comes from family papers. While many of those papers are now in the public archives, some remain within the family and the stories they tell are incorporated into this book.

I write this history also as one of the Métis Nation's lawyers. Over the past twenty-five years, I, along with other Métis legal warriors, have been putting the history of Canada on trial.[3] As a defence lawyer in many Métis rights cases, I have litigated the history of the Métis Nation and in so doing have challenged the accepted history of the settlement of this country. Most of those Métis rights trials were a contest over access to the lands and resources of the Canadian North-West. Some of what I have learned of the history of the Métis Nation is informed by my experiences in the courts litigating that history. In the course of preparing for many trials, I have read hundreds of thousands of primary source documents and dozens of expert historical and anthropological reports. I have also conducted over two hundred interviews with Métis Nation citizens.

One challenge that has become apparent through my litigation experience and in writing this history is that some of this ground has been covered by historians who wrote largely in reliance on primary source documents produced by priests, fur traders, explorers, tourists and the British and Canadian governments. Though many of those documents were written at the time of the event or shortly thereafter, they must be read cautiously, because they rarely tell the Métis side of the story. The existing records that produced those histories, and the histories themselves, are anything but neutral and unbiased.

One priest called the Métis the "one-and-a-half men . . . half Indian, half white and half devil."[4] Historian Alexander Begg described the Métis as "wild and improvident in their nature . . . often the tools of their superiors."[5] Anthropologist Marcel Giraud claimed the Métis could be characterized by their "propensity for introversion . . . lack of conviction . . . and absence of a clearly defined morality."[6] Another historian, George Stanley, starts his history (still considered a standard text) by describing the Métis as "indolent, thoughtless and improvident, unrestrained in their desires, restless, clannish and vain";[7] and then there is Thomas Flanagan, the political scientist who regretted what he sees as the error of including the Métis as one of the "aboriginal peoples of Canada" in the Constitution Act, 1982, and found their justice to be "morally repugnant."[8] The fact that these versions of history have until very recently been accepted uncritically as *the* history tells us much about the writers and Canada but little about the Métis Nation.

Having now drawn attention to these other histories, I lay out my own perspectives. I have tried to present this history from the perspective of the Métis Nation. I have tried to place myself in the footsteps of the old ones and to walk with them as I tell their stories. In each situation I asked myself: What did the Métis know at the time? What did they want? What were they thinking? Why did they act as they did? Knowing what they thought and understood, how does this all fit together? What does it tell us about them? It is my contention that the evidence contradicts the message in the standard histories that the Métis were not a nation, were thoughtless, without morals and lacking in conviction, and were never agents in their own cause. I believe, and it is my hope that this book proves, there is a better way to understand the history of the Métis Nation, one that is well supported by the evidence in the historical record. The stories in this book are meant to add a Métis perspective to the Canadian historical knowledge about the Métis Nation. It is my hope that any errors and any differences of perspective in these stories will initiate a dialogue that will enrich the history of this country. Many fine people contributed to the facts and the perspective in this book, but they are responsible for none of the errors. That responsibility is all mine.

This book contains the best-known stories of the Métis Nation as well as some forgotten ones. There are thousands of stories that, for lack of space, I have had to leave out. In telling these stories I have tried to use Métis words where they are available. I have also tried to include the stories of Métis women wherever I could find them. It has been a somewhat daunting task. Until the 1850s the words of the Métis were rarely recorded, and women's stories are mostly lost. I have used whatever I could find.

Writing this history has also raised some family ghosts. I am writing this history and these stories one hundred years after my grandfather Camille Teillet worked on the first history of the Métis Nation published by the Métis, *Histoire de la Nation Métisse dans l'Ouest Canadien*.[9] This book and the book my grandfather helped to publish both begin in the Riel House parlour in 1909. That house is now a Canadian national historic site. It is named Riel House, which suggests to the average person that it was Louis Riel's house. But Louis never lived there. It was my great-grandfather Joseph's house. Like the histories I mentioned earlier, names that are other-ascribed must also be approached with caution.

Both books begin in Riel House in 1909 because it was a turning point; the day the Métis Nation decided to write its own history. Why was this so important to them? Because the old ones had been silenced after their defeat in the North-West Resistance. Their brothers and sisters, fathers and mothers had given their lives for dreams and ideas that were not politically possible in their time. But the Métis men who met in my great-grandfather's parlour in 1909 took the long view. They vowed to keep those ideas and dreams alive. They were working toward the day when their dreams for the Métis Nation would become politically inevitable. For that to happen, they knew that their history had to be written down. They knew the future of the Métis Nation would stand on its past. They wrote that history for the generations to come.

So by way of commemoration of that turning point, in the spring of 2017, my family gathered in that parlour once again. On that May afternoon, as I read a bit from an early draft of this book to the assembled Riel descendants, I could feel our ancestors hovering, I like to think, with approval. And I think I'm right about that. I think they would approve of us because we still care about the things they fought and died for.

This book is the story of the Métis Nation. It is not the story of the many mixed-race individuals in the North-West who chose to join or identify as members of the tribes or those who did not identify as members of the Métis Nation. It is not the story of those individuals who lost their Indian Act status. It is not the story of any mixed-race individuals or Métis groups who live in other parts of Canada. This book is the story of a people who, for two hundred years, have been animated by the idea that they are a Métis collective, an Indigenous people called the Métis Nation. It is the story of when the Métis Nation acted as a collective in its own interests.

The story is set out in five movements, each defined by resistance against historical adversaries who changed over the centuries but can be identified as the Selkirk Settlers, the Hudson's Bay Company, the Canadian Party, the Orange Lodge and the Canadian state. A new adversary has recently appeared on the horizon: race-shifters, individuals in eastern Canada asserting a new identity as "Métis." Some are claiming the Métis Nation extends to Quebec and the Maritimes and are appropriating Métis Nation symbols.[10] These individuals assert that a single drop of Indigenous ancestry, sometimes originating three hundred years in the past, is enough to recast themselves as a Métis culture. This is a new challenge for the Métis Nation and it has already had to defend itself in court from these new groups.[11] It is a battle that will play out in the future. But the race-shifters can be identified as another adversary that will force the Métis Nation to defend its existence and to resist with collective action.

As it travelled on its long resistance road, the Métis Nation carved out a unique identity as an intensely political creature. The Métis of the North-West have always called themselves a nation. Their stories are of great battles for rights, their life of freedom, their dispossession and diaspora, their heroes and villains, and always their resistance to any who would fail to recognize them as an Indigenous nation. Their stories and songs are of their ongoing fight to stay and prosper in the North-West, the land they love, their motherland.

The identity of the Métis Nation has also been forged in juxtaposition to Canada's development as a nation. Sir John A. Macdonald tried twice to crush the Métis Nation out of existence, once in 1870 and again in 1885. It is certainly true that the Métis Nation was a thorn in his side. Perhaps he tried to eliminate them because the Métis Nation, by its very nature (a strong, fiercely independent, well-armed group with an inherent military nature, able leadership and collective political instincts), posed too great a threat to the fledgling nation that was Canada. Canada's own embryonic identity had no room for another collective. Canada could not then envision itself as a federation that included powerful Indigenous nations. Canada would swallow land, water, resources and immigrants, but it would not, in its early days, permit a collective, especially one with the collective nature and power of the Métis Nation, to exist.

It is a lesson in politics and history that Canada's attempts to eliminate the Métis Nation have only succeeded in reinforcing its collective identity. The Métis Nation absorbed the blows but never gave up its collective identity as a nation. Today its identity as a distinct nation is stronger than it was in Riel's day. It shows no signs of disappearing.

A NOTE ABOUT LANGUAGE

The names of the Indigenous peoples in this book have changed over time. "Indians," "natives," "Aboriginal" and "Indigenous" are all terms used to describe the First Nations, Inuit and Métis peoples of Canada. I have generally tried to use the term "Indigenous" to describe these people when referring to them overall. But all of these terms will appear in this history.

Many geographic place names have changed over time as well. Indigenous names were replaced by French names, which were subsequently anglicized. The Catholic Church also renamed places after the churches they erected. So one place could have three or four names. I have tried to simplify this place naming.

The names of individuals in this book also change. The Métis Nation was an oral culture until the beginning of the twentieth century. Individuals often had more than one name and spellings vary wildly. I have simply picked one name and one spelling, usually the one that appears most often in the records.

Finally, I have tried to add a small introduction to Michif, the Métis Nation language.

THE NORTH-WEST IS OUR MOTHER

PART ONE

THE BIRTH OF THE NATION

CHAPTER I

THE OLD WOLVES

In 1909 the leaders of the Métis Nation met in Joseph Riel's home in St. Vital, Manitoba. These were the men who survived the Red River Resistance of 1869–70 and the North-West Resistance of 1885. With them that evening were their younger siblings and some younger men, the next generation of Métis. These men who met in 1909 have many names: *les anciens, lii vyeu, les fidèles à Riel.*[1] In this book they are the Old Wolves.

The men gathered at Joseph's home that night were on a mission to tell the truth—they would have called it God's truth—about their people, the Métis Nation of the Canadian North-West. They were gathered that night for one purpose. They wanted to carve out a strategy that would counter the many stories of the Métis Nation and Louis Riel that were being printed in the Canadian media and books of their day. For the Old Wolves these stories were illegitimate and one-sided, a propaganda campaign that justified the government's denial of the Métis Nation's existence and the dispossession of the Métis from their lands.

That night the Old Wolves vowed to take action. They vowed to tell their own stories and rebut inaccuracies and attacks on the Métis Nation. They were determined to keep the Nation alive by commemorating Louis Riel, promoting their Michif language and defending Métis Nation rights. They would tell their history as they knew it and as their people had experienced it.

They were already taking action. In 1887 they had established the Union Nationale Métisse Saint-Joseph, an organization intended to keep the Nation alive.[2] In 1889 they were inspired to continue in their efforts when Gabriel Dumont, one of their famous hunters and military leaders, visited St. Vital and encouraged them to keep up the fight for Métis rights. In 1891 they erected a monument on Louis Riel's grave. In 1910 they created a new national flag and a national historical committee.[3] It is impossible to miss the constant references to "nation" and "national" in their institutions. They have always considered themselves a political entity, a nation.

The Old Wolves created a historical committee charged with telling their story. They focused their efforts on what Canadians call the "Riel Rebellions." They hated the word "rebellion." To their minds a "rebellion" was a group of people who took up arms to separate from the country or to overthrow or undermine the government. This, the Métis Nation had never done. They had taken up arms only to defend their lands and their rights. They never believed fighting for their rights was a rebellion, and this was a distinction they insisted on; it mattered deeply to them. In a letter published in *Le Devoir* in 1913, Joseph Riel chastised Henri Bourassa for just that transgression. Joseph insisted that the Métis were "fighting for their rights and never wanted independence or annexation to the United States, and it is not fitting for the grandson of the great Papineau to talk of struggles in such a good cause as 'rebellions.'"[4]

The Old Wolves and Union Nationale Métisse, 28th anniversary of the hanging of Louis Riel, November 16, 1913 (*Société Historique de Saint-Boniface 14482*)

Such an objection might not seem, in this day, to be anything out of the ordinary. But the Métis still vividly remembered their defeat at Batoche, the final battle in the North-West Resistance of 1885. So objecting to the term "rebellion" was a calculated decision.[5] The defeated are not supposed to throw pebbles at the victors, not even forty years later. A deferential manner is expected. But wolves are not deferential. It's not in their nature.

It took time for the historical committee to gather their facts and to work with the legacy of fear and silence that continued to oppress their people. When Canada hanged Louis Riel on November 16, 1885, their best and brightest voice, all the Métis voices fell silent. Silence was the price of defeat. But in the minds of the Old Wolves, that silence roared with injustice. Their bones were waxing old but they would not go silent to their graves.

The committee's first public foray was a recounting of their history of 1869 to 1870, the Red River Resistance. Guillaume Charette, the Métis Nation's "Old Storyteller," also a historian and lawyer, spoke to a shocked audience at the Jesuit college in St. Boniface on November 25, 1923.[6] They were shocked because, as the editor of the *Queen's Quarterly* in Kingston, Ontario, would later write,

> [T]he public of our country is not yet prepared to face frankly the facts . . . and those of us who are interested in the ultimate victory of truth must be content with slow and gradual progress in that direction . . . the opinion in Ontario . . . has been largely tinged by the reports sent East by such men as Charles Mair . . . and . . . Toronto papers such as the *Globe*, created an attitude of mind which succeeding years have not been able to modify substantially.[7]

In 1931 when the editor of *La Liberté* began to regurgitate all the old lies about the rebellions and labelled the Métis defence of their rights as criminal and crazy, the Old Wolves called an assembly of all the Manitoba Métis to debate how they would respond.

The Old Wolves decided to publish their own history of the Métis Nation. The historical committee began to take sworn declarations from Métis survivors, the men still alive who had played key roles in the Red River Resistance of 1869–70 and in the North-West Resistance of 1885. There are affidavits taken in 1909, and twice in 1929 the committee visited Batoche, the site of the last battle in the North-West Resistance. Virtually the whole town came to their community meetings. They hired Auguste de Trémaudan to be the author of their history.

The Old Wolves left their papers and notes behind. There are copies of Louis Riel's writings and Métis Nation meeting minutes from the early 1870s. There are sworn declarations from Métis. There are attempts to organize the facts of the resistance movements and to answer the questions that would eventually form the appendix to Trémaudan's book, a 1930s version of FAQs (frequently asked questions). The committee's original intention was to publish a simple narrative followed by a complete work supported with references. Unfortunately, Trémaudan died before he completed his task. It was a terrible setback, but the historical committee stubbornly kept editing Trémaudan's work for years.

The committee exercised great control over the content of Trémaudan's history book while he was alive. They demanded that he tone down some of the language in the book. It was not that they disagreed with what he wrote, but they wanted Canadians to hear their story. If the tone was bitter, too accusatory or just too anti-English, Canadians would not listen. Trémaudan resisted this instruction. He thought the book should be a direct attack on *lii Canadas*, the Canadian Party who so violently stole the North-West away from the Métis Nation. But the historical committee insisted that Trémaudan sweeten his words. The published version of the book describes the Canadian Party as a "band of cheats, criminals and thieves."[8] That is the toned-down version!

The historical committee understood the power of words. They knew that in addition to countering the "rebel" label, they had to counter the claim that Riel was insane. The Métis have always seen Riel as a man of God, a prophet and a great leader who was dedicated to his people and did everything in his power to help them. For the Métis, Riel's sanity has never been particularly relevant. Still, the Old Wolves knew the Canadian obsession with Riel's sanity. They knew that if Riel was labelled insane, his actions and the cause he fought for could be dismissed. This they would not allow. Louis Riel was their greatest leader, a comet that appeared on the horizon in 1868, shone brightly for seventeen years and flamed out in 1885. The Riel years have left an indelible mark on the Métis Nation, which now mostly describes itself as Riel's people. Though the Riel years are the best-known parts of the Métis Nation's history, they are only a small part of a history that really began in the 1790s and continues today.

On July 9, 1935, the Old Wolves proudly announced the forthcoming publication of their book, *Histoire de la Nation Métisse dans l'Ouest Canadien*, at an annual Métis gathering of over two thousand members of the Union Nationale Métisse.[9]

> For 27 years the members of that Committee stuck together and worked consistently and arduously with the one and almost unique object in mind: The publication of what they considered a true version of . . . history. Old ones dropped out or disappeared, but new ones replaced them and kept on going and working stubbornly. Many of them cherished the idea of reading the book, their history, the history they themselves made and really wrote with their blood and sacrifices. At the same time their children and grand-children are proud and justly so of their deeds . . .[10]

Until that book was published, the Métis Nation's history was passed down orally. These are the stories they told their children and grandchildren. They are the stories most Métis still know and tell today.

The Old Wolves' book is mainly concerned with two Métis Nation resistance movements, the Red River Resistance of 1869–70 and the North-West Resistance of 1885. This book covers that same ground but benefits from access to new analyses and evidence. It also attempts to fill in more detail of the early years leading up to the Red River Resistance and continues the story of this new nation, the Métis Nation of the Canadian North-West, into the twenty-first century.

CHAPTER 2

THE VOYAGEURS

SOCIAL GLUE

Glue. That is what we need to find in order to understand the beginnings of the Métis Nation. Not the white glue children use to paste pictures in school. This is a search for social glue, the circumstances, values and dreams that bound individuals so tightly that they began to see themselves as a separate and distinct collective entity. The social glue that originally bound people together to create ancient cultures is often buried deep in history and predates our written accounts and historical memories. This is not the case for the culture that named itself *la nouvelle nation* in 1816 and now calls itself the Métis Nation. The social glue that originally bound these people together has not been lost in the mists of history. It can be traced directly to the voyageurs—not all the voyageurs, but a subset of the voyageurs, the men of the north who married First Nation women and then "went free" in the Canadian North-West with their new families. This is where we find the social glue that created the Métis Nation.

The men of the north are the voyageur fathers of the Métis Nation. They occupy a rich and romantic spot in Canadian history. They are depicted as larger than life, courageous and powerful men who braved wild animals, freezing waters, abominable weather and starvation. They boldly voyaged where no Euro-Canadians had gone before.

The voyageurs were their own best promoters. They were famous for their stories and songs. Around the campfires at night, they would boast about their horses, canoes, friends and dogs. In their songs and stories, they celebrated their exploits, tragedies and famous deeds. Storytelling was a voyageur tradition, and exaggeration played no small part in those stories. So, the wolves and bears were gigantic, vicious monsters handled with cool expertise. Storms were always hurricane force, and any loss was a tragedy of such magnitude that it moved them all to tears. No matter that they had heard all the stories before. No matter that one man claimed to be the hero in a gallant deed one night and another man claimed the same part the next night.

This story tradition was consistent with the oral traditions of other peoples around the world. The voyageurs knew what this was all about. They never confused their tales with fact, but as consummate actors they believed them passionately during the performance. Other observers, especially the English, were cynical about the voyageur storytelling tradition, thought it all childish lies and failed to appreciate the art. But for the voyageurs, the telling of their stories, and especially the performance of them, confirmed their traditions, their uniqueness and the essence of who they were. They were voyageurs. As they said, they lived hard, slept hard and ate dogs.[1]

The term "voyageur" originally described all the explorers, fur-traders and travellers in the North-West. Later it came to describe only the boatmen and canoeists. The *mangeurs de lard* or pork-eaters (named after the main food they ate) were the voyageurs plying the large boats on the Great Lakes and the St. Lawrence River. *Les hommes du nord*, the northmen, paddled smaller craft into the lands northwest of the Great Lakes. It is the northmen who are of interest to this history.

THE VOYAGEUR HIGHWAY

The routes the voyageurs travelled are called the "voyageur highway." The voyageurs gradually pushed the highway up the St. Lawrence River and into the Great Lakes region. Until the 1780s the Great Lakes area and what is now northern Quebec and Ontario supplied many of the furs. At that time there were approximately thirty thousand people in the Great Lakes. As the voyageurs intermarried with the Great Lakes Indigenous peoples a new group of Métis, dedicated to the fur trade, began to appear. By the 1790s, the areas surrounding the upper Great Lakes had been trapped out. The Nor'Westers relocated their main trade depot to the western edge of Lake Superior. Now the North-West began on the height of land west of Lake Superior. It was on this height of land that a voyageur took a vow of loyalty to his brothers and was baptized into the elite of the voyageurs—the northmen.

The period between 1790 and 1821 was a time of great change. The War of 1812, a new American border, over-trapping in the lands surrounding the Great Lakes, and an American law prohibiting anyone other than an American citizen from trading in the United States caused a great reorganization of the peoples of the Great Lakes. In 1821 the two great rival fur trade companies merged. Since 1670 the Hudson's Bay Company had held a British charter of incorporation. For years its employees, mostly Orkneymen, "slept by the bay"—the Hudson Bay that is—and waited for Indigenous people to bring furs to them.

They moved inland to seek out furs only in response to competition from a group of Montreal traders who eagerly ventured out into the North-West. The Montreal traders were loosely organized and generally known as the North West Company or the Nor'Westers. The two companies engaged in a vicious fur-trade war, which only ended in 1821 when they were forced to merge under the name of the Hudson's Bay Company.

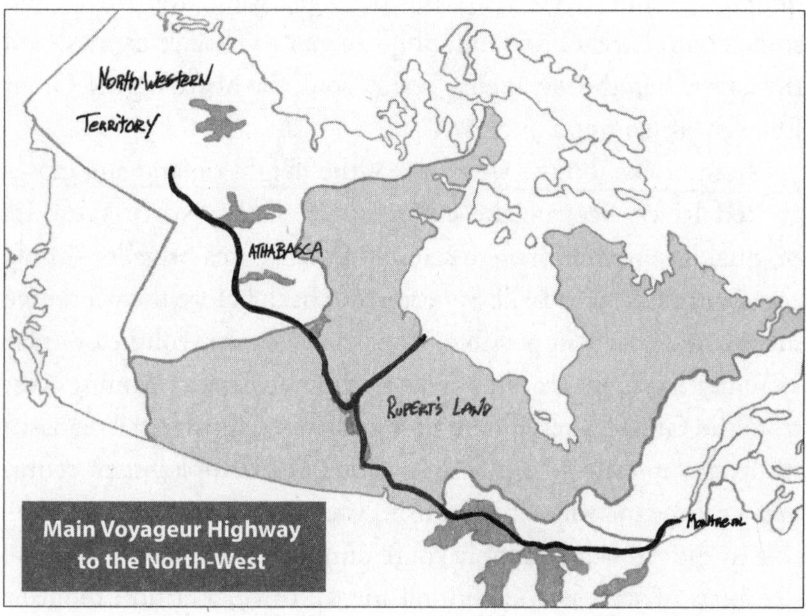

Main Voyageur Highway to the North-West

These events caused trade patterns to shift and people to relocate. By 1820 those who wanted to continue the life of freedom and independence offered by the fur trade had begun to leave the Great Lakes. Métis families like the Nolins, originally from the Great Lakes, relocated to Red River.[2] Some Métis men, the Sayers and Cadottes, traded in and out of the North-West, but the numbers of men who moved between the Great Lakes and the North-West dwindled.

From the 1790s until the merger in 1821, men travelled regularly from Montreal to Red River and beyond. But the merger changed everything. After the merger the new Hudson's Bay Company shipped through Hudson Bay, and the voyageur highway no longer criss-crossed the Great Lakes. Red River began to assume more importance, and the connections between the North-West and the Great Lakes, once so solid, rapidly deteriorated. Within a few years the portages were overgrown and some could barely be found. Ships began to replace canoes, and the days when the voyageurs' songs could be heard on the Great Lakes were ending.

Rainy Lake, on the west side of the height of land and closer to Red River, became the eastern gate of the North-West. Its original importance arose because the Athabasca brigades simply could not make it to Lake Superior and back before the winter ice made canoe travel impossible. The brigades came southeast as far as Rainy Lake, where they were met by voyageurs coming west from the Great Lakes. There they exchanged furs from Athabasca for fresh supplies. The post also served as an employment centre and a source for wild rice and fish. After the merger, Rainy Lake's role in the Athabasca supply route diminished. Instead it became the focus of intense competition for wild rice, a critical food for the traders. Wild rice, geography, family ties and proximity to Red River kept Rainy Lake on the voyageur highway, in the North-West and within the boundaries of the Métis Nation.

The voyageur highway played a crucial role in the development of the Métis Nation. It was the artery that connected the people to the land and to each other.

At their peak, before 1821, there were over five thousand voyageurs. They were a culture unto themselves, and although it may seem too obvious to point out, the culture was all male;

there were no female voyageurs. The voyageur brotherhood was Catholic and French Canadian, mostly from the parishes between Trois-Rivières and Montreal. When they first signed up, they were usually single, young, and for the first time in their lives, away from the oversight of their parents and their priests.

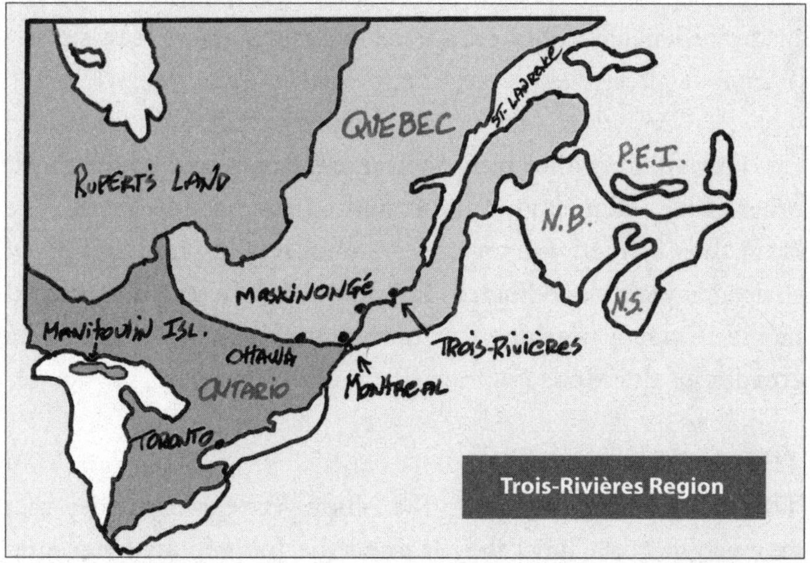

Trois-Rivières Region

The voyageurs bonded through shared adventures. Thrown together for months or years at a time, they formed the bonds of wayfarers who share celebrations and ceremonies, abundance and deprivation, hard work and danger. Washington Irving captured their bonds of brotherhood well:

> The lives of the voyageurs are passed in wild and extensive rovings . . . They are generally of French descent, and inherit much of the gaiety and lightness of heart of their ancestors, being full of anecdote and song, and ever ready for the dance. They inherit, too, a fund of civility and complaisance; and, instead of

> that hardness and grossness which men in laborious life are apt to indulge towards each other, they are mutually obliging and accommodating; interchanging kind offices, yielding each other assistance and comfort in every emergency, and using the familiar appellations of "cousin" and "brother," when there is in fact no relationship. Their natural good will is probably heightened by a community of adventure and hardship in their precarious and wandering life.[3]

Through it all they learned to appreciate and depend on each other. They competed in sport and harmonized in song. The bond thus formed was constantly reinforced by their values of sharing, equality and liberty. This bond and these values, forged by the voyageur northmen, were the social glue that enabled the creation of the Métis Nation.

THE SONGS

The voyageurs paddled into the North-West, where they met new peoples, but until they learned the Indigenous languages, they were able to speak only to their brothers. While they were initially limited in their conversation partners, their songs filled the North-West. Their stories may have been heavily embroidered, but their songs were simple. Everyone who encountered the voyageurs remembered their songs and the emotions the songs elicited. Robert Ballantyne, a Hudson's Bay Company employee whose writing later influenced Robert Louis Stevenson, provided a vivid description of the beauty of the voyageurs' songs:

> I have seen . . . canoes sweep round a promontory suddenly, and burst upon my view; while at the same moment, the wild, romantic song of the voyageurs, as they plied their brisk pad-

> dles, struck upon my ear, and I have felt the thrilling enthusiasm caused by such a scene . . . when thirty or forty of these picturesque canoes . . . half inshrouded in the spray that flew from the bright, vermilion paddles . . . with joyful hearts . . . sang, with all the force of three hundred manly voices, one of their lively airs.[4]

The voyageurs sang all day. They sang to mark the timing of their paddle strokes, to lift their mood, to increase their speed, to give themselves energy and sometimes just for the sheer joy of the sound. A voyageur with a good singing voice might be hired because of his voice and paid more than other voyageurs. They even tracked their days by the number of songs they sang. A really good day was a fifty-song day.

They sang romantic French ballads, lamentations (*complaintes*), work songs, and their own compositions, which they called *chansons de voyageur*. The *chansons* were improvised, long and repetitive, and much influenced by the lands the voyageurs were paddling through. If there was an echo off a rock wall in a canyon or their voices carried unusually in the mist, notes, a rhyme or a word would be repeated in variations, and the voyageurs were delighted with the effect. The sound of a word or its rhyming capacity caught their ear and their fancy as much and sometimes more than the word's actual meaning. Some songs were jazzy improvisations of the sounds of the water or the land. John Bigsby, a doctor and member of the commission established to confirm the international boundary in the early 1800s, provided a description of the voyageur improvisational tradition:

> [He] sang it as only the true voyageur can do, imitating the action of the paddle, and in their high, resounding, and yet musical tones. His practised voice enabled him to give us the

> various swells and falls of sounds upon the waters driven about by the winds, dispersed and softened in the wide expanses, or brought close again to the ear by neighboring rocks. He finished, as is usual, with the piercing Indian shriek.[5]

Song tempos were fitted to the speed of the canoe or boat. The pork-eaters in the large canoes and boats on the Great Lakes with their larger paddles or oars sang slower songs, *chansons à la rame*. The northmen in the *canots du nord* sang songs with livelier tempos, and the small express canoes called for the quickest rhythms of all.

Some of the songs chronicled the history of the voyageurs and were handed down from father to son. *Complaintes* were composed as eulogies for those who died *en voyage*, or memorialized a well-known event. Sometimes the songs were survival, teaching or warning songs. One of the most famous songs, “Petit Rocher” (“O Little Rock”), told the story of Jean Cadieux, who died after defending his family from an Iroquois attack. He diverted the Iroquois while his family escaped. This part of the song may even be true. Certainly, early relations between the Iroquois and the voyageurs were not always peaceful. But the poignancy and tragic romance of the song comes in the last part. Exhausted by hunger and fear, Cadieux lay down on the rocks, too weak to call out to the search party that passed him by on the river. Days later Cadieux was found dead, lying in a grave he dug for himself. In his dead hands he held the words to “Petit Rocher.”

The voyageur songs gave satisfaction to everyone who heard them. To be sure, each passenger in the boats was a captive audience, but many commented on how the songs allowed them to endure the rain and the tedium of the long voyages, during which they had to sit for hours, unable to move even the slightest bit. Thomas Moore, the Irish poet, was entranced by the songs.

> Our Voyageurs had good voices, and sung perfectly in tune together . . . I remember when we have entered, at sunset, upon one of those beautiful lakes . . . I have heard this simple air with a pleasure which the finest compositions of the first masters have never given me; and now, there is not a note of it which does not recall to my memory the dip of our oars in the St. Lawrence, the flight of our boat down the Rapids, and all those new and fanciful impressions to which my heart was alive . . .[6]

While the discipline of the work provided needed structure to the lives of the voyageurs, their daily working conditions were demanding and dangerous. The physical demands were beyond belief to those who witnessed their work.[7] An early American treaty negotiator, James McKenney, described a voyageur day as follows:

> At seven o'clock, and while the voyageurs were resting on their paddles, I inquired if they did not wish to go ashore for the night—they answered, they were fresh yet. They had been almost constantly paddling since three o'clock this morning. They make sixty strokes in a minute. This, for one hour, is three thousand six hundred: and for sixteen hours, fifty-seven thousand six hundred strokes with the paddle, and "*fresh yet!*" No human beings, except the Canadian French, could stand this.[8]

Their dress was distinctive and a unique combination of Indigenous and Canadian influences. It included a short, striped cotton shirt, a red woollen cap, a pair of deerskin leggings that went from the ankle to just above the knee and were held up by a string secured to a waist belt, an *azōin* (breech cloth), and deerskin moccasins without socks. Some kept their thighs bare in summer and winter. Others wore cloth trousers. In winter a blue *capot* made from a blanket tied with a brightly coloured *ceinture fléchée* (sash) completed the outfit. From the sash hung a knife, a cup and a beaded *sac-à-feu* (tobacco pouch).

The voyageurs loved feathers. Each northman, on getting hired, received a red feather for his cap. Northmen were distinguished from pork-eaters by the colour of their feathers. They also decorated their canoes with feathers, one in the stern and one in the bow, which was a signal that the canoe was a seasoned and worthy vessel. Before pulling into a fort, the voyageurs always stopped out of sight to tidy themselves up. They landed in their own unique style, all decked out with feathers and beads, in full song and with a merry mood.

While the voyageurs are mostly known for their canoeing, that was only their means of travelling during the good weather. These were men of the Canadian North-West, where winter held sway for six months or more. The voyageurs were not idle during those frozen months. They continued to travel by dogsled and snowshoe.

Four dogs could pull up to six hundred pounds on a narrow oak sled and travel up to seventy miles a day. The men followed on snowshoes or rode. It was a balancing act between riding, which was restful but cold, and running, which was warm but tiring. The dogs were huskies. They were left behind in summer, and Red River was known to have at least one dog hotel that housed up to one hundred dogs. The voyageurs loved to dress their horses and their dogs. Often the dogs wore fringed or embroidered saddlecloths with small bells and feathers. They also had shoes. If the rough ice cut into their paws, the dogs would lie on their backs whining and pawing, hoping the voyageurs would bring out their leather shoes, which were tied on with deerskin thongs.

The voyageurs began to create a new language. In their attempt to communicate with First Nations and to describe their unique work and situation, they created new words and embroidered their native French with First Nation words and phrases, mostly taken from Ojibwa and Cree. This is the foundation for the Métis Nation language that would later be called Michif. According to linguists, teenagers develop most new words, and Michif was no different. Its origins began with the young voyageurs.

The fact that the voyageurs were young accounts for some of the Métis traditional practices. If one can attribute a character to the voyageurs and later the Métis Nation, it is the wolf, which does actually grace one of their flags. The young voyageurs were very physical. They loved to howl, wrestle, play and hunt. They lived and travelled together like a pack. They were exuberant young male wolves, and this character fertilized the Métis culture from the beginning. The voyageur life fed an appetite for risk, exploration and novelty. In a time when there were no professional sports teams, being a voyageur was the ideal profession for a young man who liked physical challenges and wanted to travel, hang out with the guys and compete with other men. Once this lifestyle was hard-wired into their developing brains, many gave their lives to it. Despite the gruelling labour, it seems that only the rare voyageur did not love the life. One old voyageur said, "I should glory in commencing the same career again. I would spend another half-century in the same fields of enjoyment. There is no life so happy as a voyageur's life; none so independent; no place where a man enjoys so much variety and freedom as in the Indian country."[9]

Independence and freedom were their most treasured values. They sought their freedom in the wilds of the North-West, and they were willing to endure any hardship to keep their liberty. Officially they may have been servants, but when the master was a thousand miles away, the voyageurs were able to taste freedom and independence.

While outside observers uniformly thought the voyageur life was more akin to drudgery, it appealed to these young Canadiens whose future otherwise offered a different kind of drudgery, endlessly the same: working on a small family farm. In addition to the physical challenges of the voyageur life, the exciting possibility of danger and the adventure of travelling into the unknown, there were other inducements to entice a young man, including pleasures largely unavailable to a young farm boy in Quebec living under the eye of his priest: smoking, gambling, drinking, wrestling and girls.

CHAPTER 3

THE MOTHERS OF THE MÉTIS NATION

The mothers of the Métis Nation were the Indigenous daughters of the land, beautiful and exotic to a young man from Quebec. The attraction was often reciprocated when young Indigenous women met these young voyageurs.

The daughters provided access to the land and resources. The whole point of voyaging into the North-West was to trade with the Indigenous peoples who supplied the furs. To obtain the furs, one needed to establish a relationship with the bands. The best way to do that, sometimes the only way, was to marry one of their daughters. This was a general practice in the North-West. Sometimes couples married for love; sometimes it was a pragmatic arrangement. Either way, most of the voyageurs wanted women and needed them. For those who were hungry for female companionship or sex, the beautiful young Indigenous women were the only women available in the North-West. Beyond companionship and sex, when a voyageur stayed with a band, it was the daughters who looked after their domestic needs.

The voyageurs had to adapt to the customs of the Indigenous peoples. The lure of independence and freedom from their old lives in Canada was often sufficient inducement for a voyageur to embrace a new life and adapt to the customs of the Indigenous people he now began to live with. Generally, there was much goodwill between Indigenous peoples and the voyageurs. This is not to say that relations between voyageurs and Indigenous peoples were always smooth. Trading partners usually have disputes, and the Euro-Canadian trade competition, often quite brutal, had an impact on their Indigenous partners. Sometimes there were Indigenous attacks and sometimes the voyageurs instigated a conflict. Cultural misunderstandings were common, and until secure trading alliances were established with a particular band, caution was necessary on both sides.

It took a voyageur with unique skills to successfully establish a trade relationship with Indigenous people. By marrying into a band, *à la façon du pays* (in the fashion of the country), the voyageur took on familial obligations. He became the son in a new family and contributed whatever talents and skills he had to the betterment of this family and her band. In this way the new son earned access to and learned about the land and necessary hunting, fishing and trapping skills. In return he provided the family and the band with his connections to the fur-trading companies.

Entering into a relationship with an Indigenous woman, *à la façon du pays*, was marriage without the benefit of clergy or state sanction. This was not marriage as understood by Euro-Canadians at the time, their ideas being framed by the strict rules of Christianity and European property laws. It was marriage as the Indigenous people understood it and as the voyageurs learned to understand it. Indigenous custom was that if the marriage was not working out for the woman, the man, her family or the band, it could be dissolved with little fuss. That doesn't mean that all dissolved marriages ended at the mutual desire of both partners. There are many tales of love in the North-West, unrequited, deeply cherished or scorned.

A TALE OF LOVE SCORNED

In 1799 a young man from Maskinongé in the Trois-Rivières region of Quebec signed on as a voyageur with the North West Company (Nor'Westers). Jean-Baptiste Lagimodière paddled into a new, exciting life, but he also signed on in the middle of the fur-trade war, when the Nor'Westers were hiring increasing numbers of young men. In 1804, during one of the few truces in the trade war, Jean-Baptiste was terminated along with dozens of other young voyageurs.

Losing his job didn't dampen his romantic reputation as a voyageur when he returned to Maskinongé. Voyageurs were much admired in Quebec and people were hungry for their stories. Jean-Baptiste obliged with tales of his adventures in the North-West, some of which may even have been true. In 1805 at a soiree where he was invited to recount his tall tales, he met the lovely and spirited Marie-Anne Gaboury. They fell in love and got engaged based on her understanding that Jean-Baptiste intended to settle down as a farmer in Maskinongé. But Jean-Baptiste was never going to be content with such a life after tasting the freedom and independence of life in the North-West. So Marie-Anne had a choice. She could become a fur-trade widow, which meant staying in Quebec, seeing her husband once every few years, running the farm and raising her children alone. Or she could go where no white woman had gone before.

Apparently Jean-Baptiste agreed to Marie-Anne coming with him because he was confident, erroneously as it turns out, that the North West Company would refuse a female passenger. When the Nor'Westers proved indifferent to this unusual passenger, Marie-Anne headed into the North-West in May of 1806 with a bigamist. Jean-Baptiste was married, according to the customs of the country, to an Indigenous woman in the North-West. He also had children. One can only wonder how many excuses flitted through his head as he paddled with his new wife at his side, slowly but steadily heading straight toward his first wife and family.

The inevitable collision occurred when the newlyweds arrived in Pembina at the end of July. His first wife, not a woman to be scorned, tried to murder Marie-Anne. The tales vary widely. One version of the story is that the murder attempt was by knife. Another version says fire. Yet another version tells a tale of poison. In that version Marie-Anne escaped because a dog ate the poisoned food and died instead. The accounts are only consistent on one fact: there was at least one murder attempt. Jean-Baptiste, acquiring a bit of wisdom a tad late, scooped up his new wife and took her some forty miles away. The first wife, unnamed, along with her children, is never heard from again.

Fluid relationships and serial monogamy among the voyageurs were common. The voyageurs changed their postings regularly and might never return to a wife. The termination of a relationship in those circumstances was often mutual. Her family would not want to lose a daughter, and the relationship might end when her hunting band left the area. Other voyageurs returned to Lower Canada and abandoned North-West wives. Lifetime commitments were not the norm.

But some of the sons were deeply attached to their Indigenous wives. Some of these women, with their children, travelled in their own canoes and followed a voyageur as he moved from post to post. So, the woman was paddling, portaging, changing diapers, feeding and caring for her children and keeping up with the voyageurs. The fact that women with their children could and did keep up with the voyageurs doesn't dent the male superhero reputation; it does give some indication of the strength and skills of Indigenous women. Perhaps they should be added to the superhero legends.

Women were particularly important to the fisheries. They were often the ones who did the fishing, and when one considers the important role fish played as a food source, it is possible that the women may have provided as much or even more food than the men did. One particular story about Marguerite Kirkness highlights the role women played in the fisheries.

MARGUERITE KIRKNESS

The Marguerite Kirkness story is set in July and August of 1810 in Île-à-la-Crosse, where her husband, Andrew Kirkness, was employed by the Hudson's Bay Company as a fisherman. On July 6 Andrew and Marguerite had a fight and she left him, crossing over to the nearby Nor'Wester post. In the ensuing weeks officials from the Company sought, more than once, to get Marguerite back, which was highly unusual behaviour. It was not the norm in those days for traders to stir themselves simply to restore strained marital arrangements, especially for a First Nation woman.

Unusual, that is, unless she had some value, which she did—her fishing skills. While it was Andrew who had the contract to provide fish, Marguerite was the real fisher in the family. Without her, Andrew was simply unable to provide the fish necessary for the post. This is why the Company officials went to such efforts to get Marguerite back. She was their food source. It didn't take long for the Nor'Westers to figure out they were hosting a valuable woman.

The Bay men were convinced that Marguerite was being held by the Nor'Westers against her will, which may have been true. The fur-trade war was ruthless and the Nor'Westers were not above trying to starve out the Bay men. Whether or not Marguerite was a willing partner in this offensive, the tactic worked, and the Company was forced to close its post at Île-à-la-Crosse. This story provides us with insight into the remarkable fishing skills possessed by First Nation women and how many men depended on their skills. Marguerite and Andrew appear to have reunited and relocated to Red River.[1]

It is the northmen of the Nor'Westers who established the bonds that enabled the creation of the Métis Nation. Forged in freedom and independence, engraved by constant travel and shared companionship, nurtured by songs and stories, unbreakable bonds began to form. The bonds were strengthened when they married First Nation women with similar values of freedom and independence and with deep attachments to the North-West. These bonds were the framework and consciousness that were necessary to develop a new nation in the North-West.

CHAPTER 4

GOING FREE

One more step was necessary for the development of a new nation. The northmen had to go free. "Going free" meant disengaging from their employers, their attachments in eastern Canada and from the tribes.

The merger of the two fur-trade companies in 1821 led to more than a thousand men losing their jobs. Many of these men went free and stayed in the North-West. They stayed because they had married Indigenous women. These "Freemen" began to move to Red River from the Great Lakes, Athabasca, Fort Edmonton, the Saskatchewan, York Factory and the Pacific slopes of the Rockies.[1] Between 1831 and 1840 the population of Red River almost doubled. In 1832 it was 2,417 and in 1840 it was 4,369.

Once free from his contract with a company, a Freeman became an independent hunter-trader. Travelling in groups of two or three with their families, the Freemen hunted buffalo and other large animals for their food. In the first two decades of the nineteenth century, they began to roam throughout the North-West. If the product of their hunts did not provide enough for their families, they did odd jobs, freighting or voyageur work for the trading companies. But their preference more and more was to hunt buffalo.

The Freemen found a niche as suppliers and traders providing the posts and the brigades with buffalo meat, fish, baked bread, salt, and maple or birch syrup. They operated taverns and restaurants on trade routes and provided the voyageurs with the means to repair canoes. They also played the role of middlemen. Obtaining goods from Canadian posts, they would trade with Indians for furs and sell the furs back to the Canadian traders, making a bit of profit along the way. Some had visions of their own grandeur. One old Freeman claimed a sturgeon fishery for himself with the title "King of the Lake." Another Freeman called himself "Lord of Lake Winnipick." Yet another proclaimed himself a "sovereign."

Jean-Baptiste Lagimodière was one of the Freemen. When he and Marie-Anne arrived in Pembina, his partners reunited with their Cree wives, and this small party of Freemen with their families went out onto the Plains to hunt buffalo. Pembina is where the first two non-Indigenous children in the North-West were born. Both were born the same week in 1807. One child was born to Isobel Gunn, a young woman who had been masquerading as a man and was forced to reveal her gender only when she went into labour. The second child was Reine, a daughter born to Marie-Anne and Jean-Baptiste Lagimodière. By 1810 the Lagimodières had three children. Their third child, Josephte, was nicknamed *La Cyprès* after the Cypress Hills where she was born.

The 1790s was when the northmen began to move onto the Plains and hunt buffalo on horseback. It was the beginning of the transformation of the voyageurs into Plains buffalo hunters. At first they lived on the edges of the Plains, in places such as

Pembina. In 1805 Alexander Henry's census listed 176 Freemen and their families in what is now southern Manitoba.[2] The first rough Freemen settlements began to appear around 1801, first at Pembina and farther up the Red River at the forks of the Red and Assiniboine Rivers. At Rainy Lake a small village was established in 1817. Fort Edmonton, Île-à-la-Crosse, Cumberland House and other regional forts became home bases for Freemen with their families. By 1814 the Freemen and their families moving throughout the Red River region numbered about two hundred. At Pembina there was a similar-size group.

The Freemen first adopted and then adapted the Plains tribal horse culture. Previously, as voyageurs, they were bound to their canoes and dogsleds. After going free they took up the horse. For thousands of years the Plains tribes followed the buffalo on foot. The arrival of the horse in the northern Plains in the 1600s did not create a new Plains Indigenous culture. It didn't change the range of territory the people covered, their pursuit of the buffalo herds or their practice of congregating in small bands of a few families. What it did was allow the people to carry more. The Freemen added another adaptation to the carrying capacity of the horse: their new invention, the Red River cart.

Red River carts were made entirely of wood with strips of leather *(babiche)* wrapped around the wooden wheels. Horses or oxen pulled the carts. If pulled by a horse, they carried less but could travel farther. A cart could become a boat by detaching the wheels and floating it over a river.

On land the carts were loud—very loud. They emitted a high-pitched shriek that could be heard several miles away. The sound came from wooden wheels grinding on wooden axles. No axle grease was used because it served only to collect the dust of the Prairies, which clogged up the wheels. The carts were so identified with the Métis that the Sioux sign language gesture for the Métis was the sign for a man followed by the sign for a cart.

Red River carts with teepee poles (*Library and Archives Canada C-087158*)

The Freemen also adapted the hunting partnership custom from the boreal forest and Plains tribes. These partnerships formed when several men combined families and labour to exploit a particular winter hunting ground. The families in the partnership depended on each other. There was more security in numbers than could be achieved by a single family travelling and hunting on its own. The adaptation of the Plains Freemen was to take the partnership idea and move it to a much larger territory and to a larger group of hunters.

One of the central tenets of the partnership custom was sharing, which quickly became part of the developing Métis Nation ethic. Sharing was spontaneous and unstructured. It was in no way changed by the fact that part of the hunters' catch was destined for the commercial market. The production of buffalo meat for market was important to the Freemen hunters, but it was subordinate to their subsistence requirements. Sharing was not charity. Because starvation was a constant visitor, no one hesitated to turn to others for help. Not only would help always be forthcoming, the giver felt the obligation deeply and would be ashamed of himself if he did not provide it. One hunter, after having given the last of his flour and lard to two men from a neighbouring band—food he likely needed himself—said, "Suppose now, not give them flour, lard—just dead inside."[3]

The Freemen made one other adaptation to facilitate their movement to the Plains. They adopted the Plains tribes' staple diet: pemmican. Robert Kennicott, an American naturalist and herpetologist, was less than enthused about it: "Pemmican is supposed by the benighted world outside to consist only of pounded meat and grease; an egregious error; for, from experience on the subject, I am authorized to state that hair, sticks, bark, spruce leaves, stones, sand, etc., enter into its composition, often quite largely."[4] It was pemmican that allowed the Freemen to be independent, to live separately from the tribes, the traders and the fur-trade posts.

The Hudson's Bay Company thought the Freemen a great nuisance, dishonest scoundrels and a threat that took away business. But the Freemen had tasted a new and different life based on an egalitarian theory of opportunity with no company boss. More and more Freemen took their families to the Plains.

It was the emotional commitment to independence and freedom that led the children of the Freemen to the acquisition of a national consciousness. They were "bred and brought up in the very hotbed of liberty & equality."[5] Being free was an identity that would embed itself deeply in the Métis Nation, whether they were buffalo hunters, farmers, hunter-trappers or voyageurs. Their attachment to liberty was inherited, at least in part, from their Indigenous mothers, a fact that the English only understood after a hundred years on the continent, when they admitted, "We know them now to . . . have the highest notions of Liberty of any people on Earth."[6] But their deep attachment to freedom also came from their voyageur fathers, the northmen who went free.

The British were far away across the sea, and Canada was on the other side of the Great Lakes. In the North-West there was no call of loyalty to country. There was no monarchy, no one to represent the law, no government and no authorities. There was only the Hudson's Bay Company, and its power was limited to the small areas around its few forts.

The Nor'Westers and the Company men may have thought they were in charge of the North-West, but it was a hollow claim, much like the preposterous claims of Radisson and Des Groseilliers, who arrived at the end of Lake Superior in 1659 to 1660 and proclaimed themselves "Caesars" who had taken the First Nations under their protection. According to their own marketing, which was aimed at their European audiences, they were able to make thirty thousand Indigenous people scattered over a thousand miles comply with their wishes.[7] Whatever else they were, Radisson and Des Groseilliers were brilliant self-promoters, and their propaganda set the tone for the Euro-Canadian attitude toward the Indigenous peoples of the Great Lakes and the North-West for centuries to come.

In reality the traders, until well into the second half of the nineteenth century, were insignificant in the face of the vast tribes, the growing body of Freemen families, and a newly developing people, the Métis Nation. Most of the people in the North-West spent the bulk of their lives far away from the Company forts and outside the sphere of Euro-Canadians' purportedly overwhelming influence.

The Freemen formed their own families, their own partnerships and their own loyalties. They began to see the North-West as theirs. This established a sharp contrast between them and the Canadians or Europeans, who, as tourists, adventurers or traders in a foreign land, would eventually go home. The North-West became home for the Freemen and their young families. Going free changed the focus of their economic livelihood. According to the Hudson's Bay Company and the American government, the Freemen were smugglers. They preferred to think of themselves as free traders.

This is the fertile soil into which the Métis Nation was born. The men had bonded initially as voyageurs. In that milieu they forged indelible relationships with roots in the companionship, hardship, songs and travels of the voyageur northmen. They formed alliances with Indigenous peoples, married Indigenous women and began to have families. Then they went free from the tribes. At first the separation from a wife's band was seasonal. But as time went on, the Freemen families lived completely separate lives from the bands.

It was the generation born to the Freemen families in the 1790s that became a recognizable group when they hit their twenties. While the previous decades saw the birth of many such children, by the late 1700s their numbers in the North-West had reached a critical mass. These children were now marrying each other and beginning to create a new culture and language. In all parts of the North-West, this cohort began to attract recognition. When they reached maturity in the early 1800s, they were no longer identified as the sons and daughters of the northmen or Freemen. They did not identify as members of the tribes and they had never considered themselves to be connected to eastern Canada. They began to think, act and identify as a separate group. They gave themselves a collective name: the Bois-Brûlés.

They learned to live in and love the North-West as their motherland, and they were fiercely proud of their independence and freedom. There was no authority that could interfere with their developing network of families and nothing to dampen their aspirations. They were free to become anything they wanted. They chose to become a new nation.

CHAPTER 5

THE FIRST NATIONAL RESISTANCE

The Métis Nation was born in a battle, a bloody show that took place in June 1816. Midwives call the birth process a "bloody show" for a good reason. Child or nation, birth is a long, messy business usually accompanied by blood and pain, and sometimes death. The birth of the Métis Nation was no different. It was painful, bloody and deadly.

When the Métis Nation's birth took place in the early 1800s, the world had been in a mini–ice age for about three hundred years. Then, in the spring of 1815, a volcano in Indonesia erupted. Mount Tambora spewed so much ash into the air that it caused a worldwide decrease in sunlight and a drop in temperature that lasted for three years. The English painter J. M. W. Turner may have revelled in the visual drama of purple, pink and yellow skies, but the beauty belied the devastation wreaked on the entire planet by the fallout of the volcano.

The Canadian North-West began to feel the effects of Tambora a year later. In 1816 it snowed throughout the summer, the rivers were low and the creeks dried up. The grass was thin and short and the land was as dry as a bone. There were very few crops and even those failed. Fishing was terrible, and the buffalo roamed far away in search of grass. Everyone was cold and hungry.

THE PLACE

The birth of the Nation took place in Red River, which despite its name, is not just a river. It's a region that covered much of the southern part of two Canadian provinces, the northwestern corner of Minnesota and a large chunk of North Dakota. Two major rivers, the Assiniboine and the Red, dominate the region. The Métis thought of both rivers as one system, so they called the Red River "the Lower Red" and the Assiniboine River "the Upper Red." The Lower Red was a canoe route down to the headwaters of the Mississippi River. The Upper Red meanders eastward from its origin in Saskatchewan to where it joins with the Lower Red in present-day Winnipeg at the Forks. When the Métis Nation refers to Red River, they have always meant the entire region.

THE PARTICIPANTS

By 1816 there were four different groups of people in Red River: Freemen, fur traders, newly arrived settlers and Indigenous peoples. The population was small but divided. The two Indigenous groups in Red River, the Ojibwa and the Bois-Brûlés, considered each other family. The Bois-Brûlés, or Brûlés, would later become the Métis Nation. The Freemen were the fathers of the Bois-Brûlés and close allies of the Ojibwa, largely because they had married Ojibwa women and were raising families in the region. As former employees and traders, the Freemen had necessarily fluid alliances with the fur-trading companies.

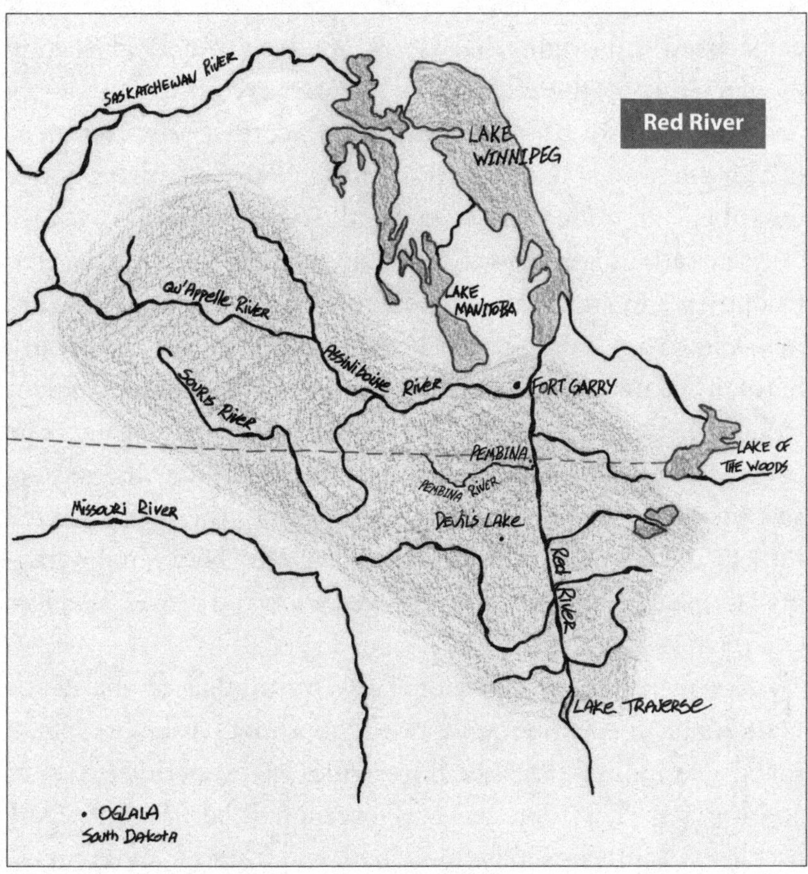

The fur traders were French Canadians and Scots employed by the Nor'Westers, or English and Scots employed by the Hudson's Bay Company. Both companies had multiple trading posts in Red River. The Hudson's Bay Company is usually described as an English company, while the North West Company is thought of as a French-Canadian consortium. The French-Canadian face of the North West Company came not from its owners but from its employees, *engagés* and voyageurs, men who were invariably from the Trois-Rivières region of Quebec. The British face of the Hudson's Bay Company came from the original charter granted by the English king in 1670. But by the early 1800s, Scots were either in control or taking control of both companies. Scottish clan warfare is not an unreasonable description of the rivalry—perhaps better described as a trade war—between the two companies.

The settlers were mostly Highlanders who had been ejected from their ancestral lands in Scotland. These victims of what are now known as the Highland clearances were called "the Selkirk Settlers" because they were brought over by and under contract to Lord Selkirk, a director of the Hudson's Bay Company. The Bois-Brûlés were mostly Nor'Wester allies and saw the settlers as a threat. The Ojibwa were sympathetic to the newly arrived settlers and relatively neutral about the rivalry between the trading companies. Red River was indeed a tangled web of alliances and relationships.

Everyone was involved one way or another in the Métis Nation's birth story, but only two groups met on the battlefield that day in June of 1816: the Bois-Brûlés led by Cuthbert Grant, and the Selkirk Settlers led by Governor Robert Semple. The battle was a fifteen-minute bloodbath and it wasn't about furs.

Lord Selkirk and the Selkirk Settlers

The Scottish Lord Selkirk was an altruistic experimenter in colonialism. His impetus to set up colonies had two sources: the Highland clearances and the French Revolution. The Highland clearances were the sad result of the destruction of the Scottish clan system. The clansmen were slaughtered at the Battle of Culloden in 1746, the culmination of the failed Jacobite uprisings. The British victors, under the guise of keeping the peace, exacted their vengeance on the Highlanders by expropriating any remaining wealth and resources, brutally suppressing the

Highlanders and executing or transporting survivors and clan leaders. Clan lands had always been collectively held by the clan members under the leadership of their chieftain. But as the clan system degenerated in the aftermath of the uprisings, clan leaders began to claim ownership of clan lands. Perceiving that more profit could be made from sheep than tenants, clan leaders demanded steep rents they knew could never be paid. Evictions followed as they squeezed out their poor. Between 1763 and 1775 over thirty thousand people were forced out of the Highlands. The clearances continued until the middle of the nineteenth century.

The French Revolution provided Lord Selkirk with an example of what happened when the dispossessed and poor, with nothing to lose, became violent and rebelled. With this lesson in mind, Lord Selkirk developed compassionate as well as pragmatic reasons for believing the dispossessed Highlanders needed to be settled with homes and work. He worried that they would slide into rebellion and violence that would destroy Scotland. His solution was to move them to new colonies in British North America.

After mixed results from his first two Canadian experiments, Lord Selkirk wanted to set his third colony in Red River.[1] But under British law the Hudson's Bay Company owned Red River. So, Selkirk acquired shares in the Company. He purchased some and he married a Scottish heiress with a sizable amount of stock. This gave him the opportunity to put his colony proposal to the Company. Under his influence and with close relatives and friends of his on the board of directors, the Company agreed to "sell" him 116,000 square miles of territory in Red River for a mere ten shillings. With this land Selkirk proceeded to implement his colonization scheme.

If Lord Selkirk was operating from sincere altruistic concerns about the dispossessed Highlanders, and it seems that he was, the Hudson's Bay Company's board of directors was grounded in more earthly interests when it approved the Red River settlement scheme. The colony had several benefits to recommend it to the Company. It would provide a home not just for the displaced Highlanders but also for the Company's retired servants—a future source of cheap manpower.[2] The fertile land in Red River would enable the colonists to become farmers and supply the Company posts with provisions, which would be cheaper than having them transported from Britain. The colonists would divert supplies and cut off the North West Company trade routes and connections and undermine its viability. If successful, the colony would be the death of the Company's hated trading rival, the Nor'Westers.

Lord Selkirk's plan in Red River unfolded in a mirror image of the Highland clearances. For ten pieces of silver, a Scottish lord now claimed the land in Red River as his own. His settlers would make the land more profitable, and the current Indigenous occupants would have to be cleared out. If Lord Selkirk's plan dispossessed those he firmly believed were not as evolved as the white race, so be it.

The Selkirk Settlers began arriving in Red River in August 1812. The first group comprised one hundred exhausted and starved men with a governor in tow. The governor put on a bright face, but the men were angry and bitter as reality replaced the fantasy of the "golden but delusive promises" they had purchased from Lord Selkirk.[3] In Red River the settlers were helpless and rather pathetic. Their clothes were inadequate for a winter in the North-West and they had few useful skills or tools for this country. They knew nothing of how to build, farm, hunt or produce food in a land that was so different from their own. They had little money, their families were far away and they were homesick. And then there was the weather—remember, it was a mini–ice age.

Before they had left Scotland, the settlers had consumed a steady diet of dire warnings about the "savage natives" they would encounter at Red River. The Nor'Westers, actively trying to scuttle Selkirk's settlement project, were the authors of these accounts:

> [When they arrive at Red River] they will be surrounded by warlike Savage natives . . . who will consider them as intruders come to spoil their hunting ground, to drive away the wild animals and to destroy the Indians as the white men have already done in Canada and the United States. Even if [they] escape the scalping knife, they will be subject to constant alarm and terror. Their habitations, their Crops, their Cattle will be destroyed and they will find it impossible to exist in the Country.[4]

Knowing the source of these warnings likely made little difference to the settlers, who did not have much else to frame their expectations. It must have been surprising, then, for the settlers to actually meet the Indigenous people in Red River, who were kind to them and extended many courtesies and assistance when they first arrived. The Freemen, Bois-Brûlés and Ojibwa all hunted for the new immigrants. They provided horses, Red River carts and canoes. They loaned their tools, provided seed grain and offered furs to the newcomers. The early days were difficult for the Selkirk Settlers, but they were not marked by animosity from those already living there.

Shortly after they arrived in Red River, the immigrants'

governor, Miles Macdonell, convened a gathering on the east bank of the Red River. With entirely unsuitable pomp and ceremony, the governor proclaimed, in English and then in French, the grant of the territory of Assiniboia to Lord Selkirk. This performance to the wind, the prairie and a few people, was followed by a riveting reading of whereas . . . heretofore . . . and hereby . . . , all to say that the commission of the Hudson's Bay Company was appointing him, Miles Macdonell, as the governor of Assiniboia. The guns were fired and cheers were given. The gentlemen in attendance (though not the Indigenous men—these people being understood by the British to not have any man worthy of the designation "gentleman") retired to a tent for a celebratory snack and some toasts.

The declaration of ownership started the Bois-Brûlés, the Freemen and the Ojibwa talking. Strangers who arrived and became new neighbours were one thing. Strangers who claimed they owned everything, well, that was something else. The young Bois-Brûlés had never seen or heard of anything like this before. And the strangers were neither traders nor hunters. What on earth were they going to do? Rely on farming? Remember the weather? Canadians today call this place, only half in jest, "Winterpeg." And this was the home where the buffalo roamed. To the Bois-Brûlés the whole idea was slightly crazy.

The settlers had only a precarious hold on their newly acquired farms. They had immigrated to Red River for a new chance at life. They might have been grateful for the chance, at least at first, but the support Lord Selkirk had promised by way of food and tools had not materialized. Many fled as soon as they could. Anywhere else appeared better than Red River. For those who stayed, the Company was absolutely necessary. It had food stores, a fort and cannon. It had canoes, ships and systems for mail and goods to arrive. The Company offered the settlers at least some possibility of protection. The remaining settlers needed the Company no matter how badly it supported them. But the Company's support was so inadequate that the settlers' loyalty to the Company and Lord Selkirk grew thin. What the settlers really cared about were their farms and their families—all they had in the world. They might be out of their depth—and they were—but they were not going to give up without a fight.

Governor Macdonell

Lord Selkirk was a racist. In his view the Bois-Brûlés were bastards, men who had thrown off decency by cohabiting with Indian women and who combined the vices of civilized and savage life. His bigotry was housed, at least for the time being, on the other side of the Atlantic Ocean. His governor, Macdonell, was much worse, and he was on location. Macdonell condescended to bestow his pity on the Ojibwa, whom he regarded as savages. He was openly contemptuous of the Bois-Brûlés.

The Brûlés and the Nor'Westers quickly dubbed Macdonell "Captain Cartouche," after a famous Parisian bandit much admired for his dashing appearance, wild exploits, strength, bravery and cunning. The Brûlés had adopted the French tradition of *soubriquet*, or nicknaming, but their tendency was to choose a nickname that was the opposite of a man's character. So naming Macdonell "Captain Cartouche" suggests that they were not much impressed with Macdonell. Even that small regard soon deteriorated.

Providing shelter for the settlers and securing food and firewood for them became Macdonell's most immediate task. To that end, he issued a series of orders. Because bark was used for roofing material and there were few trees near Red River, he issued an order prohibiting the barking of trees by anyone other than the settlers. Again because of the scarcity of nearby trees, he issued an order prohibiting the taking of larger trees for firewood by anyone other than the settlers. Despite the abundance of fish in the Red River, he issued an order prohibiting camping on certain parts (the best parts) of the river for fishing by anyone other than the settlers. Licences were now required by anyone other than the settlers, and only Macdonell could authorize them. Under his orders, food on what was now called "Selkirk's territory" was seized and appropriated for the settlers.

The settlers never questioned their right to take over the lands and resources on arrival. Macdonell sent instructions to the posts:

> You must give them . . . solemn warning that the land belongs to the Hudson's Bay Company and that they must remove from it; after this warning they should not be allowed to cut any timber either for building or fuel. What they have cut ought to be openly and forcibly seized, and their buildings destroyed. In like manner they should be warned not to fish in your waters, and if they put down nets seize them, as you would in England those of a poacher. We are so fully advised by the unimpeachable validity of the rights of property that there can be no scruple in enforcing them, wherever you have the physical means.[5]

"The physical means"—ah, that was the rub! Macdonell's proclamation amounted to a declaration of war, but he simply did not have the physical means to sustain the claim of ownership. Not that this stopped his series of orders and proclamations. On January 8, 1814, Macdonell issued a new proclamation: For a period of one year, no one within Selkirk's territory could remove provisions except for travelling food necessary for trading journeys. To make it even worse, in order to transport even this limited amount, one had to apply to Macdonell for a licence. This new proclamation placed control of food in the hands of the Hudson's Bay Company.

The relationship between the Brûlés and the settlers began to deteriorate. After Governor Macdonell began to issue his orders and as the list of prohibitions grew, the Brûlés began to withdraw their support and then to retaliate. They began running buffalo away from the settlement, which was of little matter to the well-mounted Brûlés, who simply allowed the herd to settle and then chased it wherever it went. The dispersal of the herd was a problem, however, for the settlers and the Ojibwa, who hunted on foot.

When Macdonell ordered that pemmican be seized from the Nor'Westers, he exposed his willingness to use violence. Both sides took prisoners and began recruiting men. The Freemen and Brûlés took up arms. Ojibwa and Cree warriors joined them. This was not a fight the settlers could win. They were vastly outnumbered. Macdonell backed down in time to avoid an open confrontation, but the tensions continued to escalate.

The last straw came on July 21, 1814, when the governor prohibited running buffalo. The penalty was three months' imprisonment for the first offence, and forfeiture of the horse plus imprisonment for the second offence. This was the order that went too far. The initial orders were an irritation; the ones that followed were a nuisance; but this latest one was unacceptable and arrogant.[6] Macdonell had no ability to force the Brûlés to obey his orders, but he was an autocrat to the bone, and the North-West in the first half of the nineteenth century was not a democracy. Macdonell's assertion of authority was not designed to obtain friends, allies or loyalty. It was colonialism—rule by the new and few in their own interest and damn to the rest.

When the settlers began to claim priority rights to the buffalo, to restrict how and where the Brûlés hunted, to confiscate provisions, and to restrict the flow of people and goods, the settlers were no longer a potential enemy but a real one. Their actions pushed the Brûlés even closer to the Nor'Westers, who understood them better and nurtured their alliance. There was no way the Brûlés were going to let the newcomers stop them from hunting buffalo when and where they thought best. The settlers did not consult or negotiate. They arrived and claimed everything for themselves. They had no thought of sharing. The Brûlés came to the logical conclusion that there was no way to live with the settlers—they would have to go.

The Bois-Brûlés

The Bois-Brûlés, like the settlers, wanted to protect their way of life and their families. But their values and way of life were very different from those of the newly arrived Selkirk Settlers. Every experience the Brûlés had had so far with strangers was with traders, and they had developed a relationship. But these newcomers were different. They were farmers, settlers, but it wasn't their way of life or their existence that posed a threat. It wasn't even their rules, which they were free to inflict on their own. It was the attempt to impose their rules on the Bois-Brûlés. The Indigenous peoples and the settlers now shared a common territory and resources in Red River, but they shared few basic assumptions or values. There was no social glue to keep these disparate groups together.

After only a few weeks in Red River, the settlers began to insist that the Indigenous peoples accept and adapt to *their* new order—an order based on settlement. But the Bois-Brûlés lived lives of constant movement as voyageurs, traders and buffalo hunters. Though they generally had vegetable gardens and a few grew some grain, they were not farmers. Their life depended on movement by horse, dog or canoe. They needed access to the resources of the land, especially the buffalo. Theirs was a large and expansive lifestyle based on freedom of movement. Their hunting grounds were of the utmost importance to them. Other Indigenous peoples had gone to war to protect their hunting grounds. Only after many deaths and many years had the British in the Great Lakes come to understand that Indigenous peoples were more afraid of losing their hunting grounds than their lives. The settlers and their new governor, ignorant of this history, were condemned to repeat the mistake.

The Bois-Brûlés had their own expectations. They expected the newcomers to establish themselves as allies according to Indigenous traditions of diplomacy, just as the traders had learned to do. But the settlers had no intention of even trying to establish an alliance with the Bois-Brûlés. The settlers brought colonialism to Red River. They thought Lord Selkirk's piece of paper proved that he now owned the land and, because they were under contract to him, that they had ownership rights. They came with a righteous belief in British laws and their right to force those laws on the Bois-Brûlés.

The trouble really began in January 1814, when the settlers' governor attempted to assert his law and to police Red River. He aimed squarely at the Brûlés and their attachment to the buffalo hunt. The young Brûlés excelled at running buffalo. They ran their horses alongside the buffalo and shot with bow and arrow or gun. They loaded on the fly, picked out another animal and shot again. They had perfected this dangerous skill, and they regarded the practice as their right. The buffalo were precious to the Brûlés and provided everything needed: food, clothing and material for shelter. The hunt was a right to be protected at all costs. So the Bois-Brûlés listened when their leader, Cuthbert Grant, and the Nor'Westers suggested that the settlers' new laws threatened their hunting rights. When their warning turned out to be correct and the governor did restrict their hunting, Grant's stature was reinforced.

Cuthbert Grant

Indigenous leaders were chosen for their gifts of grace and fine oratory, qualities of courage and vision, and their charisma. Outsiders view such leaders as emotional, illogical and irrational—exactly the opposite of leaders in the European mould, who are creatures of hierarchical training. But Indigenous peoples had no such system of hierarchy. An Indigenous leader gained his place because he inspired the people who loved and respected him. He was expected to work only for the benefit of his people, not in his own interest. Just such a man was Cuthbert Grant, the first leader of the Bois-Brûlés.

Cuthbert Grant, in a painting by Jill Sellers, which now hangs at Grant's Old Mill (*J. Teillet*)

Grant, like many Brûlés of his day, had two names. To the French and the English, he was Cuthbert Grant.[7] To the Brûlés and First Nations, he was Wappeston (White Ermine.) He was born in the North-West and, after being educated in Montreal, returned home in 1812 under contract to the Nor'Westers. He arrived in Red River at about the same time as the Selkirk Settlers and was posted to Fort Espérance on the Qu'Appelle River in Saskatchewan.

Grant lived in separate but overlapping cultures, the Indigenous cultures of the Cree and Ojibwa, the developing culture of the Brûlés, and the bourgeois corporate culture of the Nor'Westers. As a Nor'Wester he mixed easily with the other men, spoke their English or French language and behaved as a gentleman with the manners of an educated easterner. But though Grant was educated away and worked for the Nor'Westers, neither of those institutions formed his identity. He travelled, hunted and lived with his own people, and he was particularly attached to and was admired by the new generation of Brûlés, his *jeunes gens*.

While Grant was an employee of the Nor'Westers, many of his *jeunes gens*, like their fathers, were Freemen. For the sons, the term "Freemen" did not mean the same thing as it did for their fathers. The fathers were Freemen because they were former employees of the fur-trade companies. Their Brûlés sons were also Freemen, but many had never been employees of either company. The Freemen fathers were not particularly loyal to their former company. They traded for their own advantage, sometimes with one company, sometimes with another. Their Brûlés sons had even less inclination to give a company their loyalty.

This new generation of Freemen, the Bois-Brûlés, were different from their fathers in other ways too. While their fathers had some previous experience of law in Quebec or Britain, most of their sons had no experience of the white man's law, either of the judicial or religious kind. It had never been part of their lives. At the time, the only laws they knew were First Nation laws.

The Freemen fathers travelled in small groups of hunters and traders. They learned to avoid confrontation. By 1815, with the escalation of violence in Red River, the Freemen fathers put their avoidance skills to good use. They often melted away from the settlement and moved out onto the Plains, hunting and trading far away, where the air, the land and the people were less complicated. Their sons, however, had developed a gang mentality. They were hanging out in large armed groups and had little need for the avoidance techniques their fathers favoured. As their gang size grew, they could go anywhere and do what they wanted. They were a young, cocky, armed, dangerous, independent and mobile gang. Running buffalo had made them excellent marksmen and horsemen.

For readers who are familiar with the careful, quasi-military organization of the Métis buffalo hunts, it is important to remember that in 1816 those hunts had not yet been established. Grant and his young Brûlés took much of their warrior traditions from their Cree and Ojibwa families, and those traditions included what we would today likely call guerrilla warfare tactics. They avoided direct confrontations and excelled at small-scale actions—ambushes, raids, hit-and-run tactics and sabotage—that were heavily reliant on mobility and familiarity with the land.

The Nor'Westers named Grant as the Captain-General of all the Half-Breeds in the Country.[8] But the Nor'Westers could not command the young Brûlés who were not in their employ to follow Grant. Grant was not the commander of an army, and his followers were under no obligation to follow or obey him. For Grant to successfully take up the mantle of war chief—which is how the Brûlés would have understood the title captain-general—he had to earn it from the Brûlés. He could lead only when they accepted him as war chief.

Grant became their leader because of his character and his charisma. He was competent, had good oratorical skills, represented his people to outsiders and mediated disputes among allies. He was celebrated for his expertise as a hunter. He was not higher in rank or esteem than his men. He would have been, in their eyes, beyond such conceits. Furthermore, Grant was their leader only in matters his followers authorized—to develop and channel his people's military power. He did become their war chief, but by tradition, when the war was over, the war chief melted back into the populace. It is crucial to understand all of this when looking at the relationship between Cuthbert Grant, the Brûlés and the Nor'Westers. To a certain extent the Nor'Westers understood some of this. It could be said that, with some exceptions, the Hudson's Bay Company, the Selkirk Settlers and their governors never understood any of it.

The Nor'Westers knew that issuing orders did not work in the North-West. The First Nations and Freemen, and now the young Brûlés, were all too independent for that. If the Nor'Westers wanted co-operation from the Brûlés, it had to be based on aligned interests. So, the Nor'Westers didn't create Grant as war chief. They had no ability to do that. But they did observe and they saw a young man with great ability. To the extent they gave him a title, captain-general, it was merely decoration on a cake already baked.

The Nor'Westers thought they saw in Grant and his *jeunes gens* a perfect pre-existing military force they could use to their advantage in their trade war against the Hudson's Bay Company. The Nor'Westers may have been the first to recognize the skills of the Métis and to try to harness that into a military force, but they weren't the last. Wanting to cast their dispute with the Hudson's Bay Company as a war, the Nor'Westers donned their War of 1812 uniforms. Grant and his young Brûlés adopted the Cree and Ojibwa custom of declaring war. By 1815 they were painting their faces with war paint, decorating their horses and hats with feathers, and wearing their guns, ammunition, knives and bows and arrows strapped to their bodies and their horses.

The infinity flag (*Courtesy of the Métis National Council*)

Cuthbert Grant led the Bois-Brûlés in their battle to protect their way of life, land and resources. By September 1815 the Brûlés forces were flying their own flag in Qu'Appelle, a white horizontal infinity symbol on a red background.[9] On June 1, 1816, Cuthbert Grant led forty-eight Brûlés to take the Hudson's Bay Company post at Brandon House. There the Brûlés flag was a white infinity symbol on a blue background.

While the central action took place in Red River, with Grant and Alexander Fraser mobilizing the men from Qu'Appelle, the Brûlés were also organizing throughout the North-West. William Shaw organized young Brûlés at Île-à-la-Crosse in the English River district of northwest Saskatchewan. Simon McGillivray did the same at Fort des Prairies (Edmonton), in the district of Athabasca. Carlton House and Cumberland House also supplied Brûlés for the cause.

The Brûlés throughout the North-West were well aware of the troubles that were brewing in Red River. The Bay men at the posts were worried and tried to get the Brûlés to pass on information. A Brûlé at Edmonton, Musqua, spoke of Nor'Wester canoes recently departed eastward from Cumberland House that were "full of Arms" and said that the men "in those Canoes will attack the Colonists or Servants of the Company in Red River." Musqua assured the Edmonton chief factor that he would not "attack any of our people."[10] They didn't attack, but within a month the Brûlés at Edmonton began to organize under their own officers. The idea of acting collectively as Brûlés was spreading.

When Grant called in his men, they came from all over the North-West, from Athabasca, the English River district, the Saskatchewan, and Swan River. It was this group, the boys Grant called his *jeunes gens*, that would come together at the Frog Plain on June 19, 1816, to fight the Selkirk Settlers. They gave the name and the origin story to the new nation of the North-West.

To the extent that Grant and the Brûlés were operating as allies and operatives of the Nor'Westers, the battle was corporate competition at its most brutal. To the extent that the Bois-Brûlés were a group operating on its own behalf, the battle was about expelling the strangers who were trying to impose new laws, structures and institutions that would greatly disadvantage the Brûlés. To some extent it was a mixture of both.

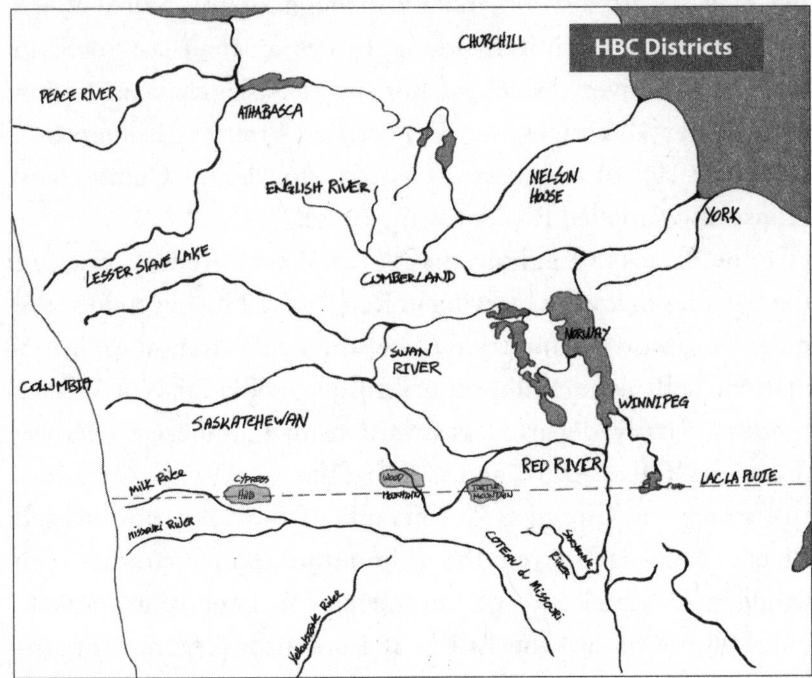

Who had the moral high ground in this dispute? In Red River the settlers had just arrived with their own imported system of British values and their own idea about appropriate conduct. The instant importation of British law privileged the newcomers' claims to land and resources and denied the previous Indigenous owners of the land. To the Brûlés there was no morality to be found in the settlers' claims. For the Brûlés it was simple: the newcomers were trying to steal the land and resources.

Bois-Brûlés morality was a mixture of what they learned from their parents. But it was far more than the sum of those parts. It was a creative mixing that was evolving into something new. From their mothers' Ojibwa and Cree cultures, the young

Brûlés were taught to place the highest value on an individual's right to independent thought and action. Young men were taught to be warriors and hunters and to take great pride in their skills. It was by means of those skills that they understood their manhood. It was by means of those skills that they provided the necessities for their people. A central part of those skills was their concept of protector and provider, which involved protecting the lands and resources regarded as the source of their people's livelihood. They could accept people who arrived and wanted to live in Red River. What they could not accept was that these outlanders could push them out. They were prepared to fight for their rights.

The Fur Trade Companies

Governor Macdonell, with his indelible ties to the Hudson's Bay Company, did not restrict his orders to the Métis. He also hit hard at the Nor'Westers. He sent his sheriff to confiscate pemmican from the Nor'Westers and ordered them to vacate Lord Selkirk's territory. The Nor'Westers could hardly be expected to remain passive spectators in light of these seizures and orders. But despite the escalating tension, the gentlemen of both companies were initially at pains to maintain the facade of geniality. In the early days of the settlement, Governor Macdonell dined often with his cousin Alexander Macdonell, who was a Nor'Wester at Fort Gibraltar. The gentlemen of both companies spent evenings together and played hurl (an early form of hockey). When the Nor'Westers requested the Company piper to perform at their evening dances, the governor agreed. The conviviality masked a growing hostility.

By June 1815 there were daily skirmishes between the Brûlés and the Nor'Westers on one side and the settlers and the Hudson's Bay Company men on the other. The Brûlés were often encamped at the Frog Plain, and from there they harried the settlement and the fort. Colonists began to abandon Macdonell. The Nor'Westers took advantage of his weakened position and aimed most of their attacks squarely at him. They claimed that if Macdonell gave himself up, there would be peace with the settlers. Macdonell eventually did give himself up in exchange, he thought, for two guarantees: that the settlers could stay in Red River and that there would be an end to the hostilities aimed at them.

The Nor'Westers whisked Macdonell out of Red River, ostensibly heading to Montreal for trial. But there was really no need to take him all the way to Montreal. They only needed him out of Red River. The Nor'Westers then proceeded to implement a propaganda campaign to persuade the settlers that life anywhere else was better than in Red River. Many more settlers fled.

On June 25, 1815, Cuthbert Grant issued an exit order to the remaining settlers. In Macdonell's absence, Peter Fidler, a Hudson's Bay Company employee, became the temporary leader of the Red River Settlement. Fidler tried to negotiate with Grant, but his offer was based on the premise that the settlers had a right to stay and make law for the settlement. He offered benevolence only. Grant flatly rejected the premise. The Brûlés claimed the right to control what they saw as "Red River Indian Territory." They would let the Hudson's Bay Company in and out to trade, but no government would be allowed to stay—certainly no government that could unilaterally affect the rights of the Brûlés. Fidler had no option but to sign their counter-proposal. The few remaining settlers packed their belongings, left the colony and headed north.

The Brûlés thought the settlers were gone for good. They were wrong. To the surprise of the Brûlés, and to the disgust of the Nor'Westers, the settlers returned in August 1815 with Colin Robertson, a former Nor'Wester now working for the Hudson's Bay Company and a man with long experience in the North-West. Robertson was smart enough to play the diplomat instead of the autocrat, and was therefore more successful than Macdonell had been in dealing with the Brûlés. Robertson also listened to them—something that Macdonell had thought himself above—offered work and made it known that he would not stop the Brûlés from engaging in their hunting practices.[11]

The Brûlés now found themselves in the sweet position of being courted with some success by both companies. Their sympathies, from long acquaintance, were certainly with the North West Company. But the Nor'Westers were often absent, and in the vacuum the young Brûlés came to appreciate offers of work and sympathy from Robertson. They could be convinced that their interests and loyalties were not always aligned with the Nor'Westers'.

Robertson tactic was to separate the young Brûlés from their allies, the Nor'Westers. He used a combination of carrot and stick. He held out a carrot to all the peoples in Red River—the Ojibwa, the Brûlés and the settlers. He used his stick on the Nor'Westers, and to good effect. When he seized the Nor'Westers' Fort Gibraltar in the spring of 1816, no Brûlés came seeking retribution.

While Robertson's tactics worked to some extent, they were too little and much too late. Then a new governor arrived.

Governor Robert Semple

Governor Robert Semple quickly became known as "Mr. Simple." He was a blunderbuss, full of his own importance and righteousness. He arrived fully equipped with a strong sense of moral superiority and shared Macdonell's truth, that the Brûlés were the unfortunate result of a violation of one of the most basic social rules—the intermarriage between two different races.

Where Robertson had calmed the waters, Semple poured gasoline on an increasingly tense situation. He was facing superior forces and had few resources other than the few remaining frightened settlers, who, despite some basic arms training, were not warriors. The governor's best asset was Fort Douglas, which came equipped with cannons, walls and a gate. While the fort provided him with a strategic advantage, that advantage would be lost if he did not keep his people behind the fort walls with the gate shut. Semple had no strategic goals and ignored the tactical advice he was given. Strategy and tactics do not seem to have been Semple's stronger suits.

The British government was warned about the poor governance Lord Selkirk was establishing in Red River, but England was far away and inclined toward a policy of wilful blindness as far as the Company was concerned. Meanwhile, Semple proceeded to dismantle the détente Robertson had so carefully engineered. Robertson tried to maintain his tactics, but Semple would have none of it. It was the worst possible time for the settlement leadership to get into an internal power dispute, but that is what happened. Semple prevailed—he was the governor, after all—and Robertson, the one man who might have averted the coming clash, left Red River. Things deteriorated quickly after that.

Jean-Baptiste Lagimodière

Louis Riel is considered the greatest hero of the Métis Nation, but his grandparents, Jean-Baptiste Lagimodière and Marie-Anne Gaboury, who were in Red River at this time, did not stand with the Brûlés; they were firmly on the side of the Hudson's Bay Company and the fledgling colony. Jean-Baptiste had formed a partnership with three other Canadians. These Freemen and their wives and families headed up the Saskatchewan River and in 1808 made their way to Fort Edmonton. Jean Baptiste and Marie-Anne spent the next three years hunting and trading in and around Alberta. Generally, men such as Lagimodière sold their services and furs to the North West Company, but when the factor at Fort Edmonton offered cash and a pound more than the Nor'Westers, Lagimodière switched companies.

In the spring of 1812, after hearing about the proposal to establish a settlement at Red River, the Lagimodières arrived and built a small cabin. They wanted to be part of the new settlement and were willing to make whatever investment it took to make that happen. When the settlers arrived, Jean-Baptiste became one of their hunters. He worked hand in hand with Robertson, and in 1815, with only eighteen colonists left and the colony in danger of collapse, accepted a dangerous mission. He agreed to travel to Montreal alone and as fast as possible to inform Lord Selkirk of the dangers facing the colony. Jean-Baptiste left Red River on October 17, 1815. He travelled eighteen hundred miles in three months—most of it, approximately twenty miles a day, on snowshoes. It took him five months to make the journey there and back again. It was a heroic feat of strength and endurance.

Lagimodière succeeded in warning Lord Selkirk and thus set

in motion the retaliation that followed. When Jean-Baptiste had left Red River that October morning, Marie-Anne moved into Fort Douglas with her five children. That is where Louis Riel's grandmother was on the day of the battle, and that is where Chief Peguis rescued her, the wife of a man he considered his brother, the next night.

CHAPTER 6

VICTORY AT THE FROG PLAIN

THE MÉTIS NATION ORIGIN STORY

Describing this time with an emphasis on the fur-trade "war" suggests that both companies were only fighting. But that, of course, is not true. They were still actively trading, and that work included gathering supplies to feed the canoe brigades and the new settlement at Red River. Governor Semple had set up a blockade at the Forks with the intention of inflicting severe damage on the Nor'Wester supply lines. Meanwhile the Brûlés and Nor'Westers were harassing the settlement's supply lines. In order to provide supplies to the Nor'Wester brigades, Cuthbert Grant and a force made up of Brûlés, Freemen and First Nations left Portage la Prairie on June 18, 1816. Their two carts were packed with eighteen hundred pounds of pemmican. They headed for the Frog Plain on the banks of the Red River, where they were to meet a brigade that was expected any day.

Grant and his Brûlés had two plans: One was to meet the brigade, pass on the pemmican and thereby break Semple's blockade. The second was to continue their ongoing harassment of the colony with the aim of inducing the settlers to surrender and leave. The Brûlés travelled a bit off the usual path, hoping to pass the settlement and the fort without being seen. They arrived at the Frog Plain at about five o'clock on the evening of June 19 and their plans unravelled immediately. They had been seen by the lookout at Fort Douglas.

Inside the fort, the alarm sounded. Governor Semple gathered a group of twenty-eight settlers and ordered the men to arm themselves, which they hastily did, though they had only what have been described as "useless muskets."[1] Following Semple's lead, the men, mostly young and inexperienced, left the fort and headed toward the Brûlés. They walked in single file and finally stopped at a grove of oak trees.

Settler witnesses claimed afterwards that Semple simply wanted to talk to the Brûlés to find out their intentions. But that claim is hardly credible. Semple was impulsive by nature, and to suggest that he was innocently engaged in a fact-finding mission does not square with the known facts. If he had wanted to engage in diplomacy, he should never have left the fort with such a large, armed party.

Grant's men were setting up camp at the Frog Plain and unloading their carts when their lookout saw Semple's party. Some of the men jumped on their horses and headed out to meet the settlers. Others secured the carts and supplies and deployed guards before they joined Grant. Men who arrived in the rear guard joined Grant's party as well. Gradually, the full force of the Brûlés came together. As they drew nearer, they saw the settlers halt and some men detach themselves from the party and head back to the fort. Semple had sent the men back for the cannon. Then the two forces met.

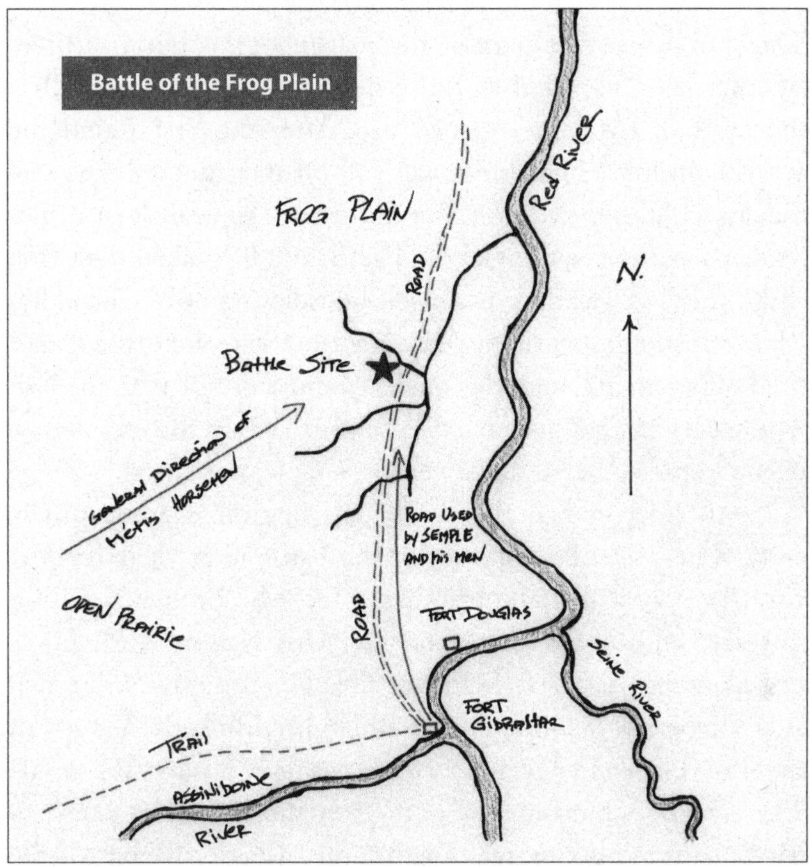

Grant had sixty-two men in his party, mostly Brûlés but also some Freemen and at least one Ojibwa. They were wearing war paint and bristling with arms, so this was not a casual group merely transporting pemmican. Grant's men surrounded the governor and the settlers in a menacing half-moon, a move that forced the settlers back and cut off any possibility of retreat. Grant sent Firmin Boucher forward to challenge Semple.

Boucher, like Governor Semple, was no diplomat, and the exchange quickly descended into snarls and challenges. The offended governor reached up to grab Boucher's bridle or gun.

Then, from another part of the half-moon, a shot was fired. Another shot was fired and a settler lay mortally wounded on the ground. Everyone opened fire. After the first round the settlers cheered. The Brûlés were all off their horses. The settlers thought they had won. But the settlers knew little of Brûlés horsemanship or battle tactics. The Brûlés had taken their first shots, then, as was their practice, slid sideways off their saddles while reloading. Before the settlers' cheers were done, the Brûlés fired off another round, this one even more deadly than the last. The settlers hadn't even tried to reload. Within fifteen minutes twenty settlers, including Governor Semple, were dead.

Both sides named the battle but they did it quite differently. The Métis Nation named the battle after their rendezvous, la Prayrii di la Goornouyayr (or "the Frog Plain"). To this day the battle is known to the Métis Nation in Michif as Paashkiiyaakanaan daan la Prayrii di la Goornouyayr, in French as la Victoire de la Grenouillière and in English as the Victory of the Frog Plain.[2] In Michif, *paashkiiyaakanaan* means "We won!" The term does not translate as mere victory; it carries a tone of triumphant self-congratulation. You get a better flavour of the word if you imagine it shouted with a fist shooting into the air with pride and satisfaction.

The Hudson's Bay Company and the Selkirk Settlers called it a massacre and named it after the nearby grove of oak trees. In our politically correct age it is now described as the Battle of Seven Oaks.

The different names given to the battle by the opposing sides tell us that there were different perspectives on the facts. Even the biological facts are incompatible. Frogs and oak trees do not cohabitate. Frogs live in and near water; oak trees don't like to get their feet wet.

Word of the battle spread across the land, and so did the blame. The settler accounts seethe with bitterness, rage and resentment. Prior to the battle the Company had given notice that it would blame the Nor'Westers if anything happened, and historians have generally picked up on this idea. Most historians depict the Brûlés as without agency in their own right and as the tools of the Nor'Westers. But Fidler, a Hudson's Bay Company man who is given great credit for his accounts in all other circumstances, has generally been ignored when he stated that he believed the Brûlés were "nearly master" of the Nor'Westers. According to Fidler, if the Nor'Westers wanted to execute their plans and work with the Brûlés to do that, they had to avoid interfering with the Brûlés' plans.[3] This suggests that the Brûlés did indeed have independent agency to act in their own interests, which at some points aligned with those of the Nor'Westers.

For their part, the Nor'Westers denied that they had incited the Brûlés into battle against the settlers. They claimed they had not taken part in the battle and were perfectly innocent. They would never, they loudly and repeatedly proclaimed, use any influence they possessed to instigate "the massacre of Lord Selkirk's helpless and deluded settlement." And the Nor'Westers would take no blame for the actions of the Brûlés, who were "personally responsible for their own criminal acts."[4]

But the Bois-Brûlés didn't care what the settlers, the Nor'Westers or the Hudson's Bay Company thought. They didn't see themselves as the tools of the Nor'Westers, and in fact, only one-fourth of their force worked for the North West Company.

After the victory the Bois-Brûlés were fierce, defiant and proud. Cuthbert Grant became their hero, and *la nouvelle nation* sang itself into being with a newly composed anthem, "La

Chanson des Bois-Brûlés." The lyrics of the song provide the Métis perspective on the battle. The Brûlés are "men of honour." There is no mention of the Nor'Westers, and the settlers are the "men who came across the sea," men who came to "steal our country."

The Victory of the Frog Plain established the Bois-Brûlés as a collective of warriors and resisters against any who would interfere with their rights. They claimed an identity as an independent Indigenous people—*la nouvelle nation*. The Métis Nation also began a bardic tradition that has continued to this day. Pierre Falcon, the composer, became the most famous of the Métis bards. His songs were taken up by the northmen voyageurs and "La Chanson des Bois-Brûlés" was sung throughout the North-West. The Métis have always sung this song. Sometimes so often that passengers in canoes complained they were sick to death of hearing it. Seventy years later it was still a song that could rouse patriotism and inspire the Métis. The Métis Nation continues to sing it two hundred years later.

The Victory of the Frog Plain is the story consciously chosen by the Métis Nation as its origin story, and "La Chanson des Bois-Brûlés" is the song that celebrates the birth of the new nation.

WHO SHOT FIRST

The Victory of the Frog Plain looms large in Métis Nation history. It also remains an important story for the Selkirk Settlers. The two-hundredth anniversary of the battle was commemorated in Winnipeg in 2016, and the two sides clearly still had different perspectives on what had happened that day and why. One of the major points of dispute is who shot first at the battle. Who was the attacker and who was the defender? The two sides of the story are really about who is to blame. No one can prove who actually shot first that day on the Frog Plain, but it is worth a walk through the story to try to understand why this issue is still so sensitive two hundred years later.

It is unlikely that one of the settlers shot first on purpose. Imagine being on foot and surrounded by sixty-plus armed, mounted and painted warriors, all with their guns pointed at you. It would have been suicidal for a settler to shoot first on purpose. But could a settler have shot first accidentally? In setting out from the fort, the settlers had loaded their muskets too quickly. They had at least one misfire on their march to the battle. And they were scared. In a panic, a man could easily squeeze his finger too tightly on the trigger. So, it is possible that one of the settlers shot first by accident.

It is also quite possible that one of the Brûlés shot first. After all, while the confrontation was accidental, the Brûlés were not out on an innocent ride that day. They had captured three settlers in order to keep them from raising the alarm, and they had been escalating the conflict for months. The tension that day was so high, someone could have sneezed and set off the conflagration. The governor had grabbed at Boucher. Most eyes would have been on that exchange. Perhaps one Brûlé took preemptive action.

Commissioner William Bacheler Coltman, who was appointed to investigate the deaths of Governor Semple and the settlers, provided an early opinion on the question when he noted that five witnesses said a settler shot first and only one witness said the Brûlés shot first. In seeking to convince Cuthbert Grant to testify before him, Coltman proposed that the Brûlés claim their actions were self-defence. "It is always understood that the Colony people pursued you, or came forward to meet you and fired the first shot while Boucher was speaking to them."[5]

Before we take Coltman's statements at face value, it is worth remembering that all the witnesses who survived, except for two, were Brûlés. And then there is the question of Coltman's loyalties. He was hardly neutral. Indeed, he was known to be sympathetic to, if not an outright advocate for, the North West Company. Coltman conceptualized the problem as a private war between the companies that needed to be settled. He also perceived a need to keep the Brûlés in British territory, in large part because he worried about the loss of the Canadian West to the Americans. He saw Cuthbert Grant, the young Métis leader, as the lever through which all of this mess could eventually be straightened out. This early conceptualization of the problem framed his tactics, his inquiry and his recommendations. To achieve his pacifist and nationalist goals, he needed Grant to co-operate and he needed the Nor'Westers to ply their influence in the courts. So, Lord Selkirk was entirely accurate when he worried about the "burrs of intimacy" between Coltman and the Nor'Westers.[6]

The battle at the Frog Plain was a spontaneous combustion. Both sides went to the scene prepared for trouble, but neither side had a premeditated plan to kill. Laying the blame on the settlers for shooting first in no way diminishes what happened after the initial explosion. From the Euro-Canadian perspective, the actions of the Métis after the initial shots were fired were the cause of grave indignation. According to their accounts, the wounded were slain, one settler was shot in the back while fleeing, and a man was killed while begging for mercy on his knees. The "savage force" of the Brûlés horrified the Euro-Canadians.[7]

The use of the term "savage" had by this time become habitual for the English and French. The Indigenous peoples of North America were seen as savage, wild, ferocious and, worst of all, unpredictable. Indigenous peoples resisted the cultural assumptions buried in the rules and law that Euro-Canadians saw as neutral and sought to enforce. The misunderstandings were legion, and because the Hudson's Bay Company had no ability to win a battle at arms, as the battle at the Frog Plain had just so eloquently proved, there was no middle ground, no place where peace could be negotiated.[8] Such middle ground requires a stalemate of force, and that was patently not the case in Red River. The Brûlés had the upper hand in all respects when it came to force.

For the Bois-Brûlés, on the other hand, the battle that had just taken place—although not the brutality afterwards—was simply the custom of war as they knew it. They were well "habituated to all the arts of Indian warfare."[9] The settlers were outlanders with no social standing in the Brûlés' world and had two options for survival: they could either fight to establish themselves as the dominant force, or they could forge alliances and personal ties with the Ojibwa and Brûlés.

The Hudson's Bay Company and Lord Selkirk didn't like either of those options. They didn't want their settlers descending into savages, and that is what they thought would happen if their values and rules did not prevail. They wanted to keep their men within the control of what they considered their legitimate authority. The English did not perceive the Brûlés to be the legitimate or authorized representatives of a society. They were something new, unpredictable and dangerous—a threat to the existing elites of the fur trade and the burgeoning colonial empire. The English were horrified by what had happened at the Frog Plain, in part because the Brûlés had prevailed and proved the English to be incompetent in battle. They were also infuriated that the Métis gloried in their victory. Pierre

Falcon dared to mock the English in his song. This, the English thought, was a world without a centre, a world without order.

But several things must be said about the early nineteenth century and violence. First, violence and the fur trade were old friends. The history of the fur trade had always been violent and bloody. But both sides also brought their own cultural understandings to the bloodshed on that June day in 1816. Euro-Canadians make a distinction between death in war and death in peace, which they call murder. For Euro-Canadians, war deaths usually carry no retribution when the war ends. The state's response to murder in the nineteenth century was the death penalty.

This distinction was important after the events at the Frog Plain. Was it war, albeit a private war between the two fur-trade companies with Brûlés and settler soldiers? Or was it murder of innocent civilians by the Brûlés? If it was war, what penalty could be enacted against the Brûlés for the death of the settlers? Logically, if one followed the values of the Euro-Canadians, no penalty could ensue. But if the battle at the Frog Plain was not war, then under Euro-Canadian rules, one must determine exactly who killed whom, and whether there was any justification for the killing, such as self-defence. Lord Selkirk and the surviving settlers characterized the events at the Frog Plain as murder.

The Brûlés had a very different perspective. When someone was killed, the Brûlés, like their Cree and Ojibwa cousins, did not distinguish between war and peace. They distinguished between ally and enemy. For a dead ally, compensation and restitution would be negotiated. For a dead enemy, blood revenge, a life for a life, was expected as retaliation. The settlers had the opportunity when they first arrived in Red River to establish themselves as friends and allies, but they had long since moved into the realm of enemy. For the Brûlés, the battle at the Frog Plain was a battle with an enemy. The death of Governor Semple was also blood revenge. Semple was wounded in the initial round of firing but not fatally. The First Nations man who administered the fatal shot to Governor Semple claimed that he was taking his blood revenge for Semple's killing of his relatives.[10] There was no meeting of the minds between the Brûlés and the Euro-Canadians on this point.

The settlers also complained about the actions of the Brûlés after their compatriots had already fallen in the battle. They claimed that "on the bodies of the dead were practised all those horrible barbarities that characterise the inhuman heart of the savage."[11] The Brûlés have always denied collective responsibility for those deeds. The Brûlés say the cruelties committed after the battle were the acts of the notorious Deschamps family and that it was the Brûlés who shamed them into stopping.

The Coltman Report reiterated the statement that Commissioner Coltman had first suggested to Grant: that the settlers pursued the Brûlés, instigated the confrontation and shot first. The Brûlés, in song and story, told the same self-defence story. The settlers maintained their version, that they were the innocent victims of Brûlés brutality and that the Brûlés shot first. The discrepancies cannot be resolved by reference to the facts. But the dispute continues to be a bone of contention between the Métis Nation and the descendants of the Selkirk Settlers.

From the very first day when Pierre Falcon enshrined the battle in song, the Brûlés claimed the settlers shot first. For two hundred years, the Métis have told and retold this story. A battle in which your ancestors successfully defended themselves against outlanders who came to take their land makes for a good story, one that a people can be pleased with, one that teaches them about their noble origins as a good people who fought to defend their lands and their families.

SELKIRK, COLTMAN AND GRANT

Lord Selkirk was furious about the death of his governor and the settlers. He was determined to make those responsible pay for their crimes. After Jean-Baptiste Lagimodière warned him about the dangers facing the colony, Selkirk sent an official complaint to Great Britain. He never bothered to register a complaint in Montreal. It doesn't seem to have occurred to him that he might need the co-operation of Canadian law enforcement. That oversight would cost him dearly in the end.

Instead, he took the law into his own hands. He put together a band of discharged soldiers from Canada (about one hundred Swiss mercenaries, veterans of the De Meuron Regiment) and headed to the North-West to administer his own vigilante justice. He captured Nor'Wester depots and forts, arrested partners and seized their goods. He also tried, and failed, to woo Freemen and Brûlés to his side with enticements of food, amusements and a ball—all of which was sweetly satirized by Pierre Falcon in the song "Lord Selkirk at Fort William."

Meanwhile the Nor'Westers were busy on their side taking retaliatory action. Both sides were blockading passage of provisions on the rivers. Then a proclamation from the governor-general arrived in January 1817.[12] All parties were ordered to keep the peace. A commission of inquiry was established and due authority was given to Commissioners Coltman and John Fletcher to investigate the events that led to the death of Governor Semple and the settlers at Red River.

The Nor'Westers and the Bay men were disposed to ignore the governor-general's order and the Coltman Commission of Inquiry. They simply continued their violent trade war. But some Brûlés and particularly their Freemen fathers began to pay attention. Cuthbert Grant was still harassing the Hudson's Bay Company forts and supply lines, and even tried to force some reluctant Brûlés to accompany him. But the Freemen fathers of the young Brûlés began to exert pressure on their sons to stay out of the ongoing trade war. If the law was indeed coming, the Freemen didn't want their sons to be the only ones in its path.

The Brûlés were able to separate Grant into two men: one was the man who acted in the interests of the Nor'Westers; the other was their chief, who acted to protect and assert the interests of the Brûlés. With the coming law, resistance to Grant the Nor'Wester began to grow. If the Métis could be convinced that a call from their leader to take up arms was in their interests, they would answer. But when Grant was seen to be acting solely in the interests of the Nor'Westers, the Brûlés could and did exercise their option to refuse.

When Lord Selkirk and his mercenaries arrived in the North-West and sought to capture the Nor'Wester post at Rainy Lake, Grant the Nor'Wester tried to persuade the Brûlés to assist him in holding the post against Selkirk's advancing forces. Many said no. Unlike Selkirk's De Meurons, they did not see themselves as mercenaries who could be deployed at the will of Grant on behalf of the Nor'Westers. Only a few followed Grant to defend the Nor'Wester fort at Rainy Lake. When the Nor'Westers urged them to move farther east to defend their post at Fort William, the Brûlés declined. They were persuaded that their interests extended to Rainy Lake, but most would only defend their lands in Red River. Fort William was much too far east. It was outside their understanding of where their land and resource interests lay.

The young Brûlés flew to arms to protect their leader Grant when the Hudson's Bay Company men tried to arrest him. Yet only a few days later when Grant the Nor'Wester sought to deploy the Métis against Lord Selkirk's forces at Fort Douglas, they declined. This was not simply quixotic behaviour on the part of the Métis. They followed Grant when he initiated projects they cared about. They felt no compunction to follow him everywhere. They did not serve and obey.

"Farce or folly" was Lord Selkirk's lawyer's description of Commissioner Coltman's associate John Fletcher.[13] The description can just as aptly be applied to the Coltman Commission of Inquiry, Lord Selkirk and the biased legal process that followed. In 1816 the North-West was not devoid of law. In fact there was a smorgasbord of laws to choose from. The First Nations had their own laws, and traders spending time in their camps would be expected to abide by those laws. The Métis were just starting to develop their Laws of the Prairie, which would apply to those who lived in their camps or travelled with them on their buffalo hunts. The Company and the Nor'Westers each had corporate rules to discipline their employees and those in their posts. Canada had criminal law that theoretically applied in the North-West, but because of the distance and thin population, it was enforced only in the most egregious cases. The Selkirk Settlers, being for the most part displaced Highlanders, were likely more familiar with Scottish law than English law.

There were places in the North-West, such as Red River, where every one of these legal traditions was operating at the same time. There were also places out on the Plains where there was no law at all. There were people who adhered to one of these systems of law, and there were others who chose from the smorgasbord at their convenience. Despite the multiplicity of available law, actually enforcing law in the North-West was often impossible. So, the different sides in the battle at the Frog Plain gathered their witnesses and evidence, and everyone—Lord Selkirk, Commissioner Coltman, Cuthbert Grant and many Brûlés—went to Montreal, where the second act of the legal farce was about to begin.

In order to secure Grant's voluntary surrender, Coltman virtually offered him a pardon based on self-defence. Grant saw his out and took it. He called on his friend and fellow trader Joseph Cadotte and together they rode into Coltman's camp. In surrendering with Cadotte at his side, Grant was drawing attention to his deep ties with the Nor'Westers. Cadotte was the son, nephew and grandson of important Nor'Westers. Grant himself had ties to the highest Nor'Westers. So when Grant and Cadotte surrendered to Coltman, they were really surrendering to the Nor'Westers. Grant gave his deposition and then travelled to Montreal in style as Coltman's guest.

THE TRIALS

In the courts in Montreal hundreds of charges were laid. Lord Selkirk laid charges against the North West Company, several of its employees and its partners. The North West Company laid charges against the Hudson's Bay Company and against Lord Selkirk. Charges were laid against several Brûlés, including Cuthbert Grant. The trials stumbled from adjournment to adjournment.

Several North West Company agents were on the grand juries, and the chief justice declined to ask them to recuse themselves. There were no judges to be found in Montreal who were not connected to the North West Company, related to the partners, or in the actual pockets of the Nor'Westers. Two of the three judges recused themselves for conflict of interest. At least the judges admitted their conflict. The same could not be said for the lawyers. John Beverley Robinson, the attorney-general and prosecutor, had deep connections with the North West Company but never admitted to having a conflict of interest.

Eventually the trials were transferred to the courts of Upper Canada. Many of the charges were dismissed in the transfer and lawyers from Lower Canada were not allowed to appear, which caused further delays. Selkirk's lawyer Samuel Gale, never at a loss for a sarcastic turn of phrase, commented that the conspiracy charges were so vague they failed to specify who was conspired against, the governor of the Red River Settlement or "the Emperor of Morocco or the Cham of Tartary."[14]

Lord Selkirk protested to anyone who would listen. His governor and settlers had been killed and yet the Canadian justice system appeared to be taking no action. Selkirk thought the inaction was due to the interference of the North West Company, and he was not wrong in his suspicion. Bail set against him by Commissioner Coltman for the misdemeanour of resisting arrest was at least double the amounts set against the Brûlés and the Nor'Westers for murder and complicity to murder. In response to his many protests, he was told quite bluntly that Canadian officials were acting on orders from higher-ups, meaning the British Colonial Office in London, which had issued orders that an indictment was to be preferred against Lord Selkirk and for his arrest. This influenced Canadian officials, who consequently acted on the assumption that they were to take all measures to bring Lord Selkirk to justice. In addition, no Canadian court or Crown law office would let Lord Selkirk use his British lawyers.

They hated the idea of a British lord waltzing into Canada, raising his own army of mercenaries and then coming into court with his own lawyers seeking to pursue private prosecutions. Lord Selkirk's search for justice was doomed, and it was very late in the day before he began to understand the full array of the forces he was facing.

Meanwhile Commissioner Coltman was still taking depositions, trying in vain to make peace between the two companies and working to keep Grant out of the fray. To Coltman's way of thinking, two things were needed: First, peace had to be made between the companies. This was a tall order, but the courts could not stand in the way of this goal. Second, the important Freemen and Brûlés, like Cuthbert Grant, had to be encouraged to stay in British territory. In order to do so, they could not be facing charges in Montreal. They needed to be in the North-West.

Coltman wrote a report, submitted it to the court and then wrote to the lieutenant-governor. Shortly after receiving the report, the legal process, which had long been delaying, convened a grand jury and immediately freed Grant on a small recognizance. Fermin Boucher and Paul Brown, both participants in the battle at the Frog Plain, were tried and acquitted, and it was likely that Grant would have been too, but he didn't wait around to find out. Grant skipped bail and headed back to Red River. Every effort had been made by the Nor'Westers to enable Grant to go free.

Years passed as trials were transferred from place to place and adjourned frequently. The years consumed an extraordinary amount of money, including a considerable chunk of Lord Selkirk's fortune. For all the trials, the money and the years, there was nothing to show when it was all over. There were no convictions for the events on the Frog Plain. Most of the cases were dismissed or allowed to languish for years. No one cared. The trials ended when Lord Selkirk, in ill health, left the country at the end of 1818. His departure brought down the curtain on the legal farce. It had been Selkirk's folly to fan the flames of the legal farce, and when he exited, everyone was happy to leave the theatre.

PART TWO

MAKING THE NATION

CHAPTER 7

AFTER THE MERGER

The British government finally turned its full attention to the trade war in the North-West and insisted on peace and union between the companies. A hard negotiation followed, and eventually, in 1821, a new company was forged under the name of the Hudson's Bay Company. The Ojibwa, the Brûlés and the Freemen were not happy about the loss of jobs, lack of competition and higher prices. On paper, the Hudson's Bay Company had been a monopoly since 1670. On the ground, however, there had long been competition. When the competition was eliminated, the Company imposed harsh new rules. There were now tight limitations on credit, and the settlers were given a priority right to goods at the forts. The Ojibwa were sent to the back of the trading line. The Company also cut back on the traditional practice of giving generous ceremonial presents, the means by which the alliance between the Ojibwa and the Company had always been reaffirmed.

The Ojibwa retaliated by obstructing the passes and setting fire to the Plains, all to keep the buffalo herds away from Red River. They arrived at the Company's new fort at the Forks with their faces painted black. It was a visible symbol of their anger and grief at the death of a valued trading relationship. The Brûlés understood the message and shared the Ojibwa concern. The Company ignored them both. The settlers were oblivious.

From the Ojibwa and Brûlés perspective, the relationship was damaged further when the Company, shortly after the merger, in August 1821, welcomed a party of their traditional enemy, the Sioux, into the fort. Assuming the Sioux were there to attack, Cuthbert Grant gathered a group and galloped to the rescue. It was a dangerous move to bring the Sioux right into the middle of Ojibwa and Brûlés territory. It could have started a war. The Sioux departed peacefully and a confrontation with the Ojibwa was narrowly avoided. But the Company's action was reckless. Still furious with Grant for the battle at the Frog Plain, the Company men took the opportunity to ridicule Grant for his effort to defend the colony. Their disrespect toward Grant may have played well among their own people, but it further distanced the Company from the Ojibwa and the Brûlés.

The merger was followed by a downsizing operation. Brûlés across the North-West were cut loose from their contracts and became Freemen. They attached themselves to several different settlements, such as Île-à-la-Crosse in northwest Saskatchewan, but Red River absorbed the bulk of the men and their families.

After the merger, the Brûlés Freemen were reluctant to lose the trading contacts and influence they had enjoyed when they were under employment with the Nor'Westers. There were influential Brûlés and Canadian Freemen at large in the area. Joseph Cadotte, Augustin Nolin and Régis Larante were all nearby, either just south of the border or at Rainy Lake. Grant himself was now a Freeman. The Brûlés Freemen came up with a plan to create their own version of the North West Company, which they thought to headquarter on the American side of the border in Pembina. From there they would be ideally placed to work with American traders coming from the Mississippi and Wisconsin and those heading farther west to the Missouri and Oregon country. They were perfectly situated to pick up the trade war exactly where the Nor'Westers had left it. It was a good plan and it was exactly the situation Commissioner Coltman had envisaged and feared. But Coltman was out of the picture now, and Grant was an important piece on the chessboard, roaming at large, unattached, very influential and possibly dangerous to the new Company.

The Brûlés Freemen wanted Grant to be the leader in their grand scheme. Unfortunately, their call came too late. Unbeknownst to them, George Simpson, the new governor of the Hudson's Bay Company's Northern Department, had already met with Grant. In Simpson, the Company had, for the first time, a leader with the kind of energy and ambition that had fuelled the Nor'Westers. Simpson saw in Cuthbert Grant exactly what Coltman had seen: a young man with influence that could be employed on the Freemen, the Brûlés and First Nations. Simpson wanted Grant inside the new Hudson's Bay Company tent, not outside causing trouble. So, he made Grant an offer of a new working relationship with the Company and Grant accepted. He declined the offer from the Brûlés Freemen, and his loss to their scheme was fatal. No one else had the strength of character or leadership skills to carry out the plan.

Why did Grant accept Simpson's offer? He didn't do it for the money. The potential for making the most money lay with the Brûlés Freemen plan, not with the Company. He didn't do it for prestige. Grant would have no partnership track in the new Hudson's Bay Company and no high position. He didn't do it for the land he was offered either. Grant could have taken as much land as he wanted in Pembina and been welcomed there. Simply put, Grant had a vision, a nationalist vision, for the Bois-Brûlés. His main concern was his *jeunes gens*, the future of *la nouvelle nation*. Grant's national vision was born in the trade war but needed to grow in peace. Taking up a leadership role in a new version of the Nor'Westers would continue the war. Grant opted for peace.

At first Simpson tried making Grant a clerk, but for the Company employees and the settlers, the memory of the Frog Plain was too raw. So, Simpson created a new role for Grant as a private trader and freighter. Simpson wanted Grant settled in Red River, and he persuaded the Company to provide Grant with land at the White Horse Plain (a few miles west of the Forks, on the Assiniboine River). Grant built his home there and gradually created a settlement of over eighty families that became known as Grantown. He was no longer the rash young man who so recklessly took his young men into battle. The man who returned from Montreal had grown wiser. After the merger, true to Indigenous custom, the war chief of the Brûlés melted back into the population and began to take on the role of a mature Indigenous leader. Grant fully embraced this new role and wielded it well for the next many decades.

The Company appointed Grant "Warden of the Plains of Red River" in July 1828 with an annual salary of two hundred pounds. From Turtle Mountain to Qu'Appelle, he was licensed to trade and freight. He was also hired to prevent the illicit trade in furs, enforce the Company monopoly, keep the Brûlés loyal to the Company, and stop Americans from encroaching. In addition to his leadership role, Grant became a healer and was well known for his medical skills. Under Grant's leadership, the Brûlés honed their military skills and used them to protect themselves and the colony at Red River from the Sioux. To all appearances the Brûlés were settling down and merging into the Red River settlement. The settlers heard little talk of the new nation and believed it to be a victim of the new order. Appearances can be deceptive.

FROM PEOPLE TO NATION

There is a distinction between an ethnic group, or a people, and a nation. There are six indicators of an ethnic group: (1) a collective name, (2) a common myth of descent or an originating story, (3) a shared history, (4) a distinctive shared culture, (5) an association with a specific territory, and (6) a sense of solidarity. By 1816 the Bois-Brûlés had acquired a foothold on all six indicators of an ethnic group. They had named themselves and had an origin story. They shared some history now and were developing their own language and distinctive culture.

They called the North-West their motherland and with good reason. They were forming strong roots in Red River. But there were many Métis families who were only loosely connected with Red River. A large and mobile group of Métis families, linked by the pemmican provisioning trade network, was arising west of Red River in Qu'Appelle, around Fort des Prairies (Edmonton), the Milk River and the North Saskatchewan River region.

The Bois-Brulés had a sense of solidarity, which was greatly in evidence before, during and after the events that took place on the Frog Plain in June 1816. At the time, they were recognized as a distinct group and called by their name. But no one, not even the Nor'Westers, really believed they were a distinct ethnic group, a people or a nation. Despite the lack of recognition, the Bois-Brûlés proclaimed themselves to be a new nation. Were they?

An ethnic group becomes a nation when it enters the political arena and attempts to influence the distribution of power. Once a group crosses the political threshold, it remains a political actor. Its political force may wax and wane. It may be more successful at times, may lay dormant for a period, or may burst onto the world stage. But once the group has tasted political activity, there is no going back. If the group continues to exist, it will not willingly give up its identity as a political actor—a nation.

The Brûlés origin story celebrates the birth of the political entity, the nation. It is not the story of the birth of the Bois-Brûlés as an Indigenous people. The origin story was the distinct ethnic group asserting its new collective political consciousness. They intended to expel the settlers "and never see any of them again in the Colonizing way in Red River."[1] There is nothing quite like the expulsion of the "other" to bring a collective consciousness to the forefront. The battle at the Frog Plain fully demonstrated the Brûlés' collective power to conquer and, perhaps more importantly, their awareness of that power.

In 1816 the Brûlés had a common goal—the protection of their land, resources and way of life—and they used a combination of force and negotiation to obtain that goal. Perhaps they were not a full-fledged nation at the time, despite their claims, but they were certainly a nascent one. At the time, the name *la nouvelle nation* was an awkward fit. It was a bit too large for these exuberant youth who were still flexing their collective muscles and lacking in the organization that is usually associated with the concept of a nation. Still, they had a sense of a collective identity and rights, and the political genie had been let out of the bottle. In those early days of 1815 to 1816 when they were first proclaiming their nationhood, the awkward fit didn't disturb them. They saw themselves as a group that was different and unique. That was the fertile idea that began to take root.

A nation comes into existence when a sizable group of people say they have formed one, act to protect their interests and, over time, grow into that proclamation. It doesn't matter if, at the time of the declaration, the bulk of those included do not see themselves as members of the nation. Massimo d'Azeglio was famous for noting the distinction when he said, "Italy is made, but who will now make the Italians?"[2] From the generation of Brûlés born in the North-West of the 1790s, the idea that they were a distinct people took root and flourished. They loudly proclaimed themselves to be a nation in 1816 and then proceeded to make it so.

Some say the whole idea of *la nouvelle nation* was a fraud from the beginning. Some say the Brûlés were not acting as an Indigenous collective but instead were simply acting as the "tools" of the Nor'Westers. Some say the Nor'Westers came up with the nation idea and that the Brûlés were so suggestible, so naive, so gullible, they simply parroted their master. The suggestion that the Brûlés were incapable of coming up with worthy ideas is a narrative we will see repeated often in this history. But it really doesn't matter who came up with the nationhood idea first. Such ideas do not take root in infertile soil. If the young Brûlés had not already seen themselves as a separate group, the idea of proclaiming themselves a nation would never have taken hold, even as precariously as it did in those first heady days. The idea that the Brûlés were a new nation took root because the ground had already been prepared. The Brûlés already had feelings of collective belonging. The northmen voyageurs who went free had established the social glue that was required to bind the

Brûlés into a people and a nation. They needed only time and freedom to reinforce the bond, and that reinforcement came from their families.

The Family

The Métis Nation created only two institutions. One was the self-governance they developed on the buffalo hunts. The second was a central and lasting Métis Nation institution: the family. The Métis Nation cannot be understood without a full understanding of the Métis family. "Family" as understood by the Métis was very different from "family" as understood by Euro-Canadians. For the Métis, family was the basic unit of life, the relationship, or *wahkootowin*, around which all life revolved, including social customs, marriage, trade and the economy.[3] The family was a world view that guided all Métis values and behaviour. Family was deeply treasured and no man or woman advanced alone. Reciprocity, mutual support and the sharing ethic were the central values of the Métis family.

The Freemen, who had originally lived with the bands, began to live independently with their wives and children. They formed hunting bands with other Freemen families. Their children intermarried and spread out across the North-West, forming large, extended-family hunting brigades. It was the women, often sisters, who held these brigades together.[4]

In their respect for their extended family, the Métis were at odds with Euro-Canadians and with their priests. The priests often admonished the Métis for visiting, partying and sharing—all practices that reinforced the family—and Euro-Canadians constantly derided the Métis for their large, often dependent, families. The Métis loved and cherished their large and extended families.

Métis women and children in the lee of a Red River cart (*Saskatoon Public Library LH-907*)

The central tenet of the Métis family was a belief that relatives do no harm to each other and in fact are obligated to support family members financially and physically. This included those who were made family by ceremony or by a significant and continuing relationship. The Métis brought this view to their trading partners. Once a relationship was acknowledged, the Métis would see it as an obligation to provide support when called on. Conversely, the Métis would expect a trading partner, especially one with whom they had long traded, to provide support in the form of food, tools or shelter at need. This difference of world view was a constant source of discord between the Métis and the Company.

Despite the extended kinship foundation, the nuclear family was the basic social grouping for the Métis. But it was a different nuclear family than what Western Christians are used to. Before the clergy arrived in the North-West, Métis families were often polygamous, with all of the wives living together. One old Métis told the story of King Beaulieu, which sheds some light on Métis families as they were when the priests arrived:

> [O]ld King Beaulieu . . . had seven wives . . . Then the priest came into the country and said to him . . . "You will have to send away all but one wife." King Beaulieu said, "Why?" The priest said, "Because it's against the Catholic Church." So they argued a long time, and finally Beaulieu said, "All right; I'll only keep two of them." . . . The priest said, "All right. But you can only have one wife. The other will have to be your housekeeper." They didn't know what was a housekeeper in this country. Didn't even know the word. But all right. So they lived that way.[5]

In the story, the priest walked away convinced he had stopped a polygamous relationship and, on that basis, brought old King Beaulieu into the Christian fold. But old King Beaulieu kept his two wives, although one had the new and exotic title "housekeeper." He probably kept his other wives as well.

The trading companies had little good to say about the fact that the Métis always travelled with their families and could not be separated from them. But Métis life required the family to travel and work together. Women were possessed of prized fishing skills and were largely responsible for small game, which became important food sources when large game animals became scarce. As the buffalo robe trade increased in the 1840s, it became crucial to have female labour in preparing the robes, which had to be done on the killing fields. Manufacturing the products of the hunt—pemmican, tallow and robes—was very labour intensive and required the participation of all of the family. It was not something that a single male hunter could do alone.

Every Métis family was embedded in a wide network of kin relationships, and loyalty to family superseded all other loyalties. This was one of the aspects of Métis culture that separated them from the Euro-Canadians in the North-West. The Métis Nation has one large kinship system with subgroups identified by family surnames. Métis surname groups were large and the families covered the entirety of the North-West. Their constant mobility reinforced the family networks for generations. The family surname groups began in the early 1800s and they continue today.

CHAPTER 8

THE BUFFALO HUNTERS

THEY LIVE ENTIRELY BY THE CHASE

Buffalo meat was both food and currency. Wages were paid in buffalo meat, as was the price of land and payment to the missionaries for educating Brûlés children. While the Selkirk Settlers made valiant efforts to produce crops, there is no question that agriculture at Red River was mostly a failure until after 1870. In thirty of the years between 1813 and 1870, the crops were destroyed. Crop destruction came in many forms: grasshoppers, spring and fall frosts, fires, mice, disease, hail, floods and lack of or too much rain. The 1820s were a particularly bad decade. While the fisheries of Lake Manitoba and at Red River provided an important backstop, buffalo was the food everyone relied on, and the Brûlés buffalo hunters were the main providers of that food. They earned good money for their work, and this too was an incentive to remain on the Plains and follow the herds. Alexander Ross wrote, "[D]uring the years 1839, 40, and 41, the Company expended £5,000 on the purchase of plain provisions, of which the hunters got last year the sum of £1,200, being rather more money than all the agricultural class obtained for their produce in the same year."[1]

Buffalo running through grass (*Saskatoon Public Library LH-3065*)

Some of the Freemen settled down to farm in Red River, but farming had little appeal for most Brûlés. Their Freemen fathers had not escaped farm life in Quebec, gone free and earned prestige as hunters and traders in order to trade all that in for farms in the North-West. For their sons, the monotonous toil of the settlers had virtually no appeal. They lived, as George Simpson said, "entirely by the chase."[2] They liked the freedom of the Plains, the wind in their faces and the constant change that mobility brought. They might like eating potatoes, but not enough to hang around and watch them grow.

In the early years of the nineteenth century, the Selkirk Settlers wintered at Pembina, and the Freemen and Brûlés hunters gathered there in order to hunt in the buffalo preserve at Turtle Mountain. Virtually everyone deserted the colony at Red River in the winter. They might stay in Red River over Christmas for celebrations, but they would quickly return to Pembina, the Plains or the fisheries on Lake Manitoba or Lake Winnipeg. Life was easier at Pembina. The weather was milder and it provided easier access to the buffalo.

In those early days the hunters went out in every season. Spring travel was difficult because the melting snow left the ground soggy, but there were summer, winter and fall hunts. By 1826 this irregularity had been replaced by two annual hunts, one in summer and one in winter. They would often hunt around Turtle Mountain, but other times they headed farther north around Brandon House. Freemen and Brûlés hunted both with and apart from the organized hunts. But if they travelled apart, it was in a group. It was always necessary to guard against attacks, particularly from the Sioux.

The growing numbers of Freemen and Brûlés congregating in Pembina made George Simpson, the governor of the Hudson's Bay Company uneasy. They were too close to the American traders and their presence provoked the Sioux. Simpson moved the Company's Pembina post some sixty miles north to the Forks of the Red and Assiniboine Rivers. He pressed the small Pembina settlement to relocate north of the border. Many did just that. Some relocated to the land Cuthbert Grant had received from Simpson on the White Horse Plain. From Grantown the Brûlés continued to hunt buffalo under the leadership of Grant.

After 1816 the Freemen and Brûlés buffalo hunt began to grow in earnest. This is where the genius of Cuthbert Grant can be seen. It was Grant who set up the organization that would grow into the legendary Métis hunts. Grant brought the wild and independent Freemen and Brûlés together. He fostered an atmosphere where they maintained their pride and freedom and yet still learned to work together as a unit. And Grant devised the democratic rules—the command structure, the elections and the laws of the hunt. Rarely has a charismatic leader been so effective on the administrative and organizational front. Rarely has such a leader been able to transform enthusiasm and exuberance into an institution built on everything the Métis cherished—freedom, mobility, democracy, the family and the hunt. Grant forged this raw material, this ragtag lot, into a mobile, armed host.

In the 1820s the Freemen and Brûlés hunters on the great buffalo hunts came together from three locations: Pembina, the Forks and the White Horse Plain. The rendezvous was on the Pembina River, just south of the border. When all the families arrived at the rendezvous, an assembly was called. The chief captain of the hunt was elected, and in those early days it was often Cuthbert Grant. The chief captain of the hunt then chose ten *dizaines* (captains), "the old hunters," who subsequently chose ten scouts and camp guards. The chief captain of the hunt and the ten captains became the Council of the Hunt.

The organization of the buffalo hunt with its captains, chain of command and laws of the hunt evolved into an efficient, effective and democratic Bois-Brûlés government. Orders from the Council of the Hunt were strictly obeyed and enforced. The Council assigned all duties. The first assignment, and one of the most important, was guard duty. This was a highly respected office and required men who were prepared to live in a state of constant vigilance for the duration of the hunt. Guarding the horses was one of their important jobs. The entire party relied on the horses. If they were stolen, lost or damaged, everyone would suffer.

The next task of the Council was to choose the hunters. These were men who were good shots and owned fast buffalo runners—horses trained to the chase. The hunters were tasked with choosing buffalo with good hides. They all wanted healthy, fatty animals, usually young cows.

The scouts were appointed next. They acted as sentries for the protection of the camp. Depending on where the hunt was taking place, the scouts always wanted to know where the various bands of First Nations were. If the Métis hunting camp was in Sioux territory or near Blackfoot territory, extra caution was needed.

Before departing on the hunt, the participants met in assembly to make all the decisions about the conduct of the hunt. At these assemblies they also considered other matters. In 1850 the assembly considered and voted on the representatives they hoped would be appointed to the Council of Assiniboia. They elected Narcisse Marion and Maximilien Dauphine to represent the Canadians, and François Bruneau, Pascal Breland and Salomon Hamelin to represent the Métis. The Council of the Hunt also dispensed justice for offences that occurred during the hunt. Their rules became known as the Laws of the Hunt.[3] The decisions of the Council formed a body of laws that became known as the Laws of the Prairie.

THE NOISY MUSICAL RIDE

Moving from the rendezvous onto the Plains was slow and orderly, but not quiet. The people sang, talked, laughed, gossiped, quarrelled and joked as they travelled, all at full volume over the ear-splitting shrieks made by their Red River carts.

The buffalo contributed in their own way to the symphony of sounds on the hunt. A stampeding herd made the grass crackle like a fire, and this sound too could be felt and heard for a long way off. Add to this the barking of hundreds of dogs accompanying the moving camp. The final addition to this musical ride was the mosquitoes. Joseph Kinsey Howard penned a vivid description of them:

> Wind-borne swarms of mosquitoes, often preceding thunderstorms, bore down upon the cart brigades in such numbers that horses, dogs and drivers were overwhelmed within a few seconds. While the horses pitched and screamed under the attack of the savage insects and the dogs writhed in agony on the ground, the men fled under their carts and wound themselves, head to foot, in blankets, though the temperature might be in the nineties. The torment might last only a few minutes, but it frequently killed horses and dogs and disabled the men for days.
>
> Sometimes, the approaching swarm could be heard: a high, unbroken and terrifying hum. This gave the drivers time to throw wagon sheets over their animals. Mounted men would attempt to outrun the flying horde. Though they were almost always overtaken, the breeze created by their horses' panic flight saved them from the worst agony; but they pulled out of the gallop, miles away, with faces and arms streaming blood and with the insects six deep on their ponies. Animals heard or sensed the approach of a swarm before men could, and horses sometimes broke into a dead run without warning, unseating their riders.[4]

No one was ever surprised by the arrival of the Métis hunters. And the noise didn't stop when the Métis halted. One might think that some relief for the ears would be appreciated when the camp stopped for the night, but no. On arrival at camp, the fiddles immediately came out and music, singing and dancing could be heard long into the night.

Métis music is described as "crooked," which refers to their phrasing and the fact that they frequently drop or add notes. Métis music is learned and handed down through the generations orally. There was virtually no practice of teaching the music by reading written notes on paper. A song was learned from listening to an uncle or a grandfather play. Today there are many women who play the fiddle, but in the old days it seems to have been mostly a male purview. The oral transmission of each song came complete with many idiosyncratic musical contours or variations in tune or phrase.

Métis music often contains in-jokes or references. For example, adding a particular flourish in one piece (no matter how discordant it sounds to outsiders) will remind everyone present of an old uncle who played it just that way. Métis fiddle music is distinct from the fiddle traditions of Quebec or the Maritimes and is said to be "more crooked" than they are. Some of the variations reveal underlying First Nation musical patterns. The crooked nature of Métis fiddling may reflect the Indian song structure, which emphasizes more the idea of a continual beat than grouping into phrases as is more common in other fiddle traditions.

Métis music is a creative blend of British and French-Canadian tunes with First Nation influences. Most Métis fiddle music is dance music. The Métis always refer to the songs as jigs, even though their dances include a wide variety of step dances, only a few of which are performed in the traditional jig rhythm of 6/8 time. In fact the use of the word "jig" is a Métis version of the French word *gigue*, meaning "a lively dance." The "Red River Jig" was the best known and called, in Michif, "Oayâche Mannin."

Métis musical instruments were small and portable. That's because the music followed them on their canoe trips or buffalo hunts or trading trips. Mouth harps, small drums, spoons and fiddles were the common instruments of the nineteenth century. Guitars and accordions were also used in the early days if available.

Dancing was a much-favoured accompaniment to the fiddle music. Most Euro-Canadians hated it, which had absolutely no deterrent effect on the Métis. Their dancing, singing and drumming may have been vexing and disagreeable to Euro-Canadians, but the Métis loved it and often danced through the night until they wore through their moccasins.

Métis songs proclaimed who they were and their beliefs. "We are Bois-Brûles, Freemen of the Plains / We choose our chief! We are no man's slave!" sang Pierre Falcon in his song "The Buffalo Hunt." The songs sung in Michif often reflect the Métis love of the irreverent, the joke and the just plain rude. The "Turtle Mountain Song" is a perfect example of this. The song originates in the Métis buffalo hunt. It was sung on the way to the rendezvous at Turtle Mountain and likely dates from the 1820s. It's a long call-and-answer song perfect for whiling away the time on a long journey. The last verse goes like this:

La Montagne Tortue ka-itohtânân
We're going to Turtle Mountain
En charette kawîtapasonân
We're going in a Red River cart

Les souliers moux kakiskênân
We're going to wear moccasins
L'écorce de boulot kamisâhonân
We'll wipe our asses with birchbark!

Smell was another accompaniment to life on the hunt. Once contact with the buffalo herd was made, the smell of the herd permeated the camp. Buffalo bulls emitted a reeking odour of musk and the smell followed in their wake. Men and buffalo were very sensitive to each other's smell and could detect each other at two or more miles.

The scouts spread out ahead of the train, searching for buffalo. When the buffalo were sighted, the train was halted. The women took over at this point and began setting up the camp, which they called *nick-ah-wah*. They arranged the carts in a circle, and put their livestock and teepees inside the circle. Meanwhile the men mounted their buffalo-running horses and rode out toward the herd. At the signal from the captain of the hunt, the men would fan out and charge the herd at full speed.

It was at this point that the horsemanship and marksmanship skills of the Métis shone. Everyone who saw them commented on it. They were commonly said to be the best horsemen in the world, and the most expert and successful of the buffalo hunters in America. When the hunt signal was given, the hunters sprang forward and the herd would stampede. Each hunter singled out an animal, pursued it and then, coming alongside it, would shoot. The speed was ferocious. Once the buffalo was down, the hunter dropped a piece of cloth, a glove or some other token on the dead animal to mark his kill. That was kill number one.

Métis buffalo hunters' encampment (*Glenbow Archives NA-1406*)

The hunters shot from the hip, dropped the token and, still galloping at full speed in the middle of the herd, reloaded, selected another animal and shot again. The best hunters could kill ten buffalo at a "course," but it was more usual for each hunter to bag between three and eight animals. Jerry McKay, armed with a single-barrel flintlock, was said to have killed thirteen buffalo in a single run, a feat that he apparently repeated more than once.

The hunt was exciting and very dangerous. A buffalo could gore a horse, and a fall in the midst of a stampeding herd was certain death. Reloading at full speed was perilous and not a practice for the novice. The men kept their powder loose in their pockets and their bullets in their mouths. While the horse kept charging through the herd, the hunter poured powder into the barrel of his gun, spat in a bullet, smacked the stock of the gun hard on the saddle and shot. Francis Parkman described the obvious danger of the practice:

> Should the blow on the pommel fail to send the bullet home, or should the latter, in the act of aiming, start from its place and roll toward the muzzle, the gun would probably burst in discharging. Many a shattered hand and worse casualties besides have been the result of such an accident. To obviate it, some hunters make use of a ramrod, usually hung by a string from the neck, but this materially increases the difficulty of loading.[5]

The buffalo-runner horse was a prized possession, dearly bought, tended with great care and gorgeously decked out with colourful beads, porcupine quills and ribbons. This prize never drew the Red River cart and was rarely mounted except for the chase. Horses were the most valuable possession a Métis family owned, and they were beautiful horses originally from the southern parts of New Spain.

The Métis habit of pursuing the chase was universally frowned on by Euro-Canadians, the priests and everyone else who observed it. As the following examples show, the disparaging critique of the Métis was relentless and, in the case of those who actually resided in Red River and were dependent on the product of the Métis hunting, hypocritical.

> RED RIVER RESIDENT: After the expedition starts, there is not a man-servant or maid-servant to be found in the colony. At any season but seed time and harvest time, the settlement is literally swarming with idlers; but at these urgent periods, money cannot procure them. This alone is most injurious to the agricultural class.[6]

> EXPLORER: The settlement [Pembina] consists of about three hundred and fifty souls . . . they do not appear to possess the

qualifications for good settlers . . . most of them are half-breeds . . . Accustomed from their early infancy to the arts of the fur trade, which may be considered as one of the worst schools for morals, they have acquired no small share of cunning and artifice. These form at least two-thirds of the male inhabitants . . . who therefore devote much of their time to hunting . . . experience shows, that men addicted to hunting never can make good farmers.[7]

OUTSIDE OBSERVERS: The French half-breeds . . . the most unreliable and unprofitable members of society . . . have an utter distaste for all useful labour . . . But as hunters, guides, and voyageurs they are unequalled . . . The two great events of the year at Red River are the Spring and Fall Hunt . . . At these seasons the whole able-bodied half-breed population set out for the Plains in a body, with their carts.[8]

PRIEST: The greatest social crime of our French Half-breeds is that they are hunters . . . Born very often on the prairies, brought up in distant and adventurous excursions, horsemen and ready marksmen from their very infancy, it is not very surprising that the Halfbreeds are passionately fond of hunting, and prefer it to the quiet, regular and monotonous life of the farmer.[9]

Patrice Fleury explained that the Métis hunters exercised the greatest care and no waste was permitted. A strict rule of his camp was that the meat and skin were preserved and cured before any more buffalo were slaughtered. According to Fleury, on hunts with fewer groups of families, no more than five or six buffalo a week could be taken. The meat was dried in strips (dried meat) or pounded into small flakes (pounded meat). The bones were broken up to extract the marrow, which was melted and poured over the pemmican before it was sewed up tightly in skin bags. The horns were used for cups, hooks and ornaments. Sinews as fine as thread were used to sew tents, moccasins and pemmican bags made from the tanned skins.

Babiche, the Métis version of duct tape, was made from long thin strips of hide from an old buffalo. They used it for everything. They stored it dry and when they wanted to use it, they soaked it in water and wrapped it around the necessary item. One of its uses was to bind the rims of the Red River cartwheels, which gave the wood greater strength but had no dampening effect on the awful shrieking sound. A *babiche*-bound cartwheel rim would last a whole summer of hard use.

In the 1840s buffalo robes became a new product of the Métis hunts—so much so that the robe trade began to eclipse the trade in pemmican and meat. The robes were made from the tanned hides of buffalo, complete with their luscious winter wool. As the robes became more and more popular in the United States, they commanded premium prices, which drew increasing numbers of Brûlés onto the Plains for the winter hunt. This new trade in robes depended much on women. It is generally thought that all the preparation of the hides was women's work. But Louis Goulet said that scraping the hides was men's work, and that while the men were scraping the hides, the women were cutting up the meat into thin strips for drying. All of this processing had to be done on the spot. This meant that entire families continued to accompany the male hunters on the hunts.

The major market for buffalo robes was not the Hudson's Bay Company. Buffalo robes were too heavy and bulky for the Company to ship to England profitably. They also had a major deficiency: they could not be dyed. Like the buffalo and the Brûlés, the robes could not be finessed. They stubbornly retained their own character.

Although the Company encouraged the robe trade north of the border, largely because this kept the robes from the Americans, the Company's low prices were not an incentive for the hunters, who mainly hunted in the United States, to bring the robes over the border and home. So the great majority of the robes were sold south of the border, especially in St. Paul, Minnesota.

The location of the hunts constantly changed as the buffalo migrated, but the Brûlés were able to identify migration patterns in the herds early on. In 1828 there were Brûlés and Freemen hunting groups that travelled a hundred miles past the Sheyenne River to find the buffalo herds. In the 1840s, '50s and '60s, the Brûlés from Red River followed the same routes they had used for fifty or more years. The difference by the 1860s was that they had to travel farther west. As time went on, the hunting expeditions grew in size. In 1822 there were 150 carts in an expedition. In 1840 there were over 1,200 carts and 1,630 people. But the hunting camps were not always large. Patrice Fleury described a camp in the 1860s of about twenty men with their families.

Pembina River was the great rendezvous. In order to obtain easier access to the herds, some Métis from Red River moved back to Pembina in the 1840s and 50s. They much preferred Pembina and regretted relocating to the Forks in the 1820s under the combined pressure of the Hudson's Bay Company and the priests. In 1816 there were swarms of buffalo to be seen from Brandon House. By the 1850s the herds were farther south and west. In

1859 the buffalo were plentiful in the Plains to the east, west and south of where the city of Saskatoon now stands, which was an area described as a famed buffalo feeding ground.[10]

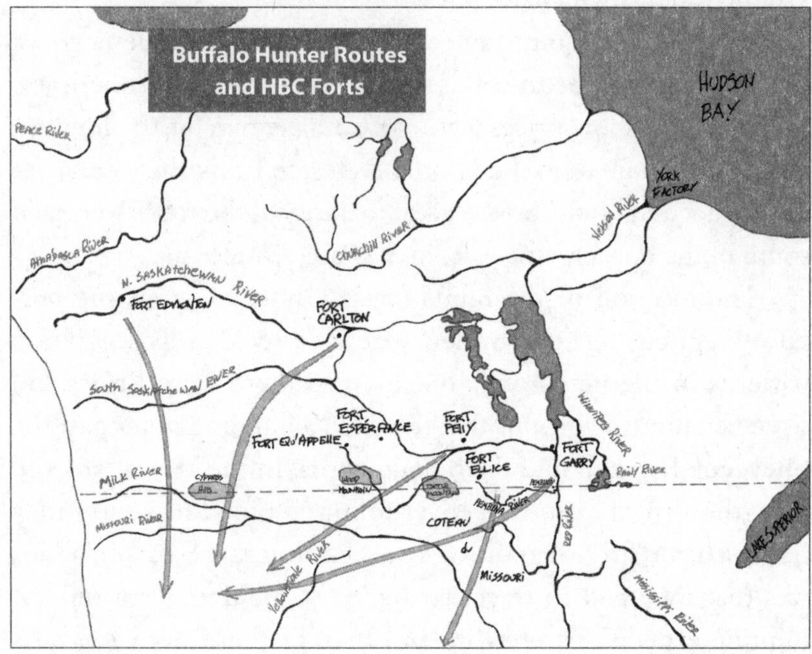

In 1845 Father Belcourt described a hunt that left the Pembina River and finished in St. Paul, Minnesota. In 1849 Brûlés traders were seen in a group of twenty-five carts travelling a well-known route for the Red River people, along the west bank of the Mississippi River, heading north to Pembina. In 1856 the Bois-Brûlés hunted in two groups, one from Red River and the other from White Horse Plain. The Red River hunters headed to the Coteau du Missouri and even as far as the Yellowstone River. The White Horse Plain Métis generally hunted west of the Souris River and between the branches of the Saskatchewan River.

The buffalo hunt is what fully established the Métis Nation. The wild boys had matured. Grant had taken a gang and turned it into a deadly and efficient hunting and military force. The whole nation, men, women and children, were capable of being called up at a moment's notice. They were a formidable defensive and attack force, drilled now to obey command.

By the 1830s *la nouvelle nation* had begun to change its name. The English generally used the term "half-breed." The French still used "Bois-Brûlés," but more and more they took to calling themselves Métis, which they would have pronounced "Michif." They used it also as the name for their language and for their nation—the Métis Nation. Naming was fluid and one individual might add a language descriptor. An English-speaking Métis might call herself an English Métis or a half-breed. Another might say he was a French Métis, a Michif or a Bois-Brûlés. Some used more than one term within the space of a few sentences. Regardless of the name, however, *la nouvelle nation*, the Métis Nation, was now known far and wide as "the best hunters, the best horsemen and the bravest warriors" of the Plains.[11]

CHAPTER 9

THE IRON ALLIANCE

THE BORDER—FROM FICTION TO FACT

The Jay Treaty, which came into effect in 1796, established the International Boundary Commission, which was given the task of surveying and mapping the border between the United States and Great Britain. The international border, a feat of imagination based on ignorance of the watersheds, remained a fiction for the next two decades. After the War of 1812, the Boundary Commission abandoned the watershed boundary theory. Straight lines are easier to map than watersheds, and so in 1818 the forty-ninth parallel became the new fictional boundary in the North-West.

Fiction became fact as both countries began to rearrange their forts, fur-trade empires, and lines of travel and communication. On the Plains, where only the horizon forms a vaguely straight line, the international border was known mainly by its absence. Not for decades would the boundary become known as the "medicine line," a name it acquired when it stopped American soldiers from crossing into Canada in the 1880s. But in the early days of the nineteenth century in the North-West, permanent settlements and international boundaries were still the dreams of eastern outlanders.

For the Indigenous peoples of the Plains, a boundary was a claim that could be enforced. Territories shifted as alliances changed and also because the animals knew no boundaries. Migratory peoples dependent on a migratory buffalo herd could maintain a claimed territory only if the buffalo always appeared within that claim. If the buffalo stayed away, the people had to sneak, negotiate, marry or fight their way into a neighbour's claimed territory. As the fictional international border began to solidify into fact, it cut through the pre-existing Indigenous territories like a knife. It forced people to choose a nationality where previously they had only an ethnic affiliation. For most, the knife cut brutally through their families, their lifestyle, their lands, their stories and their economies.

We tend to think of medicine as a healing substance, but the medicine line was anything but for the Métis Nation. Indeed, borders are antithetical to everything the Métis are. The Métis cross all the borders that societies erect, including borders of race, nationality and territory. Some peoples are like that; some places are like that.

The Red River Valley was one of those places. By the end of the eighteenth century, the Red River Valley was a contested hunting ground for the Sioux, Cree, Ojibwa and Assiniboine. The valley, both north and south of what would become the international border, was a war road. Today there is still a town named Warroad in Minnesota, a remainder of the Sioux war road.

The Cree, Ojibwa and Assiniboine were allied against the Sioux. Their alliance was called the Nehiyaw Pwat (the "Iron Alliance"), which took its English name from European metal technology (guns, needles, pots, etc.). The peoples of the Iron

Alliance took advantage of this technology to control access to Rupert's Land, the western Great Lakes and the Plains for over a hundred years. They worked and lived within the Iron Alliance but maintained their own identities and languages. It was a fluid alliance. Alliance members were intermarried and they hunted, traded and fought together. Their territory was unmarked by hard borders. They shared histories, stories and cultures. It was not until Canada absorbed Rupert's Land and the North-West Territories and implemented scrip and treaties in the 1870s that the Iron Alliance began to falter.

The lands from the end of Lake Superior to the Plains were Sioux territory until the late eighteenth century. That is when the Ojibwa joined forces with the Cree and Assiniboine and began to force their way onto the Plains. The Sioux slowly moved farther west. The Cree, Ojibwa and Assiniboine cemented the Iron Alliance with marriages and by travelling and hunting together. They all adopted an equestrian buffalo-hunting lifestyle. They joined together to defend themselves against the Sioux, often in the Red River Valley war road. When the Freemen arrived, many married into the Iron Alliance bands. After the Freemen separated from the bands and their Brûlés children began to marry each other and coalesce into the Métis Nation, it too became part of the Iron Alliance. Buffalo hunting groups could contain any combination of these groups.

PEMBINA

In the early days the Red River Settlement was really two settlements, one at Pembina and the other at the Forks. When the priests arrived in 1818, a chapel and priest were established at each place. The dual locations worked well until the Company conspired with the priests to dismantle the settlement at Pembina regardless of the wishes or needs of the Métis. Pembina was a problem for the Company because it undermined its trade monopoly by facilitating Métis trade with its rival, the American Fur Company. Bishop Plessis, situated in far-away Quebec, promised to do his utmost to discredit the settlement at Pembina and have it moved to the Forks. Despite the fact that the bulk of the Métis children were either at Pembina or on the Plains, the Bishop claimed the move would facilitate the spiritual administration and education of the children.

The priests on location knew better and demurred, knowing "the majority of the Catholics and all the Métis were at Pembina, and absolutely could not leave that post to come to the forks, where they would not have been able to get a living."[1] Lake Manitoba was suggested as a better location than the Forks because it would provide fishing and hunting, "which suit bois brûlés better than the pickax."[2] But it was a losing battle. Pembina may have been the preferred Métis anchor point, but that didn't matter. The Company wanted the Métis located on the British side of the border.

While the British were busy moving their posts, priests and people, the Americans, at the urging of the American Fur Company, passed legislation that prohibited non-Americans from trading with Indians south of the border. In 1819 the American army established Fort Snelling at what would later become Minneapolis. The Americans also proceeded to mark the border with symbols and ceremony.

All this activity had little effect on most of the Métis, who had little respect for distant authorities they could not see with their own eyes. Obtaining proof of American citizenship required a great deal of effort, and the few Métis who went to the trouble were denounced, as "Mississippi demi-civilized

Canadian mongrel English-American citizens."[3] Many Métis simply did not know which side of the line they were born on. The buffalo hunters meandered back and forth over the line several times in the course of one hunt. A child born on the hunt—and many were—would have no way of knowing whether he or she was born in the United States or Canada. Most simply ignored the invisible line that followed no river or height of land and was devoid of any geographic logic.

At Pembina, on August 8, 1823, the American army, under Major Stephen Long, surveyed the border and planted an oak post with the letters "G.B." (Great Britain) on the north side and "U.S." on the south side. Several Brûlés and Freemen were in attendance and watched the performance with interest. Opinions were divided. Those who were relocating north into British territory were skeptical. Those who wanted to remain at Pembina were delighted, noting the line put them on the same side as the buffalo. They drafted an address to the United States, asking for a priest and a judge.

Many Brûlés who moved north to the Forks in the 1820s moved back to Pembina again in the 1840s when Norman Kittson, an American fur trader, established a post at Pembina. The relocation provided easy access to the American market but diminished access to the Canadian market. The Métis could slip over the border—which might sound easy, but in fact it was time consuming and difficult. Travelling during the day between the Forks and Pembina was a two-day trip on a trail that was fairly well marked. Smuggling involved a tortuous canoe trip that took three days and difficult night travel. The Iron Alliance peoples, including the Métis Nation, flowed along and across the border but paid little attention to it. Decades passed before the border became a reality in their lives.

CHAPTER 10

THE MÉTIS NATION ARMY

"GENERAL" DICKSON

By 1836 the fame of the Métis hunters had spread far and wide. The Nor'Westers were the first to try to co-opt the Métis into an armed force. James Dickson was the second. Dickson had a grand liberation scheme that required an army. Not a man given to petty dreams and schemes, he was gave himself the title "General Dickson" or "Montezuma II, Liberator of the Indian Nations." His plan was to liberate the Indians in Santa Fe and relocate them to California, where he would set up a kingdom with himself, naturally, as the king. His liberation army would be the Red River Métis.

Dickson was by all accounts a wealthy, charming, educated scam artist. He was fully costumed in a colourful uniform finished with gold lace and braid. He sported a sword and even packed a coat of mail. He recruited officers and attendants for his army from Montreal and fully equipped them. His many officers—a general, a brigadier-general, a major of artillery, six captains, three lieutenants and two ensigns—all oversaw less than sixty men. The recruits were Métis. Apparently, Dickson thought his own credentials as a trader, his familiarity with Red River, and his Métis recruits would gain him access to more Métis soldiers for his army. With a party of about sixty, the general headed from Buffalo to the North-West. It was a rather roundabout route to Santa Fe via Red River, but the general embarked with great pomp and even greater expectations.

No one in authority liked the idea of a mercenary army, whatever its stated purpose, drifting freely around North America. Dickson's party was shipwrecked before it reached Sault Ste. Marie, and the Americans took advantage of the situation to arrest them. The adventure cost Dickson several of his officers and attendants, and by the time he resumed his trip, his party was reduced to about twenty men. The episode at Sault Ste. Marie did not go unnoticed. A newspaper in Detroit published a fabulous account of the general's adventures in an article entitled "Pirates on the Lakes." The Hudson's Bay Company's governor, Simpson, was not at all amused by the idea of losing "his" Métis hunters to another adventurer.

Dickson proceeded through the Great Lakes to the Mississippi and began to head north to Red River in what was now the dead of winter. Travelling by dogsled and on foot, the party disintegrated. Men got separated, some deserted and some died. Dickson and eleven others finally limped into Red River in December, half frozen, hungry, and a far cry from the gallant liberation army that had departed from Buffalo in August.

Governor Simpson put a quick end to Dickson's plan by the simple expedient of issuing orders to the Company office in Red River. Under no account were they to honour any of Dickson's money drafts. No money, no Métis army. It was as simple as that. More of his officers deserted, and when the Hudson's Bay Company scooped his remaining officers with employment offers, Dickson conceded with good grace. He spent the winter in Red River parading about in his costume uniform and drinking with Cuthbert Grant. Unable to resist such a strange tale, the Métis bard Pierre Falcon memorialized the story in a satiric song. On Dickson's departure in the spring, Grant provided him with food, transport and guides to Santa Fe. Dickson presented Grant with his epaulettes and sword, and with great style he rode out of Red River, never to be heard from again.

THE OREGON BOUNDARY DISPUTE

In 1845 two British officers were sent into the North-West to report on its status to the imperial government.[1] The Oregon boundary was in dispute and the Americans were building a series of armed forts that were progressing steadily westward. They had already set up Fort Snelling (later Minneapolis) in 1819 and were looking to establish a new fort at Pembina. This was right at the front door of the Red River settlement, and the British were worried that the West would be lost to the Americans. The two British officers' report was illuminating. They suggested that men could be sent in via the Great Lakes and Fort William but that ordnance would have to come in from York Factory. A local corps of Métis cavalry would be the perfect regiment. Of course these officers knew nothing about General Dickson, the Métis or the history of their voyageur fathers during the War of 1812.

The Nor'Westers had raised a voyageur regiment to fight for Britain in the War of 1812. The Corps of Canadian Voyageurs took part in at least two engagements during the war, but they are best remembered for their part in the capture of Michilimackinac and Fort Shelby. The stories of the voyageur soldiers during the War of 1812 are quite wonderful. The regiment performed well and the voyageurs were respected for their daring exploits. But the stories also illustrate just how untameable the voyageurs were. There is a delightful account of the voyageurs' attitude to army discipline from Joseph McGillivray:

> When on duty in company with the regular forces or the militia they [the voyageurs] were guilty of much insubordination, and it was quite impossible to make them amenable to military law. They generally came on parade with a pipe in their mouths and their rations of pork and bread stuck on their bayonets. On seeing an officer, whether general, colonel, or subaltern, they took off their hats and made a low bow, with the common salutation of *Bon jour, Monsieur le Général*, or *le Colonel*, as the case might be, and, if they happened to know that the officer was married, never failed to inquire after the health of *Madame et les enfants*. On parade they talked incessantly, called each other "pork eaters," quarrelled about their rations, wished they were back in the Indian country again, &c., and when called to order by their officers and told to hold their tongues, one or more would reply, "Ah, dear captain, let us off as quick as you can; some of us have not yet breakfasted, and it's upwards of an hour since I had a smoke" . . . In moments when danger ought to have produced a little steadiness, they completely set discipline at defiance, and the volatile volunteer broke out into all the unrestrained mirth and anti-military familiarity of the thoughtless voyageur. [No officer] could restrain the vivacious laugh, silence the noisy tongue, or compose the ever changing features into anything like military seriousness . . . They could not be got to wear stocks; and such as did not use cravats came on parade with naked necks, and very often with rough beards . . . Notwithstanding these peculiarities the voyageurs were excellent partisans, and, from

> their superior knowledge of the country, were able to render material service during the war.[2]

Granted, this is a snapshot of the voyageurs, but it was their sons, the Métis of Red River, who were now being proposed to form the core of the new regiment. Cuthbert Grant had by this time instilled some discipline into the Métis through the buffalo hunt. They knew how to obey orders, but it is highly doubtful that they could be persuaded to act collectively in anyone's interest but their own.

THE BRITISH ARMY ARRIVES IN RED RIVER IN 1846

For the Métis there was little to recommend obedience to the foreign British, and they were always in a low boil about the British face in the North-West, the Hudson's Bay Company. The Métis were much more sympathetic to the republican sentiments of the Americans. Governor Simpson, well aware of the Métis trade with and ideological affinity for the Americans, flatly rejected the proposal to use the Métis as the core of a regiment against the Americans. The boundary dispute provoked a prolonged discussion about sending the army out west. Governor Simpson badly wanted troops. He thought they were "absolutely necessary to the existence of the Fur trade . . . a means of protection against the inhabitants of the Settlement, as with the feeling at present existing on the minds of the half-breeds, it will be quite impossible to protect the trade or inforce [*sic*] our laws without the presence of military at that point . . ."[3]

As a result of Simpson's pressure, several companies of the 6th Royal Regiment of Foot, numbering some 383, arrived in Red River in the fall of 1846. They were not there to deal with the Americans, for the Oregon boundary dispute had been settled before they arrived. Clearly, they were sent to Red River at the behest of Simpson. With the arrival of the army, the Métis Nation, for the first time, was outgunned. The Métis were far superior in numbers to the army, but they had no artillery and were savvy enough to know when to keep their heads low. The presence of the army was a boon for the economy of the colony and thus to the Hudson's Bay Company, but tensions between the Company and the Métis were growing, and the army provided only a short respite. By the summer of 1848, the army was gone.

Simpson was not blind to the American threat either. In his opinion the Americans wanted influence over the Red River Métis to "facilitate the conquest of Red River, and other settlements within our territories in case of a rupture with Great Britain."[4] The Americans did encourage the Métis to relocate to their side of the border. In 1845 a Red River Métis group hunting near the Sheyenne River encountered the American cavalry. Captain Sumner told the Métis that if they wanted to hunt in the United States, they would have to settle on that side of the border. He suggested Pembina as an appropriate place for them to settle. The Métis sat in Council to discuss the matter but deferred the decision until they returned to the Forks.

No one ever succeeded in co-opting the Métis Nation. It remained independent and focused on protecting its own interests, and took aim at a target much nearer than Santa Fe—the Sioux.

CHAPTER 11

THE BATTLE OF THE GRAND COTEAU

In 1849 about three hundred Métis relocated to Pembina, adding to the existing population of five hundred hunters and their families. The Pembina group also spread out to a new location farther west, St. Joseph. This was just the beginning of what was to become a western migration following the buffalo as the herds receded farther and farther away from Red River.

For years the Sioux and the Métis had been sparring. Large Métis hunting parties now moved regularly into lands the Sioux regarded as its traditional territory. The Métis moved with caution, always ready for an encounter with the Sioux, but the large size of their hunting parties, their shooting skills and military discipline allowed them to penetrate farther and farther into Sioux territory. The Sioux hated the Métis coming into their territory, and they were further angered when Iron Alliance hunting groups included Ojibwa hunters.

The Ojibwa were the close relatives of the Métis but a bitter enemy of the Sioux. The animosity between the two traditional enemies was of long standing. The Sioux believed the Métis and the Ojibwa were trespassing, and they were prepared to kill both on sight. Peace broke out occasionally between the two tribes, and some Métis married Sioux and lived among them, including the influential Bottineau family. But these were small islands in the general animosity that characterized the relationship between the Sioux and the people who made up the Iron Alliance—the Assiniboine, the Ojibwa, the Cree and the Métis Nation.

Cuthbert Grant had a complicated relationship with the Sioux. He was the Warden of the Plains and it was part of his job to keep the peace in Red River. The Sioux were a constant source of worry for Red River and Pembina. In 1822 the Sioux killed twelve Métis. In 1834 the Sioux sent a delegation under one of their chiefs, La Terre Qui Brule, to the Forks. They wanted the Company to set up a post at Lake Traverse in Minnesota to provide competition to the American Fur Company. Hearing that the Sioux had appeared in the settlement, Cuthbert Grant, as he had in 1821, sprang into action. This time the encounter turned into an ugly standoff, which was defused with difficulty. All parties stood down, and fifty English Métis and settlers eventually escorted the Sioux out of the colony. It turned out the Sioux had been escorted into the settlement specifically in order to avoid an Ojibwa attack. If so, it was a poorly executed plan.

The Sioux were a large and magnificent group of warriors. They were well armed and mounted. The possibility that the Métis Nation and the Sioux would join forces was a constant worry for Governor Simpson, who was at Red River when another large Sioux delegation arrived in 1836. In 1839 the Métis travelled to Devil's Lake in North Dakota to make peace with the Yankton and Sisseton Sioux of Lake Traverse. But the peace was fleeting. One of the problems was that although peace would be made with one group of Sioux, another group would not feel bound by the peace agreement, especially if family members had been killed. In that case deadly retribution was practically guaranteed, and this rough justice prevailed between the Sioux, the Ojibwa and the Métis. In 1844 there was a deadly confrontation between some Métis and the Sioux. Cuthbert Grant brokered the peace through an exchange of letters with Sioux chiefs.

This peace lasted for only a few years. In 1848 there was another large battle between the Red River Métis and the Sioux near present-day Oglala in South Dakota. The Métis captain of the hunt was Jean-Baptiste Wilkie, and the hunting camp was made up of eight hundred Métis men and two hundred Chippewa men. They all had their families, horses and over one thousand Red River carts. One final and decisive battle between the Métis and the Sioux, the Battle of the Grand Coteau, took place in 1851. It has remained an important story for the Métis Nation.

The Grand Coteau du Missouri is a stony plateau. At its foot flows one of the great bends of the Missouri River. The battle took place northeast of Maison du Chien, or Dog Den Butte, a very conspicuous butte that is visible for miles. It has a dark, sinister and dangerous air to it. At the time it was a well-known ambush location for the Sioux.

In 1851 the Métis hunters departed for the annual hunt as usual from the Forks, Pembina and the White Horse Plain. On June 15 the Pembina group and the Forks group merged at the rendezvous south and west of Pembina. Together they numbered about 318 hunters. With the women and children, the camp numbered thirteen hundred people in eleven hundred carts. The White Horse Plain group arrived with a smaller party.

When the White Horse Plain group arrived at the rendezvous, a general council was held and Jean-Baptiste Falcon, from the White Horse Plain group, was elected chief captain of the hunt.[1] The groups decided to proceed in two columns. Separated by a few miles, the columns kept in contact and travelled in a generally parallel course. In fairly short order the White Horse Plain group encountered a Sioux camp, and not a small one. There were eight thousand Sioux against two hundred Métis carts with only sixty-seven men. Gabriel Dumont, who would become one of the great Métis hunters and their famous general, was in the Métis group. He was thirteen years old.

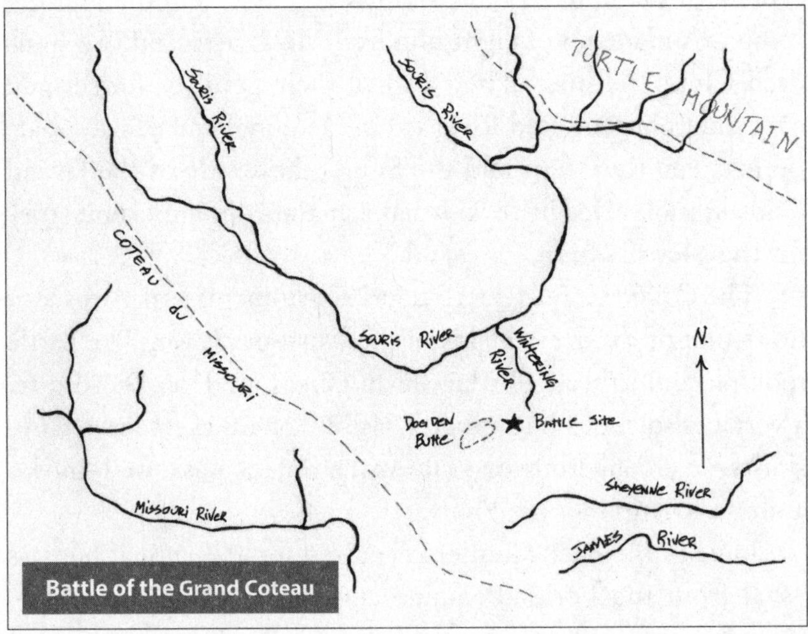

Battle of the Grand Coteau

Scouts were immediately sent off to the larger Métis group, but the Sioux captured them before they could get very far. The Métis, with the precision of a veteran army, went into military defence mode, circling their carts, digging protective pits, readying their ammunition and guns, and settling in for a protracted siege.

The Sioux attacked. So sure were they of an easy victory and anticipating spoils, they brought women and children in tow. They brought the three hostage scouts closer to taunt the Métis. Two hostages took the opportunity to make a run for it. One made it to the Métis camp unscathed. One made it wounded. The third hostage was killed.

The Sioux thought the Métis would surrender when they saw the thousands of men attacking them. They were wrong. The Métis had no intention of surrendering. They vowed to fight to the death and fully expected that to be their fate. The Sioux were so surprised that the Métis didn't scatter, they tried to scare them into flight. Their shots were not aimed at the Métis hunters, and they were more engaged in making noise and threats than in actually shooting to kill or disarm. The Métis had no such scruples. Their discipline and military prowess came to the fore, and they held up under six hours of sustained attack. Isabelle Falcon, sister of the captain of the hunt, was an impressive warrior.

> [W]hen Jean Baptiste Falcon was going around acting as captain, his sister Isabelle was fighting in his place. She never left him alone during the three days battle, she would force him to rest and during that time she would shoot and she was a good shot too. Every time they would shoot, it was sure a Sioux would fall. And they would shoot from sunrise to sunset everyday.[2]

The Sioux withdrew to their own camp for the night, and under cover of darkness, the Métis sent two men to the other Métis caravan for help. The next dawn brought a renewal of the battle. The Sioux pressed harder but after five hours made no dent in the Métis defence. Then, to the surprise and relief of the Métis camp, the Sioux quit. They gave honour to the Métis as victors, gathered their dead and withdrew. It is estimated that by the end of the battle, the Sioux had lost between eighty and ninety warriors. The Métis lost one man.

That was the last such battle. Thereafter the Sioux acknowledged the Métis as "Masters of the Plains" and would fight them no more. The Métis Nation had fully come of age. No longer was this the gang of 1816 who claimed to be a nation. Generations had grown up in the belief that the Métis were a nation. Their organizational and military skills garnered them a victory that no one expected. The Sioux, the terror of the Plains for decades, had been defeated. The Métis had acted as a disciplined army, protected their interests as a collective and were victorious as one.

The Métis Nation had now carved out a place for itself. By marriage they were kin with the Assiniboine, Ojibwa and Cree. They travelled and hunted together and in mixed parties, and they were part of the Iron Alliance. According to the Assiniboine, the Métis were born on the same soil and had the same blood in their veins. "These we cannot and will not harm, they have the same right on these prairies as ourselves."[3]

Now the Métis were a nation in fact, not just in aspiration or name. In 1816 they had proclaimed the Métis Nation and now they had made it so. They celebrated their victory over the Sioux with songs and dances that carried on for days.

PART THREE

NO COMPANY'S SLAVE

CHAPTER 12

THE SECOND NATIONAL RESISTANCE

The Métis Nation was conceived in a cry for freedom. That core value has never left the national identity. It underlies everything the Métis value and everything they did. They believed themselves free to use the lands and resources of the North-West, and they very much wanted to be free of the Hudson's Bay Company.

By the 1830s and '40s, the North-West was awash with talk of responsible government, equality, liberty and freedom, ideas that flowed over the ocean from France, north from the Americans and east from Lower Canada. The ideas coming from Lower Canada included a pushback against "Anglifying the country." This phrase, coined by Joseph Papineau in 1822, expressed the French belief that despite their majority numbers in Lower Canada, Anglification would result in the loss of everything they held dear—their laws, religion, language, institutions and customs.

The Métis wholeheartedly embraced the ideas of Papineau and the Patriotes, and it's easy to see why. Their circumstances were virtually identical. Both were denied meaningful participation in the institutions of power. In Lower Canada there was an elected assembly, but a council of English elites appointed by Britain held all the real power. If there had been responsible government in Lower Canada, the French would have had much more power. In the North-West the Métis elected their own governments in their winter camps and on their hunts. But there was nothing resembling responsible or representative government in Red River. Governance in Red River was in the hands of a corporation, the Hudson's Bay Company and its appointed Council of Assiniboia. If there had been responsible government in Red River, the majority Métis would have had more power.

Louis Riel's father, Jean-Louis, was an ardent Papineau supporter and Patriote. He was in Lower Canada, mourning the death of his first wife, during the turmoil that eventually concluded in the Rebellions of 1837–38. Before his wife died, he had been living in Rainy Lake. On his return to the North-West, he went to Red River. Jean-Louis Riel became one of the major agitators fighting against the Company rule in Red River. The goals of the Lower Canada Patriotes so resonated with the Métis Nation that they flew the Papineau standard and sang the Patriotes' songs for many years.

The British demonstrated no inclination to share power with the French in Lower Canada, and the Company followed suit with the Métis in the North-West. In Lower Canada, Lord Durham produced a report in which he recommended that the British assimilate the French as quickly as possible. According to Durham, the French Canadians were an inferior race with no literature or history. In Red River the Hudson's Bay Company appointed one of the Durham Report's authors, Adam Thom, to a judicial post in the newly created office of "Recorder of

Rupert's Land and President of the Red River Court." Thom was a lawyer, a former newspaper editor in Montreal, and an assistant commissioner on the Durham Report. He had called for the state to execute all 750 Patriotes arrested following the Papineau Rebellion. The French-Canadian press branded Thom as a hateful fanatic.

This man, Adam Thom, who didn't speak French and wanted a mass execution of hundreds of French Catholics, was the man Simpson appointed as the first judge in Red River, where the majority of the population was French-Catholic. The Métis hated him on sight. They saw him as a hanging judge, a paid employee of the Company who served at its pleasure. As Métis trader Peter Garrioch said, Thom was a "judge for the sole benefit of the Hudson's Bay Company."[1] The Métis expected Thom to "have a special eye to his employer's interest, above that of all others."[2] He more than met their expectations.

THE WANING OF CUTHBERT GRANT'S LEADERSHIP

In 1835, after the Selkirk family sold its land back to the Hudson's Bay Company, the Company reorganized its governance system and created the Council of Assiniboia. The appointed councillors, other than three local clergymen, were all Company men. Cuthbert Grant was appointed to the council, which further tarnished his reputation among the French Métis. The younger generation of Métis were cynical of Grant's role on the council and described him as a "mute and neutral Under Chairman."[3]

But there was much more to Grant than his participation on the Council of Assiniboia and his role as Warden of the Plains. In his own community of Grantown and out on the Plains, Grant was highly respected as a doctor. According to his descendants he acquired his medical training during a visit to Britain in 1822 to 1823. His medical skills were much in demand as a succession of diseases—influenza, mumps, whooping cough, scarlet fever, measles, smallpox and cholera—ravaged the North-West between 1830 and 1850. Influenza epidemics occurred six times within that twenty-year period.[4] The largest toll was on the women, because they were the main caregivers, and on the children and elderly, because they were the most vulnerable.

In 1842 to 1843, a whooping cough epidemic in Red River was immediately followed by scarlet fever. The diseases spread rapidly and almost every family was affected. Over one hundred people died of scarlet fever, most of them children. The outbreak was followed by another fever in 1844, and many more died from the unnamed scourge. Mortality rates from the measles epidemic of 1846–47 were very high, and complications from the disease added to the heavy loss of life. In 1846 in Red River, three epidemics hit in quick succession—influenza, measles and cholera. The community was devastated. The "bloody flux," following shortly after influenza and measles, carried off one-sixth of the population of Grantown. Beginning in January and lasting well into the autumn, disease took about seven people every day and 321 in all. Alexander Ross, a prominent citizen of Red River at the time, said there was "hardly anything to be seen but the dead on their way to their last home; nothing to be heard but the tolling of bells, nothing talked of but the sick, the dying, and the dead."[5] Two-thirds of them were Métis. The deaths had a demoralizing effect on the Métis society, which contributed to the tensions in the North-West during the 1830s to 60s.

Grant the doctor was a Métis hero. But increasingly, Grant the loyal Company man came to be seen by a new generation of Métis as a sellout. More and more the younger generation turned away from Grant's leadership and began to follow the lead of two young educated Métis, Jean-Louis Riel and James Sinclair. It was Riel and Sinclair who now led the growing resistance of the Métis against the rule imposed by the Hudson's Bay Company.

This was the situation in the North-West when the Hudson's Bay Company sought to double down on its moral, legal and economic authority. But when death stalks the land, deference to any authority other than the grim reaper is hard to come by.

CHAFING UNDER COMPANY RULE

The Company, like most corporations, operated within an established hierarchy populated by two main groups: masters and servants. The masters were the owners, partners and managers. The servants were the employees, who worked at the pleasure of their masters. The system rewarded those who provided the most profits, those who displayed open and continuous loyalty to the Company, and those who were ambitious to advance within the corporation. The system punished those who were seen as disloyal, interested in personal profit, resistant to following orders or unconcerned whether the Company prospered or not. The reward and punishment system is not a bad way to govern a corporation, but it was poor governance for those who were not employees or servants and who had the misfortune of trying to make a living in the same geographic territory as the Company.

To put it simply, the Hudson's Bay Company governed Rupert's Land as a corporate despot and it harvested the predictable results of its tyranny. Observers at the time had no difficulty in putting their finger on the problem. Alexander Ross wrote, "so long as the courts and council are the haunts of favourites and sinecurists, to the exclusion of others . . . a thorough change in the administration of justice . . . [is] imperiously demanded;

and the Hudson's Bay Company would be well advised to look to it."[6] Peter Erasmus, a famous Métis trader and interpreter, wrote in the 1850s that he hated the "autocratic power which some of the officials used to assert their authority."[7]

The Company provided no forum for discussion and debate about its laws, policies or rules. It ruled as an autocrat and as if the North-West in the first part of the nineteenth century were ignorant of the democratic values of liberty, equality and responsible government. The Company ruled the North-West with blinkers on, its systems built on its belief in its own moral and intellectual superiority, but also on fear that largely arose as an awareness of its vulnerability. As Sir George Simpson noted in his opening speech to the first meeting of the Council of Assiniboia, "we have not the means at command of enforcing obedience and . . . it must be evident to one and all of you."[8] Anyone who questioned Company rule—generally the Métis—was considered disloyal and rebellious. When challenged, the Company pointed to its charter, and when that didn't work, issued orders. The Métis, as we saw in the events that led up to the battle at the Frog Plain, did not react well to arbitrary orders.

By the 1830s the Métis Nation had created its own successful lifestyle. The English Métis became more agrarian and settled into the Protestant parishes in Red River. Many still participated in the buffalo hunts, but these Métis increasingly became farmers. The French Métis were more committed to the lifestyle of the buffalo hunt. They remained more mobile and formed the bulk of the Métis Nation's Plains hunters.

The colony was largely dependent on the Métis hunters for its food and safety, and the Métis, not unreasonably, expected some respect for the crucial role they played. Instead they were looked down on. Everyone wanted the Métis to change. Everyone portrayed the Métis as improvident, irrational, lazy idlers. The clergy wanted to change them into Christian farmers. The Company wanted them to be loyal servants, to provide provisions only in the exact amount the Company required and then to go away and not bother the righteous settlers. In truth the colony was happy that most Métis were absent for much of the year; it made it easier for the colonists to sustain their belief in the moral superiority of their agrarian society.

The Bay men may have been good businessmen but they were terrible governors. Macdonell, the first governor of Red River, was incompetent to say the least. As the legal historian Dale Gibson has noted, Macdonell enjoyed a "hedonistic existence in the company of cronies and sycophants."[9] He was also "despised and held in contempt by every person connected with the place . . . accused of partiality, dishonest, untruth, drunkenness, in short, a total dereliction of every moral and honourable feeling."[10] The Company replaced him with a series of equally autocratic, incompetent or corrupt governors.

The Company governors and most of its senior staff were British, mostly Protestants who were educated in England. They governed based on imported English law, custom and values. Under its 1670 charter the Company asserted ownership and law-making powers over everything in Rupert's Land—the land, the resources and the people. Decisions about Rupert's Land were made far away at Company headquarters in London and then handed down as proclamations to the First Nations and the Métis Nation. Company officers were parachuted into Red River, many for short terms. These officers gave their loyalty to the Company and the British Crown.

The Company rules, under which the Métis Nation was

forced to live and trade, made no sense geographically, economically or socially. The Company had never achieved the social licence with the Métis that the Nor'Westers had enjoyed. Because it was so unloved, it had little political capital to spend. It hoarded that capital and spent it against the Métis, a people the Company in equal parts needed and felt threatened by. The Métis Nation chafed under the weight of Company rule, which took little notice or consideration of the Métis customs, traditions or practices. The Company believed the Métis were tools to further its and the settlers' ambitions. It regarded this as natural and essential to its well-being.

A NEW GENERATION OF MÉTIS NATION LEADERS

The Métis began to resist. In 1834 a Company officer seriously injured a Métis man named Antoine Larocque when he struck him over the head with a poker. Larocque's offence was insolence for requesting his wages in advance of a trip, which was a common practice. Within hours of a bleeding Larocque appealing to the Métis community, Métis surrounded Fort Garry and began to sing their war songs and dance their war dances. They demanded the officer be delivered up to them to face justice according to their laws. The matter was only settled after hours of negotiations. The Company agreed to pay Larocque his wages without him having to work the trip. He also got a keg of rum and some tobacco.

In 1835 the Métis protested about food shortages and were successful in loosening the Company stores. The divergence of views in this case again reflected the different values of the two main parties. The Métis understood themselves to be the primary food provider of the colony, and in this assessment they were correct. As such, they saw nothing inappropriate in asking for some food back when they were in need. With their hunter's ethic they expected those who worked with them on the hunt, including the Company, their partner, to share.

The Company saw it differently. They asserted ownership over everything in the country, including the buffalo. From the Company's perspective it paid the Métis to hunt its animals and to bring its meat back to Red River. The Métis believed that if anyone owned the land and resources, it was the "Natives," by which they meant the First Nations and the Métis Nation. The Métis perspective was that they were hunting buffalo freely available to them as Natives of the country and then selling the meat and hides to the Company.

Other than the Company's bold declaration of ownership, there was little on the ground to reinforce the Company's claims. The Métis and First Nations went wherever they wanted. They hunted for their own needs when and where they chose. They provided the meat, furs and robes the Company based its business on. The colony was dependent on the Métis for most of its food. Nothing in this demonstrated Company ownership of any kind.

The Métis and the Company had a financial relationship based on credit. But credit is a two-way street. Both sides needed each other to make the system work. The Company extended credit. In exchange Métis hunters provided meat, fur and hides. When they brought their provisions to the Company post, they traded for other goods, such as tea, sugar, clothing, etc. The Métis saw this trading system as partners who were sharing. In part this is why they believed that credit, or sharing, should be extended when the hunt failed.

The Company was oblivious to what the Métis would have seen as its sharing obligation. The fight to get the Company to share food in times of deprivation added to the cultural divide.

The Métis saw the Company's behaviour as shameful. Hoarding food broke the bond of obligation in the relationship they had long established. The two sides simply did not understand each other. From the Métis perspective the Company took, demanded and invoked loyalty at its own convenience but gave nothing back.

The fight to get the Company to loosen its stores to feed the hungry fed a growing tension between the Company and the Métis. The Métis presented a list of demands to Governor Simpson, and while they did not obtain all their goals, they did succeed in getting the Company to pay a better price for pemmican. With this small victory the Métis quieted, for the time being. Gaining some advantage with the Company eased the political tensions for the moment but did nothing to address the root of the problem, which was the Company's attitude to the Métis. The Métis continued to resent the Company's attitude and the Company continued its autocracy.

Winning a series of small victories made the Métis very conscious of their own strength. They knew Company rule depended on them. The Company knew it too. Throughout the 1830s and 40s, the Métis continued to press their advantage with periodic shows of protest that flared up and died out. Their resistance should not have surprised the Company. After all, it had been relying on the Métis since its earliest days. The Métis were the colony's protection against the Sioux as well as being its main providers of buffalo meat. Both of these tasks required the Métis to keep their fighting attitude and skills well honed. They were a virtual army, and an army is always a double-edged sword. It must be kept sharpened to be of any use, but it also must be kept firmly pointed in the right direction. The Company had some influence, but not enough to keep the Métis aligned with their interests. The Métis obeyed their own inclinations.

Describing the situation in Lower Canada, Lord Durham said it was a "world of misconceptions, in which each party was set against the other not only by diversity of feelings and opinions, but by an actual belief in an utterly different set of facts."[11] The situation in Red River was identical. The misconceptions did nothing to mellow the relationship between the Company, the settlers and the Métis. Every experience in the history of the Métis Nation had reinforced the use of resistance as a means of obtaining their wants and needs. Collisions between the ruling English and the Métis now became a matter of course.

The Company raised its levies. Métis protests forced them to back down. The Company began to demand exorbitant prices for milling their wheat. The Métis forced them to construct a new mill among the French Métis. In 1836 the Company sentenced Louis St. Denis to be flogged for the crime of exporting furs without a Company export licence. The Métis organized a rescue too late. St. Denis was flogged in public, but Métis outrage forced the man who carried out the flogging to flee. The Company learned not to flog in public.

A Métis brigade crew went on strike and refused to make a second trip to York Factory. The Company managed to settle the strike by negotiation and eventually gave in to many of the demands. Cuthbert Grant, probably the one person who could prevent future strikes, was dispatched from then on to accompany the boats and keep the peace.

In the early 1840s the Company began to search Métis carts and even their homes for contraband furs. If furs were found they were forfeited to the Company. The search of Régis Larante's home and the seizure of his furs riled the entire Métis population. Furs were also seized from the homes of other Métis. One man's furs were seized, his house burned, and he was taken to York Factory, where he was threatened with deportation to England, a threat that would have been doubly insulting given that he was not English. But the seizures were premature. The Company could not prove the furs were actually contraband since they had not been taken out of Canada or sold to anyone. These orders were subsequently overturned, and the accused were indemnified by the Company's head office in England. The seizures succeeded in uniting the Freemen and the Métis, whether of French or English extraction; all now stood together against the Company.

The Company declared that no furs could be used in the country or sent out of the country unless they were purchased from the Company. Then in 1844 the Company demanded a declaration about the provenance of the furs and gave themselves a lien on the goods should the declaration prove to be false. The declaration read as follows:

> I hereby declare that since the 8th day of December instant I have neither directly nor indirectly trafficked in furs on my own account, nor given goods on credit, or advanced money to such as may be generally suspected of trafficking in furs; moreover, if before the middle of August next I shall appear to have acted contrary to any part of this declaration, I hereby agree that the Hudson's Bay Company shall be entitled either to detain my imports of next season at York Factory for a whole year, or to purchase them at the original cost of the goods alone.

When the Company tried to prosecute an American trader who had married into the Red River community, over 150 Métis gathered to discuss possible action against Judge Thom, whom they believed to be biased against the Métis.

Requests by Métis traders, such as James Sinclair, to work with the Company on supporting fledgling businesses were met with silence. When the Council of Assiniboia attempted to prosecute a Métis woman for theft, Jean-Louis Riel went to Governor Andrew Colville to object to the participation of Judge Thom in the prosecution. His prejudice against the Métis was obvious to all in Red River, and the Métis were determined to keep him from inflicting his biases on Métis accused. The magistrates, fearing a row with the Métis, abandoned the prosecution. When a young English Métis, William Hallett, sought to marry the daughter of the chief factor of the Company, he was reprimanded for even dreaming of marrying a girl so far out of his social class. Hallett was a leading young man of the English Métis, and they took his rejection as a collective insult.

Governor Simpson was not unaware of the animosity, and in 1857 he wrote, "The whole of the population of the Red River, with very rare exceptions, is unfavourable to us."[12] He was right. The entire population of Red River wanted to be out from under the Company's rigid control. The warning signs from the Métis Nation had been manifesting for decades. And others also warned the Company that it was "useless to attempt keeping things as they were 100 years ago."[13]

The buffalo also undermined the Company's efforts at rigid control. The herds were most often south of the border and the Métis followed the herds. The hunters kept their meat, but they often sold the robes, tongues and some pemmican in

Pembina before they went home. In this way the Métis evaded the Company monopoly and traded with the Americans. The Company sporadically attempted to enforce its charter, but as Governor Simpson noted, "The Company's rights are treated . . . as fictions of law which we cannot and dare not attempt to enforce, and in our present position this is correct."[14]

The younger generation of Métis was not at all interested in obeying Company rules. They openly derided the Company men. Peter Garrioch called the chief factor James Bird an "old fool" and commented that if he "waits till people go to him, he'd better drink more strong tea, to keep . . . awake."[15] By 1846 the derision was also directed at Cuthbert Grant. It was said that no Métis jury would have convicted an accused man if he attempted to kill Grant.

In 1845 the Company passed a resolution that imposed even more restrictions on exports, rescinded any of the licences the Company had previously issued and put an immediate halt to any intermediary traders by declaring that it would purchase only from the actual hunters of the furs. The resolution was aimed squarely at Métis traders and hunters.

The Métis drafted a petition. They wanted their rights set out clearly in black and white so the Company could not continue to make up the rules. The petition read, "Having . . . a strong belief that we, as natives of this country . . . have the right to hunt furs in the Hudson's Bay Company's territories wherever we think proper and again sell those furs to the highest bidder, likewise having a doubt that natives of this country can be prevented from trading and trafficking with one another . . ."[16] The Métis were stating their belief that, as "natives of this country," they had a right to hunt and sell furs in the North-West, and they included a list of fourteen questions seeking further nuance to the Company's declaration. Twenty-three Métis and Freemen signed the petition.

Governor Alexander Christie began his response by noting he was deigning to answer the petition even though it was unusual for rulers to answer legal inquiries outside the courts. But in Red River there was no forum for resolution of grievances against the Company. The Company proclaimed law one day, rescinded the next, exercised arbitrary authority, and then sat on its privilege. Sometimes it condescended to respond, making sure its subjects knew they were to be duly grateful for the condescension. The governor's response to the petition can be briefly summed up as no, the Métis have no rights as natives of the country. The response did little to calm the waters in Red River. The Métis continued to demand freedom from the Company's monopoly, and James Sinclair was particularly vocal in his opposition.

Father Belcourt persuaded the Métis to make a list of their grievances and send them to London. They reluctantly agreed. Their reluctance stemmed from a deep cynicism. They simply did not believe headquarters in London would respond any differently than its servants in Red River had. They also worried, correctly as it turned out, that the petition would only stir the Company to further acts of tyranny and reprisal. Sinclair drafted the petition, dated June 1, 1846, and carried it to England, where A. K. Isbister, a Red River Métis lawyer now living in London, presented it. The petition sought free trade, a governor independent of the Company, and an elected legislature. The petition carried the signatures of 977 Métis.[17]

The Company acknowledged that the Métis were born in the country and entitled to call themselves "Native," but denied that this carried any rights or privileges. Isbister acknowledged a distinction between Métis and Indians but asserted that the distinction did not mean the Métis had no Native rights. The Company simply reasserted its position: the Métis were fully subject to Company laws. The Company put the petition down to outside agitators who were using the Métis to attack the monopoly through the mask of Métis rights. Despite the educated Métis—Grant, Riel, Garrioch, Sinclair and Isbister—the Company could not believe the Métis were capable of coming up with articulate opposition to its rule.

The British government considered sending out commissioners to investigate, but Sinclair and Isbister were probably thoroughly justified in rejecting this proposal. The Métis believed the Company would prejudice any investigators sent out to Red River. In the end the secretary of state for the colonies advised Isbister that it was a matter for the courts, where, by the way, the Métis would not be permitted to challenge the company charter or its monopoly.

In Red River, retaliation followed. James Sinclair, Jean-Louis Riel and Father Belcourt had made themselves too prominent in their protests on behalf of the Métis. Governor Christie informed Sinclair that henceforth Company ships would carry no goods in his name. Sinclair's export business, at least the part that exported to Great Britain, was ruined. Father Belcourt was forced to leave Red River. Retaliation against Jean-Louis Riel continued for the rest of his life. Despite being one of the few educated Métis in the settlement, he was never given a place on the Council of Assiniboia or any official participation in the established government of the colony. He had simply made himself too vocal and active in protecting Métis.

Thus a pattern was established. The Company passed laws to restrain the Métis. The Métis complained and evaded the restraints. The Company tried to enforce its laws. The Métis petitioned. The Company would concede a few points in one area and double down in another. The Métis anger and resentment boiled over, and they resorted to collective, sometimes violent, opposition. The Company would back down and make concessions. Things would settle down for a while. This cycle repeated itself from the 1820s to the 1860s. The Company did not take advantage of any of these potential learning moments, and the Métis Nation further coalesced around a growing self-respect for its own ability to command compliance by means of collective action and armed resistance.

The Council of Assiniboia fed the smouldering flame by enacting more laws. It appeared woefully ignorant of the basic fact underlying the rule of law: law must rely on general compliance by the majority of the population or be implemented by force. The Métis Nation had little incentive to comply and the Company had no ability to enforce. More liberal legal mechanisms, institutions and policies would have availed the Company much better, but instead it aggravated the situation.

THE LAND AND MÉTIS MOBILITY

The Company tried to impose a land title system on Red River, with itself as sole authority for any sales. It passed a resolution that no servants would be permitted to settle at Red River unless they purchased at least fifty acres of land at a set price. The Company wanted to stop the Métis' customary practice of land transfers, which it regarded as squatters selling something they had no right to sell.

The Métis Nation, of course, saw it quite differently. They believed they were the owners of the land, not squatters, and as such had the right to sell, share or trade their land according to their customs without the interference of the Company. And the Company's interference, to their minds, was legion. The Métis were deeply suspicious of the Company's motives. Title to land purchased or provided by the Company had several covenants tying the landholder to the Company. The lots were leased in a feudal manner. The lease was for a thousand years and had rents payable, a requirement to contribute to the civil, military and religious requirements of the colony, as well as a requirement that the leaseholder give several days of free labour each year to the maintenance of the roads. There were also several restrictive covenants, including a prohibition on distilling liquor. But the most galling restriction for the Métis was the covenant that prohibited trading furs with or importing goods from the Americans.

Most Métis resisted any attempt by the Company to regulate land title or their traditional landholding practices. Some may not have objected to having it regularized, but most objected to the onerous conditions the Company attached. Most preferred to continue with their customary landholding practices and the Company was unable to collect on its covenants. The Métis resistance to the Company's attempt at controlling the land, and especially to the hated covenant prohibiting trading, was predictable. Few bothered to obtain land title from the Company, and they avoided bringing their furs back to Red River. By the 1840s there were more than five thousand Métis in Red River, most holding land without paper title. The Company could not force five thousand Métis to register their title, so title to the land in Red River continued with the two separate systems—Métis customary title and a few titles registered with the Company.

The Company never recognized or made any attempt to accommodate Métis Nation customs, values, preferences or laws.

Its failure to recognize the Métis as a collective was in part because of Métis mobility and their long absences from Red River. The Company saw little reason to accommodate people who merely used Red River as a rendezvous and who really belonged elsewhere. As Alexander Ross put it,

> [N]ot a tenth part of their number really belong to Red River, although they have from choice made it the land of their adoption. Hither, in fact, have flocked the half-breeds from all quarters east of the rocky mountain ridge, making the colony their great rendezvous and nursing place; while their restless habits lead them from place to place, from camp to camp, from the colony to the Plains, and from the Plains to the colony, like the wandering Arabs, or the more restless Mamelukes, wherever hunting or fishing hold out to them a precarious subsistence.[18]

But the Métis Nation did belong to Red River and indeed saw it as the heart of their motherland. What the Company and settlers missed was the purpose, the patterns and the catalysts that animated the Métis. Their movement was not aimless or without purpose. The Métis Nation's mobility was a murmuration, the shape-shifting movement of a flock of starlings. If it were possible to map the social movements of the Métis Nation on the Plains and in the boreal forest in the mid to late 1800s, Métis mobility would reveal itself with the same fluidity. The Métis were closely connected and moved in family groupings. They reacted swiftly to danger, shifting their focus to face the danger as a group. Their movements were coordinated. Small family units shifted and feinted, gathered, separated and regathered within the vast North-West—their motherland, their place. They lived always on the cusp of change, ready for the next shift.

Their lifestyle was the antithesis of settling. They might set for a time, but it was more like the quiet before taking flight again. The catalyst for this movement could be the Sioux or the Blackfoot causing a hunting group to shift ground or bundle together to face the danger or avoid it. The catalyst could be a joyous wedding that brought hundreds of family and friends together from far and wide. They gathered into great assemblies when called by their leaders for political decisions. Winter caused large groups to splinter into small family units seeking a favourite wintering site. The catalyst could be that first blue-sky day in the spring when the newly dry ground made movement out onto the Plains possible. Often it was the buffalo that drew the Métis from all over the Plains to come together.

One event would affect them all because of their family connections and because they were so intensely aware of each other. Communication spread rapidly across the North-West. Each individual living within the group saw, felt and reacted as the entire group. That is what made the Métis stand tall and proud. Each man or woman was one person and all of them. They were a connected people, a living, fluid, synchronized system where thousands of people came together at Red River, Pembina, Turtle Mountain, Cypress Hills or Qu'Appelle and then split off to gather again in different formations.

Many Métis had homes on the Plains and homes in Red River. So, the Métis did belong to Red River. They saw the entire North-West as theirs, just as they claimed Qu'Appelle, Cypress Hills, Wood Mountain, Fort Edmonton, Rainy Lake and Île-à-la-Crosse—all the places where they built homes, traded, hunted, wintered and visited. They saw it all as their motherland, and Red River was the beating heart of that motherland.

CHAPTER 13

TAKING THE FIGHT TO THE COURT

Until 1835 there was no real system of courts in the North-West. The Hudson's Bay Company charter of 1670 had enabled a court of the governor and council, but it rarely sat. In 1835 the Council of Assiniboia, headed by Governor Simpson, passed a resolution creating a new General Quarterly Court of Assiniboia. The new court was to sit regularly. It was the first attempt to establish a Western-style justice system in the North-West. Unfortunately, the Court of Assiniboia was not independent of the Company. It was established by the Company and staffed by Company appointees and employees. Thus, anyone who wished to bring a suit against the Company immediately placed the court in a conflict of interest. This happened in 1845 when James Sinclair sued the Company, claiming that it had underpaid him for freighting services. The court had a simple answer to the conflict: it would not hear a case against itself.

The Company's conflict of interest arose again a year later when a trader named Peter Hayden was charged with manslaughter for the accidental shooting of a boy who was in his charge.[1]

Hayden was one of the free traders the Company had been trying to shut down. He had heard that Cuthbert Grant was coming to confiscate his furs, and as he was getting his gun out in preparation to defend himself, it accidently discharged and killed the boy. Hayden was "crazy" with guilt and "attempted to lay violent hands on himself."[2] He was taken into custody and confined in the new jail the Company had built next to Fort Garry.

The Métis and all the independent traders were furious about what they considered to be a gross injustice. They held a large protest meeting and many wanted to free Hayden. Father Belcourt persuaded them to petition the British authorities, but the general feeling in the settlement was that the Company was directly responsible for the death of the boy, which had occurred as a result of the Company's efforts to impose its monopoly. As far as the Métis were concerned, the Company, not Hayden, should be charged with manslaughter, and the Company's court had no right to sit in judgment of Hayden.

At Hayden's trial Cuthbert Grant was absent—perhaps for the best. The court's sentence handed to Hayden was lenient. He paid a fine of one shilling and gave security for his good behaviour for two years. The court's lenient sentence simply damped down a predictable eruption. It didn't put out the fire. The Métis remained angry.

THE FIRST MÉTIS LAND TITLE CASE

In 1847 the Métis defended their rights in what could be considered the first Métis land title case.[3] The Company had granted title to land to Andrew McDermot. The Métis defendants were charged with cutting timber on that land. The Métis admitted cutting the timber but claimed they had a right, as Métis, to do so. In argument before the court, they said they did not recognize the Company's right to grant title or that the

Company had lawfully purchased the native right to the timber.

In effect, the Métis were arguing that their native title had not been extinguished and they were thus able to enjoy the resources—the timber—on their title lands. In the Court of Assiniboia, this kind of argument was a non-starter. The court was presented with the title deed and the 1817 Selkirk Treaty, in which two-mile tracts of land on both sides of the rivers were granted to Lord Selkirk in exchange for an annual payment to the "chiefs and warriors of the Chippeway or Sautaux Nation, and the Killistine or Cree Nation." Neither document was an agreement to purchase Métis rights. But in the Court of Assiniboia, these documents were considered proof of the Company's right to grant title and its purchase of all native timber rights, First Nation and Métis. The court found the Métis defendants liable for five shillings in damages plus costs.

During the trial, Pascal Breland testified that the Métis had allowed the case to come before the court. The statement suggests that the Métis controlled matters that went to court. Judge Thom made no attempt to correct this bold statement, perhaps because it was a fair assessment of the Métis power at the time. The court's decision, and documents issued by the Company, had no effect on the firm belief of the Métis Nation that it had native title to the land and resource access rights.

THE SAYER TRIAL

We now approach the final act in the Métis Nation's second resistance. The first resistance was against the Selkirk Settlers and their attempt to monopolize the land and resources in a manner that the Brûlés thought jeopardized their existence. This new resistance was not aimed at the settlers. It was focused on the Hudson's Bay Company and specifically resisted the Company's monopoly. This time the resistance was not carried out with the use of force. Instead the Métis Nation used the Company's court.

In 1849 Guillaume Sayer and three other traders, McGillis, Laronde and Goulet, were charged with illicitly trafficking in furs. The Company had charged others since passing its law in 1845, but this was the first case that actually went to trial. Governor William Caldwell and Judge Thom had made the decision to lay the charges, and from the beginning the case was a mess of conflicts.

Sayer and the other three Métis traders were sued by the Company, so the case was titled *Hudson's Bay Company vs. Sayer et al.*, not *The Public Interest vs. Sayer et al.*[4] In other words, the Company brought a private civil suit in its own court but treated it as a criminal prosecution, charging the three defendants with violating Company trading laws.

According to the Company's charter, a governor had to sit as a judge in any lawsuit that involved the Company. With no disinterested judge, the Company was vulnerable to charges that its courts were inherently biased and in a conflict of interest. In the Sayer trial, the Company instigated the charges, its governor and paid employee, Adam Thom, sat as judges, and the Company's chief factor, John Ballenden, was the prosecutor and gave evidence. Since the case involved the Company's monopoly, it was the quintessential definition of bias and conflict of interest. Apparently in 1849 the inherent conflicts of interest were of concern only to the Métis and the other traders. The Métis were so incensed at the injustice that they rallied to the cause.

May 17, 1849, was the date set for the trial. It was Ascension Day, which was a Catholic holiday. In setting the trial date, Thom would have known that the Métis, largely Catholic, would be at

church. It was one of the Company's tactics. They were in the habit of holding court when the Métis were out on the hunt, seeing an opportunity to avoid Métis protests. After Mass on the Sunday before the trial, Jean-Louis Riel read a letter from Father Belcourt urging the Métis to challenge the Company's monopoly. The Métis had every intention of doing just that and likely needed little urging. On the day of the trial, they persuaded the priest to hold an early Mass, and afterwards Riel again read Father Belcourt's letter and made a rousing speech in which he inspired the Métis to go to the court to assert their rights.

Jean-Louis Riel (*Glenbow Archives, NA-47-28*)

Dozens of small craft carried hundreds of men over to the other side of the river (the church was in St. Boniface), toward the courthouse in Fort Garry. Governor Caldwell, well aware of the Métis anger over the charges and of past instances when they displayed their anger at the Company's injustices, threatened to call in reinforcements. Unfortunately for Caldwell, his reinforcements were a drunken lot of pensioners who boasted about their determination to put the Métis in their place—all hot air as it turned out. The pensioners never appeared, which was just as well, for they were no match for the angry crowd of Métis.

About four hundred armed Métis surrounded the courthouse, and at eleven o'clock the authorities had to push their way through the hostile crowd to get inside. Sayer was outside with his fellow Métis and didn't go in when his case was called. Judge Thom and the other members of the court delayed until 1:00, at which time they sent a message saying Sayer might have a deputation to speak for him in his defence. James Sinclair, Peter Garrioch and Jean-Louis Riel entered the courthouse with Sayer while twenty other Métis took up a station at the courthouse door. At the outer gate of the courtyard, another fifty stood guard.

Sinclair and Garrioch addressed the court as the delegates of the people and tried to set out a wide range of grievances. They began by presenting a petition challenging the legality of the Company's trade monopoly. The petition demanded the immediate removal of Recorder Thom, equal use of French and English in the courts, rescission of the law restricting imports from the United States and the appointment of Métis to the Council of Assiniboia. The final demand was for free trade in furs.

Judge Thom launched into an hour-long "bombastic sort of an address," the climax of which had him in tears—though these were perhaps crocodile tears.[5] He gave a fierce refusal of the deputation. Thom informed Sinclair and Garrioch that the court would not receive them as "delegates of the people," and that if they wished to present their petition and make submissions about grievances other than the matter before the court, they could do so at the next meeting of the Council of Assiniboia.

With the assurance that there would soon be a chance to put their grievances before the council, the Métis agreed to restrict their submissions to the issues concerning the charges faced by Sayer and the other accused. Sinclair played the lawyer rather well. He succeeded in having several of the jury members replaced with men acceptable to him.[6] On taking the stand, Sayer admitted he had traded furs but offered two lawful excuses. First, he had traded with other Métis, not with Indians, and the law did not restrict trading with Métis. Second, he had been told by John Harriott, a Company official, that he was only restricted from trading with Indians. In effect Sayer testified that he had Company permission.

The jury found Sayer guilty but, taking note of the officially induced error, recommended mercy. With hundreds of armed and angry Métis outside the court building, Prosecutor Ballenden seized upon the mercy recommendation and claimed that he would seek no punishment. He merely wanted the court to confirm the legality of the Company's monopoly. Ballenden also offered to drop the charges against Goulet, McGillis and Laronde. The icing on the cake was that he even offered to give back the furs Sayer had just been found guilty of trading illegally. The Company's monopoly remained intact legally, if it had ever been lawful to begin with. Practically speaking, however, the monopoly was forever broken.

The consequences of the Sayer trial were immediate. The

petition the court declined to hear was subsequently presented to the Council of Assiniboia. This time it was seriously considered and met with partial success. Thom stayed on the court but began to speak in both languages when French interests were at issue, and the council promised to continue this procedure in future. The council reduced the tariffs on American goods to the same rate as for English goods, and it agreed to recommend to the Company more appointments of Canadians and Métis to the council. Free trade in furs was declared beyond the council's competence, but that no longer mattered. The Sayer trial had already broken the Company's monopoly.

When Ballenden conceded he would seek no punishment, the shout went out: *Le commerce est libre! Vive la liberté! Paashkiiyaakanaan* (we won)! Jean-Louis Riel emerged from the courthouse with Sayer on his shoulders. The scene outside the courthouse was wild. The crowd whooped and yelled and fired off a *feu de joie* (celebratory shots). The Métis surged to the banks of the river and boated across to the other side, where they continued their raucous celebration of *la liberté*. Men, women and children cheered, sang and danced in celebration of their victory.

Jean-Louis Riel's speech after Mass had inspired the crowd and made an impression on all the Métis. In the gathering that day, a small five-year-old boy had listened to his father speak passionately on behalf of the Métis. For the rest of his life, Louis Riel would recall that day. It was among his earliest memories, and his father's passionate speech and actions in defence of the Métis Nation left an indelible mark on the young Louis.

PART FOUR

THE RED RIVER RESISTANCE

CHAPTER 14

THE THIRD NATIONAL RESISTANCE

LII CANADAS

The Métis Nation settled into a pattern after the Sayer trial. They had successfully asserted their rights as a nation, as a collective force to be reckoned with in Red River. They continued to assert their existence as a "Native" nation, distinguishing themselves from First Nations and Euro-Canadians.

But there was a sense that change was coming. The leading minds of the Métis Nation could see that Britain's interest in the North-West was waning. And men of a different ilk were beginning to arrive in Red River. Before 1850 the Métis Nation had known mostly fur traders and Selkirk Settlers. But the population of Red River was growing, and by 1856 there were 6,523 people.

The newcomers were different. They were aligned with the Canada First movement in Ontario. They had two goals: ensuring that Canada became British and Protestant, and annexing the North-West to Canada.[1] The Canada First movement campaigned for exclusively British immigration and championed the idea of an Anglo-Saxon, Protestant northern race with superior values and institutions. Ontario premier Edward Blake and the Conservative minister of public works William McDougall were both members of the Canada First movement. Their point man in Red River was John Christian Schultz, the founder of the Canada First branch in the North-West, which he named the Canadian Party. Schultz was a shady manipulator and fraud artist.[2] Many years later when he died, it was said, "Pity we knew him."[3] Unfortunately, we will get to know him quite well. The Métis called these men *lii Canadas*, the Canadas. It wasn't a compliment.

The Canadian Party established a newspaper in Red River, called *The Nor'-Wester*. Although the term "yellow journalism" would not be coined for another thirty years, *The Nor'-Wester* was an early practitioner of this sensationalist style of reporting. Facts and integrity were not entirely absent in *The Nor'-Wester*, but the slant of the message was more important than inconvenient facts. The Canadian Party was in the newspaper business so they could control messaging to their target audience, Ontario. But their main interest was land. They wanted Canada to annex the North-West so the land could be opened up to the market. As the earliest opportunists on site, they dreamed of fortunes—a dream that required a significant investment in time and effort.

Converting the lands of the North-West into a market was a multi-step process. The North-West would have to change hands four times before the Canadian Party men could turn a profit. First the Hudson's Bay Company would have to transfer Rupert's Land back to Britain. Then Britain would have to transfer Rupert's Land and the North-Western Territory to Canada. Once the entire North-West (Rupert's Land and the

North-Western Territory) was annexed to Canada, the Canadian Party speculators could buy plots of land. Then they needed people. Hence the message of the Canadian Party newspaper to Ontario, praising the glories of the North-West. They wanted mass immigration of a very specific kind—farmers, preferably white, Protestant, English-speaking people from Ontario. When the proper kind of Ontario immigrants arrived, the speculators could sell them land and only then realize a profit.

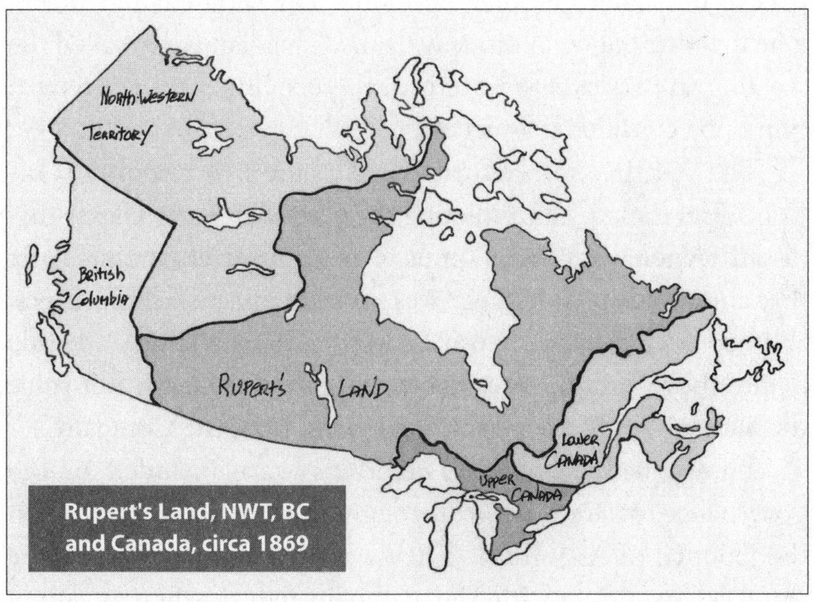

Rupert's Land, NWT, BC and Canada, circa 1869

Step one was to eliminate the Hudson's Bay Company, the owners of Rupert's Land. Using their newspaper, *The Nor'-Wester*, Schultz and his party mounted an assault on the Company. They had great supporters in Ontario and in the Canadian government, but they also needed to convince the residents of Red River of their plan. In particular they wanted to convince the Métis Nation leaders, men like Pascal Breland and Jean-Louis Riel, that annexation to Canada was good for Red River.

Jean-Louis Riel seemed like a natural ally because he had been one of those who led the charge against the Company in the 1840s. So, Schultz and his party set up an annexation meeting and asked Riel to chair it. The Canadian Party came out in full force and the meeting quickly descended into a bash-the-Company session. Seeking to provide some balance, Riel invited Father Bermond to speak in support of the Company. But the Canadian Party men were not subtle practitioners of the art of persuasion. They heckled Bermond and shouted him down. The meeting ended in disarray. If the Canadian Party called the meeting to persuade the Métis of the benefits of annexation, it cannot be considered a success.

The meeting sparked the Métis Nation to respond. Jean-Louis Riel took to contradicting the Canadian Party claims that dissatisfaction with the Company was universal, stating flatly that among his people there was no such dissatisfaction. It was an interesting change of position for the Métis Nation. A decade before they were the ones haranguing the Company. But since the Sayer trial, they were less inclined to fight the Company.

Things had changed. The Métis were included in the governance of Red River through their representatives on the Council of Assiniboia. They were trading freely and they were co-operating with the company court when it suited them. Perhaps more to the point, the Métis were less dependent on the Company. Many Métis were spending more time away from Red River as their buffalo hunts took them farther west for longer periods of time. They were fostering a trading relationship with the Americans and building their own wintering settlements on the Plains. Because the Company no longer ruled every aspect of Métis lives, their attitude toward the Company had mellowed.

It was the Canadian Party, trying to set up at Red River, that felt the bite of the Company's monopoly over governance (from which they were excluded) and its court (which more than once found against Schultz). And it was these newcomers who created the insecurity everyone in Red River now began to feel about their land title. In taking the first steps to create a market for land, they drew attention to the fact that most land in Red River was held under Métis customary law. Very few Métis had paper title from the Company proving their ownership. It drove the Métis Nation to hold a large meeting in 1862 to assert their native claim to the land.

WEATHER, DISEASE AND INSECTS

Floods, fires, drought, disease and insects all took a toll on the Métis Nation during the 1860s. There was famine in 1862 and 1864, and scarlet fever, typhus and dysentery in 1864 and 1865. In 1865 the French Métis parishes in Red River buried three people a day. Floods in 1865 and 1866 brought clouds of mosquitoes in 1867. And then the grasshoppers appeared. In the course of destroying the crops, the insects laid their eggs, and in the spring of 1868 a new generation appeared. The grasshoppers stripped the woods and fields bare and devoured every last leaf and head of grain. The entire country looked and was destitute. The loss of all vegetation meant the buffalo kept a wide berth. The hunters arrived back in the settlement starving, their hunt having failed. The fisheries failed and even the rabbits and pheasants disappeared. Many people died from the collective toll taken by the floods, fires, drought, disease and grasshoppers. Famine stalked the North-West.

There were celebrations in eastern Canada for the first birthday of the country on July 1, 1867, but few celebrated in Red

River. Canada's reputation in Red River was, to say the least, not good. As Louis Goulet said, "These émigrés from Ontario, all of them Orangemen, looked as if their one dream in life was to make war on the Hudson's Bay Company, the Catholic Church and anyone who spoke French. In a word, as my father put it, the devil was in the woodpile. The latest arrivals were looking to be masters of everything, everywhere."[4]

The Canadian Party was sowing seeds of racism, bigotry and religious conflict. The Canadian Party and the insects were both wreaking havoc. At least the grasshoppers ate and left. The Canadian Party stayed, thrived on the conflict it sowed, and gave the Métis Nation its first indication that it had something to fear and a lot to lose by joining Canada. The conflict began with a road.

THE ROAD RELIEF SCAM

Since Confederation in 1867 Canada had been preparing to accept the North-West from Great Britain. In 1868 the complicated negotiations began. Until the North-West was officially transferred, Canada was a foreign country with no rights or claims west of Ontario. But Canada was lusting after the North-West, and the famine in Red River provided an opportunity for Canada to send men to the North-West. Under the guise of a work relief project and with no prior permission from the Company, Canada authorized the construction of a road between Lake of the Woods in Ontario and Red River.

The project was a Conservative Party boondoggle. John Snow, the lead surveyor, arrived in Red River in September 1868 with his paymaster, Charles Mair. Mair was one of the founding members of the Canada First movement. Both men fell into a natural alliance with Schultz and the Canadian Party. Their

Canada First brother, who was the Canadian minister of public works, McDougall, provided $30,000 for the road relief project, money that was supposed to benefit the people of Red River who were suffering from the famine. Most of that money stayed in the hands of the Canadian Party.

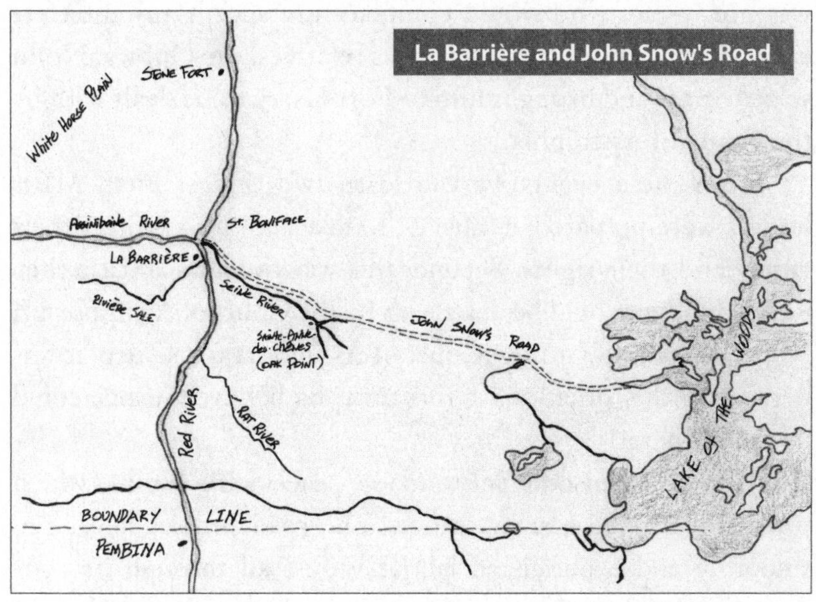

Schultz opened up a store in the Métis community of Oak Point (Sainte-Anne-des-Chênes).[5] Road workers were paid in goods from Schultz's store, where provisions cost more than the men earned. Shopping at Schultz's store was particularly galling to the Métis workers on the road project because Schultz made no secret of his utter contempt for the Métis.

Snow and the Canadian Party then developed a scheme to buy land nearby. Snow sold liquor to the Ojibwa and then held a meeting at which they, under the influence, "agreed" to sell their Aboriginal title. Snow's men plowed out claims for large tracts of land. They boasted that as soon as Canada took possession, their claims would be secured. The road workers broke into Métis houses and took them over for long dancing and drinking parties. The terrified women and children were held prisoner and prevented from escaping for help. The Métis leader in Sainte-Anne-des-Chênes was Augustin Nolin, and he was not a man who would complacently accept any interference with his family, his land or his relatives, the Ojibwa. Nolin seized Snow and brought him to Fort Garry to be dealt with by the Court of Assiniboia.

From these events we can learn two things: First, Métis leaders were prepared, as always, to take action to protect their family and their rights. Second, this was the kind of case they were confident could be dealt with by the Court of Assiniboia. If Nolin threw Snow to the Court of Assiniboia for justice, it was because in this situation, at this time, he believed justice could be found there.

After this episode Snow made peace with Nolin, which turned out to be a smart move. The road project never ran smoothly and experienced labour unrest all through its construction. It is here, on the relief project, that we first catch sight of Thomas Scott, the man who would cause so much trouble over the next three years. Scott was one of the road workers on the relief project. After a wage dispute, Scott and his road worker buddies tried to drown Snow, and it was Nolin who came to Snow's rescue.

Hudson's Bay Company governor William McTavish eventually registered a mild complaint about Canada's trespass in building the road on Company land. McDougall justified the trespass by claiming that Canada felt obligated to provide assistance because the Company had done nothing for the starving people of Red River. This was blatantly false, but McDougall saw the road as an opportunity to get into the North-West. He wanted to see just what future opportunity and fortune Canada was about to purchase.

The road became a symbol for the Métis of what could be expected from Canada: corruption, violence and land swindles, all accompanied by a racist, anti-French, anti-Catholic, anti-Métis agenda. The first view of what it would mean to become Canadian was bleak. It was slightly less offensive for the English Métis. Though they were held to be inferior because of their Indigenous blood, they were more acceptable because they were Protestant, more invested in agriculture and spoke English. The French Métis had three strikes against them. They were "too Indian, too Catholic and too French."[6]

ANNIE McDERMOT BANNATYNE AND LOUIS RIEL

In addition to his Canada First activities, the paymaster of the road relief project, Charlie Mair, was something of a literary man. His letters, published in the Toronto *Globe*, claimed the Métis were making undeserved claims on the Red River Famine Relief Fund. They were, he claimed, "the only people here who are starving. Five thousand of them have to be fed this winter, and it is their own fault—they won't farm."[7] Mair was living off the proceeds of the so-called famine relief project, so his comment about the Métis irritated everyone in Red River.

Many Métis did farm, but farming saved no one from the grasshoppers, which were equal opportunity pests, affecting the entire community. Most people needed help. In fact the starvation faced by the Métis hunters in the settlement was unusual. The hunt seldom failed; the crops failed regularly. Generally, it was the hunters who came to the rescue of the farmers. The Canadian Party may have appreciated Mair's wit, but his letters wouldn't make him friends in a community where the Métis formed over three-quarters of the population.

Mair's published literary efforts also included a gossipy snarl aimed at the Métis women. "Many wealthy people are married to half-breed women, who, having no coat of arms but a 'totem' to look back to, make up for the deficiency by biting at the backs of their 'white' sisters."[8] Given that almost no Canadians looked back to a coat of arms, Mair's comments were snobbish in the extreme. His British Protestant superiority influenced him to commend the hospitality he had received from Governor McTavish and his brother-in-law Andrew Bannatyne, but in the next breath he commented on the "deficiency" in their wives, the Métis sisters Annie and Mary Sarah McDermot.[9]

Annie McDermot Bannatyne is remembered rather fondly in Métis lore because she took on Charlie Mair. When by chance Annie met Mair at the local store, she took her horsewhip to him. Everyone in the settlement was delighted with Annie. They appreciated her method of administering what they saw as a well-deserved public humiliation of a man who had abused their women. Mair kept his opinions on Métis women to himself after this public chastising. But of course the whipping didn't change his contempt for the Métis.

Jean-Louis Riel's son Louis raised his voice in public for the first time and challenged Mair in the press. In a letter to the editor of *Le Nouveau Monde*, Riel pointed out that the famine struck members of all segments of Red River society and that Mair had his facts wrong. Riel gave voice to the Métis' low opinion of Mair: "[I]f we had only you as a specimen of civilized men, we should not have a very high idea of them."[10]

Riel had been away in Quebec and in the United States. He arrived back in Red River on July 26, 1868. He was twenty-four years old and came home to find his people obsessed with the coming transfer. They were all talking politics. The Métis Nation's political force, always simmering, was starting to boil up again. In the past the Nation had faced off against the Selkirk Settlers and the Hudson's Bay Company. Now it was facing a new threat: Canada as represented by the Canadian Party. Riel's letter marked his first foray as the voice of the Métis Nation, and with it he burst onto the Canadian consciousness. The comet had appeared in the sky.

Louis Riel (*Glenbow Archives NA-47-28*)

SOLD

It occurred to no one in the government of Great Britain or of Canada to inform the Métis or anyone in the North-West about their plans. To the extent that the Canadian government gave it any thought at all—and it really didn't—the scattered nomadic First Nations and the Métis were not considered worth the effort. Canada gave no legal credit to the Hudson's Bay Company charter and dismissed its government, the Council of Assiniboia, as a nonentity. As far as Canada was concerned, the North-West was a vast and empty land, theirs for the taking.

Canada knew there were Indigenous people in the North-West, although they didn't know who, where or how many they were. To Canada's way of thinking, the only issue was the extinguishment of Indian title, a matter they considered a mere administrative detail that could be dealt with later by treaties. The idea that there was such a thing as a collective Métis people, the Métis Nation, never entered their minds. The poet e. e. cummings's line "down they forgot as up they grew" captures Canada's convenient memory lapse perfectly.[11] Canada had forgotten the 1816 battle at the Frog Plain and succumbed to the propaganda published by the Canadian Party.

Both Britain and Canada proceeded as if only land were being transferred. Britain hoped it could transfer the land without Canada looking too deeply into the fact that the natives in the North-West had proven themselves restive in the past and could likely be counted on to behave so again. Britain also wanted to avoid any legal battle over the legitimacy of the three-hundred-year-old Hudson's Bay Company charter. Canada was urged to keep its eye on the main issue, the land, and just cut a deal. In the end Canada decided it could overlook the legitimacy of the charter. A bargain was made—and a bargain it was: 1.5 million square miles for £300,000 ($1.5 million). To put it in perspective, the United States had recently paid Russia $7.2 million for nearly 600,000 square miles when it purchased Alaska.

Both Britain and Canada were warned about the rising discontent in the North-West. All warnings were dismissed. Canada purported to be fully aware of everything it needed to know about the people and issues in the North-West and had everything entirely under control.

THE MÉTIS NATION FORCE BEGINS TO STIR

The Métis Nation was worried about the security of their motherland, and they suspected, correctly, that they would be excluded in the new government. Their objections were published in the *The New Nation*, a newspaper printed in Red River between January and September of 1870 that generally supported the Métis:

> They aver that they do not belong to Canada, and have never been made over to that Dominion. That although the Canadian Government has given £300,000 to the Hudson Bay Company for certain territories which belonged to the latter, they are not included in this bargain, seeing that they never were an appendage to the Hudson Bay Company; that Canada could not buy what it was not the company's to sell; that, in any case, they ought not to be transferred to a third power without their leave and consent; that, if they have been a British settlement hitherto, they have as much right to be consulted as to their disposition as were the people of Prince Edward's Island, Newfoundland, and British Columbia, all of whom have been

> invited, but have declined, to enter the Confederation, and yet whom the Canadian Government has never pretended to have the right to coerce, or to bring within the Union, whether they would or not. The people of the Red River territory, in fact, decline to be sold as a chattel of the Hudson Bay territory . . . and they protest that, if they are British subjects at all, they are the subjects not of Canada but of England; that they are a colony of England, and not "a colony of a colony."[12]

Their worst fears were confirmed in June 1869 when Canada revealed its plans for governance of the North-West. Canada would henceforth have its own Crown colony in the North-West with a lieutenant-governor and a council appointed from Ottawa. The lieutenant-governor was to be the "Paternal despot, as in other small Crown Colonies, his Council being one of advice, he and they, however, being governed by instructions from HeadQuarters."[13]

The proposal was a great step backwards for the people of the North-West. While the Council of Assiniboia was not an elected government, it did contain appointed members recommended by the residents, and it had learned to ensure that the various sectors of the colony were given voice in the council. This is why Jean-Louis Riel had confidently stated that the Métis had no complaints about the Company. Canada's proposal of a government composed only of easterners accountable to, appointed by and directed from far away was unacceptable to the Métis Nation.

The English-speaking population of Red River, largely made up of English Métis, was concerned about its future but inclined to believe that everything would be fine and there was no need to get involved. The French Métis were not so complacent. Everyone had heard the Canadian Party boast that they "would take up arms and drive out the half-breeds."[14] They "would all be driven back from the river & their land given to others."[15] There was no way the French Métis were going to sit quietly and let this happen.

CHAPTER 15

THE RESISTANCE BEGINS

THE FRENCH MÉTIS TAKE ACTION

The Red River Resistance began on July 5, 1869. Prior to this the Métis Nation had been passionately debating how to protect its rights and existence as a nation. Now they began to take action. It began when the French Métis in St. Vital and St. Norbert found men from Canada's road project, including Charlie Mair, staking claims on their lands. The Métis ordered them off and began to send out regular mounted patrols with orders to protect Métis lands from the speculators. The Métis patrols evicted squatters, chased away claim-stakers, removed stakes and signs of occupation, and filled in any wells they found. They chased *lii Canadas* to lands near Portage la Prairie.

They also claimed a specific territory, which they described as their collective lands, recognized by the custom of the people or by agreement of their nation.[1] They expressly excluded strangers. At this point, July 1869, the French Métis marked out only their own territory. They did not include the English Métis parishes.

While the French Métis were taking action to identify and protect their territory, the Canadian Party was trying to drum up support for annexation to Canada. Some prominent Métis traders such as William Dease, Georges Racette and Pascal Breland stood to gain a great deal from more customers and new markets for their goods. Dease had particularly ambitious plans. In addition to annexation he wanted to overthrow the Council of Assiniboia, be named governor and appropriate the £300,000 Canada was paying Great Britain for the North-West. He announced his grand plan at a public meeting on July 29, 1869. It didn't go well.

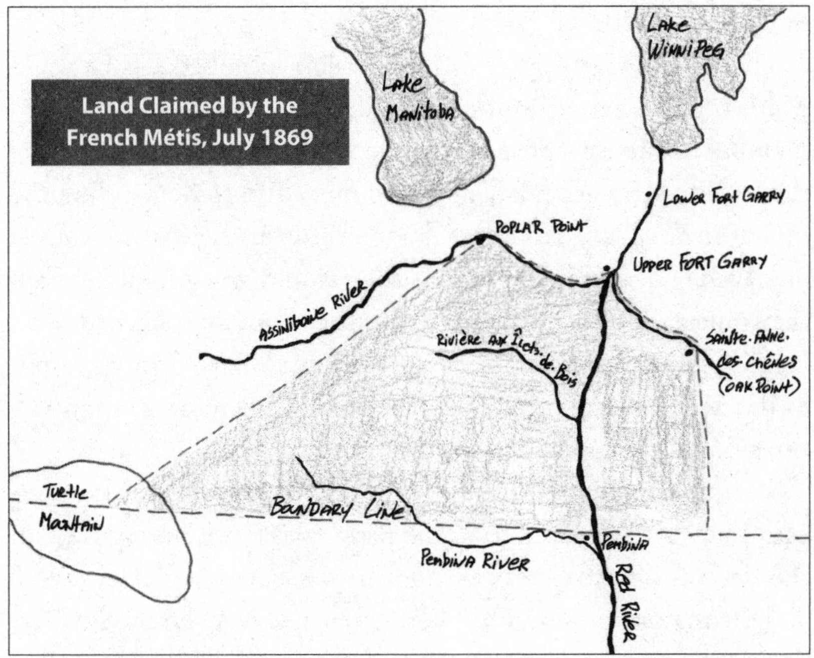

Land Claimed by the French Métis, July 1869

The Métis were ready to listen to someone with a plan. But they didn't like his. They were suspicious of Dease's connections to the Canadian Party, and they knew that overthrowing the Council of Assiniboia could not be done without them. If the Canadian Party, via Dease, could get the Métis to overthrow the council, Company rule would collapse like a house of cards. The resulting chaos would open the way for ambitious men to claim land and make fortunes. It was a classic example of what Naomi Klein calls "the shock doctrine," where planned chaos provides opportunities for speculators. Overthrowing the Company government would have benefited the men of the Canadian Party and perhaps a few traders like Dease. It would be of no benefit to the Métis. Schultz and his ilk didn't believe the Métis had rights, but they knew the Métis claimed them. This would be a cheap and easy way to overthrow the Company and use its money to buy off the Métis.

Dease's proposal was particularly shocking because he was a Métis representative on the Council of Assiniboia, an appointed member of the very government he was now proposing to overthrow. Those in attendance had no objection to demanding the money from Canada. There was nothing to be lost by such a demand, and who knew, maybe they would get something. But they objected to everything else Dease proposed. John Bruce, an English Métis, rose to object. Bruce was a man of some stature in the Métis community. So when he expressed his disapproval, the people listened and most agreed.

The Métis Nation has never made its decisions by consensus. They are prepared to argue passionately for a long time in the decision-making process, but in the end, they always vote and the majority rules. They vote often and on even the smallest decision. So Dease's proposal went to a vote. A few supported Dease, but the majority, by a long shot, were opposed and left the meeting considering a petition to publicly condemn Dease. Dease's attempt to become the governor of Red River and the leader of the Métis Nation failed.

The Métis would not go down the route Dease had mapped

out, and for good reason. The problem didn't lie with the Company, which the Métis saw as a spent force. The problem was Canada. Overthrowing the wrong target would be foolish. And the Métis were not prepared to follow a leader who urged them to act in what was so obviously his own self-interest. Dease left the meeting ashamed, "like a fox caught by a hen."[2] The French Métis in St. Norbert and St. Vital continued protecting their territory with their mounted patrols, and they continued meeting to make their own plans.

THE SURVEYORS ARRIVE

The next step toward colonization of the North-West began in July 1869. Canada still had no legal right to do anything in the North-West until after the land was transferred from Great Britain to Canada on December 1, 1869. But the legalities didn't trouble William McDougall. After all, he had sent in the road crew with only a mild protest from the Company. Anticipating no resistance from it, McDougall sent in surveyors.

The surveyors, led by Colonel John Stoughton Dennis, arrived in Red River in August 1869 and, like the road relief crew before them, immediately took up with the Canadian Party. This made the Métis suspicious of their survey objectives. Augustin Nolin sent Dennis a letter telling him not to come out to Sainte-Anne-des-Chênes if he wanted to keep his head on his shoulders. Despite the warning several surveyors began staking out claims at Sainte-Anne-des-Chênes, again boasting that such claims would be recognized by Canada. Nolin and his men forcibly removed them and obliterated any signs of their claims.

The French Métis saw the survey as a move by Protestant Ontarians to take their lands and to interfere with their rights. Their worry about the vulnerability of their lands was not misplaced. The draft plan for bringing the North-West into Canada provided no protection for the Métis Nation or its lands. Canada's plan proposed to recognize and confirm only the titles conferred by the Company before March 8, 1869. But most Métis lands had not been conferred by the Company. Their lands were held according to their customary laws. Canada's proposed law left the Métis Nation in Red River feeling very vulnerable.

It is not an exaggeration to say the survey project set the North-West on fire.

CANADA BLUNDERS ALONG

On September 28, 1869, William McDougall was appointed lieutenant-governor of the North-West Territories, an appointment that was to take effect after the transfer on December 1, 1869. The appointment of McDougall was a blunder, much like so many of the previous appointees to Red River. McDougall was known, not affectionately, as Wandering Willie—a moniker earned as a result of his constant and blatant search for political opportunity. In Red River he already had a bad reputation. It was McDougall who had sent in the road relief project and the hated surveyors. Both groups had tried to claim Métis land. These were facts.

Rumours painted McDougall as a priest killer. He had had a run-in with Jesuits and Ojibwa at Manitoulin Island a few years before, but the rumours were exaggerations with respect to the priests. He hadn't killed them. Still, the Manitoulin incident provided insight into the kind of ruler he would be. At Manitoulin McDougall had imposed a law to remove Ojibwa access to an important fishery. Under the new law only those licensed could fish. The Ojibwa were not granted licences and suddenly had no right to use their traditional fishery. According to McDougall this was "the majesty of the law."[3]

The Métis Nation feared the same legal sleight of hand would obliterate their lands and resources. McDougall, a prominent member of the Canada First movement, was anti-Catholic, anti-French and anti-Métis—everything the French Métis feared from Canada. He would be in a powerful position to favour everyone in the settlement but them. He would have the power to grant their lands and resources to newcomers and then claim the majesty of the law, as he had done in Manitoulin, thus making the Métis criminals for trespassing on their own lands, and thieves for accessing their own resources. They warned McDougall that if he showed himself in the country, he would be told to go back to Toronto.

At the time, the Métis may not have known the prime minister's exact plan for Red River, but they were beginning to get the drift. They were expendable in the coming scheme. Indeed John A. Macdonald did have a plan for them. He was going to "keep those wild people quiet. In another year the present residents will be altogether swamped by the influx of strangers who will go in with the idea of becoming industrious and peaceable settlers."[4]

The appointment of McDougall provoked the French Métis leaders to increase their meetings, and they began to discuss asserting their collective identity as the Métis Nation as the means of resistance to the coming invasion from Ontario. They were already taking action against the Canadian Party attempts to claim their lands. Unfortunately, their leaders were unable to harness the discontent and gather a consensus about what to do about the coming annexation.

The younger generation of Métis were not content to sit and wait for Canada to come in on its own terms, and they were not going to follow the lead of men like Dease. Perhaps these men were seen as too connected to the Canadian Party. Perhaps they were seen to be acting in their own personal interests. Perhaps they were seen as old codgers unable to connect with the younger generation. Likely it was a combination of all of these factors.

It was in this milieu that Louis Riel—a young, articulate, well-educated Métis, with no connections to the Canadian Party, who was not seen to be acting in his own interest, and the son of a deceased but well-respected Métis leader—emerged as the one man who could organize and lead the resistance of the Métis Nation.

STOPPING THE SURVEYORS

The French Métis, especially the young men, began to listen to Riel and to ask his advice. He was educated and he spoke English, so they asked him to find out what the surveyors were doing. Riel met with Colonel Dennis, who assured him that the intention was to survey "all the lands occupied and to give the parties in possession of lands Crown deeds free."[5] Riel listened politely, but what he heard was not reassuring.

It was the "parties in possession" part that was worrisome. When the Métis spoke of the lands they possessed, they meant their lands held under paper title or pursuant to Métis custom. They also considered the lands they possessed to include their access to common lands. The commons was part of their traditional land-use system, and it worked perfectly for their small farms, which required access to the riverfront, land for a house and garden, plus access to commonly held lands for hay and wood. The surveyors were treating the common hay lands and woodlots as vacant.

Once the survey was completed, the land use in Red River

would change forever. The new system would ignore Métis land knowledge and their systems of common land use. The surveyors, newly arrived, certainly saw the existing system, but they made no attempt to protect it. There was no room in their survey system for commonly held land.

Since July Métis patrols had been stopping any attempts to stake, build or dig wells in their claimed territory. On October 11, 1869, Major Adam Clark Webb was running survey lines on Edouard Marion's hay privilege in St. Vital. A Métis patrol encountered Webb's party and attempted to stop the survey. But the patrol was made up of French-speaking Métis, and Webb and his men spoke only English. The patrol sent for Louis Riel, and on his arrival eighteen unarmed Métis confronted the survey party.[6] There was no violence. Riel simply ordered the surveyors to stop running the lines and "to leave the country on the south side of the Assiniboine, which country the party claimed as the property of the French Half-breeds, and which they would not allow to be surveyed by the Canadian Government."[7] Janvier Ritchot stood on the survey chain first and then the rest of the Métis party did the same. There would be no more surveying on Métis lands.

THE RIFLES

Riel and the Métis went unarmed to challenge the surveyors. That was before they found out about the rifles—a Canadian government shipment of one hundred Spencer carbines and two hundred and fifty Peabody rifles all equipped with bayonets and accompanied by eight to ten thousand rounds of ammunition.[8] Word of the rifles spread through Red River before they even arrived. No goods or people arrived in the North-West without the knowledge of the Métis. The new governor was coming with rifles—lots of rifles. Why would a new governor come with any arms at all, let alone so many? Who was going to be armed?

This then was what the Métis understood in October 1869. Canada was sending a well-armed governor. The surveyors were military men, with military titles such as major and colonel, and packed uniforms in their luggage. There were more ex-soldiers in the road relief crew. All these men had been sent into Red River by Canada. Canada was no longer just a political threat, something that could be talked out. It was now a military threat. Canada was taking over and it gave every indication that it was going to use force.

For the Métis Nation, knowledge of the rifles changed everything. The idea of joining Canada was not the problem. But the terms of the new relationship needed negotiation so that unity would be achieved for the right reasons—voluntary inclusion, equal participation and mutual compromise—thereby achieving a collective endorsement of what would become new and inclusive principles and institutions of Canada. That's what everyone in Red River wanted.

What Canada thought it was doing is difficult to fathom. Canada made no attempt to understand or to encompass the vastly different principles that guided the people of the North-West. Herein lies the root of all the discord between the Métis Nation and Canada that was to follow in the North-West. Even on the most basic political level, it would have made sense for Macdonald to make new friends and not alienate future voters. He had just negotiated Confederation. He knew that even small provinces have demands, one of which is respect for their jurisdiction and power. Nova Scotia in particular had resisted Confederation, at least in part, because of the lack of consultation.

Why would Macdonald think the North-West was different? In 1870 the population of Red River was approximately twelve thousand. Eighty-five per cent were what we now call Métis. Almost eight thousand were under the age of twenty-one. The four thousand adults were almost equally divided between French and English. It is difficult to avoid concluding that it was because Macdonald didn't consider the adult inhabitants of Red River, overwhelmingly Métis, capable or worthy of consultation or negotiation.

The Métis stepped on the survey chain on October 11, 1869. No Métis went to that confrontation armed. But when they learned about the stash of rifles and ammunition and put that together with the Canadian military men already in Red River, the French Métis reached for their arms and started to organize more seriously. They created the National Committee of the Red River Métis with John Bruce as president and Louis Riel as secretary.

The National Committee was charged with instituting not British law but their own Métis Nation laws—the laws they had developed since 1816, the Laws of the Prairie. They began with their usual organization, the same one they had finely honed during many years of buffalo hunts. It would be a stretch to call the Métis organizing efforts at that stage a government, but they were well organized, they were reinforced by men with quasi-military skills, and they had specific goals.

The Métis in the English parishes were not far behind. They met a few days later in St. Andrews. They agreed that Red River should enter Confederation on equal terms with the other provinces and that they were fully competent to manage their own affairs. They also thought they should have their land title and access to resources protected. They too were angry about not being consulted and were concerned about the military nature of the incoming envoy from Canada.

At this point the English Métis differed from the French Métis only in tactics. The French Métis believed that immediate direct action was required *before* Canada could be allowed to come into the territory. The English Métis were prepared to let Canada in first and hope it would all work out. Despite the fear that Canada was about to use force, everyone in Red River held meeting after meeting to peacefully debate the future. They demonstrated an astonishing faith in democracy in the face of Canada's obvious lack of the same.

LA BARRIÈRE

The French Métis didn't wait for the English Métis to come around to their way of thinking. They didn't want to lose the initiative. On October 17 they made their third move. André Nault took forty men to construct what would soon come to be known as "La Barrière" across the road at Rivière Sale.[9] The barrier was constructed to prevent McDougall and "other suspicious persons, entering the Red River Colony . . . who might be carrying weapons or other objects considered to be dangerous to the peace."[10] By this time there were almost three hundred armed French Métis gathered at St. Norbert.

The rifles suggested that McDougall was arriving with an army. So the National Committee mounted a military expedition to stop him. When they learned that McDougall's party was an unarmed entourage that included women, they set aside their military expedition. Instead they sent a letter to McDougall warning him not to enter the colony without the express permission of the National Committee of the Red River Métis.[11]

On October 24 the Canadian Party sent Dease and Georges

Racette to St. Norbert, hoping to persuade the French Métis to dismantle La Barrière and clear the way for McDougall to enter. Dease squared off against Riel. After a long argument they did what the Métis always do; they voted. The question put to the vote was whether it was necessary to protest against the way Canada was going to impose its governance on the country. The vote carried unanimously. Even Dease and his followers agreed on the necessity of protesting. They also agreed to step aside and not hinder the efforts of the activists.

RESISTANCE NOT REBELLION

The Council of Assiniboia sent for Bruce and Riel to warn them of the potential consequences of their actions. Bruce and Riel were polite but firm. They understood the risk. The Métis Nation was not out to make an enemy of the Company, but the North-West was theirs and they would not be pushed out. Riel assured the council that the Métis recognized its authority and was not rebelling against the queen or against the Company. Riel argued that Canada was a foreign power, so resistance against Canada was not a rebellion.

Riel's argument, that the Métis action was not a rebellion against Canada, was sound. Canada was a foreign country. But was it a rebellion against Britain? According to British law, Rupert's Land and the North-Western Territory were British lands and subject to British law and rule. Under British law the actions of the Métis Nation could be considered a rebellion or at the very least as unauthorized activity.

British law did not recognize any sovereignty in the Métis Nation and recognized native title to the land as a mere property right that was only affirmed at the precise moment it was extinguished. It has always been a convenient legal argument.

Britain assumed that its assertion of sovereignty legally displaced Indigenous sovereignty. This bald assertion of sovereignty, which amounts to saying "because we said so," is the sole basis of Canada's claims of ownership and jurisdiction. One American senator put his finger close to the reality button when, with reference to Panama, he said, "It's ours. We stole it fair and square."[12] For the Métis Nation there was never anything fair or square about Canada's acquisition of the North-West.

On the ground in Red River the two world views were on a collision course. Canada and Britain were cutting a deal and didn't think they had to stoop to negotiate with the riff-raff on the ground. When the Council of Assiniboia could not dissuade Bruce and Riel from their path of resistance, they were called "malcontents who could not be reasoned with." With classic condescension the Métis were said to have "excitable temperaments, which it was impossible to control"—meaning that the French Métis could not be persuaded to remain quiet and passive.[13]

After Riel's departure the council asked Dease and Goulet, two Métis who sat on the council, to collect "the more respectable of the French community" to head to the St. Norbert camp to "procure their peaceable dispersion."[14] Goulet would have nothing to do with it. When Dease took the request as carte blanche to arm his supporters, the Council of Assiniboia quickly rescinded its order. Nevertheless, Dease rode with eighty men to La Barrière, where he squared off once again with Louis Riel.

Dease was hardly the best or an honest broker for the Council of Assiniboia in light of his attempt to overthrow it just a few short months ago. At La Barrière he argued that it was best to let McDougall in and negotiate afterwards. Riel argued that it was crucial to negotiate terms *before* Canada entered and took control. The issue again went to a vote, and the majority—a large majority—voted against Dease. For Dease it was a humiliating loss. He had set out for the meeting with eighty men. He returned with sixty. Twenty of his men had defected to Riel on the spot. Dease's confrontational style succeeded in rallying even more Métis to Riel's side. Not a man to give up, Dease approached McTavish and then Colonel Dennis, offering to go and get McDougall if they would supply the guns and ammunition for a party of fifteen. McTavish and Dennis both said no.

Meanwhile rumours ran wildly through Red River. It was said that hundreds of armed men had come from all over the country, which was a fact—the Métis were gathering and there were hundreds of them. Another rumour, not based in fact, spoke of a major battle that had been stopped in its tracks by fear of the souls of dead Métis who had risen from their graves to aid their brothers at La Barrière.

THE MÉTIS LAWS OF THE PRAIRIE AND THE RED RIVER CODE

Every effort to stop the French Métis activists had the opposite effect. Their numbers grew every day. Métis tripmen as far away as northwest Saskatchewan deserted their brigades and went to Red River when they heard of the resistance led by Riel. As they grew in size and purpose, Riel knew they needed laws. They resolved to organize not according to British or Canadian culture, but according to their own culture. They resolved to codify the Métis Laws of the Prairie, which would remain in place until supplanted by another authority. On October 30, 1869, at a large Métis assembly at La Barrière, a Red River Code was proclaimed and adopted.[15]

In four short months the Métis Nation had gathered its forces, evicted strangers off their lands, taken up arms, enacted their own laws and elected a Council of the Métis Senate to act as their representatives. They did all this in a democratic manner and with the support of their people. By November 1, 1869, the St. Norbert camp had over five hundred Métis in arms. All swore an oath of fidelity and to refrain from drinking alcohol. The camp was a model of discipline with everyone obeying the new laws. The Métis Nation now had an operating government.

THE MÉTIS EXPEL McDOUGALL

Meanwhile Canada's would-be governor was faring rather poorly. When McDougall arrived at the international border on October 30, Governor McTavish ordered him to stay put. So McDougall's party was stuck in Pembina living in sod huts with winter fast approaching. Colonel Dennis tried to raise a party from the Scottish and English settlers to escort McDougall into the settlement, but the settlers declined, saying bluntly that they mostly agreed with their Métis friends and neighbours.

McDougall was staying at the Company post in Pembina on the Canadian side of the international border. But Riel wanted him out of the country, so on November 1 Ambroise Lépine rode to Pembina and ordered McDougall to move south of the border onto American soil. When McDougall demanded to know who sent him, he replied, "The government." McDougall asked, "What government?" Lépine answered, "The government we made."[16]

McDougall tried to laugh it off and flourished his papers, which likely looked impressive and official with signatures and seals. But Lépine proved immune to fancy props, simply saying he was there to execute Riel's orders and McDougall would leave whether he liked it or not. At that point it seemed to have finally dawned on McDougall that he was powerless, isolated and vulnerable. His party left in such a hurry they forgot one of their horses and had to come back to beg for it. The request was cheerfully granted with a display of Métis gallantry.

McDougall had been outmanoeuvred. He was a would-be governor, not wanted by anyone, with no place to go and nothing to govern. The Métis had turned McDougall into an international joke. Everyone poked fun at his helplessness, his dreams of grandeur and even his furniture. Apparently he had packed two thrones. One was said to be finer than the throne in Ottawa. The other, hitherto unknown in Red River, was a toilet, which Pierre Falcon sweetly satirized in "The Ballad of the Trials of an Unfortunate King." Everyone had a good laugh at McDougall's expense. Sir John A. Macdonald laughed, and so did the American press: "A King without a Kingdom is said to be poorer than a peasant. And I can assure you that a live Governor with a full complement of officials and menials from Attorney-General down to cooks and scullions without one poor foot of territory is a spectacle sufficiently sad to move the hardest heart."[17]

TAKING FORT GARRY

Rumours continued to swirl throughout the settlement. One rumour was that the Canadian Party was planning to take control of Fort Garry from the HBC. The Métis could not allow that to happen because the party in control of the Upper Fort controlled Red River. The Council of the Métis Senate and the Métis Nation's war council authorized a detachment to capture Fort Garry and to stand guard in Winnipeg. André Nault, in command of a small Métis force, captured the fort. It was easily done; the gates were wide open with no one on guard. The Métis simply walked in and took the fort. Shortly after their arrival Nault reported that he saw the Canadian Party men approach and then retreat when they realized the Métis were in occupation.

The Métis began to patrol the settlement at night. They had guards on the roads coming in and out of Winnipeg, in Winnipeg itself and in Fort Garry. There were now an additional sixty guards, equally selected to represent St. François Xavier, St. Norbert, St. Boniface, Ste. Anne and St. Vital. The discipline and sacrifices of the Métis guards made an impression on Alexander Begg, who wrote:

> Some idea may be formed of the earnestness of these French people when it is stated that at this moment some of them have been eighteen days on guard—sleeping at night on the snow with no tents or other covering except their ordinary clothes and this without the least prospect of pay—the food they eat is the only thing they get and that is furnished them by the more wealthy among their own people.[18]

CHAPTER 16

BRINGING IN THE ENGLISH MÉTIS

The French Métis were moving too quickly for the other residents of Red River, who were, quite frankly, stunned. So was everyone else. Riel had successfully blocked the plans of Great Britain and Canada and halted the largest peaceful land transfer in the world. The surprise and anger of the Canadian Party and Canadian politicians, including Prime Minister Macdonald, came in no small part from their racism, which they bragged about in the press. The prime minister thought he could entice Riel to come to Ottawa, where he would soon be one "gone coon."[1] Simply put, they all had trouble believing that Riel and the Métis had successfully got the upper hand.

Up until now the French Métis had been acting alone. But Riel knew he could not force negotiations with Canada unless he had the backing of the English Métis and the other residents of Red River. He sent a public notice inviting the parishes to send representatives to form a council. The notice announced a gathering of representatives of all the people of Red River, including

St. Peters parish, an Ojibwa community. Every representative could speak and vote—every male representative, that is.

In the days leading up to the November 16 meeting, rumours about the rifles continued to float around Red River, and the Métis began to search for them in each trader's cart that passed through La Barrière. The traders didn't take kindly to these searches. Riel and Bruce successfully made the rounds trying to persuade the English Métis to leave McDougall to cool his heels in Pembina. The English Métis made small noises about sending a delegation to welcome McDougall, but when the Canadian Party tried to raise an escort, their efforts mustered fewer than fifty men.

THE CONVENTIONS

The meeting in November was the start of three months of conventions. From mid-November 1869 to the end of January 1870, the citizens of Red River convened repeatedly in an attempt to hammer out a negotiating position. At the first convention twenty-four delegates met. The Métis celebrated the beginning of the convention with a *feu de joie*, a twenty-four-gun salute (twelve for the English, twelve for the French), a burst of enthusiasm not much appreciated by the English Métis. But the French Métis were undaunted; they were enthusiastic and happy. They had succeeded in bringing the English Métis and the French Métis together.

All residents of Red River agreed with the basic complaint of the Métis. They may not have agreed with the methods used by the French Métis, but they were all of one mind when it came to disapproval of the Canadian Party and the way the transfer was proceeding without their input. That's why they came when Riel called them.

The delegates settled in and the debate began.[2] They didn't agree on the next steps. The English Métis wanted elections; the French Métis wanted to ascertain the intentions of both sides first. The English Métis wanted the French Métis to lay down their arms, vacate the fort and let McDougall into Red River. The French Métis said no. They had always protected their interests and the colony with arms. They had learned from experience that to be sure of peace, they had to prepare for war. Occupying the fort was necessary, and opposition to McDougall's entry was even more necessary. The French Métis would not let their liberties pass to an alien power before assuring them. Riel's notes, which are the only record of the convention, describe what followed as "animated discussion."[3]

The two most able men in the room controlled the debate, Louis Riel for the French Métis and James Ross for the English Métis. They were both persuasive and cogent, but neither scored a decisive argument that captured everyone. At the end of the day, the delegates read a proclamation from Hudson's Bay Company governor McTavish. It scolded the Métis, saying they should have adopted "lawful and constitutional means, which, under the enlightened rule of Her Most Gracious Majesty our Queen, are sufficient for the ultimate attainment of every object that rests upon reason and justice."[4] But there were no lawful and constitutional means for the about-to-be-colonized to negotiate the terms that would transfer their government, their people and their land from one country to another. Day one of the convention adjourned with no resolution on anything.

Day two continued with the Riel-Ross debate and then adjourned for the quarterly court session, during which John Snow, the road relief manager, was fined for his extracurricular activities of selling alcohol to the Ojibwa (to induce them to sell their land title). It was one of the cases the Métis wanted the court to deal with. This was Augustin Nolin's business. The French Métis would set aside the convention to accommodate the injustices inflicted on the Sainte-Anne-des-Chênes Métis, the Nolin family and the Ojibwa.

On November 19, 1869, the Hudson's Bay Company surrendered its charter to the Imperial Government, and Canada finally woke up to the situation it had created and claimed to have under control. Prime Minister Macdonald sent out two commissioners, Lieutenant-Colonel Charles de Salaberry and Father Thibault, men Macdonald believed would be able to exercise some moral suasion over Riel. But the commissioners had no authority to do anything about the terms on which the North-West would join Canada. The prime minister suggested putting two leading Métis on the council and offering Riel a position as an officer in the future police. Macdonald was trying to get away with tokenism to get McDougall into Red River.

Meanwhile the convention continued with the Riel-Ross debate. One must admire the sheer perseverance of these men and their faith that differences can be resolved by means of debate. But at the end of day four, Riel's notes say, "No understanding, little hope of one."[5]

RIEL PROPOSES A PROVISIONAL GOVERNMENT

The French Métis then took full possession of Fort Garry and began to discuss the formation of a provisional government. Riel wanted to force Canada to negotiate with a public body, but his own people were initially reluctant. Establishing a government, even a provisional one, might be seen as a rebellion against the queen. After seven long hours the French Métis delegates finally agreed to establish a provisional government, but only after Riel promised not to announce it until after December 1, the day on which the transfer from Great Britain to Canada was scheduled to take place. The decision suggests that the Métis were reluctant to be seen as rebels against Great Britain but were perhaps more willing to assume that role against Canada. In the course of the debate, Riel also proposed seizing the Company accounts. No one agreed with that.

On day five of the convention, the English representatives learned about the full occupation of the fort and hesitated before reconvening. Still, they did appear. Riel proposed the formation of a provisional government and invited the English to join. The government would be composed equally of French and English, and he stressed it would only be provisional. The English delegates demurred. They had no authority to agree to such a proposal. The convention adjourned to allow the English to consult with the people in their parishes.

The French Métis then seized the Company provisions, strongbox and books at Fort Garry. Riel had finally persuaded them that they needed money to feed their men. Many of the French Métis were greatly disturbed by this move. Even Lépine, one of Riel's strongest supporters, didn't like it. Riel kept them on his side, barely, by characterizing it as a loan. Credit was a system they were well used to. It was how the Company invested in the buffalo hunt. The Métis would have taken that seriously. It was a promise that the money would be fully accounted for and paid back. They were confident they were going to win, and with local control they could make things right with the Company later, if it was still around. No one inquired into just how the payback would be accomplished if they failed.

The English Métis were outraged by the move and refused to

come to the next meeting of the convention. Still trying desperately to become even a bit player in the local politics of Red River, the Canadian Party circulated a public statement saying they were willing to do everything in their power to conciliate the parties if the French put down their arms. No one paid any attention.

In the absence of public meetings, men met in private to discuss a counter-proposal to Riel's provisional government. The idea was to set up an executive council to negotiate terms with Canada upon which Red River would enter Confederation. The difference was in the name—"council" versus "government." Riel never liked the council proposal. Such a body had no authority. Riel made a rousing speech arguing for a provisional government. The movement was wholly French, but he invited the English to join. They would not coerce anyone and they would not interfere with anyone's rights. Riel's speech roused everyone, and apparently even Schultz applauded. They may have applauded, but they still disagreed with him about a provisional government. Under pressure from all sides, Riel reluctantly agreed to abandon his provisional government idea and set up an executive council. Everyone breathed a sigh of relief.

Meanwhile Prime Minister Macdonald was having second thoughts about accepting Rupert's Land and the North Western Territory from Great Britain. He wanted the land with *peaceful* possession. He didn't want to pay £300,000 for a hornets' nest, and he really didn't want the financial burden of suppressing the unruly Métis. So he delayed the transfer without informing anyone in Red River—not even his would-be governor.

On December 1, 1869, in the wee hours of the morning, McDougall sneaked across the border and read a proclamation to the night wind, the stars and the lone prairie, that all should take notice and act accordingly. Then he ran back over the border, and his nickname changed from Wandering Willie to Silly Wandering Willie.

THE FIRST LIST OF RIGHTS

McDougall's proclamation was distributed throughout Red River. There was some skepticism about the authenticity of his proclamation, but because no one knew the transfer had been delayed, there appeared to be no reason to doubt his bona fides. The English Métis and the French Métis were still at odds, though. Riel said that if McDougall would guarantee their rights, he would escort McDougall in himself. That raised the question of just what the rights were. So, the French Métis took up the pen and began drafting a List of Rights.

The List of Rights is notable for the absence of any mention of the Métis Nation. The explanation lies in the need to be inclusive of all the residents of Red River. The conventions brought the residents of Red River together to negotiate the terms of a *public* government, not a Métis-only government. The Métis Nation was operating under the assumption that the majority Métis would form the government they negotiated and would have the jurisdiction to legally protect their rights. The List of Rights reflects this assumption.

The first three clauses demand the right of local control even to the extent of an override of Ottawa's hand-picked executive. This would provide the Métis Nation with the jurisdiction and authority to protect itself. Another clause demanded respect and protection for *all* privileges, customs and usages. This too would provide the legal basis to protect the Métis lands and their customary use practices—specifically, the hay and wood commons. Everyone agreed that the List of Rights formed the basis for a joint claim to be presented to Canada.

Sending the List of Rights to McDougall was the obvious next move. But Riel still wanted a guarantee that the rights would be protected before they let McDougall in. The English Métis said no. They thought Riel and the French Métis were unreasonable. Riel thought the English Métis were too timid. The convention dissolved, but many men tried to persuade Riel that a delegation should go to McDougall. Riel's party was not opposed, mostly because they all believed the transfer had actually taken place. Discussions about how to approach McDougall were underway when Colonel Dennis and the Canadian Party threw everything into chaos.

THE SPECTRE OF CIVIL WAR

Word came that Colonel Dennis was drilling companies in the English parishes. Schultz had convinced Dennis that the public would rise to his call. The plan was to capture Riel, put Schultz and his friends in control of the settlement and triumphantly parade in the governor. The Ojibwa Chief Prince provided fifty guards, the survey parties were called to the banner, and Major Webb was sent to Portage la Prairie to organize four companies of fifty men each. Major Charles Arkoll Boulton drilled recruits. They wrote to Sir John A. Macdonald that Louis Riel would very soon be a prisoner in the hands of loyal men, or a fugitive from justice.

The French Métis, previously at odds on any number of issues, closed ranks. Riel was warned to stay within the Upper Fort. The French Métis took control of the newspapers and began to search private homes for Canadian Party men and arms. Two Métis who were not sympathetic to the French Métis activists, James McKay and one of the Nolins, tried to find middle ground. They planned to take the List of Rights to McDougall in exchange for proof that his proclamation was authentic. But their plan was doomed from the start because McDougall's proclamation had no authority. McKay and Nolin weren't the only ones alarmed at the military nature of the Canadian Party. Judge John Black, still hopeful of the outcome of the convention, flatly refused to support them. James Ross bluntly told Dennis not to get them into a civil war, warning that the English Métis didn't want to fight their French brothers. James McKay was adamant that he would not fight anyone, not McDougall and certainly not his own people.

When the List of Rights was printed and distributed on December 5, 1869, support for the Canadian Party dissipated. The English Métis liked the list. They could see the demands of the French Métis were not unreasonable. In the end hardly anyone answered the Canadian Party's call to arms, and within two days Dennis's force, puny to begin with, dissolved.

Schultz tried to keep sixty armed men in his compound, but three hundred Métis led by Riel forced them to surrender. The attitude and demeanour of Schultz when he finally vacated the compound made Riel and Nault suspicious. It was very cold but curiously there were no fires on. Riel and Nault carefully inspected the compound and found gunpowder stashed everywhere—under beds, wrapped in blankets, tucked into furniture. Likely hoping the Métis would light a fire, Schultz and his men had also stashed gunpowder in the stoves and stovepipes and in the cold ashes. If the Métis had lit a fire, the entire compound would have exploded, taking Riel and his men with it. Schultz and his men had just made a credible effort to kill three hundred Métis.

Forty-five men, including Schultz, were taken as prisoners to Fort Garry.[6]

CHAPTER 17

CANADA SNEAKS INTO RED RIVER

THE DOMINION COMMISSIONER ARRIVES IN DISGUISE

Meanwhile back in Ottawa, the prime minister decided to get some advice. He reached out to the Hudson's Bay Company and contacted Donald Smith, the highest-ranking Company officer available. Smith had been a district manager for Labrador and eastern Canada. He knew little about Red River and had never been west. Still, he answered the prime minister's summons and was duly appointed "Dominion Commissioner to Inquire into the North West Rebellion." He was instructed to pacify the natives by whatever means possible, including bribes of money and offices. Smith was given a five-hundred-pound fund to spend as he saw fit to buy off the "Insurgent Leaders or some of them."[1] If Smith failed, Macdonald would use force: "Should these miserable half-breeds not disband, they must be put down . . . I shall be very glad to give Colonel Wolseley the chance and glory and the risk of the scalping knife!"[2]

Smith's plan was to bypass Riel and negotiate directly with the citizens of Red River. He was operating on the assumption that Riel was asserting his own agenda, which he was not. It is true that Riel had thought his way through the implications of their actions further than most residents. He understood that the Métis Nation and Métis lands and resources would only be protected with local control and that this required provincial status. Riel had ideas about setting in place governance practices that fairly represented the unique mix of cultures that made up the people of Red River. He hoped these practices would survive the expected influx of immigrants from Ontario.

Three such practices were quickly established. The first was equal representation for the two main language groups, French and English. The second was that participants in the convention could speak in their own languages and translation would be provided. The third was inclusion of the Ojibwa. Chief Prince was a full participant in the convention on behalf of his band. It was much more democratic than the government being proposed by Canada, and when Canada arrived it crushed all three practices. One can only imagine what Canada would be like today if we had followed the practices the Métis established in Red River.

Still, Macdonald and eastern Canada saw Riel as their main obstacle. They firmly believed that without Riel, the residents would accept whatever fate Canada decided to hand them. Smith met with the prime minister on November 29 and arrived in Red River, in disguise, on December 27, 1869. He presented himself as a Company trader and arrived without his commission papers.

This is where things stood in Red River at the end of December 1869: The French Métis had succeeded in bringing the English Métis into their tent. There had been no official information from Great Britain or Canada as to exactly what was going to happen in Red River. Canada's actions before it had any lawful right to act in the North-West had made everyone in Red River skeptical of Canada's bona fides. The Métis were occupying Fort Garry and holding several prisoners. The flag of the provisional government flew over Fort Garry. They thought they had held off Canada until they could negotiate terms. But unbeknownst to them Canada was already there in disguise in the person of Donald Smith.

Smith wasn't the only foreigner hovering around Red River. The Americans had several observers in Red River, including a constitutional lawyer, a consular official and a spy. The Fenians were hovering with their convoluted Irish plans, and there was even a dashing cavalry officer, Captain Norbert Gay, newly arrived from France and looking for an army—any army—to lead into glory.[3] Then on December 30, 1869, the Sioux arrived. The Métis sent a delegation to meet them at James McKay's house about six miles from Fort Garry. McKay, François Dauphinais and Pierre Poitras all made presentations to the Sioux advising them to turn back because of the troubles in the settlement. But the Sioux chief said they weren't there to cause trouble; they wanted to know what was going on and how it might affect them.

The Métis Nation needed the Sioux to remain neutral, and such an agreement could only be negotiated between leaders. So Riel met with the Sioux chief. Because the Ojibwa, the traditional enemy of the Sioux, were allied with the Canadian Party, it was unlikely that the Sioux would come in on that side. But Riel didn't want the Sioux to engage. A neutrality agreement was reached and affirmed when Riel presented the Sioux chief with twenty-five pounds of tobacco. The Sioux celebrated the agreement with a ceremonial dance and drumming, and honoured their commitment to remain neutral.

In the midst of all this, the French and English Métis delegates continued their democratic process. Everyone other than the Canadian Party was working together to form a united front. There was a growing sense of cohesion in Red River. The prospects for the new year didn't look too bad. Indeed, 1870 started on a positive note. On January 1 Riel addressed a large meeting of French Métis, mostly the Nolin family, at Sainte-Anne-des-Chênes. Also in January McDougall finally left Pembina. No one regretted his departure.

Until now Riel had been skilfully playing the American card, hinting that he might throw the Métis Nation's weight behind joining the United States rather than Canada. It was a good tactic because Macdonald was genuinely afraid of losing the North-West to the Americans. But that kind of balancing act could not continue indefinitely. Evidently, the Americans made several tempting offers to Riel, suggesting that if he proclaimed independence, the Americans would gladly take the Métis under their protection. There were offers of money and arms. They warned Riel that although Canada would make them great promises, it would not keep them. But Riel had already chosen Canada. He would not go back on his word.

PIERRE LÉVEILLÉ

On arrival in Red River, Donald Smith initiated a divide-and-conquer strategy. First, he planned to separate the English Protestants from the French Catholics. Second, he would separate as many of the French Métis as he could from Riel. Smith wrote to Sir John A. Macdonald that the "English speaking inhabitants are now moving heartily with the view of bringing their weight and influence to bear on the malcontents so as to induce them to come to terms with Canada or England."[4] That was spin. The English-speaking inhabitants of Red River had never moved heartily on anything. They also were not influencing the French to come to terms with Canada or England. Smith's spin was certainly what Macdonald wanted to hear, but it was far from an accurate assessment of the situation.

Red River gradually awoke to the fact that there was more to Smith than his guise as a Hudson's Bay Company official. Inside Fort Garry he was distributing multiple offers, bribes and promises. He had also successfully gained the confidence of a group of French Métis and, perhaps most importantly, succeeded in co-opting Pierre Léveillé. Léveillé was a St. François Xavier Métis and an influential trader. Smith's success with a Métis of Léveillé's stature was a blow to Riel's authority.

Finally, Riel demanded to see Smith's commission. Smith agreed to produce the papers, which he had left in Pembina. He sent his brother-in-law Richard Hardisty with a French Métis guard led by Léveillé. Riel, perhaps worried that the commission would not be produced or more likely wanting to see the commission first, set out for Pembina in a separate party. The Hardisty-Léveillé party collided with Riel's party. The confrontation grew heated and ended when Léveillé convinced Riel's party to stay out of it by putting a gun to Riel's head. Riel conceded. The Hardisty-Léveillé party retrieved Smith's papers from Pembina and returned to Fort Garry.

Smith had gained Léveillé's trust by promising that his commission gave him the authority to protect Métis rights. Léveillé then set up a separate Métis guard inside Fort Garry and insisted that he, not Riel, would ensure the people's rights were secured as set out in Smith's papers. There were now two separate Métis groups on guard in Fort Garry, one led by Riel and another, whose main task seemed to be watching Riel, led by Léveillé. With Léveillé at the head of a Métis guard, Donald Smith thought he had neutralized Riel. He also thought that given the chance to address the people, he could win them over. He saw his opportunity when a convention was called for January 19, 1870.

Over a thousand people, fully 25 per cent of the adult population of Red River, came to the January convention. There was no building in Red River large enough to house such a gathering, so they met in the courtyard of the Upper Fort. Meeting outside in January in Red River is not for the faint-hearted. It was minus twenty Fahrenheit—a bitterly cold day to stand around and listen to speeches you could barely hear.

Smith had a plan to take over the convention. He thought he had bribed his way into control. His plan was simple: Smith had his Métis guard, led by Léveillé, in place at the convention. He thought he had arranged it so Riel would not be nominated for an official role, which would cut off his voice and power. Then, Smith would start giving orders, which Léveillé and his Métis guards would carry out. Smith would carry the day and the Resistance would be over.

The convention began with elections. The first indication that all would not go according to Smith's plan came when Louis Riel was elected as the interpreter, thereby assuring Riel an official voice at the convention. This happened because a key player who had made promises to Smith reneged. It was a blow to Smith's plans, but not a fatal one.

What Smith didn't know was that there had been a late-night intervention at the fort. Father Lestanc and the prime minister's two hand-picked commissioners, Colonel de Salaberry and

Father Thibault, had worked out a compromise with Léveillé. Léveillé wanted to hear Smith read his commission. That wasn't a problem; they all wanted to hear it. The concern was that Smith would command Léveillé and his guards to take over, and Riel's men would resist. No one wanted a shootout in the fort. Léveillé promised not to act on Smith's commands at the convention the next day.

When Smith was introduced to the crowd as a commissioner appointed by the prime minister of Canada, he moved immediately to take control of the convention. He ordered everyone to lay down their arms, and take down the Métis flag and replace it with the British ensign. No one put their arms down and no one made a move to the flagpole. Smith stared at his Métis guard, and at Léveillé in particular. They were supposed to jump to his orders. Léveillé didn't move. Riel and the French Métis didn't gloat. They simply left Smith to absorb the fact that all his bribes and conniving had failed to gain him support. Léveillé later described the late-night intervention as a mission of peace. Smith called it a defection. Léveillé wrote, "I would state that Mr. Smith deceived himself very much if he thought it was the intention of myself and the leaders with whom I was associated, to lay down our arms, or haul down the flag which we had hoisted to obtain our rights."[5]

Louis Schmidt, Riel's Métis secretary, called Smith "the old trickster."[6] Tricky he may have been, but he clearly had no backup plan. Having no other options, Smith started to read. He read his letter of appointment, a letter from the governor-general and a message from the queen. The queen was apparently surprised and regretful that the people of Red River opposed, by force, the entry of the future lieutenant-governor. She was sure this could only be because of a misunderstanding or misrepresentation, because her course of action was only meant for their advantage. Never mind that the queen had steadfastly ignored the residents; she *now* wanted to know their wants and conciliate with them. If there were complaints, the people should make them. The queen was ready to listen to "well-founded grievances."

Nothing Smith read was very helpful. He was to ensure a peaceful transfer and to use his own judgment in doing so. This was encouraging news to the Canadian Party but much too vague for the French Métis. It didn't take long for Léveillé to be disabused of his faith in Smith. As soon as Smith read his papers, Léveillé realized he had been duped. Afterwards he apologized to Riel and the provisional council. The council welcomed him back into the ranks, and as a peace offering, Léveillé presented Riel with the gun he had pointed at his head.

In any event, it was much too cold to stand around and listen to any more talk, so the convention adjourned to the following day. When someone in the crowd called for the release of Schultz's men, who were still being held as prisoners, the mood shifted instantly. The French Métis reached for their arms and "there was a general skidaddle amongst a good many of the English."[7]

On day two of the convention, even more people gathered. This time Riel selected eight Métis to keep order in the crowd. Smith continued to read documents. The first reading was of a letter from Governor-General John Young to Hudson's Bay Company governor McTavish, which stated, "[T]he inhabitants of Ruperts Land, of all claims and persuasions, may rest assured that Her Majesty's Government has no intention of interfering with, or setting aside, or allow others to interfere with the religions, the rights or the franchise hitherto enjoyed, or to which they may hereafter prove themselves equal."[8] Some of the English in the crowd greeted this promise with cheers. The French Métis were not convinced. The governor-general's promises were as vague as the other documents read by Smith. Knowing he had not persuaded the French Métis, Smith claimed kinship via his Hardisty in-laws and his relationship to Cuthbert Grant, because his mother was a Grant from Scotland. Family claims were nice but not enough.

Riel stepped in and took control. Smith had no backup plan, but Riel had one. He proposed a convention of forty (twenty English and twenty French) to draw up a list of rights for submission to Ottawa. He wanted them all to agree to the terms on which they would enter Canada. Everyone agreed. Riel summed up the feelings of those gathered:

> Before this assembly breaks up, I cannot but express my feelings, however briefly. I came here with fears. We are not yet enemies [loud cheers] but we came very near being so. As soon as we understood each other, we joined in demanding what our English fellow subjects in common with us believe to be our just rights [loud cheers]. I am not afraid to say our rights; for we all have rights [renewed cheers]. We claim no half rights, mind you, but all the rights we are entitled to. Those rights will be set forth by our representatives, and, what is more, gentlemen, we will get them [more loud cheers].[9]

THE PROVISIONAL GOVERNMENT IS ESTABLISHED

This time when Riel again insisted on the need for a provisional government, the English Métis were prepared to listen. First, they consulted with Governor McTavish, who is said to have told them to get on with it. With his affirmation, everyone agreed to form the Provisional Government of Rupert's

Land. Riel was elected president, Thomas Bunn was secretary, William Bernard O'Donoghue was treasurer, James Ross was chief justice, Andrew Bannatyne was postmaster, Ambroise Lépine was the adjutant-general and Louis Schmidt was the assistant secretary.

The mood was festive throughout the settlement, and dances were given that night, one by Riel's party in Fort Garry and another at the McDermots'. Fireworks marked the celebration, and Riel released some sixteen prisoners with a promise to release the others very soon. Two days later most of the French Métis occupying Fort Garry left. Only a skeletal guard remained. The English and the French chose their committee members to draft a new list of rights.[10] Everyone thought they had passed through the transition.

THE SECOND LIST OF RIGHTS

On January 29 the convention of delegates began to review the new draft of the List of Rights. Among the first clauses to be approved by the convention were three important decisions. First there was an acknowledgement that the North-West was temporarily in an exceptional position. The country would become, only for the duration of the exceptional time, a territory governed by a lieutenant-governor from Canada and a legislature of three members all nominated by the governor-general of Canada. The emphasis was on the temporary nature of the territorial status.

Then the convention turned its mind to how the North-West was to be situated within Canada and governed after the expiration of the exceptional period. Afterwards the North-West was to be governed, like Ontario and Quebec, under a legislature elected by the people. There would be no interference with the local affairs by the Dominion Parliament. So strong was the insistence on local government that even during the exceptional period, the local legislature could pass laws over a veto of the lieutenant-governor by a two-thirds vote.

English and French were to be the common languages in the legislature and the courts, and all public documents and legislation would be published in both languages. Judges of the Supreme Court would be bilingual, and treaties were to be concluded as soon as possible with the tribes. Most importantly, "all properties rights and privileges as hitherto enjoyed by us be respected and that the recognition and arrangement of local customs usages and privileges be made under control of the Local Legislature."[11] This clause ensured recognition of land titles already registered but also protected the local Métis customary uses and titles, which would be dealt with locally. Another clause insisted on local control of all public lands for a radius of sixty miles.

Then they elected three delegates to negotiate these rights with Ottawa: Father Joseph-Noel Ritchot, Judge John Black and Alfred Scott.

THE CANADIAN PARTY COUNTERATTACK

The remaining prisoners in the fort took an oath to keep the peace and were released—all except James Farquharson, who was Schultz's father-in-law and known to the Métis as "Old Depravity." He was pushed out of the fort, no one believing it worth the effort to take his oath. Schultz had escaped on January 23 and had begun to make his own plans. He wanted to liberate the prisoners, capture Riel, destroy the Provisional Government, replace it with a government headed by Donald Smith, and burn the French Métis part of town. He drove around town making sure everyone knew he was free, and began to hold war councils. By February 14 there were rumours that Schultz was raising an armed force. More rumours whispered that some "loyal" Métis would bring men, Chief Prince would bring the Ojibwa, and more would come from Portage la Prairie. They were all to meet at Kildonan.

A Portage party, composed of sixty Canadians, promptly got storm-stayed in Headingley for two days. Riel sent a letter of warning to them: go home or be captured. With the release of the prisoners, one of the stated goals of Schultz's force was accomplished, but the Portage party pushed on through the blizzard. On the way to Kildonan, they took three prisoners and Thomas Scott broke into a home in an unsuccessful attempt to capture and assassinate Riel. When they arrived in the settlement, they were cold, but they had a cannon, they had been drilling and they were armed. They drew up a list of demands. The primary one was the release of the prisoners—men who had already been released. They also demanded that the Provisional Government disband. The French Métis could have their own provisional government, but it would not govern anyone else. John Norquay volunteered to take the demand letter to Riel at Fort Garry.

That is when the first violence occurred, leaving John Hugh Sutherland dead and Norbert Parisien savagely beaten and on his deathbed.

The expected Canadian Party attack, the assassination attempt on Riel, the death of Sutherland and the beating of Parisien shocked Red River. The community had just celebrated together two weeks earlier. The French rallied around Riel, called in reinforcements and prepared to defend the fort. When Norquay arrived with the demand list, Riel ripped it up. He also sent a warning: the Provisional Government wanted peace and the rights of all, but it was prepared for war.

Schultz's group numbered about 160 men from the English parishes, the Portage party of 80 men and 200 Ojibwa. But it was poorly organized. They had no provisions and it was winter. Many had joined solely to release the prisoners from the fort. On hearing that the prisoners had already been released, these men thought their task was accomplished. They wanted to, and many did, go home. Others wanted to attack the fort and rid the settlement of the objectionable Riel and his men. But they didn't have enough men to sustain an attack on the fort, and there was no possibility of taking it by surprise. Riel seemed to know everything they said and did. Slowly it dawned on them: there was simply no way they could win such a battle. Their leaders, Schultz and Mair, abandoned their compatriots and left for Ontario.

The Portage party included Thomas Scott, the man who had already tried to capture Riel and had so viciously beaten Parisien. Now reduced to forty-eight men, they began the long trudge from Kildonan back to Portage la Prairie, passing close by Fort Garry on their way. Lépine, the Métis adjutant-general, didn't like the idea of this large group of armed men heading toward the fort, so he captured them. The fort, which had just been emptied of prisoners, was full again. It was an arrangement that pleased no one, especially the Métis guards.

CHAPTER 18

FATEFUL DECISIONS

THOMAS SCOTT

The Red River Resistance lasted for 416 days.[1] During that time three people died: John Hugh Sutherland, Norbert Parisien and Thomas Scott. Sutherland's death was a tragic accident regretted by everyone. Everyone understood there was no need to pursue further justice for his death. Memories of Sutherland rest in peace. Memories of Parisien and Scott do not.

Scott was tied to the deaths of the other two. Scott was in the Portage party when they captured Parisien on February 15, 1870. Parisien escaped and in the process stole a gun. He was hiding in the bushes when Sutherland galloped by. Parisien, fearing recapture, shot him twice. Sutherland knew it had been an accident, and on his deathbed he pleaded for mercy for Parisien. But his magnanimous gesture came too late. Scott had already beaten Parisien with a club. Using Parisien's sash, Scott galloped his horse back and forth over the ice, simultaneously dragging and strangling the barely conscious man. Cooler heads prevented Scott from lynching Parisien, but it was hardly a merciful intervention. It condemned Parisien to die slowly from Scott's strangling and vicious beating.

No one seems to know whose side Parisien was on or if he was on any side at all. Riel thought he was a Schultz partisan. But it was Schultz's Canadian Party that captured Parisien. What is clear is that Parisien was Métis and he died at the hands of Thomas Scott. *The New Nation* reported that Parisien died of his wounds on April 6, 1870.[2]

Shortly after the brutal assault on Parisien, Thomas Scott was captured and imprisoned by Lépine. By all accounts Scott was an obnoxious bully boy. His character did not improve in captivity. He taunted and kicked the guards. He spat bitter racist slurs at them day and night. Riel tried several times to persuade Scott to settle down, but he said he would never be satisfied until he had walked through the blood of Louis Riel. Scott threatened repeatedly to assassinate Riel, overthrow the Métis forces, torch Métis homes and take the fort. With Schultz and Mair gone, Scott was one of the remaining leaders of the Canadian Party. According to the Métis guards, Scott was inciting the other captives to violence, and infecting the other prisoners and everyone else in the fort. According to *The New Nation*,

> Mr. Scott was very violent and abusive in his language and actions, annoying and insulting to the guards, and even threatening the President. He (Scott) vowed openly that if ever he got out, he would shoot the President; and further stated that he was at the head of the party of Portage people, who on their way to Kildonan, called at Coutu's house and searched it for the President, with the intention of shooting him.[3]

Most accounts say the guards wanted to kill Scott because he taunted and kicked them. This makes little sense. The guards had heard racist slurs all their lives. They were hunters, strong men who would not fear a man they had tied up and in their control. If he kicked them they would have just kicked him back.

The motives of the guards make more sense if we look to the strategic reasons for eliminating Scott. He was dangerous to the guards, their families and especially to Riel. Scott was inside the fort, not outside. And the fort was not a prison. It was a large wooden building. Windows could be opened, and there were visitors and many people around. Security was difficult to maintain, which could readily be seen from the number of escapes. Scott was perfectly placed to lead an attack from the inside while the Canadian Party mounted an attack from outside. The men would be forced to guard their backs and to fight on two fronts. There were too many opportunities for Scott, a man obsessed with killing Riel, to make good on his threats. Scott was a serious problem and he was inside their defences. The guards believed Scott needed to be killed.

The French Métis were men of action. They never opted for a wait-and-see approach. When they thought something needed doing, they did it. The guards dragged Scott out into the courtyard and started to beat him. They might have killed him then if one of the Provisional Government councillors had not intervened. The guards thought saving Scott was a mistake. They believed Scott had to be eliminated and they pressed Riel hard. Damase Harrison and Jerome St. Matte demanded that Riel send Scott to the war council for judgment. If Riel refused, then he would be the one facing the council.

Riel was an Indigenous leader. He was not the commander of an army. He could not command his men to blindly obey if they disagreed with his orders. Riel's men were independent volunteers, and they followed him because they believed in him. They were also free to leave at any time and free to take their own path. So, Riel was forced to concede to the guards' demands. But he would not let the Métis descend to the level of the Canadian Party, which had just acted as a mob, viciously beaten Parisien, attempted a lynching and left him on his death-bed. Riel insisted that the Provisional Government was to be respected. They would act deliberately and deliver justice with due process, in the manner of a government.

So, they put Scott to a trial before the war council. It was not a trial in the style of British justice. This was a Métis trial. It was the way they meted out justice according to the Laws of the Prairie. These were the same laws they had just codified and adopted in assembly. Articulating and codifying laws, especially those that are part of an oral tradition, is not a small endeavour. It takes considerable thought and the participation of many people. It is safe to say, then, that the Métis had been thinking a great deal about their laws and how they worked. They had been applying their laws. The Laws of the Prairie had governed the Métis throughout the North-West, everywhere except in the Red River settlement. Since many Métis spent more time on the Plains than in the settlement, the Laws of the Prairie would have been very familiar to them. They formed the basis for how the Métis dealt with justice on the hunt, and they'd been doing it this way for over fifty years. It was a system that began under Cuthbert Grant and developed over time. It was well known to the Métis buffalo hunters.

The Métis guards in the fort were buffalo hunters. During the fall and winter, they were in the settlement, supporting the Resistance. The Métis force had been bolstered because the hunters were there and not out on the Plains. They were skilled with horse and gun and they drilled often. They had even co-opted

Macdonald's commissioner, Colonel de Salaberry, into drilling their young boys with bayonets, guns and tactics. These were the men who demanded that Riel put Scott on trial.

The procedure of a Métis trial was unique. It drew from three distinct legal traditions—British common law, France's criminal process, and Cree and Ojibwa justice systems. There were some similarities in all three. Each called on witnesses to testify. All three systems used one or more decision-makers. But after that, there were significant differences.

In the British adversarial system, witnesses testified before the accused and were cross-examined by a prosecutor. In the French non-adversarial system, the evidence was primarily gathered before the trial and admitted with few restrictions. Judges decided based on their inner conviction whether there was moral proof of guilt. In the First Nations system, the hearing was concerned with the facts of the offence and the history of the accused. It was a forward-looking, non-adversarial system.

Both the British and French systems purported to seek the truth with respect to the facts of the offence. Indigenous trials sought a different goal—restoration of harmony in the community. While this required an examination of the facts of the offence, there was no belief that an adversarial system helped the decision-maker to arrive at a useful remedy. First Nation trials acknowledged societal causes and had a broad range of remedies unknown to British or French law.

Scott's trial more closely resembled the French and First Nation systems. There was more than one judge, and the trial was not conducted under an adversarial system. It was more of a review of evidence admitted without restriction, and the judges decided based on their inner conviction that there was moral proof of guilt.

Scott's trial did not focus on the details of the offence, which was vaguely described as insubordination. Two witnesses testified as to the specific incidents of Scott's wilful disobedience, his threats, his assaults on Riel, the danger he posed and his physical abuses of the guards. There was no cross-examination. A council of six heard the evidence but Scott was not present for that part of the trial. He was brought into the room to hear the verdict, which was translated for him by Riel.

In some ways the procedure at Scott's trial resembles Riel's trial in 1885. Riel was not allowed to present the defence or evidence he wanted, and he was allowed to speak only after the evidence was closed. The main difference was that Riel's trial was conducted in his presence. There was no presumption of innocence in either trial and both guilty verdicts were foregone conclusions. It is the death sentence in both trials that shocks the conscience.

The procedure of the Scott trial should not be held up against the Canadian or British justice system. By the 1860s the Court of Assiniboia in Red River had developed its own unique justice system. For example, the court, a creature of the Hudson's Bay Company, often allowed judges and legal counsel to adduce their own opinions and testimony as evidence. Often more than one Hudson's Bay Company officer (called a judge) sat on a case, the presumption of innocence played little or no role in a trial, and the court declined to hear cases that were against its own corporate interests. The court's procedures were anything but regular, and the Métis believed that it acted with a clear bias against them. This is in part why the Métis often exercised their influence to clear some cases off the docket that were not in their interests. Pure British law and trial procedure were unknown in Red River.

The trial of Thomas Scott was held before a war council composed of André Nault, Joseph Delorme, Janvier Ritchot, Elzéar Lagimodière, Elzéar Goulet and Baptiste Lépine. Joseph Nolin acted as the clerk. Ambroise Lépine was the presiding officer, and Louis Riel translated into English. Riel, Nolin and Ambroise Lépine didn't vote.

We have conflicting accounts of the trial. According to Joseph Nolin, three witnesses, Joseph Delorme, Riel and Edmund Turner, gave evidence against Scott. According to André Nault, Riel was not a witness but he spoke to the judges, urging them to spare Scott the death sentence. If they disagreed and found Scott guilty, Riel would accept his share of the responsibility.

After hearing the evidence the court unanimously voted Scott guilty. Scott was brought in and the court voted on his sentence in his presence. The majority, Ritchot, Nault, Goulet and Delorme, voted for a death sentence. Baptiste Lépine and Elzéar Lagimodière voted against execution.

Death was not their only punishment option. The Métis used shame quite effectively, to deter thieves, for example. A thief on the buffalo hunt who was tried and found guilty was marched into the centre of the camp, where his name, with "thief" added, would be shouted out three times. The entire camp would then know the thief by name, and word would spread to other camps across the North-West. Because each individual life depended on the collective, and the collective depended on trust, public shaming worked well in those situations. But it was obvious to everyone that Scott was not susceptible to shaming.

Banishment, another common punishment, and one suggested by one of the war council, Elzéar Lagimodière, was also not a realistic option. No one believed Scott would stay out of the country. They could not let Scott stay in prison, where he would continue to be a danger to them all. The decision to execute Scott stood. Ambroise Lépine ruled that the majority sentence would be carried out. Scott was executed the next day, March 4, 1870, by a firing squad.[4]

The Métis trial of Thomas Scott should not be critiqued as an absence of, or inadequate, justice. It was not mob rule and it was not primitive. It was duly deliberated with due process, not carried out in the heat of passion, and it was done according to a justice system that had been functioning in the North-West for half a century.

After the execution the Métis refused to hand over Scott's body. A wooden box was buried inside Fort Garry, but when the box was later exhumed, there was no body inside. Elzéar Goulet and Elzéar Lagimodière disposed of Scott's body, and both went to their graves without revealing where they disposed of it. The search for Scott's body continued well into the mid-twentieth century, and to this day no one knows where Scott's body is.

The death of Scott has consumed the attention of English Canadians for over a century, but there is virtually no memory of Parisien. His death does not echo down through English-Canadian history as Scott's death has. But the Métis Nation remembers Parisien. They are mystified by the intense focus on the execution of Scott and the indifference to Scott's murder of Parisien. The Métis Nation story of Thomas Scott starts with the murder of Parisien.

From the Métis perspective, the Provisional Government conducted a trial and carried out a court-ordered death sentence. Scott's death was a state execution. It was the first fateful decision that would have future consequences for the Métis Nation.

THE QU'APPELLE ASSEMBLY

The Qu'Appelle Lakes had long been one of the Métis rendezvous and wintering camps. A Métis assembly had been called at the lakes as soon as the snow disappeared and it was possible to travel in the spring of 1870. Early arrivals waited weeks for all the Plains hunter families to assemble. By April over a thousand Métis had gathered in Qu'Appelle. They came from all over the North-West, including from south of the border. They were keenly attuned to what was going on in Red River, and families talked of little else. They wanted to hear the latest news, and they were entirely sympathetic to their relatives in Red River.

The Qu'Appelle assembly was a great social event. People devoured the stories of the Red River Resistance, especially stories about Riel. It is at the Qu'Appelle assembly that we first hear the Métis begin to speak of Riel as a man inspired by heaven. There were stories that Riel had been seen with a supernatural being in the form of a man and that he conversed with this being in a strange language that was not French, English or Indigenous.

Métis elders, *lii vyeu*, all have stories about Riel. They all begin with the same words: "Riel, oh he was a saint, *aen saent.*" They all think of Riel as a holy man, a man who walked with God and the spirits. That reverence for Riel began in Red River, but by the spring of 1870, it had reached the hunters in Qu'Appelle. They took the stories of Riel with them throughout the North-West.

The hunters saw their relatives in Red River engaged in a battle to protect the Métis Nation and all that entailed—their land, religion, culture, practices and rights. The question for the thousand assembled at Qu'Appelle was whether they were going to join the action in Red River. Most wanted to go. Indeed, that appears to have been the general mood of the camp. The fight was about family, their rights and their nation. They were not naturally inclined to abstain from such a fight, and they would never take sides against their brothers and sisters in Red River.

The Hudson's Bay Company traders tried to convince the Métis winterers to stay out of it. They distributed Donald Smith's proclamation widely. But there had been too many proclamations. McDougall's proclamations had turned out to be bogus. What was different about this one? They would not believe in the proclamation just because the Hudson's Bay Company said it was authentic.

The deciding factor lay with Pascal Breland and Salomon Hamelin. Both were important Métis traders and very influential men. Both vehemently opposed Riel's activists. Breland was called *le roi de traiteurs* (the king of the traders), and his influence was greatly enhanced by being the son-in-law of Cuthbert Grant. When Breland made his speech to the assembly, he knew the mood of the gathering, so he began by situating the Métis clearly on side with the goals of those in Red River. It was wrong for Canada to impose her rule without first making terms with the Métis. All the Métis wanted to protect their lands, their language and religion, their independence and their culture. So far they all agreed.

But Breland had never supported the Riels. He was from St. François Xavier, and since the *Sayer* trial, there had been a difference of opinion between the Métis of St. François Xavier and the Métis of St. Vital and St. Norbert. It was not an irreconcilable difference. There were many marriages between the two groups. But since 1849 they had mostly hunted in separate groups, and it was not lost on the St. François Xavier Métis that Louis Riel's father had been, toward the end, one of the most vocal opponents of the Hudson's Bay Company and therefore of Cuthbert Grant. Times had changed but some of the old tensions remained. The Métis from the French parishes around the Forks and St. François Xavier were not always unanimous in their ambitions.

Breland and Hamelin, both wealthy traders, had much to gain from an alliance with Canada that would open markets for their trade goods. They also had their land registered (it had originated as a grant from the Hudson's Bay Company to Cuthbert Grant), so they were less fearful of losing their claimed lands. And unfortunately Riel had imprisoned Hamelin for a while the previous winter, a fact that did not make him disposed to assist the Riel activists. Breland and Hamelin were also associates of Dease and of an older generation of Métis who were uneasy with the brash young men leading the charge in Red River. Finally, Breland's son was working with Riel's party, and that was particularly galling for his father.

The news of Thomas Scott's execution had circulated before the assembly. In that spring of 1870, the Métis winterers gathered at Qu'Appelle were reluctant to let the execution of Scott change things. But Breland and Hamelin were persuasive. Retribution was coming for that deed. Macdonald was sending the army. If the hunters went to Red River, they would be fighting against the Canadian army and they wouldn't win that battle. Both men argued that the hunters should not go to Red River. It was the turning point. Had Breland and Hamelin not urged neutrality, the hunters, over a thousand of them, would have gone to Red River. That had been what they wanted to do before Breland and Hamelin spoke. But in the end they listened to Breland's advice and stayed out of it. Most drifted back onto the Plains, and only a few went to Red River to help. That was the second fateful decision.

THE MANITOBA ACT

At the end of March 1870, the Red River delegates, Alfred Scott, Judge Black and Father Ritchot, left Red River for Ottawa. They were armed with a new draft of the List of Rights, which the executive of the Provisional Government had drafted. Thomas Bunn had given the delegates a letter of instruction and a commission. The delegates were instructed that they had full discretion to negotiate ten of the twenty articles.[5] However the other articles were "peremptory." The delegates were not empowered to conclude any final arrangements. They were to negotiate the best deal they could and bring the proposal back to Red River for the approval of the Provisional Government.

When two of the delegates, Father Ritchot and Alfred Scott, landed in Ontario, Schultz and his friends had them arrested—twice. The Métis Nation was outraged that the delegates selected by their Provisional Government had been arrested. The court dismissed both warrants. Nevertheless, because of these antics, Scott and Ritchot were not free until April 23. It certainly started the negotiations on a sour footing.

The delegates began to negotiate with the federal government on April 25, 1870. All the while the government was preparing a force to go to Red River. On April 6, 1870, Colonel Garnet Wolseley had written to his brother, "The government is anxious that everything should be done quietly for as they expect some vagabond delegates from Mr. Riel's government to go to Ottawa they do not wish it to appear that they are preparing for war whilst they are also professing to treat amicably."[6] Privately, Macdonald wrote that the "impulsive half-breeds . . . must be kept down by a strong hand until they are swamped by the influx of settlers."[7] But there was no unanimity on the question of sending in the army. Quebec was against it, understanding, correctly as it turned out, that the troops could only have one purpose—punishment.

Ritchot began the negotiations with two crucial issues. First, he expressed his concern about sending in the army. Second, he demanded a general amnesty for all the participants. Sir John A. Macdonald and Sir George-Étienne Cartier deflected any talk of an armed force. They also led Ritchot to believe that the amnesty would be forthcoming. Macdonald and Cartier wanted to talk about the land, specifically about whether there would be control over the lands and resources. They conceded that Manitoba would enter Confederation as a province, but it was not really a concession, because under their scheme Manitoba would be a province in name only, with control of the lands and resources left in the federal government's hands. The reason Riel had been so insistent about Manitoba becoming a province was because he understood that provinces had local control over lands and resources. The List of Rights also emphasized the need for local control whether Manitoba was called a territory or a province. Macdonald's proposal, that Manitoba would be a province in name only, defeated all the aspirations of the Provisional Government.

For Ritchot, the chief negotiator, the change was profound. The Métis sent their negotiators to obtain local control of lands and resources, language and religious protections, democratic rights and the principles on which Manitoba was to enter Confederation. Instead there was no local control over lands and resources. This left Métis lands and customary land use practices particularly vulnerable. But Ritchot was determined to protect their lands, so the negotiation turned to how much land Canada would set aside for the Métis. Macdonald and Cartier initially offered 100,000 acres. Ritchot negotiated them up to 1.4 million acres.

Why did the delegates accept Macdonald and Cartier's proposal when it was contrary to their instructions? One major factor would have influenced their need to conclude an agreement quickly. They knew that Macdonald was amassing an army to send to Red River. They also accepted because of three promises Macdonald and Cartier made. The first promise was that the Métis land distribution would be supervised by the local legislature. Second, there would be legislation to ensure that the lands would continue to be held by Métis families. Finally, an amnesty was promised and would be forthcoming. Cartier was well aware of the Red River negotiators' reliance on an amnesty. He wrote to Sir John Young, "The delegates relied upon these explanations and forthwith entered upon the negotiations which resulted in the passing of the Act relating to the Government of the Province of Manitoba . . . [and without the assurance of an amnesty] it is more than probable they would not have felt themselves justified in negotiating."[8]

Macdonald and Cartier had a tough time getting their bill ratified. When the draft bill went to the House of Commons, the Canadian Party screamed its opposition. Macdonald and Cartier could not afford to have "Schultz of Red River" against the bill, so they bought him off with $11,000 and the offer of an appointment in Red River. Schultz, ever the opportunist, promptly supported the bill, a dereliction that caused much anger among his confederates.

When Father Ritchot returned to Red River with the draft bill, he worked with Riel and the council before presenting it to the people. They knew that Macdonald was sending the army. They all knew it was a take-it-or-leave-it offer. So Ritchot presented the draft bill with a fair amount of spin, leaning heavily on the promises about the amnesty and local control over land distribution. The Métis were persuaded that the promise of 1.4 million acres would allow them to secure their lands. The Provisional Government agreed to accept the terms of the draft bill that would, on May 12, 1870, become the Manitoba Act.

This was the third fateful decision.

RIEL DISARMS

Everyone in Red River knew that the army was arriving with a large number of volunteers from the Orange Lodges in Ontario. By May 25 the Canadian Expeditionary Force was at the end of Lake Superior, awaiting only the passage of the Manitoba Act before embarking overland to Red River. The "*orangistes*" in the ranks spent much of the trip to Red River boasting about how they would avenge their brother Thomas Scott by annihilating the Métis and assassinating Riel. Many of the voyageurs hired to transport the army were Métis, and they deployed the moccasin telegraph to send messages to Riel in Red River. The Métis Nation began discussions about what to do about the coming army, and whether to do anything at all.

More than one person, including Gabriel Dumont, wanted Riel to take on the army. Dumont promised five hundred warriors.[9] Old Nick Chatelain, a much-respected Métis leader at Lake of the Woods/Rainy Lake appears to have been acting as a double agent. He was retained by Canada to keep the Ojibwa on side when the Expeditionary Force came through, which he did, but only to the extent that the Ojibwa agreed not to attack the force. They wouldn't lift a finger to help. They refused to act as guides or to clear the portages.[10] That was in June. In July Chatelain was in Red River. Did Riel want the Métis from Lake of the Woods to attack the expedition? Chatelain suggested that a quick drop of logs at the right spot on the Winnipeg River would obliterate the force once and for all.[11]

It was Riel who stopped the Métis from attacking the troops.

The newspapers confirmed the vulnerability of the troops and Riel's control over his men:

> I am of opinion—and almost every officer in the detachment agrees with me—that a hundred determined men with a couple of guns, could not only have, over and over again, sent our boats to the bottom, but have kept the whole detachment at bay and in fact have caused its return . . .[12]

> [B]ut for Riel's command over his men, but for his strong personal influence and predilection for Canada and her institutions, the loss of life would, in all probability, have reached hundreds, massacre and assassination would have done their bloody work, the Canadian expedition would certainly never have reached Fort Garry this year.[13]

If Riel had known about the violence the Expeditionary Force was about to inflict on the Métis, one wonders if he would have made a different decision. It is quite certain that many Métis thought the army was only coming for slaughter and should be stopped. And Riel knew he could take the warpath; that's what would have followed if he'd agreed to Chatelain's or Dumont's suggestions. The Métis would have followed him. But Riel had never sought war. He took up arms only to defend their right to negotiate.

At this point Riel did not suspect that Canada and Manitoba would gut the key provisions of the Manitoba Act. It would have taken a devious mind to imagine that Canada would create a system that left the Métis with virtually none of the promised 1.4 million acres of land and that Manitoba would negate the French language and Catholic schools protection.

Riel was many things, but not devious. He had led his people, the Métis Nation, in a basically peaceful entry into Canada. Riel was a grand idealist, and his ideals had become reality—or so he thought.

He was inexperienced in the ways of Canadian politics. Métis politics are passionate but direct. When Léveillé set up a parallel guard at Fort Garry, he was announcing to everyone that he didn't trust Riel. There was nothing devious or covert about Léveillé's watch. Even Dease directly confronted Riel. They argued passionately, sometimes yelled at each other and never did agree. That was the kind of politics Riel knew. He was naive when it came to the kind of politics Macdonald and Cartier practised on a daily basis.

Still, Riel had done well in leading the Resistance. He obtained his goal—negotiations. He stickhandled powerful parties—the Americans, Great Britain, Macdonald, the Sioux and his own people. He was not perfect by a long shot. He misjudged the vehemence of the Canadian Party. He was sometimes furious and sometimes very frustrated. Sometimes he was barely in control. Things didn't always go the way he wanted them to and he made some bad decisions. But he had managed most of it well. Canada asked him to keep governing until the lieutenant-governor arrived and he agreed. He thought he could manage the handover peacefully. So, he didn't accept Dumont's five hundred horsemen, and he thanked Old Nick Chatelain and advised him not to go to war.[14]

This was the fourth fateful decision.

Riel sent the bulk of his men home. He met with the winterers who came back from the Plains in May. There were large meetings in Winnipeg and at the White Horse Plain. At these meetings Riel explained what had happened over the winter, about the Manitoba Act and the Métis Nation Treaty that guaranteed them 1.4 million acres of land, and he spoke of the coming troops. He printed and distributed Wolseley's "we-come-in-peace" proclamation:

> To the Loyal Inhabitants of Manitoba
> Our mission is one of peace and the sole object of the expedition is to secure Her Majesty's sovereign authority . . . Justice will be impartially administered to all races and to all classes . . . and will afford equal protection to the lives and property of all races and of all creeds. The strictest order and discipline will be maintained and private property will be carefully respected. Should any one consider himself injured by any individual attached to the force his grievance shall be promptly enquired into.[15]

Riel even had a celebration planned for the lieutenant-governor's arrival. He wanted to mark the day of the handover with grace and ceremony.

Riel wrapped up his tenure, all the while believing the amnesty was on its way. But it never came. The civil authority, the lieutenant-governor, didn't come either—at least not in time. Only the army came. Riel lingered in Fort Garry, but at the last minute he was warned that Wolseley's real intention was to imprison him and that his life was in danger. Riel stayed to watch the vanguard of the force arrive, and then he fled south of the border. That is when he had his first taste of bitterness. His ideals had taken a body blow. Even his faith in the priests was tested. He knew now just how naive they had all been.

PART FIVE

EARLY LIFE WITH CANADA

CHAPTER 19

THE REIGN OF TERROR

THE ORANGE LODGE

We come now to the second battle in the war between the Canadian Party and the Métis. Louis Riel had won the first battle. The Métis had executed Thomas Scott and forced Schultz, Charlie Mair and the other leaders of the Canadian Party out of Red River. Schultz was down, but he was not out. He made the rounds in Ontario, stirring up hatred—and he did have to stir it up, because initially Ontario was quite indifferent to the affairs of Red River. Schultz and his friends had to work their own people.

They began to hold a series of indignation meetings in Ontario in early April 1870. Their first meeting resulted in resolutions to send forces to Red River and a demand that Macdonald refuse to receive the Red River delegates of those who had "robbed, imprisoned and murdered loyal Canadians." The headline of *The New Nation* article reporting on the meeting read, "Schultz & Mair and their Associates Advocate Mob Law at Toronto to Lynch our Delegates."[1] The headline was accurate.

The plan was pretty basic. Schultz wanted to go back to Red River, but he needed an army to confront the Métis forces. So he raised his own army with lies, fear and the aim of revenge. He lied when he claimed his fortune had been wiped out and that his wife was a Métisse. But his lies gained him public sympathy for his financial woes, and claiming his wife was a Métisse created the illusion that he had no personal axe to grind against the Métis. The fear he spread was based on what would happen if the Fenians and the Métis, both Catholic peoples, joined forces. It was a potentially deadly combination to be sure and one that would have been offensive to the Protestant Orange Lodge. But Riel had long aligned himself and his men with Canada. There was virtually no danger that the Fenians and Métis would join forces. Schultz had an advantage in this game, though, because no one in Ontario knew anything about Red River. No one would fact-check Schultz about his lies or the fear he spread. He peddled revenge for the execution of Thomas Scott.

At indignation meetings throughout Ontario, Schultz and Mair called for Riel's head again and again. They made a saint of Thomas Scott. Schultz in particular had a dramatic bent. He liked props. He'd wave a piece of rope he claimed had been used to bind Scott's wrists. He even carried a small bottle said to contain Scott's blood. Schultz and Mair were very good at whipping up the crowds with anti-Riel and anti-Métis sentiments. Everywhere they went they passed the same resolutions and sent them on to Ottawa.

The Canadian Party, especially Schultz, wanted the riches of the North-West, and the Métis Nation was the only real obstacle to obtaining those riches. The Métis were a serious obstacle because they were a large, cohesive group, they were determined to protect their lands, and they were armed and organized. The only way to eliminate the Métis obstacle was for the Canadian Party to raise its own army. The men for this army were to be found in the Orange Lodges in Ontario.

The full name of the Orange Lodge was the Loyal Orange Association of British America. It was a society characterized by its penchant for violence and secrecy. Its members viewed Catholics and French as disloyal and culturally inferior. By 1860 there were over twenty lodges in Toronto alone. It is estimated that fully one-third of all Protestant men over twenty-one in Canada were members of the Orange Lodge.[2] In the late nineteenth century, Toronto was known as the "Belfast of Canada," a reference to the Orange influences in municipal government. The Orange Lodge permeated all levels of the English-Canadian establishment.[3]

Schultz offered the Orange Lodge what it wanted most: the blood of Papists, Frenchmen and the Métis. Papists and the French were the usual targets for the Orange Lodge. The Métis Nation in the North-West, previously unknown to the Orangemen in Ontario, was a new target. But Schultz and Mair needed something to activate their rage. Revenge was the perfect tool, and for Schultz's purposes, it was not a dish best served cold. Schultz and Mair needed their revenge to burn hot. Revenge for the execution of Thomas Scott turned out to be just the ticket.

The Orange Lodge made no secret of its intention to go to Red River on a mission of vengeance for the death of Thomas Scott. The Lodges passed dozens of resolutions similar to the following:

> Whereas Brother Thomas Scott, a member of our Order was cruelly murdered by the enemies of our Queen, country and religion, therefore be it resolved that . . . we, the members of L.O.L. No. 404 call upon the Government to avenge his death,

pledging ourselves to assist in rescuing Red River Territory from those who have turned it over to Popery, and bring to justice the murderers of our countrymen.[4]

RED RIVER
OUTRAGE.

A Public Meeting of the inhabitants of Hullett, Morris and Wawanosh will be held in the

Village of Blyth,

ON

WEDNESDAY, 20th APRIL,

AT 4 O'CLOCK, P. M.

To afford Loyal People an opportunity of expressing their deep indignation at the vile crimes committed in Rupert's land, by imprisoning and murdering British and Canadian subjects. The honor of England was never outraged with impunity, and never will be. Let Canada not be degraded, the honor of the country must be maintained, the blood of the Martyred Scott must not cry in vain for vengeance. Let Canada speak out now, and let the assassin Riel feel that a Canadian must be like an ancient Roman, free from injury wherever he goes. The men that went to Magdalla can go to the Red River. Come all Loyal Men to the meeting, this is the common cause of all Canadians.

DISTINGUISHED SPEAKERS WILL BE IN ATTENDANCE.

HURRAH FOR CANADA.

A ROPE FOR THE MURDERER RIEL!

GOD SAVE THE QUEEN!

Printed at the *New Era* Cheap Jo Printing Establishment, Clinton.

An Orange Lodge poster calling for a rope for Riel (*Manitoba Archives P7262A/6*)

By August 1870 the city of Toronto and villages throughout southern Ontario were full of inflammatory notices that read: "Shall French Rebels Rule Our Dominion?", "Orangemen, is Brother Scott Forgotten Already?" and "Men of Ontario, Shall Scott's Blood Cry in Vain for Vengeance?"[5]

The Canadian Party continued to make the rounds in Ontario. At first they thought they would need an amnesty for their own participation in the killings of John Hugh Sutherland and Norbert Parisien. And that should have been the case. But they soon realized that Ontarians had not even heard about Parisien, which was perfect for them. They didn't have to defend their responsibility for his death. They could continue to raise a vendetta against the Métis for the death of Thomas Scott.

The Ontario press, especially *The Globe* in Toronto, loved it. Schultz and Mair had always had the sympathy of the Ontario press. Nothing had changed there. The press in Quebec, while not sympathetic to the Orange outrage, was also not much inclined to inquire too deeply into what was happening in Red River. *The New Nation* was the only paper to challenge the obsession of the Ontario press with avenging Thomas Scott: "Three lives have been lost . . . Yet those very men who have been lionized and lauded by the Globe and its partisans, are the primary murderers of Sutherland, Parisien and Scott."[6]

THE CANADIAN EXPEDITIONARY FORCE

There was no public announcement about why Canada and Great Britain were sending the army to Red River. The silence allowed some to think the force was symbolic and others to think the purpose was punitive. The Orange Lodge insisted that the purpose was to implement what they called "justice" in Red River and turned it into an election issue. At least in part because of the Orange votes, the Conservative government in Ontario fell. Thereafter Macdonald made soft noises about the peaceful mission of the Expeditionary Force but stayed silent when Orange Lodge members enlisted with their well-known goal of vengeance.

Two-thirds of the 1,051 non-commissioned officers and men in the Expeditionary Force bound for Red River came from the Orange Lodges of Ontario. They freely admitted that the desire to avenge the death of Scott was one of their inducements to enlist. Some admitted that "they had taken a vow before leaving home to pay off all scores by shooting down any Frenchman that was in any way connected with that event."[7]

What happened next was entirely foreseeable. Sir John A. Macdonald knowingly sent into Red River an Expeditionary Force embedded with the dogs of war. These angry men from the Orange Lodges of Ontario would rape and assault, pillage and then plunder Red River. Once let out, the dogs were not easily contained. Macdonald's correspondence provides evidence of his intentions and his motive. Before the Expeditionary Force left for Red River, Macdonald wrote that the Métis were "wild people," "miserable" and "impulsive half-breeds."[8] He wanted the Métis to be "put down," "kept down" and "kept quiet."[9]

As he wrote those sentences, Macdonald was actively trying to engage Britain to send a force to Red River, and he was planning the commission of boats to ship an army out there. We know that he intended to use force because he wrote of using a "strong hand," and that he contemplated the use of excessive force because he would happily give the head of his army "the chance and glory and the risk of the scalping knife."[10] So, Macdonald's intention to use force against the Métis was clear, and these statements were all made before Thomas Scott was executed and before the Expeditionary Force was established. There is no indication that Macdonald ever backed away from these statements, and the facts show his intentions were fully carried out.

Sending troops didn't make practical sense at the time. It was expensive. And by the time they set out, everything was peaceful in Red River. Although there was a sentiment that Canada had to send a force to put down the Métis rebellion, there was nothing to put down and no need for an army in the summer of 1870. Canada and the Red River negotiators had come to an agreement. Parliament and the Provisional Government in Red River had approved the terms. If the political problem in Red River had been solved, why send in the army? The reason is that solving the political problem in Red River didn't solve the political problem Schultz had created for Macdonald in Ontario. The many voters in Ontario far outweighed the few new voters in Manitoba.

The evidence suggests that Canada had always planned to take over the North-West by force. We need only recall the shipment of rifles and ammunition sent out to Red River with the would-be Lieutenant-Governor McDougall in 1869 and the survey party bearing military titles and packing uniforms. Everyone wanted an armed force in Red River. McDougall, Donald Smith, the prime minister, and the Anglican bishop of Rupert's Land all wanted troops.

Only Britain was reluctant. It had experience with native unrest in its colonies and knew the dangers of sending in an army to "put down" the natives. Britain was not eager to send an armed force against the Métis, and they didn't want to rile the Americans either. The American Civil War had just ended, and there were a lot of American men roaming around that could quickly be gathered into an army. Britain didn't want to put troops on the U.S. doorstep.

But Macdonald was committed to the idea of sending an armed force to Red River. By the end of January 1870, he had boats ready to transport the troops across the Great Lakes. By February his correspondence to London was more strident. A Canadian Expeditionary Force was to set sail as soon as the Manitoba Act received royal assent on May 12, 1870. Great Britain, bending to Macdonald's insistence, agreed to send its own men, but only for the journey into Red River. Britain was the delivery agent for Macdonald's dogs of war. The Expeditionary Force received its standing orders on May 14, and by May 25 Wolseley's force was at the western edge of Lake Superior. There they waited until the Manitoba Act came into effect on July 15. The force left the next day, overland, for Red River. They went overland because the United States refused to allow a Canadian army or its equipment passage over American soil.

On the old voyageur route, the troops complained about the weather, mosquitoes, road conditions, and the difficulties of lugging cannon and equipment 435 miles from Lake Superior to Red River. There were still many old voyageurs in Red River. One can almost hear them laughing when they heard about the complaints.

Wolseley was supposed to be on an errand of peace. But immediately upon arrival in Red River on August 24, he dropped even the pretence of a peaceful mission. Thereafter he spoke of protecting the settlement from the tyranny of the "banditti." Wolseley was in outright defiance of his orders to be a force for peace. He even published stories about his activities. He refused to discipline his men or to use his power and influence to deter the violence perpetrated by his men. In a weird revival of the

Hudson's Bay Company authority, he asked Donald Smith to become the acting head of state until Lieutenant-Governor Adams George Archibald arrived. Smith claimed that he refused to issue warrants against Riel and Lépine during his twelve-day "rule." But Lieutenant-Governor Archibald stated, under oath, that warrants for the arrest of Riel, Lépine and O'Donoghue were issued and in the hands of constables before his arrival.[11]

The volunteers were frustrated and angry because they could not lay their hands on Riel and Lépine, who had fled to the United States. That anger never abated, and the troops went on a vicious rampage that would last two and a half years. The prime minister, so anxious to use force to put down, after the fact, what had essentially been a non-violent political movement, did nothing to stop the violence.

FEAR

There were over ten thousand people in Red River when the Expeditionary Force arrived. Eight thousand were fairly evenly split between English and French Métis. But the arrival of the troops, just over one thousand men, established the emotion that was to dominate the population for the next two and a half years—fear.

On August 24, 1870, the British Imperial Force escorted the first wave of the men into Red River. The civilian authority, Lieutenant-Governor Archibald, arrived on September 2. The British troops shipped out on September 3, and Schultz arrived on September 6.

The Expeditionary Force, officially under the command of Colonel Wolseley, was readily available to carry out the revenge envisioned by the Orange Lodge, and for that purpose it was under the virtually unopposed command of Schultz. One of

Schultz's supporters summed up their goal: "The pacification we want is extermination. We shall never be satisfied till we have driven the French half-breeds out of the country."[12]

On the first day, Wolseley claimed to have "captured" Fort Garry, which in point of fact was unoccupied. His Expeditionary Force looted the stores of the Hudson's Bay Company and the house Riel had used as a headquarters. They shot a horse out from under Father Kavanagh, injuring the priest from the White Horse Plain. Wolseley also claimed to have captured two "spies." In reality his men assaulted and then imprisoned two elderly Métis men, members of the Provisional Council, who were peacefully wending their way home. One was sixty-year-old Pierre Poitras, a famous buffalo hunter, a nephew of Cuthbert Grant, and a man who had fought at the Battle of the Grand Coteau in 1851. Poitras was seriously injured in the attack. That is how the Red River occupation began.[13]

The Métis were acting on fear even before the Expeditionary Force arrived. As word of their violent intentions spread throughout Red River, some Métis left for the Plains. Within days of the troops' arrival, many more Métis quietly gathered their families and slipped out of Red River.[14] Those who stayed quickly became immobilized and demoralized: "Our people cannot visit Winnipeg without being insulted, if not personally abused, by the soldier mob. They defy all law and authority, civil and military."[15]

Forced to live under an occupying army hell-bent on revenge, the Métis began to avoid Fort Garry. Social connections with relatives and friends in other parishes were severed. English Red River and French Red River became completely isolated from each other. For the French Métis there were serious economic consequences. Fort Garry was the trade centre and the main store. For the majority of the French population, trade was disrupted and everyday purchases at the fort became difficult if not impossible: "I do not feel safe. Certainly I would not take any money and walk between Winnipeg and Fort Garry after ten o'clock . . . I do not believe that any village was ever in so short a time so thoroughly demoralized as Winnipeg, since our arrival—for Riel, with all his faults—kept up an excellent police force."[16]

Whether they had business or family there, everyone who had even been remotely connected to Riel and the Métis cause was now afraid to "cross the river."[17] Two years later it was still not safe to cross the river.[18]

Most of the former leaders of Red River were gone. French Métis leaders such as Riel, Nault and Lépine were living in exile in the United States. The English leaders—Ross, Begg and Bannatyne—who had worked so hard to bring the people of Red River together in order to negotiate with Canada found good reason to absent themselves from Red River. The absence of leaders meant that the population had to fend for itself. Chaos was the result. The young Métis men tried to stand their ground and fight back. There were many brawls on the streets between the volunteers and young Métis. As the volunteers became increasingly violent, civil society, safety, and law and order for the French, the Catholic and especially the Métis became non-existent.

Métis women hid in their parishes and at home with their children and their elders. But nowhere was safe in the colony. While most Métis were afraid to cross the river into Fort Garry, that didn't stop the troops from crossing over into the Métis parishes. Soldier vigilante squads began to raid Métis homes.[19] No one was safe, not farmers in their fields, not women in their kitchens, not people trying to purchase goods at the fort and not those on their way to and from church.

Schultz and the Canadian Party published their intentions and broadcast them throughout the town. They took control of the press, and the Métis were not the only ones who objected. "The man [Schultz] who encourages lawlessness in a soldier . . . is not only a public enemy but a scoundrel of the deepest dye. There are such men in Canada today, and unfortunately they have control of the columns of newspapers."[20] Schultz and his men disabled the presses of *The New Nation*, the only newspaper unsympathetic to their goals. They invaded the editor's home and whipped him at gunpoint. That same day the *Telegraph* reported, "[A]lready their vigorous and not unnatural detestation of Riel, and those connected with him, has commenced to work . . . It is very probable that some rough-and-tumble work will take place here, for a Nemesis is stalking abroad here, and the friends of Riel are in a perilous state"[21]

Members of the Provisional Government and the Métis guards were the "friends of Riel" and the particular targets. Thomas Bunn would likely never have described himself as a friend of Riel. Still, he had agreed to act on the Provisional Government and had worked hard to enable the negotiations with Canada. Placards with a picture of a hanging man accompanied by a statement that this was the proper fate of Thomas Bunn were posted about town. They threatened to tar and feather him.[22]

The soldiers rarely resorted to arrest and imprisonment, likely because that was an official action with authorized supervision. They were not interested in that. "Disorder reigns in the town and in the vicinity since the arrival of the troops . . . and nobody intervenes . . . Colonel Wolseley says that he did not come here to act as a policeman."[23]

The Expeditionary Force did exactly the opposite of what

the Métis did. Except for the execution of Thomas Scott, there were few incidents of violence perpetrated by the Métis during the period when the Provisional Government was in power. They certainly did capture and confine.[24] They did not engage in random acts of revenge and violence. But the Expeditionary Force did.[25]

The press announced that the soldiers planned on "burning the houses of some obnoxious people" and they did. They burned the house James Ross was building and the home of Maurice Lowman, a Métis supporter.[26] Soldiers dragged Alfred Scott, one of the negotiators sent to Ottawa, through the mud by his heels. A dozen soldiers seized Landry, tied a rope around his neck and dragged him. He was saved only by the actions of Romain Nault and his son, and for his pains Nault was also assaulted. The soldiers were clear about why they were assaulting these men. It was revenge for Thomas Scott.

ELZÉAR GOULET

Elzéar Goulet was the first Métis man to die at the hands of the Expeditionary Force. He was murdered on September 13, 1870. Through both birth and marriage, Goulet was connected with the leading families of Red River.[27] He was one of the leaders of the Provisional Government and he served on the Scott trial. Schultz's father-in-law, James Farquharson, and three members of the Expeditionary Force were identified as the men responsible for Goulet's death. They chased Goulet into the river and pelted him with stones until he sank. His body was recovered the next day.

Judge Francis Johnson reported to the lieutenant-governor that there was insufficient evidence to prefer a charge of murder. The British Colonial Office was decidedly not of the same opinion and was not shy about criticizing Johnson for diminishing a "felonious intent to kill" to mere "drunken mischief."[28] The office noted that any man must be horribly frightened to take to the river and didn't accept drunkenness as an excuse for the soldiers' murderous actions. The British Secretary of State for the Colonies, Lord Kimberley, certainly thought there was material enough for a trial and wanted a prosecution to take place: "[I]f no evidence is forthcoming which would justify a conviction of any offence known to the law still the Govt will have done all in their power to vindicate the administration of justice and accordingly I am of opinion that legal proceedings should be taken, as suggested by the law Officers."[29]

Elzéar Goulet (*Société Historique de Saint-Boniface 03598*)

But Judge Johnson refused to issue warrants against men who were members of the Expeditionary Force. It would cause a mutiny and a riot. The volunteers believed that Schultz had brought them to Red River to kill the men who were responsible for Scott's death. Elzéar Goulet was one of the men they wanted dead, and they were unrepentant. Schultz's order, which now governed the settlement, was vengeance, and vengeance has no room for justice. No one was ever charged for Goulet's murder.

Goulet's funeral was the first opportunity for the Métis to gather in public since the Expeditionary Force had arrived. They came from far and wide to pay their respects. Riel and Lépine came back from their exile in the United States to attend prayers, though they didn't dare appear at the funeral. Despite the personal risk they could not let their friend and brother go without saying goodbye. It was a solemn and sad affair. Prayers were whispered throughout the evening. The Métis Nation shed many tears for the loss of their good man.

Men were assaulted if they spoke publicly or voted in a manner Schultz didn't like. Frederick Bird, a member of Manitoba's first legislative assembly representing Portage la Prairie, was kicked and thrown into the mud because supporters of Schultz didn't like the way he voted. Reverend James Tanner was killed after leaving a political meeting at Poplar Point. James Ross and other Métis men who left moments later were attacked with clubs, stones and snowballs. It took an exceptionally brave man to attend a public political meeting, to vote or to speak up. The Métis held their own meetings in secret.

Archibald may have carried the title of lieutenant-governor, but he did nothing, perhaps could do nothing, to restrain the wild troops, who at this point outnumbered the population of the town. According to the U.S. consul, Archibald was a virtual prisoner of the volunteers. Archibald may not have been able to stop the pogrom, but he did what he could. He offered the shelter of his home to Edmund Turner (one of Thomas Scott's guards and a witness at his trial) when the soldiers chased and threatened him—an act that did not endear him to the Expeditionary Force, Schultz and the Canadian Party.[30] The U.S. consul thought they were beginning to secretly plot the expulsion of Lieutenant-Governor Archibald.

The sheer brutality and volume of assaults was shocking in a community that had seen nothing of the kind before. Initially many people thought the newspaper accounts were exaggerated, but they weren't. David Tait and two companions were found half-dead. Louis (Henri) Hibbert, a Métis winterer who had recently arrived in Red River, was beaten with belts so savagely that an eyewitness was sickened by the brutality of the attack. Hibbert would have been killed if two women had not intervened. The witness, a man recently arrived from Ontario, reported that he had not really believed the violence was so bad until he saw it with his own eyes. The Canadian Party and the Hudson's Bay Company shrugged it off. The general thought seemed to be that the Métis should not give vent to "*Vive mon Nation*!" or "*La gloire de tous ces Bois-brûlé*" in public.[31]

It took six weeks for *The St. Paul Daily Pioneer* to put a name to the violence. This was the North-West and it was no stranger to violence. For the St. Paul paper to name it a "reign of terror" so quickly gives an indication of the level of violence in Red River. *The St. Paul Daily Pioneer* wrote that the troops intended "to drive out by threats or actual violence" all the French Métis.[32]

Soldier vigilante squads roamed throughout the settlement, and Schultz's father-in-law, Farquharson, ran one of them. He was implicated in the murder of Elzéar Goulet, and he brutally assaulted one of Riel's most brilliant cavalry officers, Jean Cyr. In December 1871, Farquharson and a gang of men invaded the Riel home. They threatened Riel's mother and sister at gunpoint, demanding to know where Louis was. They swore they would kill Riel. When the Métis heard about it, they were outraged and sent a petition to the lieutenant-governor.[33] They wanted the men who had invaded the Riel house punished.

But no one was punished for any of the violence. The Métis thought it was because Macdonald and Schultz were working in collusion. "Collusion" may be too strong a word. It suggests a secret pact. There appears to be no evidence of such a pact. But both men and the Orange Lodge, of which Macdonald was a member, did have a common goal: ascendancy, or complete control by white, English-speaking Protestants.[34] So, far from being punished for their criminal activities, some of the men involved in the reign of terror later "ascended" to high office. John Ingram attacked and beat up Joseph Dubuc. Ingram became chief of police in Winnipeg.[35] Francis Cornish was involved in the invasion of the Riel home and led a gang that liberated his fellow perpetrators from jail. He became the first mayor of Winnipeg. Macdonald and Schultz may not have been acting in collusion, but they didn't need a pact; they were acting in lockstep.

In January 1871 the soldiers murdered another member of the Provisional Government, Bob O'Lone. They also murdered François Guillemette, the man who had administered the final shot to Thomas Scott. Even living in exile in the United States provided no safety. Quite by accident Riel overheard men in Pembina discussing a plan to assassinate him, and he was able to evade them. André Nault was not as lucky and was attacked by fifteen soldiers. He attempted to run across the border to escape, but the soldiers caught him, bayonetted him and left him for dead. Nault recovered, but no one was charged with the attempted murder.[36]

The Métis didn't take all this lying down. The papers regularly described fights between the soldiers and the Métis. In the spring of 1871, there was an escalation in the level of violence. The hunters were back in the settlement, and the number of Métis on the streets rose dramatically. As their numbers increased, the Métis had less inclination to avoid confrontations with the troops. The violence also increased that spring because many of the volunteers were now free of the constraints of military life. They had signed up for two-year contracts in the spring of 1869, and they were now free to continue their rampage unrestrained by officers. The minimal restraints exercised by the officers had certainly done little to stop the violence, but now even that small restraint was gone.

Women and those who tried to protect them were particularly vulnerable. Soldiers invaded Toussaint Voudrie's home and propositioned the women in the family. Voudrie successfully evicted the men, but they returned soon after with reinforcements and Voudrie was almost beaten to death.[37] Soldiers also invaded Andrew McDermot's home, severely beat one of the servants and threatened the two daughters that their house would be burned down if they called the police.[38] A dozen soldiers attacked the home of Madame Goulet. When the occupants tried to defend themselves, they too were beaten.[39]

When a soldier raped Marie La Rivière, his punishment consisted only of being confined to barracks. Soldiers also raped Lorette Goulet, the seventeen-year-old daughter of Elzéar Goulet. Though the men were identified to Lieutenant-Colonel Samuel Peters Jarvis, the commander of the Ontario force and later an inspector in the North-West Mounted Police, his response was that rape by his soldiers was none of his business.[40] No one was charged for the rapes.

Often one soldier would initiate an assault, and if he was unsuccessful, others, sometimes as many as thirty men, would pile on. When a Métis named Bourassa successfully defended himself against a volunteer who assaulted him, other soldiers jumped in and stoned and whipped him in revenge.[41] On their way to see Lieutenant-Governor Archibald, Maxime Lépine, Pierre Léveillé and André Nault were threatened by a soldier. When they complained and the man was arrested, Lépine, Nault and Léveillé had to run a gauntlet of thirty angry volunteers armed with clubs.[42]

Le Métis ran several editorials that described the assaults as odious and brutal, and decried the violent deaths of Parisien, Tanner, Goulet, O'Lone and Guillemette, all at the hands of the people from Ontario and *orangistes*.[43] In June 1871, when the U.S. consul, James Wickes Taylor, was attacked by the soldiers, *The New York Times* ran a story with the headline "Military Reign of Terror."[44] Taylor was firmly on the side of the French and Métis and wrote a report on his assault in which he said, "Outrages upon the French population are of daily occurrence—often most flagrant and cowardly in their character, and so far this incident has tended to identify me with this long-suffering population. I do not regret it."[45]

Métis who had not sided with Riel because they thought him too radical, and other residents who had stood aloof during the resistance, now thought as one. The violence united the residents of the settlement together against Schultz, the *orangistes* and the Canadian Party.

Despite its success in murdering members of the Provisional Government and friends of Riel, the Canadian Party was still frustrated. They had not succeeded in getting Riel himself. So, they put out a $1,000 bounty on Riel's head. Not to be outdone, Ontario upped the ante by putting a $5,000 bounty out for those concerned with the death of Scott.

Wolseley had promised that justice would be "impartially administered to all," that there would be "equal protection" for everyone's lives and property, that "the strictest order and discipline" would be maintained and that if anyone suffered an injury "by any individual attached to the force his grievance shall be promptly enquired into." The Métis reminded the lieutenant-governor of that promise of justice. They petitioned and wrote letters and begged assistance in personal meetings. Nothing happened. The state in Manitoba, rapidly becoming the Orange state, made virtually no attempt to administer law and order for the protection of its Métis citizens. Riel and Lépine expressed the dismay of the Métis Nation when they wrote:

> Wolseley entered the Province as an enemy . . . he gave up to pillage . . . [he] allowed to be ill-treated by his soldiers, peaceable and respectable citizens . . . The conduct of Wolseley was a real calamity. It produced its victims . . . and [the perpetrators] have lived . . . in impunity under the eye of the authorities . . . [M]urder was also left unpunished . . . The inhabitants of the settlement generally have been attacked in their persons . . . by a large number of the men belonging to the militia. And the Canadian authorities leave us to be crushed . . . These facts are supported by affidavits of honest witnesses still living. We could cite many similar facts, but these . . . show how great an injury the policy of the Government of Canada inflicts upon us . . . During the last Federal election we . . . were attacked in every possible way, even by shots . . . As for these disturbers of public order, they can all, whoever they may be, move about freely and

> defy the law everywhere in Winnipeg. They can show themselves even in our courts of justice . . . to laugh at our laws and show clearly in the eyes of the world that we . . . [are] plunged in the horrors of anarchy . . . The Government at Ottawa acts towards us as an enemy . . . [and] causes us to suffer frightfully and has occasioned for more than two years a public strife . . .[46]

The crimes cited here represent only a small portion of the pogrom. The bulk of it went unreported. But this account does provide the flavour of the early days of Canada's reign in the North-West. The reign of terror in Red River lasted for two and a half years. Canada ignored the reign of terror when it was happening. That attitude continues. In 2018 Canada announced that the Red River Expedition of 1870 would be honoured with a new national historic designation. In the backgrounder accompanying the announcement, the minister of environment, who is responsible for Parks Canada, stated that she was "very proud" to recognize it as one of the events that "shaped our country." She called the Red River Expedition a "vibrant symbol of Canadian identity." Their story, said the minister, was one that tells us "who we are as a people," one that will "inspire us towards new endeavors and adventures."[47] After the Métis Nation objected, the minister agreed to redraft the backgrounder.

The reign of terror has left a visceral anger, resentment and sense of injustice deep in the heart of the Métis Nation, specifically about the role played by Sir John A. Macdonald.

SIR JOHN A. MACDONALD'S RESPONSIBILITY FOR THE REIGN OF TERROR

The Métis Nation has always cried out against the perpetrators of the crimes committed during the reign of terror. The Métis

Nation knows and continues to honour the names of the victims. The Métis Nation also continues to insist that the individual who bears the primary responsibility for the crimes should be named. They say that name is Sir John A. Macdonald.

During the reign of terror there was no language to describe a deliberate campaign of crimes committed by government forces against its own people. But the language came into use shortly thereafter. Today we would call such a campaign "crimes against humanity," defined as multiple, intentional acts committed by state actors, with the knowledge of the state, as part of a systematic attack directed against a civilian population. The description fits the reign of terror perfectly.

In Canada decisions as to whether to deploy the military, where the military is to be deployed and the appointment of senior military officers rest solely with the prime minister.[48] If the prime minister chooses, he may bring the matter before Parliament. But if he does, it is merely an exercise in political discretion. So, when it came to the authorization of the Canadian Expeditionary Force, the appointment of Colonel Wolseley, the decision to deploy the force to Red River and the decision not to discipline, correct or remove Wolseley, Sir John A. Macdonald made the decisions and bears the responsibility.

As prime minister, Macdonald also had a constitutional duty to protect the citizens of Canada, and that included the Métis Nation citizens in Red River. In fact he had two duties: one was to refrain from authorizing or approving crimes against his own citizens. The second duty arose once he had knowledge that such crimes were being committed. He had a duty to stop his army from continuing to commit the crimes. He failed in both duties. Macdonald knew about the violence and the deaths while they were taking place. Although he had two and a half years to stop the reign of terror, he did nothing. By wilfully remaining silent in the face of his knowledge, he approved and encouraged the crimes to continue.

It is no excuse to say that such crimes were part of the attitudes and practices of the times. Long before the phrase "crimes against humanity" was coined in the early part of the twentieth century, there was well-established international law that governments and state actors—especially those holding the highest office in the land—have an obligation to protect their citizens and not subject them to violence and death. Those responsible could not, even in those days, shelter behind their office or claim that they were enacting state policy. Common notions of justice, upheld for centuries, reveal such excuses to be flimsy and offensive. Sir John A. Macdonald cannot claim ignorance, innocence or immunity for the crimes. The Métis Nation says that for all of history Sir John A. Macdonald must answer at the bar of public sentiment for the crimes committed during the reign of terror against the Métis Nation, a people whose lives and fortunes were entrusted to his care.

THE FAILED FENIAN INVASION, 1871

Despite the horrors being perpetrated on them by the state during the reign of terror, the Red River Métis made a deliberate decision to remain loyal to Canada and proved it when Manitoba faced the threat of a Fenian invasion in the fall of 1871.

Based in the United States, the Fenians were an Irish republican organization trying to pressure Britain to withdraw from Ireland by attacking British targets in Canada. During the Red River Resistance, one of Riel's close advisers, William O'Donoghue, was suspected of being a Fenian. After the Resistance Riel and O'Donoghue went their separate ways. But in late 1871 O'Donoghue reappeared in the United States as one of the leaders of the Fenians threatening to invade Manitoba. The past connection between the Métis and O'Donoghue raised the spectre that the Métis would support the Fenians. The possibility that Manitoba could be lost if the Métis chose to support the Fenians was not something that could be easily dismissed, especially in light of their military skills, numbers and present resentment against Canada during the reign of terror.

Rumours that the Fenians were planning an invasion into Manitoba first surfaced at the beginning of September 1871, when the U.S. consul, Taylor, brought the news to Lieutenant-Governor Archibald. On September 28 twelve Métis met at the Riel house in St. Vital.[49] Louis Riel, on a clandestine visit home at the request of the Métis, set out five questions for the men to discuss:

1. Does the Government fulfil sufficiently its pledges toward us?
2. If it has not yet done so, have we reasons to believe that it will fulfil them honestly in the future?
3. Are we sure that O'Donoghue is coming with men?
4. If he is coming, what is he coming to do?
5. At all events, what conduct must we follow respecting him and respecting Canada?

The answer to the first question was an unequivocal no. The reign of terror and the lack of a general amnesty made the question barely worth discussing. The second answer followed logically on the first. Judging by Canada's actions to date, the Métis had no reason to believe Canada would honestly fulfill its pledges. Their minutes of the meeting reveal a profound disappointment in Canada "especially if one considers how the

Government dodges in the presence of the Ontarian [op]pression which is contrary to us."[50] Still, they decided to delay answering the second question.

The discussion on the third question was revealing. The Métis were widely supposed to be in league with O'Donoghue and the Fenians. But not one of the Métis leaders in attendance had communicated with O'Donoghue directly, and no one knew for sure if he was even coming with the Fenians. They had all heard the rumours and believed them, but no one had any solid information. According to the rumours the Fenians were going to arrive at Pembina. If the rumours were true, then the logical conclusion was that the Fenians would use Pembina as their foothold into Manitoba and were indeed coming to attack the province.

The last question was the crucial one. What were the Métis going to do, if anything? Whatever position they decided to take—be it to side with the Fenians, stay neutral or defend the province—they wanted their Métis people to be united behind them. They knew O'Donoghue would try to drag them into it. Perhaps he even presumed their co-operation because of his support for them during the Red River Resistance and the terrors that were going on. But the Métis leaders were determined to make the decision themselves and not be pressured by O'Donoghue. They decided to send out feelers into the various Métis parishes to find out whether their people would unite unanimously in favour of the Manitoba Act they had negotiated. They had not seen the advantages of it yet, but still they advocated loyalty and moderation.

They met again on Wednesday, October 4. By that time O'Donoghue had indeed contacted them and asked them to meet him near Pembina. Baptiste Lépine and André Nault went to see what O'Donoghue wanted and how many men he had. They also wanted to see what their brother Métis around Pembina were thinking. The meeting minutes note that the Métis in the parishes were very excited by these events. No one seemed to want to actively join the Fenians, and neutrality might be the best option if they were to stay united. In light of the terror they were being subjected to, asking them to unite and act to defend the government was anything but a foregone conclusion.

The next day, October 5, thirteen Métis leaders met again in the evening, still with no particulars about O'Donoghue and the Fenians. Nault and Lépine had not yet returned from Pembina. They voted on whether to remain neutral or to act in favour of the government. They did not even consider the option of joining the Fenians. Twelve voted to stand with the Manitoba government. Only Baptiste Touron voted for neutrality, and this was directly because of the injuries he and his family had suffered at the hands of the Expeditionary Force.

On October 6 at 9:00 AM they met again to hear from Nault and Lépine, who had arrived late the night before. Nault and Lépine had met with O'Donoghue on Tuesday night (October 3), left Pembina first thing in the morning on October 4, and ridden hard for the better part of two days to bring the news. They reported that O'Donoghue claimed he had sufficient men and money, and needed the Métis "for the success of the declaration of the country's independence." O'Donoghue intended to take Fort Pembina on Wednesday morning.[51] What Nault and Lépine did not know, because they were already on their way back, was that O'Donoghue and the Fenians did indeed take Pembina.[52] News of the fort capture had not yet reached Red River when the Métis met on October 6.

Nault and Lépine then learned of the previous day's vote

of loyalty to Canada. But that was a vote of the Métis leadership. Where would the people stand? The general opinion of the leaders in attendance was that their people would have to be persuaded to stand in favour of the government. They agreed to hold meetings in their respective parishes. Some of the Métis leaders at the meeting said they would plead in favour of the government at the meetings. Others said that while they themselves were in favour of the government, they must move cautiously in advocating that position because of the angry mood of the people against Canada.

The meetings began and continued in all the French parishes over the next day. In St. Vital the answer was that the people "wish that what Riel shall say shall govern."[53] Riel's response was to separate the injustices they were currently experiencing from the need to support the government against the Fenian invasion.[54]

On October 7 the leaders reconvened to bring the responses from the parishes. White Horse Plain, St. Boniface, Sainte-Anne-des-Chênes, Ste. Agathe, Pointe-Coupée, St. Norbert and St. Vital all voted in favour of the government. Each parish had also appointed captains and seconds to lead their men into battle to defend Manitoba against the Fenians. Riel wrote to Lieutenant-Governor Archibald later that same day to say that the Métis believed it their duty to respond to his call to arms that had been issued on October 4.

> May it please Your Excellency: We have the honour to say to you that we . . . [will] respond to your call . . . Several companies are already organized and others are being formed . . . we, without having been enthusiastic have been devoted. As long as our services shall continue to be required, you can rely on us . . .

It was only after the Métis offered their assistance to Lieutenant-Governor Archibald that news arrived of the Fenian attack on Pembina and that it had subsequently failed. The Fenians captured Fort Pembina the morning of October 5, and the Americans recaptured it later that same day. O'Donoghue escaped into Canada but was captured by two Métis that same evening and turned over to the Americans. The news did not arrive in Red River until two days later. But Red River was still on edge. Most believed that the attack on Pembina was only a feint and that the main incursion would come from St. Joseph.

The Métis had gathered a force with some cavalry and awaited orders. It was during this period of uncertainty that Lieutenant-Governor Archibald crossed over to St. Boniface to review the Métis force and shake hands with the Métis leaders, including Louis Riel. Archibald was clearly thankful for the Métis support and stated, "If the Métis had taken a different course, I do not believe the Province would now be in our possession."[55]

The danger faced by Riel and the other Métis leaders—hunted men with a price on their heads—should not be underestimated. In the absence of a general amnesty, the Métis leaders wanted assurances from the lieutenant-governor that if they appeared publicly to urge their people to stand with Canada, they would not be arrested. The lieutenant-governor assured them that "*pour la circonstance actuelle*" they should not be arrested.[56] But arrest was the least of the worries for Métis leaders. They were more at risk of being assassinated than being arrested.

Despite the danger to their persons, they came back into Manitoba to organize the Métis to resist the Fenians. They came to the defence of Canada, a country that had forced them into exile and whose armed forces were terrorizing their people and daily trying to assassinate them. Riel in particular revealed his solid commitment to Canada. The risks they took to loyally defend Canada helps us to understand today why it hurts the Métis Nation so much to have its resistance movements labelled as rebellions.

Lieutenant-Governor Archibald appreciated the loyalty of the Métis. But he was the only one. With the gracious act of shaking the hand of Louis Riel, his days as lieutenant-governor were numbered. The Canadian Party was outraged. Schultz led a campaign to have Archibald dismissed, and he eventually succeeded in hounding him out of office. Macdonald danced to Schultz's tune.

Archibald wrote to Macdonald warning him that Schultz was a dangerous man: "Anything in the world for self, cheat, lie, steal, friend or foe as opportunity offers—ready is he at all time." According to Archibald, Schultz and his cronies had been "prominent in every trouble we have had."[57] *The Volunteer Review*, a militia magazine, called Schultz a "scoundrel of the deepest dye" and said he had done "his best to bring disgrace on the military service of his country." Macdonald didn't listen; he kept his alliance with Schultz and kept rewarding him.

THE BROKEN PROMISED AMNESTY

The promise of amnesty first came to Red River via Bishop Taché when he brought Governor-General John Young's proclamation to Red River in March 1870. Young's proclamation predated the execution of Thomas Scott, but Taché believed, and assured Riel, that an updated general amnesty was on its way.[58] The List of Rights the delegates took to Ottawa stated the case for an amnesty: "that none of the Provisional government, or any of those acting under them, be in any way held liable or responsible with regard to the movement or any of the actions which led to the present negotiations." For Ritchot the success of the negotiations depended on "being satisfied that the Royal Prerogative of Mercy would be exercised by the grant of a general amnesty."[59]

Ritchot and Taché both believed an amnesty had been promised.[60] They did not misunderstand the promise. It was the politicians who began to retreat from their promise. The amnesty passed back and forth between Canada and Great Britain a few times, but by August 6, 1870, Britain had made up its mind. It would not touch the question of amnesty. Canadian politicians began to deny they had ever promised an amnesty.

Then new warrants were issued for Riel and Lépine. Lieutenant-Governor Archibald worried about what would happen if Riel and Lépine were caught. He knew the Métis would fight hard to save them. It would be bloody. Everyone in power, the Canadian government, Bishop Taché, Father Ritchot and Lieutenant-Governor Archibald decided that the solution was for Riel and Lépine to disappear and stay away, preferably for a long time. No one in power gave a thought to what the absence of the leaders would mean for the Métis Nation in Red River.

The Métis would not let go of Riel or Lépine and kept begging them to come back. Men made constant trips to visit Riel in the United States. They kept asking for Riel's advice. So, Riel and Lépine didn't disappear. They couldn't. They just kept their heads down when they came back home, which they did, often. In exile Riel questioned his own judgment. He had believed in Taché, Ritchot and Cartier, and he had wanted to believe in the amnesty. He had allowed himself to be blinded. The amnesty was not coming. Taché also felt betrayed, but he continued to push for the amnesty. Young, Macdonald and Cartier, however, were practised manipulators, and Bishop Taché was never a match for them. They played the bishop like a puppet.

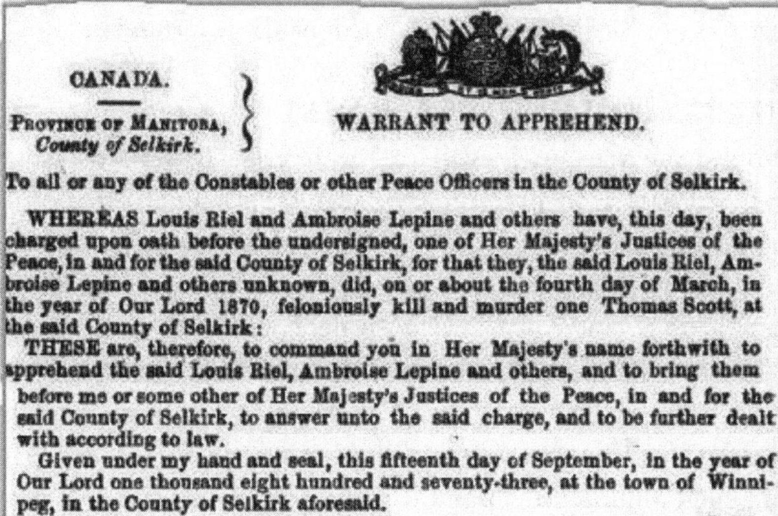
CANADA.

PROVINCE OF MANITOBA, County of Selkirk.

WARRANT TO APPREHEND.

To all or any of the Constables or other Peace Officers in the County of Selkirk.

WHEREAS Louis Riel and Ambroise Lepine and others have, this day, been charged upon oath before the undersigned, one of Her Majesty's Justices of the Peace, in and for the said County of Selkirk, for that they, the said Louis Riel, Ambroise Lepine and others unknown, did, on or about the fourth day of March, in the year of Our Lord 1870, feloniously kill and murder one Thomas Scott, at the said County of Selkirk:

THESE are, therefore, to command you in Her Majesty's name forthwith to apprehend the said Louis Riel, Ambroise Lepine and others, and to bring them before me or some other of Her Majesty's Justices of the Peace, in and for the said County of Selkirk, to answer unto the said charge, and to be further dealt with according to law.

Given under my hand and seal, this fifteenth day of September, in the year of Our Lord one thousand eight hundred and seventy-three, at the town of Winnipeg, in the County of Selkirk aforesaid.

[L.S.]

[Signed,] JOHN H. O'DONNELL, J. P.

Warrant for Riel and Lépine (*Wikipedia Commons*)

Ontario fully believed that the Catholic clergy were behind all the problems and that they were intent on making the West "another hot-bed of Jesuitism and treason."[61] Ontario considered the very idea that the Métis would bar the way to "the onward progress of British institutions and British people" unthinkable, a joke.[62] It was to appease Ontario that Macdonald and Cartier refused to grant an amnesty.

The people of Red River, of all persuasions except for the Canadian Party, hated how Ontario was interfering in their local affairs. They especially hated the $5,000 bounty that Edward Blake, Ontario's premier, had put on Riel's head. With the passage of the Manitoba Act, 1870, Manitoba now had a legislative assembly. In 1872 it passed resolutions asking for amnesty. In 1873 Macdonald suggested an amnesty for all actions except murder. This was useless. What was needed was a general amnesty and that was not forthcoming from Macdonald's government.

RIEL IS ELECTED TO PARLIAMENT

Despite the warrant issued for his arrest and the lack of an amnesty, Riel decided to run for a seat in Parliament. He began to campaign for election in the district of Provencher in June 1872 but was persuaded, largely by Bishop Taché, to give up his seat to Cartier, who had been defeated in his own riding. When Cartier died shortly after being elected, Riel won the by-election in October 1873. The reign of terror was mostly over by then, but there was still a bounty on Riel's head. He remained a hunted man and it was simply impossible for him to take his seat in Parliament.

He was elected for the second time in the general election of February 1874. This time he decided to symbolically take his seat. March 30, 1874, was the first day of the new Parliament, and Riel made no secret of his presence in Ottawa. It was a public sensation. Crowds gathered outside the Parliament buildings, and there were soldiers on the grounds to keep the crowd under control. Even the governor-general's wife, Lady Dufferin, made a special appearance at Parliament just to catch sight of the famous Riel.

Riel was there, but in disguise. Two sitting members of Parliament traditionally witnessed the oath of a new member and his signing of the register. Dr. Jean-Baptiste Romuald Fiset and Alphonse Desjardins accompanied Riel to the clerk's office in the main corridor of the old Chamber of Commerce. Riel took up the Bible. The clerk read the oath and Riel repeated it. Then he signed his name in the register. The clerk was horrified when he saw the name Louis Riel, but before he could do anything, Desjardins and Fiset whisked Riel away and off to Montreal.

Parliament was outraged. They expelled Riel and ordered a by-election. In September of 1874 the good people of Red River promptly voted Riel right back in again. Riel appreciated the support, but it was still far too dangerous for him to take his seat.

Then, on the basis of new warrants, the Canadian Party men in Red River arrested Ambroise Lépine.

THE TRIALS OF AMBROISE LÉPINE, ANDRÉ NAULT AND ELZÉAR LAGIMODIÈRE

On September 17, 1873, Ambroise Lépine was arrested. Francis Cornish was the man behind the arrest. He was an Orange lawyer recently come from Ontario, and a drunk, a brawler and a vicious bigot. Lieutenant-Governor Alexander Morris wrote to Macdonald that "Cornish is lost to all social restraint, and his orangeism gives him a [pass] for evil." He naturally fell in with Schultz and the Canadian Party. Cornish and his thugs invaded Riel's mother's home and tried several times to capture Riel. He couldn't get his hands on Riel, but he could and did arrest Lépine. He then acted as prosecutor at the trial, and for his efforts he was awarded $400 from Ontario premier Blake's $5,000 bounty.[63]

A grand jury was convened on November 12, 1873. Justice McKeagney heard the testimony, mostly in French, although he could not speak the language. The grand jury indicted Lépine, who was forced to sit in jail for six months until the new chief justice arrived in June 1874. Chief Justice Edmund Burke Wood's appointment was a reward for helping Alexander

Mackenzie's Liberals to bring down John A. Macdonald's Conservative government over the Pacific Scandal. On arrival Wood immediately fell in with Schultz.[64]

Ambroise Lépine (*Glenbow Museum NA-47-29*)

Wood was a scoundrel of the first order and a rude drunk. He was accused of multiple incidents of inappropriate judicial behaviour, and within six months of his appointment, the prime minister was inquiring into his financial problems. The chief justice also presided over a scheme to traffic in Métis land grants. This is the man who was the judge on the Lépine trial. The manner in which he conducted the trial was anything but impartial. So, it was no surprise that the jury found Lépine guilty.

The jury recommended mercy, but Chief Justice Wood saw no reason for mercy and sentenced Lépine to hang.

The Quebec Legislative Assembly passed a unanimous motion for a pardon. Ottawa received 252 petitions with 58,568 names asking for amnesty for Lépine. The Liberal cabinet refused. Finally Governor-General Lord Dufferin stepped in over the objections of cabinet. Four days before the scheduled execution, on January 15, 1875, the Colonial Office commuted Lépine's death sentence to two years in prison with a permanent forfeiture of political rights.

After Lépine's trial, in November 1874, André Nault and Elzéar Lagimodière were also tried for the murder of Thomas Scott. The evidence and argument were similar to those at Lépine's trial, but the jury simply could not agree on a verdict. Chief Justice Wood sent them back twice, demanding they come to agreement. Finally, the foreman told Wood they didn't agree and never would. The chief justice had no choice but to declare a mistrial. Stubbornly, he held Nault and Lagimodière in prison, denying all bail applications. It was months before Chief Justice Wood permitted the attorney-general to enter a *nolle prosequi*, which is Latin meaning "we shall no longer prosecute."

Parliament finally passed a motion for a full amnesty for Riel and Lépine in February 1875. The price was five years of banishment from the country. Riel accepted. Lépine refused and served out his sentence.

CHAPTER 20

CANADA TAKES THE LAND

THE MÉTIS TREATY

The Red River settlement was oriented around all of the rivers in the valley. The rivers were the source of life and the pulsing heart of the settlement. The people crossed the rivers regularly on dogsleds, snowshoes and on foot in winter, and in small boats and ferries when the water was ice-free. They swam in the rivers and fished in them. It was the rivers that connected the people of Red River to the land and to the farthest reaches of the North-West. The Métis built their homes on the rivers, on long, narrow lots they called *rangs*.[1]

The *rangs* were about eight hundred feet wide and about two miles long. Each family built their home and garden fairly close to the river. Toward the back of their *rangs*, they had a commons that provided forage lands for their livestock (their hay privilege, woodlots and other cutting areas). The close proximity of neighbours and extended family meant people could keep an eye on each other and it was easy to visit. It also fostered quick communications and nurtured community bonds. It was common for neighbouring Métis families to intermarry, and many areas were associated with a particular family. A good example of this was the Nolin extended family on the Seine River at Sainte-Anne-des-Chênes, and St. François Xavier, where Pascal Breland and Cuthbert Grant's descendants and extended family formed a large intermarried Métis community on the Assiniboine River.

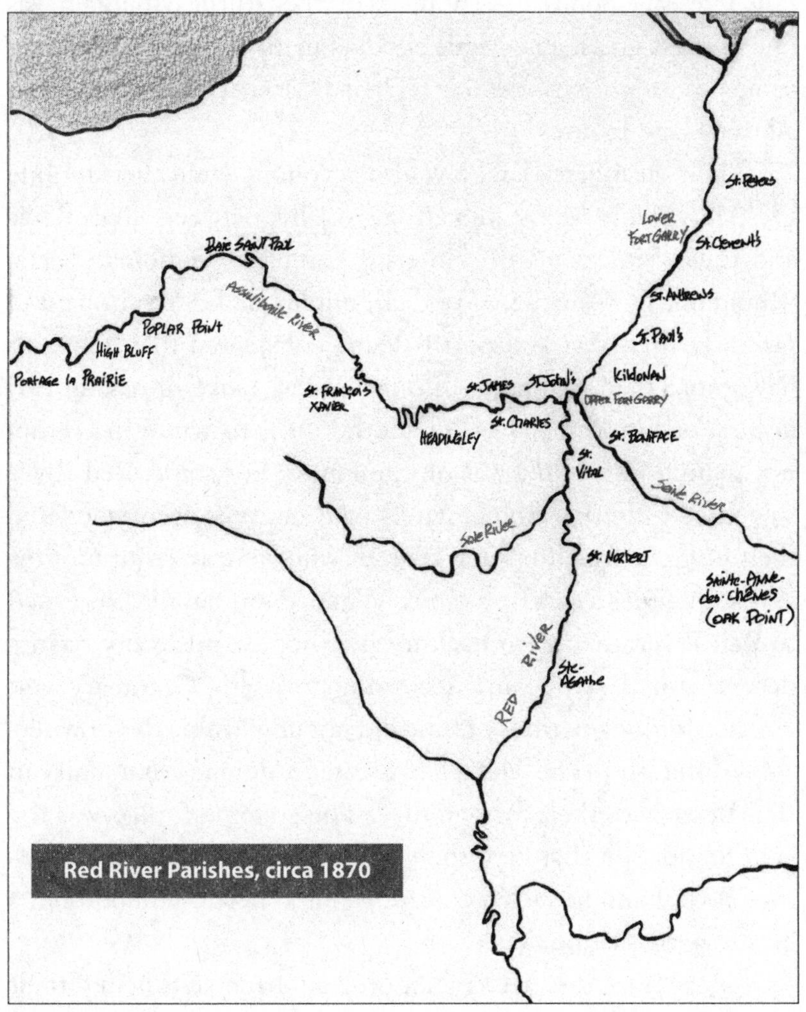

Red River Parishes, circa 1870

The two-mile area on either side of the Red and Assiniboine rivers was called the settlement belt. Most of the Métis *rangs* were within the settlement belt, but there were other lands in Red River that the Métis considered theirs. Some of their woodlots or hay privileges straddled the belt or were outside it altogether. By necessity, some of their lands were quite far away. These were the Métis rendezvous points and refuge areas—elevated points used to escape floods, grasshoppers or fires. Turtle Mountain was one of these areas. The Métis also had many fishing and hunting camps outside the settlement. Their customary law recognized all these land tenures.

Their customary land law also accommodated their mobile lifestyle. Many Métis moved seasonally between Red River and their rendezvous or wintering camps in Pembina, Turtle Mountain, Qu'Appelle, Wood Mountain, Lake Manitoba and places farther west and north. Many considered themselves to have more than one home. Louis Goulet spoke of having two homes, one in Red River and another in their wintering camp. For many Métis home was on the Plains. For some, Red River was their wintering home. Métis land customs accommodated their hunters, freighters and traders, who were away for months and sometimes years at a time. When these families returned to Red River, they went back to their homes, made any repairs necessary and settled in. According to Métis customary law, absence for long periods of time did not undermine their ownership of the land. The Métis had created a unique community in Red River with their own culture. The system of *rangs* was the land foundation that kept their families together and their culture alive. Land in such a culture is not a mere commodity in a business transaction.

Since 1816 the Métis Nation had been advancing their

land and resource claims as natives of the country. Lieutenant-Governor Archibald recognized this, writing:

> It is only because the French [Métis] . . . and their leaders treat the [land] question, not as one of business, but rather as one of Race, and Creed and Language and because they are unwilling that their people should form part of a mixed community, that they prefer having the lands to which they are entitled laid off in a block . . . The French [Métis], or their leaders, wish the lands to be so tied up, as to prevent them, at all events, for a generation, from passing out of the family of the original grantee.[2]

Today we would call these Aboriginal or Indigenous rights claims. Back in 1870 such claims to land were usually referred to as claims to "Indian title." The Métis made these claims long before they sent their delegates to Ottawa to negotiate the protection of their land and customary usage. The Métis believed that the land guarantees in the Manitoba Act protected all the lands they held at the time of the transfer in 1870, including the lands possessed by the traders and hunters who used their land as a base of operations, the lands the Métis held by peaceable occupation, by rights of common, their camps and refuge areas, and the 1.4 million new acres negotiated for the benefit of their children.

The lands for the children were particularly important because in 1870 over 60 per cent of the Métis population were children—that is, they were legal minors under the age of twenty-one. The Métis wanted these protections because if the children's lands were not near their parents', the central institution of the Métis Nation, the family, would be broken up and scattered.

The delegates who negotiated the Manitoba Act were concerned with five main issues: the amnesty, land protection, local control over land and resources, local representation in government and official bilingualism. In addition to the promises to secure land specifically set out in the Manitoba Act, Cartier provided three other land-related promises. The first was a promise to protect the lands claimed by the nomadic winterers and tripmen who regarded the Red River settlement as their home. The second was a promise of local control over the lands and resources, which Cartier promised would come by way of an order in council. The third was a promise that the regulations implementing the land "reserve, will be such as to meet the wishes of the Halfbreed residents."[3]

Canada ratified the negotiated terms when it enacted the Manitoba Act. The Provisional Government in Red River ratified them by a vote when Father Ritchot presented the terms on his return. In 1871 the Manitoba Act became part of the Canadian Constitution, which elevated the terms contained in the Manitoba Act to constitutionally protected promises.

The Métis Nation has always called the land provisions in ss. 31 and 32 their treaty, which was subsequently entrenched in the Manitoba Act:

> 31. And whereas, it is expedient, towards the extinguishment of the Indian Title to the lands in the Province, to appropriate a portion of such ungranted lands, to the extent of one million four hundred thousand acres thereof, for the benefit of the families of the half-breed residents, it is hereby enacted, that, under regulations to be from time to time made by the Governor General in Council, the Lieutenant Governor shall select such lots or tracts in such parts of the Province as he may

> deem expedient, to the extent aforesaid, and divide the same among the children of the half-breed heads of families residing in the Province at the time of the said transfer to Canada, and the same shall be granted to the said children respectively, in such mode and on such conditions as to settlement and otherwise as the Governor General in Council may from time to time determine.

Riel called it a treaty in 1885, and the Old Wolves made sure his words were reprinted in their book in 1935. Métis legal scholar Paul Chartrand, a commissioner on an influential report published by the Royal Commission on Aboriginal Peoples, called the negotiated terms in the Manitoba Act a treaty in his 1991 book *Manitoba's Métis Settlement Scheme of 1870*.[4] In the most important case that the Métis Nation has ever taken to the Supreme Court of Canada, the *Manitoba Metis Federation* case, the Métis argued that these two sections of the Manitoba Act were a treaty:

> [A] treaty was reached between the Crown in right of Canada and the Provisional Government and the people of the Red River colony. The parties exchanged solemn promises. The terms of the treaty are to be ascertained from the provisions of the Manitoba Act, the correspondence between Cartier and Ritchot, the statements made in the House of Commons by Macdonald and Cartier, and the record of the negotiations kept by Ritchot.[5]

One of the declarations the Manitoba Metis Federation asked from the court was "a declaration that there was a treaty made in 1870 between the Crown in right of Canada and the Provisional Government and the people of Red River."[6]

The Supreme Court of Canada was not prepared to go that far. They distinguished between the constitutional promise made in s. 31 of the Manitoba Act and a treaty. They looked at the "treaty-like history and character," said the promises were "no less fundamental than treaty promises," and that "like a treaty" they were adopted with the intention to create obligations and to reconcile the Métis community with the sovereignty of the Crown. The decision as to whether a negotiated agreement is a treaty never rests on what the Indigenous party to the agreement says. The Métis may have called it their treaty for over a century, but the Supreme Court of Canada gave it a new name: it was a "treaty-like promise."[7]

The benefit in the Métis treaty-like promise was land for settlement. Father Ritchot negotiated it. He believed it would take at least one generation to settle the Métis. That was why he wanted the land to go to the children, to make the land inalienable for long enough to create a "gradual regulated land settlement scheme" that would protect the land from the white speculators.

There was another provision in the Manitoba Act dealing with land protection: s. 32.[8] The Supreme Court held that this provision was not part of the "treaty-like promise" in s. 31 because it promised to protect the use and occupation of all landholders, not just the Métis. This provision must be understood in light of the fact that 85 per cent of the people in Red River were Métis. Still, the 15 per cent were enough to dismiss the claim that there were outstanding obligations to the Métis under s. 32 of the Manitoba Act. The Métis (and all other settlers) already in possession and eligible for s. 32 protection of their holdings were assured they would get their lands free. But the government made it difficult for the French Métis to actually get their s. 32 claims processed.

Louis Riel's mother, Julie, held lots 50 and 51 in the parish of St. Vital. Julie met all the requirements imposed by the policies, regulations and orders in council enacted under s. 32 of the Manitoba Act. She had established residence prior to July 15, 1870, she had been in continuous occupancy and she had fulfilled the cultivation requirements. Theoretically, her claim should have breezed through, just as the English Métis claims did. But it took nine years for her to obtain a patent for lot 51 and eighteen years for lot 50. No bureaucracy that takes nine to eighteen years to process a land claim gets a passing grade for efficiency.

Other pieces of evidence about Riel family claims remain inexplicable. One that is particularly puzzling is the signature on Joseph Riel's affidavit, which was signed with an *X* when he was eighteen. The priests and nuns had schooled all the Riel children, and Joseph was fully literate. He later became postmaster of St. Vital, and we have his journal and correspondence with some of the most important newspapers in Canada. He was legally a minor in 1875, but the affidavit and indeed the entire system was designed to be signed by or on behalf of a child applying for an allotment under s. 31 of the Manitoba Act, his share of the 1.4 million acres. Joseph should have signed it. Why is it signed with an *X*? If someone else was claiming it for him, it should still have had his signature or a statement as to who was signing on his behalf.

No one in the Riel family knows the answer to the mystery of Joseph Riel's *X* mark. But the story appears to be fairly typical. Many Métis report that they know none of the details of their ancestors' land applications. They generally know the story of the Métis dispossession from Red River. Most know their family's oral history, including their own dispossession story. But few have looked at or compiled the chain of documents in the long, sorry Métis land fraud.[9]

DOMINION OF CANADA. I. Joseph Riel
PROVINCE OF MANITOBA.
County of Provencher — of the Parish of St Vital in the County of Provencher in the Province of Manitoba, laborer make oath and say as follows:
Parish of St Vital.

1. I claim to be entitled to participate in the allotment and distribution of the 1,400,000 acres of land set apart for Half-breed children, pursuant to the Statutes in that behalf.

2. I was born on or about the fifth day of February A.D. 1857 at the Parish of St Vital in said Province; and am now of the full age of eighteen years

3. Louis Riel, a half-breed is my father
Julie Lagemodière, a French Canadian is my mother; my said father died ~~was the~~ previous to ~~head of a family resident~~ in the Parish of St Vital in the said Province, on the fifteenth day of July, A.D. 1870.

4. I was not the head of any family at the last named date and I have not made any claim other than the above in this or any other Parish, nor have I claimed or received as an Indian any annuity moneys from the Government of said Dominion.

^ the transfer, and I make the present claim as ~~a~~ half breed child who resides in

his
Joseph X Riel
mark

Sworn before me at the Parish and County aforesaid on the third day of July A.D. 1875, having been first read and explained in the French language to the said deponent, who seemed perfectly to understand the same, and affixed his mark in my presence.

Mathew Ryan
Commissioner.

Joseph Riel's Manitoba Act affidavit, signed with an *X* (*Teillet Family Papers*)

Everyone knew about the fraud; no one in government cared. Actually, it's more than that. They didn't care *and* they benefited personally from it.[10] No one in government acted promptly or fairly when Bishop Taché, Joseph Royal or leaders of the Métis Nation spoke or petitioned about the process. Part of the problem was an unwritten policy not to investigate or report fraud no matter who perpetrated the fraud. The don't-tell policy, long in play, was eventually written down in 1913. It meant that "patentees negotiating multiple sales of the land, or . . . agents claiming to act for persons they had never met" had official sanction to defraud the Métis.[11]

Canada made many promises that existing Métis landholdings would be protected. They promised that all "properties, rights and equities of every kind, as enjoyed under the Government of the Hudson's Bay Company will be continued" and in granting titles to land now occupied, "the most liberal policy will be pursued."[12] Later, Macdonald told Donald Smith to promise that "all Titles to land held by residents in peaceable possession will be confirmed" and reiterated that all would be administered under a "very liberal land policy."[13]

But Macdonald wanted the land to pass to "actual settlers," a.k.a the Ontario immigrants.[14] His choice tool to ensure the lands did not end up in Métis hands was delay. Delay was a strategy he employed in many situations and it often worked well for him. When the Manitoba Act came into effect in July 1870, Macdonald retained control over the lands and resources in Manitoba, so he kept jurisdiction in federal hands. The federal government could take its own sweet time in implementing the land protection provisions and the allocation of the lands for the children. And in this they were assisted by Charlie Mair and the Canadian Party, who were drumming up thousands of "actual settlers" from Ontario, with the first batch expected to arrive in the spring of 1871.

The passage of the Manitoba Act, 1870, was a master stroke. Passing the legislation gave the illusion—an illusion sustained for about five years—that the government was actually going to provide land for the Métis children and protect existing Métis lands and resources. The mere existence of the Manitoba Act, the reign of terror and the immigrants succeeded in keeping the "wild people" quiet until the Métis were swamped. Macdonald's plan worked.

The Métis have always maintained that Macdonald never intended to honour their treaty. That is the Old Wolves' story. It was 1909 when they started researching and collecting the historical documents to write their first history, and a large part of the book is the story of the Red River Resistance of 1869–70. The Old Wolves knew what they wanted to say about the broken promises in that first history book. In the appendix to the book, the committee inserted a piece by Louis Riel. It includes a short paragraph that tells the Métis story about what happened to the Red River Métis lands. Riel began by saying that the "Government had not properly fulfilled its obligations in the treaty with the Manitoba Métis." Then Riel provided a succinct version of the story. It is short and bitter, but not wrong:

> The Manitoba Métis never had any satisfaction. The Government neither protected them nor gave them justice. It oppressed them and it might be said, having made their country unlivable for them, distributed some land, delaying the granting of titles and patents so long, that they were either forced to sell their landed property at half or quarter-price, or were even reduced to the extremity of abandoning all.[15]

MÉTIS LAND RESERVES

The Métis wanted their land in reserves. Except for the Métis, no one liked the idea of Métis land reserves. The very idea was said to be an "improvident" use of land.[16] Chief Justice Wood was somewhat less restrained. He called Métis reserves a "curse to the country."[17] Given that the government would soon grant half a million acres in a large reserve to the Mennonites, the objection to Métis reserves was clearly not about the size of the blocks. The Mennonite land grant set aside land for their exclusive use. So, the objection to Métis reserves was not about setting aside land for a separate group. The Mennonites spoke a foreign tongue. So, the objection to Métis reserves was not about language. The obvious conclusion is that the objection was solely about who was getting the land—the Métis. Was the decision to deny Métis reserves racist, or was it revenge for the Red River Resistance? Likely it was a lethal combination of the two. The Orange Lodge and the Canadian Party didn't think the Métis should exist at all. They shouldn't live in Red River, they shouldn't be allotted land, and they definitely shouldn't get land in large blocks.

From the beginning the government, the Canadian Party, the immigrants, the bureaucrats and the speculators worked to take the land away from the Red River Métis employing means that were not always within the boundaries of the law. Some (the immigrants) wanted the land for themselves. Some (the Canadian Party and other speculators) wanted to make money. Some (the governments of Manitoba and Canada) wanted to get the land into the hands of anyone other than the Métis. The "screamers from Ontario" were outraged that the Métis lands might be turned "over to Popery."[18]

Both federal political parties disliked the grant of 1.4 million acres to the children of the Red River Métis. The difference between Macdonald's Conservatives and Mackenzie's Liberals was only that the Liberals were upfront about how much they hated it. Mackenzie liked to pose as an honest broker, so when the Liberals were in power, they implemented orders in council to ensure the land did not stay in Métis hands. Macdonald made no objections for years—fifteen years to be exact. He didn't rouse himself to defend the Métis land grant until 1885.

In the negotiations with the Red River delegates during the spring of 1870, Macdonald and Cartier put land on the table immediately. Macdonald gave land because it was the one thing he had in abundance. He could afford to give it away. Ritchot's idea was to give the Métis a chance to settle on land before the expected influx of Ontario immigrants. But that was Ritchot's plan, not Macdonald's. Ritchot's plan was only possible if land was legally in Métis hands before the immigrants arrived and if it could be protected from sale for a couple of generations. Macdonald's plan was to get the land into the hands of the immigrants as soon as possible.

Until 1876 most of the Red River Métis still lived under the illusion that the promised lands would be provided. They were enthusiastic about confirming their existing landholdings and forming committees to select and divide the 1.4 million acres of children's land according to their own customs and usages. They began to choose their lands both inside and outside the settlement belt.[19]

The Métis Nation was determined to protect its communal interests against the expected immigrants. All the parishes held meetings and nominated land selection committees. They met in large assemblies to discuss their land selections. They staked out their preferred lands and they published their claims in the newspapers.[20] In June 1871 the Métis of St. Charles, St. Boniface and St. Vital, St. François Xavier, Sainte-Anne-des Chênes, Lake Manitoba and St. Norbert all placed public land claim notices in *Le Metis*.[21]

They chose lands *en bloc* and referred to their claims as "reserves." The Métis at St. Charles posted a public notice to claim a reserve at Rivière aux Îlets-de-Bois. The St. François

Xavier Métis posted a claim to a reserve on the Assiniboine River. The Métis of Lake Manitoba posted a claim for a reserve at St. Laurent, and the St. Boniface and St. Vital Métis posted a claim on the Red River.[22] *Le Métis* reported Métis resolutions to protect their exclusive rights to their woodlot reserves.[23]

The aim of the Métis in making their claims was to stay together and not be too far from their old settlements. They didn't choose too much land and they didn't monopolize the best lands in the province. But they wanted to have their lands *en bloc*, and their understanding was that allocations for their families would be chosen from within those blocs. Out at Sainte-Anne-des-Chênes, Norbert Nolin posted claims for two separate reserves, which were situated next to his father's, Augustin Nolin's, claims.[24] Pierre Falcon and the Nolins published notices of their claims in almost every issue of *Le Métis* from January to July 1872. Pascal Breland told the government representative that the Métis would not be pleased with any arrangement that did not give them their lands *en bloc* for themselves entirely.

The blocs would keep families together and permit the Métis to continue their customary land practices of use, possession and inheritance. They elected their own people on to committees to select their reserves. They planned to divide them among the children of the families within that block. Then the local legislature would have the authority to pass laws to ensure the continuance of these lands and resources in the Métis families.

Lieutenant-Governor Archibald confirmed that he intended to honour the reserve selections made by the Métis.[25] But then Ottawa arbitrarily decided that individual lots would be drawn in a lottery. The idea of Métis bloc lands was snuffed out. Family lands might be near each other or hundreds of miles apart; all would be determined by the luck of the draw. The lottery was surgical in its cold application. The decision to cut Métis landholdings into lucky pieces lacked the surgeon's intention to wound slightly with a view to eventual healing. There was no intention to heal in the land lottery. It truly was death by a thousand cuts.

The lottery began in late February 1873. The lieutenant-governor began to draw the lots at a rate of sixty per hour. With an estimated six thousand allotments to draw, the entire lottery should have taken about one hundred hours. It took seven years. Procrastination, delay, deliberate manipulation, political intervention, bungling—take your pick of these terms to describe what happened, but it's hard to imagine how a lottery that should have taken at best a month took seven years to complete.[26]

Meanwhile Ottawa was undermining Métis claims. The evidence supports the suggestion that it was deliberate. One of Macdonald's early orders ensured that the Ontario immigrants had the right to settle wherever they found "vacant" land and their claims would be protected. Charlie Mair formed an association to assist and underwrite the costs of Ontario immigrants settling in the North-West Territories. The first lot of fifteen hundred immigrants arrived in Red River in January 1872. It is worth noting that no one else was pressing Ontarians to immigrate. Ontarians were talking about it, but they were not making immediate moves. Schultz and his men in Red River set about turning Manitoba into a "field in which to feed and fatten Canadian Government pets and robbers."[27] The fight for control of the bureaucracy and provincial government began.

Schultz's newspaper, *The Manitoba News-Letter*, and later *The Manitoba Liberal*, ran a side business as an unofficial lands office in Winnipeg. The papers posted notices telling new immigrants to come to them for information. *Le Métis* called it the "office of Sedition."[28] Schultz's newspaper provided crucial information for immigrants. Only there could an Ontario immigrant learn the location of the very best "vacant" lands suitable for settlement. In the spring of 1871, it most helpfully directed some new immigrants to "vacant" lands at Rivière aux Îlets-de-Bois.

The Métis had been occupying and using Rivière aux Îlets-de-Bois since the 1830s. They had staked it and used it as a woodlot and a winter foraging area. They posted claims to the land in their public notices. The immigrants found the "vacant" land to their liking. They removed the Métis stakes, staked out their own, set themselves down and stayed. The Métis warned them to quit, but they were "armed immigrants" and as such could ignore the Métis protests.[29] The Métis could no longer take up arms to protect their rights, especially not during the reign of terror. Macdonald's new order in council worked hand in glove with Schultz's careful directions to the immigrants as to which lands were "vacant." By this means, squatting now prevailed over customary Métis usage. The immigrants quickly renamed *their* new river after their own historic resistance, the Boyne.

That was the pattern. The forced relocation went on for over fifteen years. Law, land speculators, the army and the armed immigrants worked in sync. It was an effective four-pronged assault.

The land speculators knew how to circumvent the law. They had known since at least the 1860s. They developed workarounds using perfectly legal tools—depositions, affidavits, assignments and powers of attorney. The land speculators trolled through the parishes pretending to be lawyers and buying up assignments.

It should come as no surprise that Schultz and Donald Smith were the biggest land speculators. The chief justice of the Manitoba Court of Queen's Bench was aiding, abetting, participating in and profiting from the fraud. Chief Justice

Wood and his sons had a sweet land scheme going. They processed the children's claims in batches with "an almost utter recklessness and disregard of the interests of the Court's wards."[30] The result, of course, was that the children received much less than the market value for their lands.[31] It was particularly convenient to have a family business that included a chief justice. A man with that kind of power could and did sweep any pesky illegalities under the rug. When a commission of inquiry finally investigated and reported on the practices of the court in 1881, counsel appointed by the attorney general described the court's "pernicious" practices as the "creature of the learned Chief Justice."[32] T. Beverley Robertson summed it all up as a series of "monstrous abuses."[33]

It didn't seem to matter what the Métis did or said or what papers they filed or what hoops they jumped through. The land agents declared that Métis reserve claims were vacant lands and thus available for immigrants and speculators. The timber on their woodlots and the hay from their hay privilege was being stolen. All this was taking place over their many protests and petitions.[34]

During the negotiations of the Manitoba Act, Father Ritchot had shown Cartier and Macdonald a map of Métis lands, and he fully explained how the Métis land system worked. He explained that some lands were not inhabited but marked only by posts, lines, little houses or otherwise. He needed to explain that the Métis land use was a coherent system that could not be sliced and diced into convenient squares. The location of the *rangs* on the river provided land and water for their homes and gardens. The back of the lots provided wood for fuel and hay for their livestock. The two parts could not be severed without destroying the Métis system. This was the customary land usage the Métis wanted protected.

So, from the beginning Macdonald and Cartier had known about the Métis customary land-use system and had promised local control.[35] That was the purpose of the negotiated terms in the Manitoba Act. If the act didn't protect Métis customary usage, then arguably it was a deception, because the terms implementing the act were being used to defeat the constitutional promise.[36]

Ottawa was primed to impose a brand-new land system based on the American township model. It was a system of large square blocks with provision for road allowances. Ultimately, the system was not designed for people and community, because the people lived too far apart. It was designed for the new commercial agricultural economy, for capital investment, for the marketplace and for the expediency provided by straight lines.

There is probably no faster way to destroy a customary land system than by imposing new boundary lines on the land. The new lines change how people relate to the land and to each other. The new square-block system took no account of access to water or natural land formations. The Métis Nation's customary land use incorporated the rivers into their landholdings. The new survey system imposed large squares everywhere except for the settlement belt along the Red and Assiniboine Rivers, where the long, narrow river lots already existed. Even there, it cut into the hay lands. While it is true that most Métis in Red River lived along those two rivers, many were settled on the other rivers, such as the Seine and the Sale. The children's lands, the 1.4 million acres, would also be in the new squares.

For all the attempts by the Métis to quite literally hold the line and preserve a place for the Métis Nation on the land, they had only delayed things. The survey they stopped on October 11, 1869, began again.

THE ADHESION TO TREATY #3

The idea of asking for lands *en bloc* was not restricted to the Métis in Red River. The Métis in Rainy Lake also sought to have their lands protected in a reserve. On September 10, 1875, a Métis delegation led by Old Nick Chatelain met with John Stoughton Dennis, seeking to adhere to Treaty #3.[37] These Métis were not eligible for land under the Manitoba Act because they were resident outside the boundaries of Manitoba. Their only option to obtain land *en bloc* was to join their Ojibwa cousins in treaty.

The Rainy Lake Métis wanted to maintain their own collective on lands they controlled. They successfully negotiated a separate reserve, and on September 12, 1875, they signed an adhesion to Treaty #3.[38] After the signing Canada had second thoughts and decided that it would not approve separate "Half Breed Bands."[39] The Indian agent was instructed to inform them that they were to enter Little Eagle's band. Three reserves were laid out for Chatelain's band to be held in common with Little Eagle's band, all under the name of the Couchiching Band.[40]

Lieutenant-Governor Morris set out Canada's policy with respect to the Métis. They could choose to be recognized legally as either white or Indian.[41] There was no option to be Métis. By entering into Treaty #3, they became "Indians." Despite their registration as "Indians" and members of the Couchiching Band, they were always known and referred to as the "Halfbreeds" who continued to live mainly on the two reserves originally set aside for them.[42]

To this day, the "Half-breed Adhesion to Treaty #3" remains the only treaty south of the sixtieth parallel that specifically included a Métis group, provided them with the same benefits Indian bands received, and promised them a separate reserve.

COLLUSION AND DELAY

Most Métis stayed in Red River for five years before they gave up and began to leave. They had survived the reign of terror and tried their best to get their lands affirmed in the new system. While Lieutenant-Governor Archibald was in office, there had been some optimism and there seemed to be a chance. Archibald recommended an area of sixty townships to be laid out in the parts of the province the Métis desired. He knew the Métis wanted their lands in reserves and he knew they wanted them to be protected from alienation. He wanted to affirm the reserve selections made and publicly notified by the Métis.

But Macdonald had no intention of allowing the Métis to tie up blocks of land. So, he sidelined Archibald. The Canadian Party claimed Archibald was too sympathetic to the Métis, and he had dared to shake Riel's hand in thanks for the Métis role in stopping the Fenian raid. So, Archibald had to go. In May 1872 he announced his resignation. The Métis had found Archibald's course of action reasonably fair despite his inability to staunch the flow of immigrants or stop them from squatting on Métis lands. They put the blame for the land problems not on Archibald, but on the Canadian Party, which they described as "the party of vengeance" and "a miserable coterie of fanatics."[43]

The government had many excuses for its failure to get the land to the children. They acknowledged delays but maintained they were justifiable, even reasonable. Explaining away fifteen to twenty years of delay takes some doing. But the delays suited Macdonald's purposes. Over almost twenty years the government delayed for any number of reasons—dithering about what decision to make, and then making and reversing decisions. That happened often and years passed by. There were also inevitable delays for elections and changes of government and lieutenant-governors. More years passed.

By 1873 the Dominion Lands Office in Winnipeg was run by Donald Codd, a man who despised the Métis, used his office to exact revenge and didn't speak any French. Under his leadership the office was anxious to assist the newcomers in their settlement. The same office wrote that Métis claims were considered weak, "not entitled to any consideration at all," and any review of Métis complaints by the Department of Justice should be immediately stopped, the concern being that such a review might encourage claims to "pour in from every direction."[44] This appears to be the bureaucracy simply saying, "Don't investigate our work; we are subverting Métis claims as planned."

The Métis didn't go quietly. They didn't just fold their tents and silently steal away. They tried to press their claims. Canada's response was to change the law and make it illegal for Métis to file disputes against Canada in the court of claims set up to resolve land disputes. Canada also changed the date of occupancy from March 9 to July 15. This was the date on which the Métis had to prove occupancy in the settlement in order to advance a claim. Changing the date seems innocuous, except that July was when many Métis were out on the Plains, either hunting or freighting.[45] Another law redefined the children eligible for claims by eliminating those children whose parents were out of the province freighting and hunting on July 15, 1870.[46]

More laws, regulations and orders were to come—many more. New regulations removed "unimproved land" (read "much of the Métis lands") from river frontage claims entitled to consideration.[47] Such claims had to be occupied "in accordance with the custom of the country" before January 15, 1870. But the definition of the "custom of the country" in the order in council was not the actual custom of the country. The Métis custom was to stake out lands, most of which were only surveyed if there was a dispute. But the new definition re-envisioned the custom as one where everyone used surveyors and the Hudson's Bay Company had recorded the claims. Only a fraction of those in Red River had done this. The new law was a sweeping repudiation of everything Father Ritchot had fought for in his negotiations with Macdonald and Cartier.

Métis hay and timber claims, though the Métis had long used and occupied these lands, were denied. Their use and occupation were never sufficient. Their improvements were never valuable enough. The requirements for sufficiency of occupation went ever higher. Now one had to have a house and five acres under cultivation where there was no Hudson's Bay Company survey.[48]

Métis claims were obliterated. By the end of December 1877, at Rat River, eighty-four of ninety-three claims were rejected, and they were not allowed to clear their titles with the scrip that had been distributed.[49] The official response was that if such claims were granted, there would be little land left.[50] The reason was always staring them in the face: The Métis were not wanted. They were in the way. They had to go.

Somewhere along the line even the Catholic priests gave up and decided the endless fight to keep the Métis on the land in Manitoba was not worth the effort. And now there were other French Catholic people who could fill in as their flock; the Métis weren't the only ones available. Riel had accused Bishop Taché of abandoning the Métis in 1874, and if it wasn't exactly accurate then, it turned out to be an accurate prophecy by the end of the decade.

Schultz and the Canadian Party took control of Red River on six fronts. Their army had already taken physical control during the reign of terror. Within a few years they had bureaucratic, political and legal control by their elevation into a police force, as magistrates, as Crown counsel and as the judiciary. Their propaganda controlled Ontario, the new immigrants in Red River and the Canadian government. Finally, they took control of the land. For this the Canadian Party brought in a second army, their armed Ontario immigrants. They brought in their own people to supplant the Métis, whose political and national sympathies were not properly aligned with their goal of Anglo-Saxon dominion. *The Globe* was in full support:

> Ontario had laboured long and hard to acquire that fertile region, and now that it was within her grasp, she must see to it that the land was peopled and settled by a population liberal and intelligent, and in sympathy with her own language and traditions. As Dr. Schultz had hinted there was a determined effort being made to import another element into the population, whose political and national sympathies would be a bar to progress, and to the extension of a great Anglo-Saxon Dominion across the continent.[51]

You have to give the Canadian Party one thing: they weren't hiding their agenda. It was right there in print. The Canadian Party wanted the lands and resources of Red River. They had already cleared out the Hudson's Bay Company and they were successfully pushing out many of the Métis.

CHAPTER 21

THE DIASPORA

Gilbert McMicken ran an undercover operation for Sir John A. Macdonald. During the 1860s his efforts were concentrated on the Fenian organizations in the United States. He was appointed Dominion Police commissioner in 1869, and in September 1871 he was sent to Winnipeg to establish several federal government offices. In addition to his role as Dominion Police commissioner, he served as the agent of the Dominion Lands Branch and assistant receiver-general in Manitoba. He was also appointed the immigration agent and a member of the Intercolonial Railway Commission. With these many offices to hand, he played a major role in the disposition of Métis land claims.

McMicken arrived in Red River fully supportive of the Ontario position on Riel and the Métis. His recommendations caused many of the delays in land distribution, and he was long suspected of inappropriate involvement in Métis land transactions. He inserted himself easily into the Ontario Anglo-Saxon takeover of Red River and reported to Macdonald for years on the results of his endeavours to pressure the Métis to leave. In 1873 he wrote:

> The Métis are very uneasy at present. They are expressing themselves as greatly dissatisfied with the Canadian Government. Chiefly in regard to the lands not being given to them and alleging that injustice has been done to Riel. That good faith has not been kept with them in respect to him. There has been something said about a number of them having intention of moving up on the Saskatchewan and the Plains of the northwest.[1]

The Red River Métis diaspora began in the 1870s. Many of the people moved out onto the Plains, and from then on they would winter at Wood Mountain, Touchwood Hills, Cypress Hills, Qu'Appelle or other wintering sites in Saskatchewan, Alberta or Montana. Some of the departing Métis families went north into the boreal forest.[2] Some went east to join Chatelain in the Lake of the Woods/Rainy Lake area.[3] Many went to the South Saskatchewan River.

Métis settlement, Wood Mountain, 1873 (*Library and Archives Canada C-081758*)

The reign of terror and the broken promised amnesty forced almost one thousand Métis to flee. That was the first wave of the diaspora. It took away approximately 8 per cent of the population of Red River—no small number of people to leave the settlement. Many Métis winterers decided that Red River was now a violent place to be avoided. Their absence affected Red River's economy. If you were Métis, especially if you were a vocal Métis nationalist, Red River in the early 1870s was a bad place to live. It wasn't a good place to visit either. Métis leaders were in exile, and their people now started to join them—exiled from Manitoba.

Each wave of Métis emigration grew larger. The first wave was from 1871 to 1876; the second and larger wave was from 1877 to 1880. The largest wave was from 1881 to 1884. The total number who fled the violence and the land swindle was more than four thousand Métis. Many thought, at least at first, it was a temporary absence. Those who stayed faced the new civic powers in Winnipeg.

MARIE TROTTIER

Marie Trottier provides a sad early example of how Métis women would be treated in the newly installed Canadian courts. Marie was a witness in an abortion charge against a local doctor, somewhat ironically bearing the name Dr. Good. It was 1881 and she was so ill that she had to be carried into court on a stretcher. According to police testimony Trottier had been pressured by her partner to purchase an abortifacient from Dr. Good. She was seven months pregnant. After miscarrying, she began to hemorrhage. When her own doctor refused to treat her, a friend informed the police, who subsequently laid charges against Dr. Good.

Dr. Good brought seven doctors to testify that Trottier was an immoral woman. One wonders how one indigent Métis woman could have possibly known or even come into contact with seven doctors. The court never questioned this strange volume of character evidence. The judge concluded that the good doctor had not provided an abortifacient to Marie Trottier. Dr. Good would remain, in the eyes of the public, good. Marie was ordered to leave town within forty-eight hours.[4]

THE SOUTH SASKATCHEWAN

Where do you go when Red River is denied to you? That's what the Métis now asked themselves. The need to go was apparent now. It was becoming increasingly clear that there was no place for the Métis as a nation in Red River. If they stayed, they faced a brutal, hateful regime that would not let them in and would barely let them live. Some claimed new identities as French, which allowed them to hide in the French parishes. Others became English and kept their heads down in the English parishes. Very few of those who stayed in Red River publicly retained their Métis identity. It was easier to identify as a member of the Métis Nation elsewhere.

The Saskatchewan beckoned. That is what the Métis called the lands on the South Saskatchewan River in what is now the district of Prince Albert.[5] There, the Métis were far away from the hatred in Red River, and there was plenty of land. They knew this land and had hunted and lived there for decades.

Since at least the 1840s, the Métis had set up their *nick-ah-wahs* (wintering camps or *hivernants*) at Wood Mountain, Touchwood Hills and Cypress Hills. The Métis hunted in the area around what is now the city of Saskatoon throughout the 1850s. They tented in summer and built small winter cabins near the elbow of the south branch of the Saskatchewan. They traded at Fort Carlton and occasionally went to Red River.

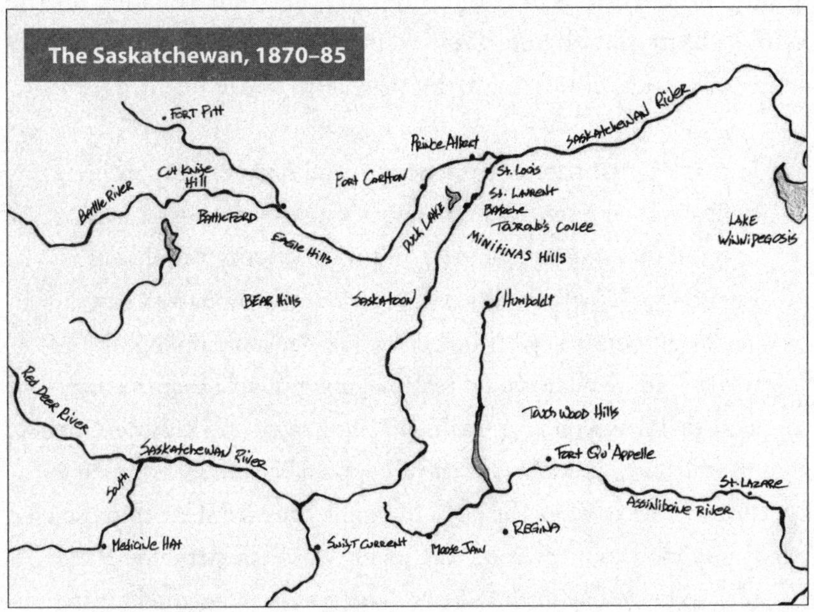

The Saskatchewan, 1870–85

By the late 1860s Métis wintering camps on the Saskatchewan were evolving beyond seasonal use. The camp at Petite-Ville later became better known as St. Laurent, an area that included Batoche, St. Louis, St. Laurent de Grandin and Tourond's Coulee. In 1866 Patrice Fleury moved to Batoche with a number of Métis families from Red River. They settled at the St. Laurent settlement and began farming and freighting. In the early 1870s more Métis hunters and winterers began to settle on the South Saskatchewan.

The troubles in Red River and a smallpox epidemic in the wintering camps convinced the Métis of the need to look for more permanent residences. On December 31, 1871, a group of Métis who were wintering near the St. Laurent de Grandin mission met to choose a site for a new community.[6] The decision was not made lightly or quickly. The patriarchs spoke eloquently about the need to work together, give up their reliance on the buffalo hunt and change their way of life. The Métis patriarchs knew of a good country for the people to settle in: St. Laurent.

> Isidore Dumont dit Aicawpow: [He] had been all his life a prairie hunter. He could remember when vast herds of buffalo covered the prairies from the foot of the Rocky Mountains to Fort Garry. Now they were only to be found in the Saskatchewan, and as the country got peopled the buffalo would disappear. He was an old man and could tell the young people that the decision they had come to was good, they must . . . cultivate the ground . . . He knew a tract of country between Carlton and Prince Albert which he thought would answer their purpose, it was good country, good soil, plenty of wood for building and fuel and wild hay in abundance. The grasses were good for the horses and the spot not too far from the buffalo country.

> Louison Letendre dit Batoche, Sr: The young people could not lead the same lives as their fathers. The country is opening out to the stranger and the Métis must . . . not be crushed in the struggle for existence. What Ecapor [Isidor Dumont dit Aicawpow] said of the country was true, he knew the place and he thought it the best situation for their colony.

> Jean Dumont dit Chakasta: He agreed with all that had been spoken. The Métis must join together like brothers and work like men, he was seventy-five years old and had seen great changes in the country, but the greatest of all was at home. The buffalo would disappear . . . They will do well to til the soil and

> make a home for themselves amongst their friends . . . where his friends went he would follow.[7]

So there the Métis settled, just as they had at Red River, in *rangs* fronting the river, and they took up small-scale farming. By 1872 there were 250 Métis families living at St. Laurent. As word got back to Red River, more Métis arrived from St. Norbert, St. François Xavier and Baie St. Paul.

The situation on the South Saskatchewan in the 1870s was an eerie echo of Red River before the Resistance. The Hudson's Bay Company was still a force to be reckoned with. The Company was the only store and the only source of a job or money. The Company hired Métis as freighters and still bought their pemmican. But the Company was also a new beast. It was still a fur-trading corporation, but it had other interests now, including real estate. So, when the Métis decided to establish a settlement close to one of the Company's main posts, the chief factor's support would have been important.

Lawrence Clarke was the chief factor for the Company in Prince Albert. Clarke was a two-faced Janus. Some people had his measure. Edgar Dewdney, the lieutenant-governor and Indian commissioner, certainly didn't trust him, and the Qu'Appelle Métis said Clarke had "fine words and flatteries," the better to "deceive" afterwards.[8] Unfortunately, Gabriel Dumont and the Métis in St. Laurent didn't see through Clarke until much too late.

Clarke gave his support for the Métis' choice to settle in the vicinity. Having a permanent community providing a secure source of freighters and pemmican was a win-win for the Company. A growing Métis population would increase competition for freighting, which would allow Clarke to drive down wages. Clarke expected the new labour force would replace two-thirds of the permanent staff with short-term contract labour and thereby save the Company "by the lowest calculation two thousand Pounds sterling per annum."[9] By 1874 the Company was paying its Métis freighters and hunters only in goods at inflated cost, sometimes jacked up by as much as 100 per cent.

Clarke was also working with Donald Smith to "avoid the necessity of again trusting to French halfbreeds."[10] This was retaliation for the Métis on the La Loche brigade abandoning four boats of goods in Grand Rapids to assist their nation during the Red River Resistance. Smith and Clarke resolved to cut out the small boats, and they started to freight goods from Fort Carlton to La Loche. When the SS *Northcote* arrived at Carlton House in 1874, it put the La Loche brigade out of business. The Métis began to sink under the weight of the Hudson's Bay Company's rule.

It was worse for the freighters than the hunters. The hunters could take the meat to Red River or they could just keep it for their own food. This gave the Métis some leverage against Clarke. But the growing scarcity of the buffalo scared them all. The Métis relied on the buffalo for their major source of protein, and the Company's northern fur-trade routes still ran on pemmican.

To make matters worse, the Company was also the law. Technically, the South Saskatchewan was governed by the North-West Council and the lieutenant-governor. But both had their headquarters a long way away in Winnipeg.[11] Despite its name, the North-West Council concentrated on Indian treaty-making and otherwise paid little attention to the North-West. There was no government, and the only way of administering Canadian laws was via the Hudson's Bay Company, which meant that Lawrence Clarke, as chief factor for Fort Carlton, was the magistrate for the South Saskatchewan. Sound familiar? It should. It was the same system that had been in place in Red River prior to the Provisional Government of 1869–70.

THE LAWS OF ST. LAURENT

Canada had asserted its sovereignty in the North-West but still had little idea of what and whom it had sovereignty over. The assertion of sovereignty meant that Canadian law was in effect in the North-West. That was the theory. On the ground there was no Canadian law. No one knew what the Canadian laws were, no one referred to them and no one enforced them. Clarke might be the official representative of Canadian law in Fort Carlton, but the Company enforced laws selectively, usually when there was a transgression against its interests.

The Métis didn't initially see this as a problem because they had their own laws, the Laws of the Prairie. The Métis Nation Laws of the Prairie were adopted with accompanying ceremonies. The ceremonies took place at a gathering of the people on the hunts, in Red River and in St. Laurent. The leadership took an oath before a priest to act in good faith and according to good conscience. They swore on the Bible to abide by and enforce their laws. Their first codified laws were the Laws of the Hunt, and the existence of that code was well known.[12] The Laws of the Prairie also included codes adopted throughout the North-West, such as the Red River Code (1869), the Qu'Appelle Code (1873) and the Laws of St. Laurent (1873).[13]

None of this law-making was done secretly or in defiance of Canadian law. In fact, wishing to be seen as loyal Canadians, the Métis of Qu'Appelle promptly informed Lieutenant-Governor Morris that they had formed a governing council in Qu'Appelle.

They acted to fill a legal vacuum because, as far as they could see, there were no laws in place. So, they said, "We make a law, and that law is strong, as it is supported by the majority." They sent messengers and received votes of support from "all the Métis of the North-West."[14]

The Qu'Appelle Métis also expressed great anxiety about how, in making a treaty at Red River, "the people of Red River being our own people," were maltreated. Sadly, they knew they would be treated the same. "Bright promises" were made but broken. More specifically, they noted that Schultz and Dennis, the main instigators of the reign of terror, had achieved good positions "in order to give them a chance of annoying the people of Red River." Finally, they asked for a general pardon for Riel and the other principal men, and noted that even in 1873 it was still too dangerous in Winnipeg for Métis to appear "without being molested and ill-treated by strangers and also by soldiers."

All of the Métis knew the Laws of the Hunt, but the codes that began to appear in 1869 were more sophisticated. With the Métis diaspora from Red River, it is quite likely that the Red River Code formed the template for the Qu'Appelle Code and the Laws of St. Laurent. George Woodcock, in his biography of Gabriel Dumont, credits the priests in St. Laurent with the idea of a governing council and the laws.[15] There it is again—the belief that all ideas about governance and law, anything seen to be civilized, are to be attributed to the priests or to outsider men. Despite all the evidence to the contrary, especially the Métis history of the Laws of the Prairie, the baseline belief was that Métis were not sophisticated or civilized enough to come up with such ideas. Woodcock acknowledged that Dumont was the leader, but he seemed to assume that because Dumont did not read or write, he could not have come up with the idea for the Laws of St. Laurent.

Most people who gain experience with Indigenous people develop a deep respect for the knowledge and memories of those who live in an oral culture. Even today it is possible to witness the near-perfect recall of men and women who recite complicated agreements that had not been looked at for months or years. They remember the language and details far better than those who rely on the written word. They are tolerant of the poor memory skills of those who live in reliance on writing, flick their fingers at papers, smile, and urge that the conversation be written down—for those dependent on written words that is, not for them. They have no need to write it down. With great accuracy they remember what has been said, when, who said it and often where it can be located in the document they cannot read.

So, the idea that the Métis in Red River or Qu'Appelle or St. Laurent needed the priests to imagine a governing council or laws is condescending to say the least. By 1873 the Métis had a long history of self-government and their Laws of the Prairie. It seems more likely that Gabriel Dumont dictated the Laws of St. Laurent to the priest. Dumont was a chief captain of the hunt, charged for years with enforcing the Laws of the Hunt. He was in Red River during the Resistance, so he would have known the Red River Code. One can imagine him flicking his fingers at the papers, smiling and suggesting the priest write it down so the priest would remember. Dumont would have had no problem dictating the terms of the Laws of St. Laurent. He spoke seven languages. Memory, words and ideas—even legal ideas—were not challenging for him. Since most of the Métis, including Dumont, could not read, the oral version of the Laws of St. Laurent, spoken to the people in a large public meeting solemnized by ceremony, was far more important than a written version most had no need of and would never look at.

On March 10, 1873, the North-West Council in Winnipeg resolved that the criminal laws in force in the rest of Canada would now apply in the North-West Territories. The council appointed several justices of the peace, usually Hudson's Bay Company officers. Lawrence Clarke was appointed for Carlton. Those justices of the peace were in office for a full year before the North-West Council acknowledged that they didn't know the law. If the justices of the peace were ignorant of Canadian laws, it seems safe to suggest that the people would not know of them either.

This was the gap the Qu'Appelle and St. Laurent Métis were trying to fill by enacting their own laws. The St. Laurent Métis met in a public assembly on December 10, 1873, in their winter camp. They elected a council of eight with Gabriel Dumont as president. As in Red River in 1869, they took an oath to act honestly and to support their president.[16] The reaction from Canadian law enforcement was anything but supportive. Lieutenant-Governor Morris was emphatic that the laws of England were in force in the North-West and there was no other council than the North-West Council, which sat in Winnipeg.

Lawrence Clarke, the chief factor of the Hudson's Bay Company at Fort Carlton and the local justice of the peace, clearly had his nose out of joint. He made it his mission to undermine the Laws of St. Laurent, in particular a section called "Laws for the Prairie and Hunting." These laws regulated when the buffalo hunt would commence in April and strictly forbid anyone from leaving for the hunt before the fixed date. There were penalties for breaking these laws—fines, equipment confiscation or both.

The laws were designed as a conservation measure and to protect access to the herd for everyone in the community.

The first violators of the Laws for the Prairie and Hunting were acting under the directions of a Hudson's Bay Company employee named Peter Ballendine. In reality the order came from Lawrence Clarke. In the spring of 1875, Ballendine's group left for the hunt before the fixed date. Gabriel Dumont reacted to the violation quickly. He led an armed party to stop Ballendine's group and informed them that they could join the Métis hunt and the matter would be forgotten. Otherwise, there would be a penalty. Ballendine and friends were having none of it. They would not submit to the authority of the St. Laurent Métis Council. Dumont confiscated their equipment and carts, imposed a twenty-five-dollar fine and promptly left for the spring hunt.

Clarke complained to Lieutenant-Governor Morris and practically demanded a protective force. Morris sent for the North-West Mounted Police, and in August fifty Mounties arrived to investigate the Ballendine incident. Major-General Edward Selby-Smith found, contrary to rumours, that the "mighty Half-Breed hunter named Gabriel Dumont"[17] had no pretension to undermine Dominion authority. The Mounties, the lieutenant-governor and the secretary of state all knew that Clarke had engineered the entire incident. But they didn't stop Clarke from charging, trying and fining Dumont and his men.

Dumont and his council knew nothing of Clarke's role. But the incident undermined the St. Laurent Council and also destroyed the Métis attempt to implement conservation measures to protect the buffalo. Clarke's next move was to send out professionals to hunt buffalo. The meat was appropriated to the Company stores and then sold to their newest customers: the police detachments now stationed at Fort Carlton and Duck Lake. It was another win-win for Clarke. The loss of Métis hunting rules didn't mean Canadian laws of conservation were put in place. It encouraged Clarke's men to leave for the hunt earlier than the Métis. What followed for the Métis was famine.

Canada's only act of governance was to stop Métis self-government. But there was no other government in the North-West to fill the gap. Canada was like a dog in the manger. It didn't govern the North-West, but it would not allow the Métis to do so. This was not good governance. It was exactly what the Métis had fought about in Red River. The government was hundreds of miles away and appointed by men even farther away. The facade of governance was what it was. It didn't exist on the ground.

The Métis who were on the North-West Council—Pascal Breland and later Pierre Delorme and James McKay—did nothing for the South Saskatchewan Métis. That's not to say they worked against the South Saskatchewan Métis, just that their main interests were trade and Red River. The St. Laurent Métis petitioned for a representative but were considered too untamed for such civilized responsibilities.[18] Even when the seat of government was transferred from Winnipeg to Battleford, there was no representative for the South Saskatchewan Métis.

With the arrival in 1878 of another fifty Métis families, St. Laurent numbered over five hundred people. More than 75 per cent of them came from Red River or the environs of Pembina and St. Joseph in North Dakota. By 1878 the Métis in the Prince Albert area numbered about twelve hundred souls with more coming every day. By 1883 there were fifteen hundred Métis on the South Saskatchewan River around St. Laurent and Duck Lake.

THE BONE PICKERS

The Métis are a stubborn lot and they held on to their life on the Plains as long as they could. They loved it. Family and friends travelled together. The food was fresh, plentiful and delicious. The camps were safe, friendly, social and filled with music and dancing. All the Métis described it as a life of beauty. For them, a life on the Plains was no hardship. They saw nothing better in a life on a farm. They held on to their life of movement as long as they could. Marie Rose Smith thought it was wonderful and said, "Oh but that was the life! Free life, camping where there was lots of green grass, fine clear water to drink, nothing to worry or bother us. No law to meddle with us . . . We always travelled with different families, whenever we would camp it would be like a nice village."[19]

For a hundred years the Métis travelled throughout the North-West, trading and hunting. They were always on the move. Then one by one, the economies that had sustained their mobile lifestyle for a century began to crash in the early 1880s. It was the end of the buffalo that forever transformed their lifestyle.

The Métis said that, toward the end, some buffalo died of an infectious bacterial disease called black-leg. Hundreds of dead buffalo were seen on the Plains. In a vicious effort to starve out its Indians, U.S. soldiers burned the Plains, slaughtered buffalo and paid a bounty for each skull recovered. The disease and the American scorched-earth policy took a huge toll on the herds. The buffalo died from a combination of over-hunting, disease and deliberate slaughter. By 1882 all that was left of the magnificent herds were millions and millions of bones, hooves and horns. The Plains were covered with large, sun-bleached white bones and skulls highlighted by ebony hooves and horns lying in the midst of the skeletal remains.

For the new settlers the bones were a pain. Land had to be cleared and broken, and the bones had to be removed. The Métis did most of it. They became bone pickers. Bones were gathered onto Red River carts and hauled off to markets. The bone pickers were paid by the ton. It took one hundred buffalo skeletons to make a ton of bones. The price per ton varied over time from three to twenty-three dollars, but by the end of the nineteenth century, a ton of bones fetched about eight dollars.

The bone trade was big business. Bones were piled in ricks, some a quarter mile long and thirty feet high. Old bones became bone meal fertilizer, a pigment called bone black, and the bone in bone china, and were used to decolour sugar. Horns were made into buttons, dice or even toothbrushes. By the end of the 1880s, the business began to dwindle, but Métis were still picking buffalo bones in quantity in Canada until 1893.

A rick of buffalo bones in Saskatoon (*Saskatoon Public Library LH-2823*)

The bone picking removed the last physical remains of the buffalo from the Plains. And then the Plains themselves began to change. The massive herds of buffalo had played a huge role in the formation of the Plains. They fertilized the grasses, kept them nibbled down to size and packed the earth with their weight. Their presence kept the trees from encroaching. The herds were a moving ecosystem that included all the other creatures that fed off the buffalo—humans, wolves, birds and insects. When the buffalo were gone, tree saplings began to encroach, and the prairie grasses changed.

Most Métis stopped picking bones by the early 1890s. But George Fleury and his father were still gathering buffalo bones from the riverbanks around Ste. Madeleine, Manitoba, in the 1950s. The Fleurys got a hundred dollars for a wagonload of bones.[20] By that time the bones were mostly buried and you couldn't just pick them. You had to dig. The Métis say that the buffalo bones can still be found if you know where to look for them.

PART SIX

THE NORTH-WEST RESISTANCE

CHAPTER 22

THE FOURTH NATIONAL RESISTANCE

GABRIEL DUMONT

If Louis Riel was a comet, Gabriel Dumont was a lodestone, a magnet firmly grounded on the earth of the Plains. At a very young age, he earned a reputation as a warrior and hunter. Dumont was thirteen years old when he fought at the Battle of the Grand Coteau in 1851. The man he became was forged in that battle. In later years Dumont was often elected the chief captain of the hunt. People followed him and they trusted him with their lives. He was a man of his word and a man who cared for the people he led. Every time Dumont hunted he gave his first kills to the needy. He was the best of men and a mighty hunter.

He had two seemingly incompatible reputations, as a peacemaker and as a warrior. It was the warrior Dumont who offered Riel five hundred men to fight Wolseley's forces at Red River in 1870. It was Dumont the peacemaker who kept a line of communication open with the Sioux and the Blackfoot throughout the 1860s, '70s and '80s. Sometimes Dumont's peacemaking skills were used to facilitate Métis access to a share of the resources. Sometimes they were offered to assist the First Nations. Assuming the role of peacemaker in such situations meant that Dumont spoke fluent Cree, Ojibwa, Sioux and Blackfoot. In the 1870s one did not acquire such language fluency from books or in school. The skill was acquired from long acquaintance, family ties and constant interaction, even with traditional enemies such as the Sioux and Blackfoot.

Gabriel Dumont, circa 1880–82 (*Glenbow Archives PA-2218*)

He was a deeply religious man, and over the years he and his wife stood as godparents for dozens of Métis children. Godparents took on important family responsibilities. Assuming the role was an agreement to care for the children if something happened to their parents. In those days, when diseases swept the Plains leaving hundreds dead, Dumont's many godchildren had a special call on him.

Dumont was educated on the Plains. He never learned to read or write, but he learned diplomacy, politics, leadership, religion and trade. Dumont's education gave him a deep knowledge of the land and the resources of the Plains. On Métis hunts and in their camps, he absorbed Michif ways, language and culture. He travelled deep into the United States and knew people of many languages, cultures and religions. He lived a life of movement on the Plains. He was an ardent Métis nationalist and a classic Métis buffalo hunter.

Dumont tried to strengthen the ties between the First Nations and the Métis Nation on the Plains. He wanted to create an alliance similar to the ancient alliances that had long existed in the North-West, such as the Blackfoot Confederacy, the Sioux Confederacy, the Dakota Confederacy and the Nehiyaw Pwat (the Iron Alliance).[1] Being part of the Iron Alliance did not preclude the Métis Nation from forming alliances with bands in the Sioux Confederacy. After 1862 there appears to have been just such an alliance between the Sioux and the Métis Nation. Gabriel Dumont and his family were credited with making that alliance. These were political alliances and the world of politics is not always smooth sailing. There are some reports of uncomfortable hunting camps where distrust and discord reigned. The people didn't always like each other and they didn't always agree. But the whole point of the alliance was not to make war on each other. They didn't have to be best friends.

When Dumont offered five hundred horsemen to Riel in 1870, it is likely he thought he could get them from the Iron Alliance. Dumont was not a man to promise support he could not deliver. Métis from the South Saskatchewan, Qu'Appelle and Fort Edmonton would have made up the bulk of the force. The Iron Alliance might have provided more warriors. This was before the treaties were signed and there were young Cree, Assiniboine and Ojibwa men who would answer a call from Dumont.

But by the 1880s things had changed. The buffalo were gone and the Iron Alliance was no more. The First Nations had been cut up by the American border and then cut further into small bands living on what the Cree call *iskonikan* or "leftovers." Canadians call them reserves. The Indian agents made sure the Cree were poorly armed, mounted and fed. Canada, like the United States, used food to control the bands.

The First Nations had treaties. They had signed solemn agreements with the Crown, with the queen. Treaties were supposed to mean something. Indeed, some of the internal disputes within the bands about whether to go to war were about loyalty to the Crown and the treaties. The ink was barely dry on some of their treaties when the promises were broken. The reserves were simmering—the loss of the buffalo, disease, starvation rations, vindictive Indian agents and Ottawa's ruthless disregard had all contributed to a mounting tension within the tribes. They were watching their people die. The taste of life in the early 1880s was bitter and hard to swallow. It made it difficult for chiefs like Poundmaker and Big Bear to control their young warriors.

Dumont travelled extensively to the reserves and he personally visited the chiefs. He kept open lines of communication because he hoped there was enough common cause for the Métis Nation and the First Nations to work together. There wasn't. They were all heading to war.

It's usually called the North-West Rebellion, but the Métis Nation has always called it the North-West Resistance. Like the Red River Resistance, the North-West Resistance was not about disloyalty and it was not an attempt to overthrow the government. The Saskatchewan Métis called their part in the North-West Resistance "La Guerre Nationale" (The National War). Like that of the Victory of the Frog Plain in 1816, the name tells us how the Métis saw things.

First Nations were also heading to war at the same time as the Métis. They were all part of the North-West Resistance. There were some Indians who fought alongside the Métis and some Métis who fought alongside the Indians. But the First Nations weren't fighting the Métis national war and the Métis weren't fighting the First Nations war. They were walking separate paths on the war road. They were both in desperate battles to defend their own people.

THE CLIQUE

In 1874 the federal government reserved whole townships for colonization companies. The idea was that the companies would find it profitable to purchase land from the government and then resell it to settlers. The scheme didn't work, largely because there were too few settlers to purchase the lands and there was little profit to be made. By 1877 none of the tracts set aside for the colonization companies had been successfully settled. But in 1882 Macdonald breathed new life into the scheme. He proposed a grant of 10 million acres to the companies. The much larger land base and the prospect of a railroad was a land speculator's dream. Fortunes would be made, and everyone wanted in on the action. The land grants went to political cronies and friends of the Conservative government. The best bets were placed on lands along the future route of the Canadian Pacific Railway. So, colonization companies made it their business to have connections within government. They all wanted to know the planned route for the railroad. The newspapers reported on bribes to officials who got stock in the companies in exchange for information about the railroad route.[2]

For the Métis Nation on the Saskatchewan River, the Prince Albert Colonization Company was a problem. When twenty-four Métis families tried to file entry for their lands, they were told that the parish of St. Louis de Langevin had been transferred to this colonization company and that they would have to register their claim with the company's agent. For the Métis, this sale of their parish to Conservative Party cronies was the single most important factor that would lead to the coming war.[3] A list of the board of directors provides evidence of the Conservative Party's inside dealing. The board members included two sitting and one about-to-be-elected Conservative member of Parliament, and two sons, one brother, one son-in-law and one brother-in-law of Conservative members of Parliament.[4] It is not too difficult to see what was going on.

Some of the players in the coming war are already familiar to us. Macdonald was still the prime minister. He had learned the value of propaganda, and in July 1884 his Indian commissioner, Edgar Dewdney, secured an interest in *The Prince Albert Times*, after which the tone of the newspaper, formerly sympathetic to the Métis, changed dramatically.[5] Schultz and Charlie Mair were carrying on their familiar activities of land speculation and the promotion of the Canadian Party's agenda, with its lethal dose of anti-Métis and anti-Riel poison. Mair wrote several articles for *The Prince Albert Times*. Colonel Dennis was the surveyor-general for a while and then jumped into the land speculation game.

Lawrence Clarke was part of a Conservative clique in Prince Albert. These were the men who held all of the political power. The Indian commissioner, Dewdney, thought the clique was intentionally stirring up the Métis in the belief that a war would bring profits. Clarke worked hard to make the Métis think he was acting in their interests, and he was very successful in hiding his real agenda. He dropped money into the coffers of the priests to get them to exercise their influence with the Métis, and that worked well for a while. The priests urged the Métis to vote Conservative and they did, even though the Conservatives did nothing to assist the Métis and actively worked against them.

Then Clarke cut the wages of the freighters. This third source of revenue for the Métis was drastically reduced at a time when they were also experiencing the loss of the buffalo and crop failures. Dewdney thought Clarke's wage cut was deliberately intended to provoke the Métis.

The clique also infiltrated and then took over the local Farmers' Union, which until then had been a staunch ally of the Métis but now began to separate itself. The surveyors fixed any survey problems for white landowners. The only outstanding claims left were those of the Métis in St. Laurent whose land was claimed by the Prince Albert Colonization Company. The excuse for not surveying the Métis lands was feeble. In a land where francophone Métis were a significant part of the population, the land office could not be bothered to get someone who spoke French.

The Métis on the Saskatchewan were fighting to keep their

land. They were poor and getting poorer, but they had chosen their land and they were prepared to defend it. Everyone, especially the priests, had pressed them to settle on the land. They did settle and they were making a go of it. But their land was under threat. In the 1870s Canada took Métis lands in Manitoba, claiming that the Métis were mere users, not owners, so the lands were empty and up for grabs. Now the Métis had come to the Saskatchewan, and the Canadian Party men were still taking their lands. The justification now was that the Métis were not settled exactly as Canadians settled. The Métis must settle on the land in squares; no other shapes were permitted. The Métis preferred their long, narrow *rangs* on the riverfront. That's what they had in Red River. That's what they had on the Saskatchewan. That's what they wanted to keep.

Not only did the Métis have to be settled on a square; they had to be on the right square. Each township had odd and even numbered squares. The Métis were permitted to settle only on the even-numbered squares. They could not be on the squares set aside for the Hudson's Bay Company or the ones set aside for the roads, the public schools or the railway. The fact that the squares were imposed after many of the Métis settled on the land didn't matter. There was no land office to view maps of the township divisions and there was no place to register their titles. Once again the Métis were seen as mere users of the land, not settlers and not proper owners. So, it really didn't matter which squares they were on. Even if they were on the right squares, their lack of title meant others could jump their claims. If they were on the wrong squares, they were squatting on someone else's land—the Canadian Pacific Railway's or the Company's. They were supposed to go.

Dumont looked around the North-West and what he saw

was not promising. He knew about the dispossession of the Métis in Red River after 1870, and he knew that in 1881 and 1882 new settlers had tried to displace the Edmonton Métis. Ignoring Métis protests, the newcomers built their cabins on Métis lands. When the Métis complained to the police, they were told that nothing could be done. So, the Edmonton Métis took things into their own hands. Some thirty Métis rigged cables to their horses and pulled the newcomers' houses down into the ravines.[6] In so doing they successfully protected their lands. That action inspired Dumont. He knew those men in Edmonton. He thought the Saskatchewan Métis could also take action to protect their lands.

The same scenario was being played out everywhere. The immigrants were taking Métis lands. The South Saskatchewan Métis believed that *all* Métis had won their rights in 1870 with the Manitoba Act, but those outside Manitoba had not received them. The Saskatchewan Métis tried to get the government's attention. Their civil protest took the form of petitions to Ottawa and the new territorial capital in Regina. They urged their priests, ministers and local representative to send petitions containing their claims and resolutions to Canada.

EIGHTY-FOUR PETITIONS

The Métis sent the government petition after petition. Later, in 1885, Macdonald told Parliament that the Métis had not presented their claims to the government. But Macdonald knew the Métis had sent petitions—eighty-four between 1878 and 1885. That averages one per month over a seven-year period. One doesn't need to read all eighty-four petitions to get the idea.[7] There is a sorry sameness to them. As one petition penned by Gabriel Dumont and addressed to Sir John A. Macdonald said,

> We are poor people and cannot pay for our land without utter ruin, and losing the fruits of our labour or seeing our lands pass into the hands of strangers . . . In our anxiety we appeal to your sense of justice as Minister of the Interior and head of government, and beg you to reassure us speedily, by directing that we shall not be disturbed on our lands . . . since which have occupied these lands in good faith.[8]

The decision-makers, far away in eastern Canada, never even bothered to respond.

In 1879 many Métis petitioned for reserves. They wanted to live in communities or close together, they wanted to exclude strangers from these lands and they wanted the lands to remain in their hands for a long time. The government disliked this idea, and because there were some Métis families who wanted to live independently, those requesting reserves were rejected. According to Ambroise Lépine the government not only dealt in deception, it liked to deceive those it dealt with. Lépine was not alone in thinking the government was deceiving the Métis. By 1880 the Métis were very bitter about Canada. They were on the move seeking places to settle, and lack of food was driving some of the movement. It drove the Métis from Cypress Hills down to the Milk River in Montana. Riel was drafting Métis petitions from there.[9]

In 1883 the Métis in St. Laurent were promised, in writing, that their lands would be surveyed in a manner that respected the *rangs*. Despite the promise no one dealt with the Métis claims in St. Laurent. The Métis sent messages to everyone. But there was only a deep silence. It was all *aen mahykamikaahk*, "going wrong."

CHAPTER 23

LA GUERRE NATIONALE

THE BLACK WINTER

The 1878 winter was called the Black Winter because there was no snow even in the North. During the Black Winter starvation was the norm for virtually all of the Plains peoples. The warm temperatures and drought caused multiple fires that drove the dwindling buffalo herds into the Cypress Hills. The people followed, and everyone congregated in the Cypress Hills, even traditional enemies. The Blackfoot, Cree, Assiniboine, Ojibwa and Métis were all jostling for buffalo in Cypress Hills. There were even professional American buffalo hunters with easy access to the Plains because the American railroad had reached Sioux territory. The professionals were hired by the army to exterminate the buffalo in an effort to starve American Indians into submission. The American extermination program pushed several thousand Sioux refugees into Canada.

It was during the Black Winter of 1878 that a great gathering of the Nehiyaw Pwat (the Iron Alliance) was held in the Cypress Hills. Two hundred and seventy-six men signed a petition asking for a reserve. The signatories were Métis Nation and

First Nations "usually resident in the neighbourhood of Cypress Hills." It was a petition from the poly-ethnic group following the buffalo along the Milk River to the Judith Basin.[1] They wanted the land to be inalienable and to exclude "all whites."[2] Basically, they were asking for a treaty, and this was not the first time the Métis in the southwest parts of the Plains had petitioned for one. In 1876 Métis from four districts of Assiniboia had petitioned to join Treaty #4 as a distinct group with their own chief. Thirteen Métis signed both of the petitions.[3]

POLICE, ARMS AND THE MILITIA COME TO THE SASKATCHEWAN

By 1880 Canada had worked itself into an agitated and fearful state, and what it most feared was the Métis Nation. The Métis were dangerous and Riel was evil. Rumours started to fly around the North-West. Louis Riel was said to be agitating about stolen ponies. The Indian agent denied the stolen ponies rumour but suggested that Riel must have "other evil designs."[4] Hugh Richardson (who would later be the judge on Louis Riel's trial) wrote that the Métis were being "subjected to the evil influences of leading spirits of the Manitoba troubles of 1870, who, during the past season, have been traversing the country, doing at least 'no good.'"[5]

Then in 1883 and 1884 there was a crop failure across the North-West. The Cree, Ojibwa and Blackfoot on the reserves were starving. The Mounties and the Métis did what they could to feed the starving people. Government policy used food as a means of subduing the First Nations, and the Indian agents got upset when the Mounties and Métis interfered by providing food to the starving people. Gabriel Dumont was outraged at how the First Nations were being treated:

> The government should not be surprised if we side with the Indians. They are our relatives and when they are starving they come to us for relief and we have to feed them . . . The government is not doing right by them. I heard the speeches and the explanations given of the Treaty, not only that they would live as well as they had before, but better . . . They are allowed to go about starving and the burden falls on us.[6]

By 1884 the starvation was terrible. Dr. John Kittson, the doctor for the North-West Mounted Police, reported that a minimum daily ration for a man in moderate health with an active life should be 1 pound of meat, 0.2 pound of bread, and 0.25 pound of fat or butter. The First Nations daily ration was 0.5 pound of meat and 0.5 pound of flour, which according to Dr. Kittson was "totally insufficient."[7] First Nations people were receiving less than half the rations provided to state prisoners in Siberia.[8]

Macdonald was unmoved. He wanted to keep the expenses down as much as possible and complained that "the Indians will always grumble."[9] His answer was to send in police.[10] Everyone wanted police. Clarke wanted the Mounties to put down what he called the lawlessness of the Métis. Lieutenant-Governor Morris wanted police to put pressure on First Nations during treaty negotiations. The commanding officer of the militia wanted a regiment to protect the surveyors, contractors and railway workers, and he warned Ottawa that "the only thing the Indians really respect, and will bow to, is actual power" and that the Métis were "unaccustomed to the restraint of any government . . . and requiring to be controlled nearly as much as the Indians."[11]

The messages coming out of the North-West were consistent on one hand and contradictory on another. The consistent message was that trouble was brewing because of the unresolved land issues. The priests, Indian Commissioner Dewdney and the Mounties all urged the government to settle the Métis land issues. To their way of thinking, settling the land title would solve the Métis unrest. But there was another message coming from the land speculators, the Hudson's Bay Company and the Conservative clique. They warned of an imminent Métis and Indian uprising that would have to be put down with arms and force.

LOUIS RIEL

By the spring of 1884 the Métis council in St. Laurent knew they needed help. Gabriel Dumont was a sturdy and devoted man, but he had taken them as far as he could. They needed someone with more experience with government, someone educated and sophisticated. They had been taking advice from the priests but were rightly suspicious of the ties between them and the clique. As Patrice Fleury put it,

> It was decided to get someone, a Métis if possible, to clearly set out the requirements of the case . . . After due consideration at a meeting attended by French and English halfbreeds, it was decided to approach Louis Riel who was then living in Montana, and get him to come here and argue our case, in a constitutional way, that is to make speeches at all the large centres and let the whole of the settlers see that we had a grievance that could be easily rectified and a delegation . . . was sent to Montana. They had great difficulty in persuading Riel to consent to come to Saskatchewan, but the fact that he had a better education than many of us, and representation being made to him that it was only an agitation for rights in which he as well as all of us were entitled, induced him to come and take part.[12]

They wanted Riel's experience and knowledge. He had led the Métis in Manitoba and obtained recognition for their land rights. The treaty had not been honoured, but that was not Riel's fault. He had successfully negotiated a deal, and that's what they needed on the Saskatchewan. Bringing Riel onboard was a calculated strategy. They wanted him to negotiate a similar deal for them.

Knowing that Riel brought controversy in his wake, the Métis council met with the leaders of the local Farmers' Union. They wanted broad support before they brought in Riel. At a joint meeting on May 6, 1884, members of the Farmers' Union and the Métis drafted a letter to Louis Riel to be delivered by a chosen delegation. Unknown to the other Métis, James Isbister, one of the men designated to go to Montana, wanted more than the approval of the Farmers' Union and the Métis. He went directly from the meeting to see Lawrence Clarke, the leader of the clique, to seek his approval of the offer to Riel. On obtaining Clarke's unqualified approval, Isbister agreed to go to Montana. Clarke sent a telegram to Dewdney telling him that the Métis were going to get Riel:

> A series of meetings have been held at which only [Métis] were allowed to be present. All were sworn to secrecy as to what transpired . . . Object was to pass resolutions complaining of their treatment by the Government . . . Two appointed to interview Riel asking him to assist them if he could not come to advise them what to do.[13]

The two delegates were Gabriel Dumont and James Isbister. Moïse Ouellette and Michel Dumas were their two travelling companions.[14] They set out on their journey to Montana on May 18, 1884, and arrived at St. Peter's Mission on Sunday, June 4. Riel was at Mass when they arrived. He went out to greet them and promised to meet them after Mass was over. The delegates presented Riel with a somewhat optimistic view of the situation on the Saskatchewan. They told Riel there was a close union between the French, the English and the Indians and that the whole of the Métis Nation was calling for him. Riel asked for a day to think and pray and retreated inside the small church.

The church is still standing. It's a charming place. One can imagine Riel kneeling for long hours as he fought an internal battle between what his reason told him to do and what his heart wanted to do. The reasonable option was to stay put in Montana. He had a teaching job, a wife and young children. Reason told him not to take risks. Reason told him he could die if he went back. Reason made him reluctant to go. But reason is a cold thing, and Riel always burned hot.

His heart was sending a different message. He wanted to go back to his people in Canada, a land he had not wanted to leave in the first place. If he could not be with his family in Red River, at least he would be in a Métis community made up in large part of Métis from Red River. And there was the call of his people to consider. They wanted him and needed him. The great hunter Gabriel Dumont himself had come to ask. No Métis, not even Riel, turned down a request from Dumont lightly. Riel had done fought this battle before, so perhaps he could do it again. He was aware that things were different this time, but Dumont and Isbister were clear that the Métis would lose their lands again if something wasn't done and soon. In the end Riel listened to his heart.

On June 10 the party left for the Saskatchewan. On the

outskirts of Batoche, seventy Métis men and women greeted Riel, the man they called their national apostle, and led him into the town, where they held a meeting in the church. Riel made his first speech the next day before a crowd that had come from miles around just to see him. His speech calmed them all as he preached patience and an orderly process to press their claims. He urged them to keep on with their petitions. At Prince Albert a few days later, Riel served up the same message, this time to six hundred people.

Riel had come back to Canada to draft petitions. And draft petitions and speak at meetings is exactly what he did. All through the spring and summer, the people on the Saskatchewan—the Métis and the settlers, sometimes all together—met. The message from Riel was always the same: be patient, don't give up, articulate your rights and press government for an answer. In November of 1884, they made a Bill of Rights for the Métis in the North-West:

1. Subdivision of the North-West Territories into Provinces.
2. Concessions of land and other benefits such as had been accorded to their brethren in Manitoba.
3. Immediate distribution of letters patent to the settlers in possession.
4. Sale of a half-million acres of Crown land for the foundation of schools, hospitals and other institutions of this kind in Métis settlements, and to buy grain and farm implements for Métis in poverty.
5. The setting aside of one hundred townships of marshy land to be distributed to Métis children during 120 years to come.
6. An allotment of $1,000 for the maintenance of a religious institution in each Métis settlement.
7. Arrangements for the welfare of Indians.[15]

All through the spring and summer of 1884, the governor-general, the 5th Marquess of Lansdowne, Prime Minister Macdonald and the minister of public works, Sir Hector-Louis Langevin, discussed Riel and the Métis issues. Langevin pressed Macdonald for good treatment of the Métis, worried that if harsh measures were taken against Riel and the Saskatchewan Métis, they would create a martyr. "A little bit would go a long way to settle matters," he said.[16]

It was clear to all three men that the situation in the North-West *could* be dealt with. It would cost them very little. They would have to recognize the river lots, and they thought they would have to give Riel money or a position. They seemed to be disposed toward trying to resolve the land issues that so worried the Métis. But by August 1884 their conciliatory mood had evaporated. Through the fall and winter of 1884, the answer to the Métis petitions and to the list of rights was the same: deafening silence.

In January 1885 the Métis got word that the secretary of state had received their List of Rights. The Métis saw this as a tremendous step forward. It shows how desperate they were for any kind of response. It was nothing more than a formal government acknowledgement of receipt. The Métis lived on that dream for a few days. Their petitions, letters and meetings all show a blind faith. They were convinced that if someone would just sit down and talk to them, they could negotiate an agreement. From the twenty-first century their actions don't seem at all unreasonable. To the nineteenth-century politicians, it was sedition in the making.

On January 28 the federal government adopted an order in council to investigate the claims and enumerate the Métis who had not participated in the Manitoba Act land grants.[17] This was not good news. Only two hundred of some thirteen hundred outstanding claims would be investigated. The Métis were decidedly unhappy. Further investigation? What further investigation? They needed action, not this waste of time. Riel continued to preach his doctrine of peace, and as they saw more of him, his stature among his own people grew. They always spoke of him with veneration. He was their hero, their prophet and their saint. He urged them to continue the agitation for the Métis rights by petition and peaceful methods, but by early 1885 the younger Métis were growing more insistent and hard to control.

THE BRIBES

The priests, the police, Macdonald, Dewdney and the clique all wanted to get rid of Riel. In their eyes he was a dangerous threat, an apostate, Satan's instrument, a crazy fool and a proud wretch. The priests, the lieutenant-governor and the clique tried to bribe him, first with a position on the North-West Council, then with a Senate seat and then with money.[18] They assumed he could be bought off.

The first bribe was the offer of a position on the North-West Council. It was meant to buy him off personally; it was not intended to address Métis grievances, since the solution to all land claims lay in Ottawa, not in the North-West Council that had no jurisdiction with respect to land. Furthermore, Pascal Breland was already holding the Métis councillor position. Putting Riel on the North-West Council would mean ousting Breland, a move that would only cause strife within the Métis Nation.

The Grant/Breland family and the Riels' somewhat acrimonious history has been set out in Chapter 18. They made peace by taking a united stand during the reign of terror, but the offer to displace Pascal Breland with Louis Riel on the North-West Council is an indication of just how removed the Canadians were from Métis politics and how little they knew of Métis Nation history. It is also an indication of how these powerful men completely misjudged Riel. He would take no position of power that would divide the Métis.

The second bribe, a seat in the Senate, was almost laughable. That kind of political patronage appointment was solely within the purview of the prime minister, and while these were indeed powerful men, they could not guarantee a Senate seat. Parliament had ejected Riel from the House of Commons, and he had never been able to take his seat despite being elected three times. It was foolish to dangle the offer of a Senate seat. Macdonald would never risk his own political neck in such a manner. We know these men thought Riel was an apostate, Satan's instrument, crazy and proud, but surely they didn't think Riel would fall for such an empty offer. Perhaps it is more of an indication of how desperate they were to find a rock, any rock, to hide him under.

The offer of public office having failed, they resorted to cash. This offer came in December 1884. There are various amounts in the records. The highest number is $100,000. It slides down from there to $35,000 to $5,000 and then to $3,000. So was Riel willing to accept the cash bribe? It is certainly true that Riel was poor. He had been making some money as a teacher in Montana, but on coming with his family to the South Saskatchewan, he was left with no income of any kind. He also felt, not unreasonably, that Canada owed him for services rendered in fighting the Fenians, in giving up his seat to Cartier, and in governing Red River in the interregnum before Wolseley arrived.

Father Alexis André was thinking ahead to the next federal election. Prior to Riel's arrival, the priests had a unique role as political rainmakers. Because the Métis were such a large majority, if the priests urged them to vote for a particular candidate, they could assure that man's victory. It was the essence of political power in the hands of the Church. It forced those running for office, like Lawrence Clarke, to drop cash offerings to placate the priests. Riel's arrival threatened the political dynamic, the cash flow and the embedded powers. The Church and the clique didn't like it.

Father André claimed Riel was going to take the money personally and the bribe failed only because Father André couldn't raise the funds. The Métis say Riel did discuss money with Father André. Riel reported everything to the Métis in St. Laurent, and they planned to use the funds to buy a printing press. They discussed how much they would need for the purchase and decided that $35,000 would do the job. They even made inquiries about where a press could be found. In the end we are left with two very different versions of the story. However the money would have been used, Riel never thought he sold out the Métis Nation, and the Métis Nation never thought Riel sold them out.

Meanwhile Riel continued to speak at meetings throughout the area. At each of the meetings, Riel's proposal was to proceed by means of petition and persuasion. He spoke at numerous meetings of the Métis throughout the district, but he also addressed meetings of the non-Indigenous population in Prince Albert. As he worked, his message of peace and persistence won over the majority of the population. Despite the tone and content of Riel's message, however, the police surveillance increased. The local Indian agents had nothing negative to report, and indeed their messages said Riel's return had calmed the waters with the

First Nations. But Riel's name alone caused a stir. It mattered not what he actually did or said. The powers-that-be wanted Riel suppressed by the strongest of measures and as quickly as possible. Their greatest fear was that the First Nations and the Métis Nation would join forces.

The Métis spent the winter preparing their final petition. Their plan was to present it in person to the governor-general. But it was obvious that none of the Métis could do the actual presentation. It would have to go through an intermediary. They chose their local member of Parliament, Lawrence Clarke. They asked him to go directly to Ottawa with the petition. He left in February. The Métis waited. And waited. But there was no word of what was happening in Ottawa. Meanwhile the rumours began to fly. It was said that the Métis were expecting a shipment of arms and ammunition from the United States. It wasn't true, but Dewdney passed that rumour on as fact to Macdonald.

More police—that was always the solution to the Riel problem.[19] According to Dewdney, they needed more police in the North-West and the "sooner they [the Métis] are put down the better."[20] The recruitment of police escalated over the year. They called for five thousand recruits for the army in March 1884. In April two hundred men were added to the police. In May twenty additional police and one hundred and fifty militia were sent to Fort Carlton. In August the Mountie detachment in Prince Albert was increased. Two hundred men were distributed between Battleford, Carlton, Prince Albert and Fort Pitt.

THE SPARK THAT STARTED THE WAR

The Métis had been trying for years to resolve their issues within constitutional means. Surely, they thought, eighty-four petitions would attract someone's attention. But Ottawa was adamant and inflexible. Nothing the Métis wanted, as little as it was, would be negotiated. By March the Métis had had enough. On March 8, 1885, they issued a ten-point "Revolutionary Bill of Rights."

Revolutionary Bill of Rights (1885)

1. That the half-breeds of the Northwest Territories be given grants similar to those accorded to the half-breeds of Manitoba by the Act of 1870.
2. That patents be issued to all half-breed and white settlers who have fairly earned the right of possession of their farms.
3. That provinces of Alberta and Saskatchewan be forthwith organized with legislatures of their own, so that the people may be no longer subjected to the despotism of Mr. Dewdney.
4. That in these new provincial legislatures, while representation according to population shall be the supreme principle, the Métis shall have a fair and reasonable share of representation.
5. That the offices of trust throughout these provinces be given to the residents of the country, as far as practicable, and that we denounce the appointment of disreputable outsiders and repudiate their authority.
6. That this region be administered for the benefit of the actual settler, and not for the advantage of the alien speculator.
7. That better provision be made for the Indians, the parliamentary grant to be increased and lands set apart as an endowment for the establishment of hospitals and schools for the use of whites, half-breeds, and Indians, at such places as the provincial legislatures may determine.
8. That all lawful customs and usages which obtain among the Métis be respected.
9. That the Land Department of the Dominion Government be administered as far as practicable from Winnipeg, so that the

settlers may not be compelled as heretofore to go to Ottawa for the settlement of questions in dispute between them and the land commissioner.

10. That the timber regulations be made more liberal, and that the settlers be treated as having rights in this country.[21]

Despite its dramatic title nothing in the bill is revolutionary. The Métis Bill of Rights asserted rights of possession to their lands, which they wanted to have administered from an office in the North-West. They were still trying to persuade Canada with words.

On March 18, 1885, only by chance, some Métis met up with the recently returned Lawrence Clarke. By this time Clarke had shed his mask. He told the Métis that the answer to their petition would be bullets.[22] Macdonald was sending armed men, and Clarke had just seen them in Humboldt. They were coming to take Riel and Dumont.[23]

Clarke's announcement that police were coming with the express purpose of taking Riel and Dumont was shocking. The Métis moved into defensive mode. Should they resist the coming onslaught? Or should they remain quiet and lose everything? They voted unanimously to resist. The Métis had anticipated that it would come to arms. They had titled their Bill of Rights "revolutionary," and on March 5 ten men had signed a pledge in which they promised to take up arms if necessary to protect their country.[24] So while they were shocked at the quick turn of events, perhaps they were not that surprised.

Riel, however, was deeply disturbed. He was not a man of violence. By this time Riel's heart and soul were embedded in his mysticism. Dumont would do battle with arms, but Riel's battle was a spiritual one. The battle to enlist God's aid was something he deeply believed in and it was all he had to offer really. He was not a soldier. He had come to draft petitions, not to foment war. This is not to say he did not fully participate in the preparation for the war. He did. Indeed, we have stories that he corresponded widely with Métis throughout the Métis Nation in an effort to gauge the level of support he might be able to call on.

But Riel was toxic. His presence made everything more dangerous and he knew it. He knew he should leave, and more than once he told the people they would be better off without him. They would be safer if he left. These were not token protests on Riel's part. There were serious debates at many meetings about his presence. Again and again, the people decided. They would not let him go.

Riel and Dumont both knew there was no possible way the Métis Nation could win this fight. But the people said they would take up arms. According to Patrice Fleury, "[A] feeling of aggression that we were being denied our rights was felt and the crowd got beyond of Riel and the older and steadier heads and a muster was held, which was about three hundred strong, the total number of guns, a greater part of which were shot guns and many muzzle loading, was sixty."[25] As old Champagne said, "When a hen's young ones are under her wings, she protects them . . . we sought to protect our women and children."[26] On that fateful day of March 19, Dumont asked the people three times if they were sure about taking up arms. The entire crowd rose to its feet and shouted, "If we are to die for our country, we will die together."[27]

They proclaimed a provisional government and appointed a council of fifteen. Riel, ever the erudite intellectual, gave it a highfalutin name the Métis never took to: the Exovedate. Gabriel Dumont was made the general. The Métis picked up their arms and began to plan. La Guerre Nationale had begun, but it had begun on a lie, Clarke's lie. There were no police on their way to arrest Dumont and Riel. But as Dumont said, that lie "put fire to the powder."[28]

Métis joining Riel, 1885 (*Glenbow Archives NA-1406*)

The priests denounced the decision to take up arms, threatened participants with excommunication from the Church and refused to hear their confessions. The decision to take up arms went against the priests' political instructions and became a rebellion against the Church, not just a rebellion against the state. In 1858 the Bishop of Montreal, Bourget, had made it clear that "No one is permitted to be free in his religious and political opinions: it is for the church to teach her children to be good citizens as well as good Christians, by instilling into them the true principles of faith and morals, of which she alone is the sole depositary."[29]

According to Church doctrine rebellion was an error, and error had no rights. Rebellion had no rights. The Métis were acting under the influence of Satan. The Church deals with such error by instruction, but if the penitents remain obdurate, "she launches her thunders against them and declares them excluded from her bosom."[30] The Church defined politics as morals and claimed absolute jurisdiction in all matters of morals. "Rebellion has a strict duty to fulfil; this duty is to repent, to come back, submission to the church."[31] The priests at St. Laurent were not of Father Ritchot's or Father Belcourt's ilk. They did not work with the Métis and they didn't stay neutral.

Ontario couldn't wait to send troops to the North-West. In Toronto *The Globe* headline read, "REBELLION: Louis Riel Again Heading an Insurrection."[32] When Macdonald called for troops, "hats were thrown into the air and the cheering renewed again and again."[33] The Toronto press constructed war fever and saw its job as one of reinforcing the message of the government.[34] The eagerness to fight the Métis consumed Ontario, and everywhere there was talk of "squelching Riel and his crowd of malcontents."[35] The Toronto newspapers used the opportunity to feed anti-French tensions, and thousands crowded the train station to see the troops off, singing, "We'll hang Louis Riel on a sour apple tree."[36]

The Métis described the events at Duck Lake, Tourond's Coulee (Fish Creek) and Batoche as a resistance or their national war. Prime Minister Macdonald used whatever term suited his purposes at the time. When he wanted to build up his forces, he elevated the events to a rebellion. When he wanted to minimize the actions of the Métis, he called it a mere riot.

Macdonald and the governor-general had no qualms about admitting to manipulation of the language, at least to each other. In the late summer of 1885, Macdonald suggested to the governor-general that they tone down their language. But the governor-general didn't quite see how they could do that at this late date. "We have all of us been doing what we could to elevate it to the rank of a rebellion and with so much success that we cannot now reduce it to the rank of a common riot."[37] They had worked hard to ensure their acts of "suppression had been described in glowing language of the press all over the world." It would surely be a bit awkward to downgrade their national effort at suppression by admitting that it had been expended on a mere "outbreak."[38] Macdonald was unrepentant about the manipulation. He wrote, "We have certainly made it assume large proportions in the public eye. This has been done however for our own purposes, and I think it wisely done."[39]

DUCK LAKE

There were three Métis battles in the North-West Resistance. The first was the battle at Duck Lake on March 25 to 26, 1885, and it began as an accident. On March 25 Riel and Dumont took thirty men to Duck Lake to confiscate guns and ammunition from the store. The Mounties had also sent a small party with sleighs hoping to secure supplies from the same store. Dumont intercepted the Mounties before they arrived at Duck Lake and the conflict began—but not with guns. Instead they shouted at each other until Dumont knocked down a Mountie. The Mounties retreated to Fort Carlton.

More Métis and some Cree from nearby reserves arrived, bringing Dumont's force up to about three hundred men. He set up an ambush and waited.

The next morning the Mounties came back with reinforcements and a cannon. They now had about one hundred men. Caught in Dumont's ambush and taking heavy Métis crossfire, Superintendent Leif Crozier, in charge of the police force, ordered an immediate retreat. The snow hindered their flight and the Métis picked them off as they fled. Dumont was injured. A bullet had grazed his head, which put him out of the real action. Still, he wanted to pursue the retreating Mounties to finish the job. It would have been a massacre, but Riel ordered them to stop. He didn't want anyone else to die that day.

The Métis lost five men in the Battle of Duck Lake—Isidore Dumont Jr., Assiyiwin (an elderly Cree headman), Joseph Montour, Jean Baptiste Montour and Auguste Laframboise. Three men were wounded.[40]

The Métis tell many stories about the battle of Duck Lake. They remember that Riel and Maxime Lépine fought armed only with crucifixes. Both men rode fearlessly, taking fire throughout. Neither was hit and both spent the battle encouraging the fighters. They seemed invincible, and the Métis believed that the spirit of God kept these holy men from being shot. Those fighting with guns took courage from Riel and Lépine.

Small, vivid pictures of the battle came later. François Tourond remembered a buffalo skull on the ground beside him. A shell hit the skull right in the middle of the forehead and penetrated so deeply that Tourond could not get it out. Why he tried to remove it is anyone's guess. Perhaps he thought to reuse the shell. The image of that bullet embedded in the buffalo skull was still in his mind nineteen years later.

Marguerite Caron remembered exactly where she was and what she was doing: "When the shooting started . . . I had just begun to wash my floor; I continued, although I was quite worried because my husband was over there [on the other side of the river]; it was all over before I had half of my floor washed."[41] Women non-combatants always see battles from a different perspective. Not on the battlefield and consigned to waiting, they find things to do. Anything to feel useful, to stave off the helpless feeling that the men you love might be dead or dying. It's a woman's way to measure a battle, by the length of time it takes to wash your floor. The Caron house was not large, and Marguerite's account gives some indication of how short the battle was. From start to finish the battle of Duck Lake took less than half an hour.

Others remembered the dogs. After the battle of Duck Lake, all the dogs were killed to maintain absolute silence. One cannot hear the land or an enemy over the barking of dogs.

The Métis on the Saskatchewan didn't all support the resistance fighters. Many left quietly before the fighting started, and men left with their families throughout the resistance. The ones who stayed were in it to the death. As Moïse Ouellette said, "I will stay to the end, or else I will not have a man's heart."[42]

After the battle at Duck Lake, there was a month of calm for the Métis.

Marguerite and Jean Caron and family, Batoche (*Société Historique de Saint-Boniface 1131*)

TOUROND'S COULEE

The next battle was at Tourond's Coulee on April 24, 1885.[40] By this time General Frederick Middleton had arrived with troops and militia, so it wasn't just Mounties facing the Métis. Not that they were seasoned soldiers. Many were volunteers who had never seen combat before.

The evening before, word had arrived that the Mounties were going to attack Batoche. Riel and Dumont split their forces and Riel rode back to Batoche with fifty men. Dumont set up another ambush. He placed two hundred Métis in the coulee and waited for Middleton's men to walk into the trap. Some of Middleton's scouts discovered the Métis position, however, and Dumont lost the advantage of surprise. The shooting began at nine o'clock in the morning. Dumont set fire to the prairie in an effort to smoke Middleton out. But the wind shifted and the fire went out. Middleton kept trying to advance, but the Métis held him off all day.

Men need to find courage in battle. That's not an easy thing to find when bullets are flying, men are dying around you, you have no more ammunition and you are surrounded by a force many times greater. At Tourond's Coulee, with the enemy closing in, the men found courage in the songs of the Métis bard Pierre Falcon. They wanted to show the soldiers they were not afraid, that they welcomed the battle and that they delighted in it. So, they sang their Métis Nation songs, shouted with joy and threw their coats and blankets into the air. Elie Dumont remembered it years later and how, at the time, he thought it was a beautiful sight.

They would not surrender. There was an English Métis scout named Thomas Ouri translating for Middleton. During the battle he shouted out in Cree to the Métis that they should surrender. Ten voices shouted back, "Go to hell!"[44]

Marguerite Caron was the deciding factor. She insisted Riel send reinforcements. Not a woman to be gainsaid, she reacted angrily to Riel's suggestion that she should pray. Her husband and two of her sons were out there taking enemy fire, and prayer was not her idea of what needed to be done. If Riel would not send reinforcements, she would go herself. Domitilde Gravelle's son was fighting and she wanted to go too. Domitilde had a wagon and the two women decided to go together. Riel finally relented, and a force of eighty men led by Edouard Dumont and Ambroise Champagne headed out to Tourond's Coulee. When the Métis reinforcements arrived, Edouard Dumont led a cavalry charge that forced Middleton's soldiers to withdraw. When it was over the Métis had seven bullets left.

Two Métis died during the battle—St. Pierre Parenteau Jr. and Joseph Vermette. Two other Métis, François Boyer and Michel Desjarlais, died of their wounds three days after the battle.[45]

For decades Canada claimed this battle was a victory and even mounted a plaque on the site that boldly stated that the Métis had been defeated in the battle. But there was no victory for the Canadian forces that day. Claiming victory when your general, with an army many times greater than the Métis, was forced to withdraw was a mixture of pure propaganda and hubris.

At the end of the day, there were only about sixty Métis still able to shoot. They lost fifty-five horses and had virtually no ammunition, but they successfully held off four hundred soldiers and forced them from the field. After Middleton's forces withdrew, the Métis picked over the terrain in search of badly needed bullets and rifles. They collected thirty-two carbine rifles and rode back to Batoche.

Middleton spent the next few days furiously drilling his green troops. The battle at Tourond's Coulee had been a shock to his confidence. The Métis were much better fighters than he had been led to expect, his own soldiers left much to be desired, and he had no idea what he would face in future confrontations. Would Métis from other parts of the North-West join the insurgents on the Saskatchewan? Would the First Nations join forces with the Métis?

Meanwhile events were unfolding elsewhere. The Cree, suffering greatly from starvation, raided the Hudson's Bay Company stores at Frog Lake, Fort Pitt, Cold Lake, Battleford and Lac la Biche. When the Cree arrived at the Métis community of Green Lake, the Company factor, James Nicol Sinclair, gave them food and they left without further trouble. Lawrence Clarke called the Cree visit "Riel's success at Green Lake." But Riel and the Métis of the South Saskatchewan had nothing to do with the incident at Green Lake. The Green Lake Métis were not acting in concert with their cousins on the South Saskatchewan. The Green Lake Métis didn't share the problems of the South Saskatchewan Métis. There was as yet no push for settlement that far north, so the problems of surveys and changing the land-use patterns had no meaning for them. Their own encounters with the land issues were twenty-five years in the future.

Riel and his council were in communication with Métis in Qu'Appelle, Red River and Edmonton. Riel sent letters to Métis men who had participated in the Red River Resistance. Letters went to Laurent Garneau and Benjamin Vandal, who were now living in Edmonton. The Saskatchewan Métis wanted to know about the situation in Edmonton and what support, if any, would be forthcoming from the Métis there. Garneau read the letter to Métis sympathizers in the area and kept it.

The Mounties were watching the Métis all over the North-West and were particularly concerned about the Métis in and around Edmonton. Acting on information, the Mounties raided the Garneau place. When the police arrived Laurent's wife, Eleanor, was doing the laundry. She grabbed the letter from Riel, dropped it into the washtub and started scrubbing. The police were not at the Garneau place on a random spot check. They went directly to the shelf where the letter had been moments before. Not finding it, they began a thorough search of the house. Eleanor quietly scrubbed the letter against the washboard until it dissolved into the tub. Her quick thinking didn't save her husband from arrest, charges or prison, but her destruction of incriminating evidence did help to save Laurent from execution.

When the army arrived in Edmonton, it declared martial law. Fearful of a local Cree uprising, the residents were ordered to move into the fort. Garneau and Vandal, on excellent terms with the local Cree and fearing no danger, ignored the order. For disobeying a military order made under martial law, Garneau and Vandal were arrested, taken before a military court, given a summary trial and sentenced to death. The execution was set for 6:00 the next morning.

The precipitate nature of the order and the death sentence shocked everyone. No one thought it was a good idea. The Hudson's Bay Company, the Protestant clergy, even the Mounties appealed to the commander. Edmonton was where the Métis had already taken collective action to push houses on their lands over into the ravine. Things were peaceful there at the moment, but executing two popular Métis would change that quickly. Bishop Grandin warned the commander that the execution could unleash bloody vengeance. The verdict and sentence were overturned only when Bishop Grandin appealed by telegram directly to the minister of national defence. Despite that, Garneau and Vandal were held in custody until after the war was over. They were then tried in a civil court and sentenced to six months' imprisonment. One can only imagine what would have happened had Eleanor Garneau not washed the Riel letter into the laundry.[46]

After his defeat at Tourond's Coulee, Middleton continued to drill his men and plan how to incorporate the new weapons he had ordered—two Gatling guns under the supervision of an American, Captain Arthur Howard. On arriving in Saskatchewan Howard demonstrated the gun's lethal power by slaughtering some poor ducks. Canada was eager to test these lethal weapons on its own people. Dick Cassels, a soldier with Middleton's troops, wrote in his diary, "These curious implements of destruction we inspect with interest, and their trial is watched eagerly . . . [T]he rapidity of fire shows us how very deadly a weapon of this kind might be on proper occasions. We want now to see one tried on the Indians."[47]

The Métis dubbed the gun *rubabou*, a term they use to this day, usually to mean something useless and ineffective. Naming the Gatling gun *rubabou* can be taken in one of two ways: it was either the Métis practice of *soubriquet*, their way of satirically naming this truly awful weapon, or it was an accurate assessment of the effect of the Gatling gun, which inflicted terrible damage on buildings but, according to Gabriel Dumont, actually killed only one horse.

BATOCHE

The first two battles were fought in Métis guerrilla style. Dumont chose the ground and he set the conditions. The final confrontation came on May 9 to 12, 1885, at Batoche, a small Métis settlement on the South Saskatchewan River of some eight hundred to a thousand souls. While Middleton drilled his soldiers, the Métis dug dozens of rifle pits. They were perfect places of concealment, could hold up to ten men and were fronted with logs, making them virtually bulletproof. The pits were strategically placed on the slopes of trails. From the pits men could slip in and out unseen, and fire across the river.

General Middleton had a two-pronged strategy for the Battle of Batoche. He divided his forces into a water-based attack and a land-based attack. He placed one of his two Gatling guns, thirty soldiers and two officers on the SS *Northcote*. To prepare the steamboat Middleton's men fortified it by boarding up the sides with plywood, mattresses, Gabriel Dumont's billiard table and his wife's washing machine.

The *Northcote* arrived in Batoche in advance of the land force and began to fire on the women and children on the bank. This infuriated the Métis because it was plain for all to see, including the soldiers on the *Northcote*, that there were no men there. The women and children scrambled out of gunshot range and no one was hurt.

The Métis then proceeded to take the *Northcote* out of action. One of the Métis, Xavier Letendre, owned a cable ferry at Batoche. In 1873 he had erected a tower on both banks of the river and run cables between the towers. As the *Northcote* lumbered up the river, the Métis lowered the ferry cable and sliced off the steamer's smokestacks. Suddenly it was a steamship with no steam, smokestacks in pieces on its deck and a crippled engine. The ship careened down the river for three miles and eventually beached itself on the bank. The Métis took potshots at anyone who came above deck, so the thirty combatants and civilian crew hid and refused to do any repairs. The inglorious fate of the *Northcote* did nothing to enhance Middleton's reputation, which had suffered when Canadians learned about the battle at Tourond's Coulee. The Métis had taken out one prong of his two-prong attack. They had also taken out one of the Gatling guns, which remained stranded on the *Northcote*. This *rubabou* really was useless.

The Métis then regrouped to face the land battle. Patrice Fleury commanded the men on the west side of the river and Ambroise Champagne patrolled the east side. As they had always done on the buffalo hunt, the men were organized into small units of ten with a captain; all reported to Gabriel Dumont.

There are wildly different reports about the number of Métis who fought at Batoche—anywhere from fifty to four hundred men. The number of men fighting varied on each day of the battle. Maxime Lépine said that on the last day, only fifty to sixty Métis were fighting. Middleton had 886 men and by the last day of the Battle of Batoche, his forces outnumbered the Métis by about four to one.[48] The Métis faced the North-West Field Force, which included Boulton's Mounted Infantry, the remaining Gatling gun, the 10th Royal Grenadiers, the 90th (Winnipeg) Battalion of Rifles, the Royal Regiment of Canadian Artillery "A" Battery with two nine-pounder field guns, the Midland Battalion and the Winnipeg Field Battery with two nine-pounder guns.

The shooting started at nine o'clock in the morning on May 9, 1885. Métis started firing from two houses. Both houses were quickly demolished by the big guns. No one was killed during the first attack. The North-West Field Force tried repeatedly but could not break through the Métis line. The Métis tried twice to capture the Gatling gun, but failed both times. They lit a prairie fire and almost succeeded in cutting off Middleton's supply line, but like the fire at Tourond's Coulee, it burned out too quickly. During a break in the fighting in the afternoon, Middleton took the opportunity to build a defensive enclosure called a zareba. His men hunkered down in it, and the Métis fired on it every ten minutes all night long.

During the battle the women, children, and elders, *lii vyeu*, hid. Most set up tents or dug small shelters on the east side of the South Saskatchewan River on flats surrounded by bluffs. They were away from the fighting but still well within earshot of the battle. They used anything they could find—robes, blankets and branches—for concealment during the day and to provide shelter and warmth for the elders and the children. There was little food and it was cold. There was snow on the ground and light snow continued to fall during the battle. The women tended the children, the elders, the sick and then the wounded.

Over the next two days, May 10 and 11, the fighting and the prayers continued. Dumont fought with bullets. Riel fought with prayers and urged the women to join him in his spiritual battle. Riel wasn't the only one who believed in the power of prayers and symbols. The priests told Marguerite Caron to leave her holy pictures on the walls to protect her house. It was demolished.

The Métis used every trick they could think of. From their pits they put their hats on the ends of their rifles and lifted them up. When the hats were shot off and then replaced, the army kept revising the number of Métis upward. By May 12 there were less than sixty Métis still fighting and only forty had rifles. Others were using double-barrelled shotguns. The soldiers advanced as the Métis firing slowed. The Métis were running out of ammunition, and Middleton knew because Father Végréville told him.

The women tried valiantly to help. Véronique Fidler and Rosalie Gariépy melted down anything they could find—the handles of frying pans, lead kettles, the linings of tea tins—anything that could be formed into bullets. The men by this time were using nails and spent bullets for ammunition. It became a siege of attrition. Victory was a simple matter of who had more ammunition, and that was not a battle the Métis could win. When their bullets ran out, the Battle of Batoche and La Guerre Nationale were over.

Fourteen Métis died at Batoche or later as a result of their injuries: Isidore Boyer, Damase Carrière, Charles Ducharme, Ambroise Dumont Sr., Ambroise Jobin Jr., André Batoche

Letendre, José Ouellette, Donald Ross, John Swain, Calixte Tourond, Elzéar Tourond, Joseph Trottier, Michel Trottier and Joseph Vandal. Reports vary but approximately twenty Métis were wounded.[49]

Batoche cemetery (*Glenbow Archives NA-935-8*)

CHAPTER 24

AFTER BATOCHE

La Guerre Nationale ended on May 12, 1885, and the Métis fled. The combatants, the women, the children, the sick and the elderly, fearing for their lives, abandoned everything they had and headed for the Minitinas Hills south of Batoche, eighteen miles away. There they hid for three days. They had no food and many were sick or injured. Some were pregnant, including Louis Riel's wife, Marguerite. Josephte Tourond had just given birth.

The men did their best to come to their aid. Always avoiding the soldiers who were searching the area, Gabriel Dumont scrounged for hides and took the time to make moccasins for barefoot children. He found food and blankets and distributed them among the sick, the young and the old. Louis Riel visited his wife and their two children three times.

The question for the men was whether to surrender to Middleton or to head to the United States. Most of the women wanted their sons, fathers and husbands to go to the United States. There the men would be safe and the women might be able to join them later. The women wanted their men alive, even if that meant they were far away. They didn't want their men imprisoned and they didn't want them executed. There was no blame for their men. Blame was reserved for the government they felt had pursued and mistreated them. But in the immediate aftermath of the war, it wasn't a question of blame. There was bitterness and anger to swallow, but the immediate need was survival. It would be better for the men to go over the line.

The women would manage, somehow. They were not afraid to stand up for themselves when they needed to. When Marguerite Caron saw the medical officer on one of her best mares, she marched straight up to the horse, unsaddled it and took it away. The soldiers were so stunned, they didn't say anything. In the midst of the battle and the men who were dying, Josephte Tourond gave birth in the cold and the snow. The women helping her were afraid light would attract bullets, so they only lit a fire during the final moments of the birth. After May 12 the English soldiers started looting and helped themselves to all manner of Métis goods. They stacked up their loot in a big pile. Madame Tourond searched the collection, and when she saw her own case, she tried to pick it up. Some soldiers shoved her away. But Madame Tourond spoke fluent English and took them to task for their rudeness. She demanded they hand over her case. Fortunately, an officer came to her assistance and when she told him that she had just given birth and the case contained clothes for herself and her new child, the officer kindly gave her the case and reprimanded his soldiers. It is one of the few stories that show any kindness on the part of the soldiers toward the Métis. In Edmonton the families of Garneau and Vandal, who were still in prison, were left destitute. Cree chief Papaschayo fed and cared for them.

There are many stories of wanton theft and destruction by the soldiers. Two of those stories are "The Bell of Batoche" and "Bremner's Furs."

THE BELL OF BATOCHE

After the Battle of Batoche, the soldiers looted the town, stealing money, furs, horses and anything they fancied. They burned and destroyed farms, houses and stores. Middleton's soldiers stole a church bell, which ended up in Millbrook, Ontario, as a trophy of war. Quite a bit of pressure was put on the town to return the bell. But Millbrook was staunchly Orange and there was no way they were going to give back a trophy they thought they had earned. A letter to the editor of *The Port Hope Evening Guide* provides the attitude of the day:

> What are you giving us about the bell that our Boys brought from the North-West rebellion? You say that the Bell was stole . . . The Bell was not stole. It was taken from the church where the rebels got together to arrange to shoot our brave boys—or at least that is where the priest said service and preached to them, and I don't see much difference. Mr. Ward [the local MP] need not come out to Millbrook to coax the bell away from our Hall so as to hang it up in a Catholic steeple again. I tell you the boys ain't going to give it up . . . I tell you we would have a Catholic bell in every Orange Lodge in Durham, and we wouldn't have to go as far as Frog Lake for them too. It's time us Protestants got together and put a stop to all this talk about stealing a bell from the Catholics. That kind of people have no right to have a Bell to ring in this country. I'd put a stop to it and take all their property from them and divide it among the true men of this country who are all Orangemen.

> You needn't fret your gizzard about the Catholics and the Bell . . . No, sir, we mean business now, both about keeping this Bell that our boys got in the North-West and everything else about Protestantism, and you can yell the wind out of your carcass until you have none left and we will keep the Bell . . . and don't you forget it.
>
> No Surrender
> Millbrook, July 7, 1888[1]

The bell remained in Millbrook, first hidden in a farmer's field, then used in the local fire hall and finally displayed in a showcase in the Legion Hall. A hundred years later, in 1990, the Saskatchewan Métis sent a letter to the Millbrook Legion requesting the return of the bell to Batoche. The response from one Millbrook Legion member was, "We got it. You tried to wreck the country and we stopped ya. And we got the bell. It's ours. Can ya get it any plainer than that?"[2] As far as Millbrook was concerned, nothing much had changed since 1888.[3] But the bell has now been reacquired by the Métis Nation of Alberta.

BREMNER'S FURS

The soldiers also stole Métis furs. The loss and wanton destruction of furs was a financial disaster for the Métis. The wealth of the community didn't come from farming. What they could grow on their farms provided subsistence food only. Their economy depended on their hunting and trapping. And since the buffalo were gone, they now trapped fur-bearers.

The soldiers destroyed any furs they found in the villages. Baptiste Boyer, one of the best trappers, had been storing his large stash of furs in his attic. The soldiers took his furs and cut them into shreds as they travelled away from Batoche. Bits and pieces of beaver, otter and mink pelts were scattered over twelve miles. Madame Fisher reported that Middleton had his men dig a large hole in front of Batoche's store, where they buried thousands of dollars of furs.

The soldiers also helped themselves to Charles Bremner's furs. Bremner was not one of the Métis insurgents. He had arrived from a Protestant, English-speaking Métis parish in Red River and settled on the Saskatchewan.[5] While the Métis were engaged in their battles at Duck Lake and Tourond's Coulee, the Cree had been engaged in their own battles. Many others, including those like Bremner who identified as "half-breeds" and did not support Riel and Dumont, were caught in the middle. Bremner's family and other settlers were taken hostage by Chief Poundmaker's Cree band and forced to move as the camp moved. Finally, on May 23, 1885, Poundmaker's band surrendered. Throughout his captivity with Poundmaker, Bremner had carefully guarded his furs. They were worth between $5,000 and $7,000, and Poundmaker had honoured Bremner's property.

When the soldiers captured Poundmaker's band, they simply did not believe that Bremner's group were captives. Bremner was a "half-breed" and to the soldiers, all such people were rebels. All were sent to Regina, where Bremner was taken into custody and charged with treason felony. When his case finally came to trial, the Crown admitted that it had no evidence against him and Bremner was discharged on his own recognizance.[6] But Bremner wanted his furs. He needed them to rebuild his farm.

It was General Middleton and two men on his staff who stole some of Bremner's furs. The rest of the furs were handed out to other officers. All of this was done under signed orders from General Middleton or Colonel Otter. The theft of Bremner's furs is what brought Middleton down. The articles of war stated that property could only be confiscated by judicial or legislative action, and even the property of a man convicted of treason devolved to his children. Middleton was a general and he knew the law. But he testified that he thought he could do pretty much as he liked.

Bremner pressed for compensation for five long years. Eventually, a committee of inquiry found the general's appropriation of the furs highly improper. In Parliament, Macdonald went further and said it was an illegal act that could not be defended. By this point some members of the House were out for the general's blood. They insisted that Middleton compensate Bremner and be dismissed from his command of the military force in Canada. Finally, the House unanimously adopted the conclusions of the inquiry. It was May 16, 1890.

During the inquiry, after five years of denial, Middleton finally admitted he had ordered the furs confiscated for himself and his staff. He also promised to indemnify Bremner. But he claimed the furs had mysteriously disappeared, that he never received them and never profited from his order. Middleton resigned in July 1890, bitter about his treatment in Canada. He felt he had risked his life for Canada and that he was sacrificed for the French vote. He warned that the Canadian press would be sorry and left the country in disgrace. Once safely in England, Middleton refused to pay Bremner.

Bremner continued his fight for compensation. It took him until 1899 to get payment for his furs from Canada. Canada finally paid him because they were sick to death of the stubborn man and the only way to make him go away was to pay him for his stolen furs.

THE AFTERMATH

After Batoche many of the Métis fled south of the border. There they joined the four Métis settlements in Montana and North

Dakota—St. Peter's Mission, Lewistown, Poplar River Agency and Turtle Mountain. The Canadian government sent spies to follow them. One of the spies reported that thirty Métis from the South Saskatchewan arrived in Lewistown, Montana, in the fall of 1885 and spent the winter there. This is where Gabriel Dumont and his family landed.

According to the spies, the general feeling in Montana was against Riel, though it seems support for Riel depended on whether one was a Republican (for Riel) or a Democrat (against Riel). By the end of December 1885, the spy's assessment was that there was no danger of a future rising from the Métis living south of the line, and if there was one, it would come from Turtle Mountain, where Gabriel Dumont intended to settle in the spring.

There are stories that Dumont tried to organize a rescue for Riel, but if that is so, it came to naught. When his wife, Madeleine, died in the spring of 1886, Dumont was at loose ends. He accepted an offer to join Buffalo Bill Cody's Wild West show. Along with Annie Oakley, he performed trick shots for audiences throughout the eastern United States. He began a series of speaking engagements at meetings of French-Canadian nationalists in Quebec, where they were eager to hear about the North-West Resistance. The nationalist movement of the Métis Nation resonated with their Quebec nationalist aspirations. But Dumont was not Riel. He was not erudite like Riel and he was bitterly critical of the Church. It was not what the Association Saint-Jean-Baptiste de Montréal wanted to hear. They dropped him as quickly as they had picked him up. The *idea* of the mighty Métis hunter of the Plains who had fought for the Métis Nation was much better than the man in person. The Canadian government granted the participants in the North-West Resistance amnesty in 1886. After his brief stint as a showman and the unsuccessful attempt at public speaking, Dumont went back home to Batoche.

Some Métis men fled south of the border, some surrendered and some simply went home and waited to see whether they would be arrested or not. The Métis leaders who stayed were all arrested. Some who surrendered began to work for the soldiers. There was no rhyme or reason to how they were treated. Patrice Fleury, despite being a captain of the scouts and participating fully in the battles, was hired to take the police to Qu'Appelle and got paid well for his work. Damase Carrière suffered a broken leg during the battle of Batoche. He died after soldiers tied a rope around his neck and dragged him. The soldiers thought he was Riel.

The relationship between the Métis and the priests was irreparably damaged. The priests had used all their energy to undermine Riel and denounce the Métis recourse to arms. They had actively worked to stop Métis in other settlements from joining their brothers. Archbishop Taché had ordered Father St-Germain to Wood Mountain to quiet the Métis there. In the Métis settlement at Green Lake the priests threatened excommunication from the Church if the men went to join their brothers in arms at Batoche. The priests were both afraid of a general Métis uprising and panicked that their missions would be destroyed. They abandoned their mission at Île-à-la-Crosse in a wild fear that Riel held them responsible for his sister Sara's death and would order the massacre of the nuns there. In fact the only action the Métis took with respect to the Church was to confine Fathers Végréville and Moulin and six nuns at Batoche. The Métis did not pillage any missions.

But they knew that the priests had been in constant communication with the soldiers during Batoche and always believed that was a betrayal. Middleton knew they were short of ammunition because of Father Végréville. When Father André told the imprisoned Métis they got what they deserved, Patrice Tourond turned on him angrily and said, "When we wanted to go to confession on the eve of the Battle of Batoche, you refused. My two brothers were killed and they had been refused that sacrament. Now that we don't need you, you spend all your time trying to get us to confession. We don't want you."[7]

Despite the animosity, the priests tried to salvage their relationship with the rank and file Métis. Father Lacombe sent a long letter to Public Works Minister Hector Langevin, providing a character reference for many of the Métis prisoners. This was accompanied by a plea for leniency.

The priests began working with the one-man-to-blame theory. Father Lacombe blamed it all on Riel and claimed that the Métis were just "poor ignorant people"[8] who had been duped and exploited by Riel. Father André provided a long deposition as to the character of the Métis in the trial of Joseph Arcand. He declared that with the exception of Gabriel Dumont, Napoléon Neault and Damase Carrière, the Métis were the poor deluded dupes of Riel.

The one-man-to-blame theory of the Métis national war continued and has persisted ever since. According to Father Lacombe, Riel forced the men to take up arms. The priests spread this story, but they knew it wasn't true. They knew the Métis were defending their lands, their women and their children. The priests knew this was the reason the Saskatchewan Métis sent for Riel in the first place. Still, the priests claimed they pitied the poor Métis, who would never have done this if it hadn't been for Riel. The priests saved their hostility—and there was a great deal of it—for Riel.

According to the priests Riel had usurped their role as intermediaries with God. He had manipulated the Métis and terrorized them. He was an agent of Satan. Riel alone deserved to be punished. The priests found a way of neatly framing the story: Riel was insane and therefore not responsible for his wild religious beliefs. But it was a temporary fit of insanity because Riel reconciled with Father André just before his death. It was a convenient argument that allowed the priests to sweep the participation of hundreds of Métis under the carpet.

The Métis of Batoche were not the only ones who repudiated the priests after 1885. The Métis of Green Lake accused the priests of deceiving them and provoking Riel to revolt. The Métis of Lesser Slave Lake accused Father Lacombe of selling their lands to the government. Father Moulin in Batoche complained that the Métis were not going to confession anymore. The Métis in St. Laurent stopped attending vespers or taking communion regularly. The Métis no longer introduced themselves to priests and they no longer took the priests' political advice. The young people absorbed the new antagonism to the Church. After Batoche, the relationship between the Métis and the Church was strained almost to the breaking point. Tourond was not the only Métis who decided he no longer wanted or needed the priests or the Church.

In the first brutal days after Batoche, Riel and Dumont tried to maintain contact with their families and avoid capture at the same time. Dumont was better at this than Riel, and he was defiant. He would not surrender and he didn't want Riel to surrender either. Middleton sent Moïse Ouellette with letters for Dumont and Riel. The letters were surrender demands. Dumont took the letter and asked what it said. The letter promised justice,

Ouellette said, justice that would be granted in exchange for Dumont's surrender. Dumont didn't believe in that kind of justice. Justice in the hands of Canada meant one thing only: death at the end of a rope. He continued to evade the search parties. Father André basically laughed when the Mounties asked him where Dumont was: "You are looking for Gabriel? Well, you are wasting your time, there isn't a blade of grass on the prairie he does not know."[9] Father André was right. No soldier had the skills or knew the land well enough to find Dumont. Dumont continued to search for Louis. He remained defiant, saying, "I will not lay down my arms—I will fight forever . . . never to be taken alive . . . I will not surrender, but I will keep searching for Riel—not to make him surrender, but escape. If I find him before the law does, I won't let him surrender."

Riel had different ideas. Unlike Dumont, Riel had already tasted the bitterness of exile in the United States. He knew exactly what it would be like. He would always be looking over his shoulder for the next attack. This time there would be no amnesty, no way to quietly visit his family in St. Vital. He would have no way of making money and no supporters. Riel knew they wanted him more than any of the others. Perhaps if he surrendered, they would be lenient with the men. Maybe the Métis would have a chance to get some justice if he could present their case. Maybe they would be happy with his head.

Riel and Dumont had hidden in the Minitinas Hills south of Batoche for three days. After assuring himself that his family was cared for, Riel spent most of the time praying. The soldiers were scouring the hills in search of the combatants. By May 15, 1885, Riel had decided. He walked up to a soldier, introduced himself and surrendered. Other than the clothing on his back, Riel had nothing but a bible, some papers and pencils, and his marriage certificate.

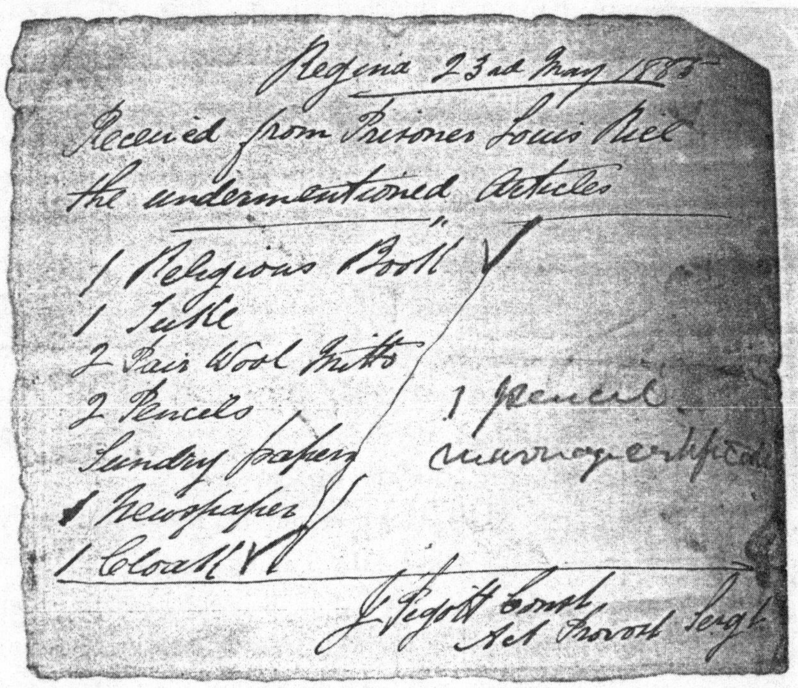

Regina 23rd May 188

Received from Prisoner Louis Riel the undermentioned Articles

1 Religious Book
1 Tuke
2 Pair Wool Mitts
2 Pencils
Sundry papers
1 Newspaper
1 Cloak

1 pencil
marriage certificate

J. Pigott Corpl.
Act Provost Sergt.

List of the items Louis Riel had on his person when he surrendered (*Teillet family papers*)

CHAPTER 25

THE TRIAL OF LOUIS RIEL

Riel was held under tight security. The soldiers were afraid the Métis would attempt a rescue. But Riel was not focused on rescue. His mind was on his wife, Marguerite, and his two children. Marguerite was sick with tuberculosis, she had no home, she was pregnant and she was now the sole support for their two children. Louis's brother Joseph went to Saskatchewan to pick up Marguerite and the children. He took them back to St. Vital, where the Riel family cared for Marguerite and eased the fears of Louis's two children—each now a war child with all the trauma and scars that war leaves on a child's body, heart and mind. It eased Louis's heart that his family would be cared for.

Louis also worried about the Métis left back in Batoche. When he heard that Gabriel Dumont had escaped, he was pleased. But he had no idea what was happening to the rest of the people. The truth is it was bad there. The Métis combatants who were captured were transferred to Regina. Twenty-four men were charged with treason felony.[1] The other men fled, mostly to the United States. The women were left in houses that had been burned or shelled or looted by the army. Money, horses, cattle and food were stolen and fields were destroyed.

The women back at Batoche lived in the ruins. Nine of the women of Batoche died shortly after from consumption, flu or miscarriages. Madeleine Dumont died shortly after joining Gabriel in the Montana Territory in 1886. Younger widows had to depend on other families for shelter and sustenance, or else they had to remarry. One woman found a job teaching at Vandal School near Fish Creek, but the only job available for most of the women was as a domestic servant. Josephte Tourond, Marguerite Caron and Marie Champagne rebuilt and managed their family farms.

Louis Riel was transferred under heavy guard to Regina. On July 6, 1885, he was charged with high treason. Friends in Montreal put together a legal defence team, and the matter moved quickly to the courts. Knowing that lawyers were coming to represent him, Riel began to write. He saw the trial as his chance to speak, to justify what the Métis had done. He was being watched carefully and his writing became the subject of intense speculation. His brother Joseph was anxious to preserve his writings.[2] But Riel's immediate purpose in writing was not for his family or for posterity. It was meant to educate his lawyers. Knowing they were coming from Quebec and not fully versed in the issues, he wrote his justification for the North-West Resistance.

His lawyers thanked him for his efforts. At this point they were still humouring him. They arrived in Regina with a fully formed agenda, and nothing Riel said or did was going to change that. They had already decided on an insanity defence, and they were going to ram that through the court whether Riel liked it or not. He didn't. He was adamant: if he was to die, it would not be as a madman.

(T. Form K.)

This Blank to be used for Commercial Messages only.

Canadian Pacific Railway Company's Telegraph.

Terms and Conditions.—All messages are received by this company for transmission subject to the terms and conditions printed on their blank Form I., which terms and conditions have been agreed to by the sender of the following message.

Sent by R Rec'd by

Check 22 pd 106

No. 248 Time 1250p Aug 18 1885

By Telegraph from St Boniface 11

To Louis Riel. Regina

Jai appris. Que tu
Ecris La vie ne
donne ce Livre a personne
Gardes le pour moi
Jy tiens beaucoup
Surtout la femme
Irai le voir bientot
Reponds de suite
Reponse payee

Joseph Riel

To secure prompt despatch send reply to

Joseph Riel's telegram to Louis asking him to save the book for him (*Teillet family papers*)

RIEL'S SANITY

Riel's sanity is a touchy issue. The Riel family has never believed that Louis was insane. Joseph Riel firmly believed that Louis only pretended to be insane. Members of the Riel family to this day insist that Louis was not insane and that he only feigned insanity.[3] Despite these claims there is evidence that Louis had periods in his life when he suffered from mental depressions, hallucinations and emotional disturbances. He suffered from depression after his father died in 1864. From 1875 to 1876 he was placed in an asylum under the name of Mr. David in Longue-Pointe, Quebec. Fearing the vengeance of the Orange Lodge, Dr. Howard later transferred Riel to the Beauport asylum.[4] There is evidence that while Riel lived at Beauport, he was able to come and go freely and had several visitors. He met people in other villages and towns, such as Trois-Rivières. He even met with Wilfrid Laurier. Whether he was a voluntary inmate or not, Riel remained at Beauport until January 21, 1878.

The Riel family was not alone in its assertions that Louis was only feigning insanity. Three doctors who were his physicians over the years signed sworn affidavits attesting to the fact that notwithstanding "Riel's peculiar views upon religious subjects which so strongly impress the ignorant and unreflecting with an idea of his madness," he was perfectly sane.[5]

Was Riel insane or was he feigning insanity and seeking asylum from the Orange Lodge in the asylum? Riel's own words likely provide the best insight into his mental state during the late 1870s:

> I had come to believe myself a prophet. It seemed to me that the papacy should leave the moth-eaten soil of Europe for the new world. I saw the light of civilization grow from the Orient, the Euphrates, Palestine, Rome. It seemed to me that it was America's turn, and I believed that I had an important role to play in the new order of things. By pen and sword I tried to make converts.

> However, one day tired of fighting opposition, I asked myself if I was right or if everyone else was right. At that moment, the light came to me. Today I am better, I laugh myself at my hallucinations of my brain. I have a free spirit, but when one speaks to me of the Métis, those poor tragic people, the fanatic Orangemen, of the brave hunters who are treated like savages, who are of my blood, of my religion, who have chosen me as their leader, who love me, and whom I love as brothers, ah, alas! My blood boils, my head gets on fire, and it is wiser if I speak of other things.[6]

Riel's sanity has never been an issue for the Métis. But it is an obsession with Canadian historians. The Métis Nation knows that, but generally finds the whole issue irrelevant to what the man did, what he stood for and their reverence for him. This is not to say that all Métis have always been without criticism of Riel. Some thought everything he did was wrong, and some thought everything he did was right, only he should have done more of it. Some wish he had given Dumont more freedom to direct the fighting in La Guerre Nationale. Some wish he had never been brought to the Saskatchewan at all.

But for most Métis, Riel continues to be their saint, *aen saent*, an intensely religious man who saw, talked and walked with God, the angels and the souls of the dead. They saw and continue to see his mysticism and visions as evidence that he was a man of God. They have generally thought the best of Riel, and the best of him includes, and has always included, his connection with God in his everyday world. Indeed, it is that very connection that recommends Riel to the Métis. Because of it, he was seen as being above corruption and above the commonplace world of opportunity.

The Métis also see the Canadian focus on Riel's sanity as a double standard. They often point out that Sir John A. Macdonald was a drunk who disappeared for great periods of time into the bottle. During those times Macdonald was non-functional. It was a serious problem for the governance of the country, but no one tried to dismiss everything Macdonald did because of it. No one dismisses the political party he led or the people of Canada because Macdonald was a binge alcoholic.

At bottom, the Métis Nation wants Riel to be judged for his actions only. By that they mean one simple fact: Riel fought for them and he died for them. He was a mystic and deeply religious. He believed he had a mission from God. The Métis do not see any of this as evidence of insanity. They will not judge Riel by the mental illness standards of others. For the Métis, Riel's actions amount to a grand gesture of defiance. Riel was their prophet, their inspiration and their leader. He died for the Métis Nation, for their rights, their lives, their lands and their very existence. Like him or not, think him insane or not, in the end all that matters is that Riel stood up for the Métis over and over again. That is what they remember him for. That is what they revere him for.

What Canadians remember Riel for is something quite different. French Canadians see Riel as the defender of their language. For others he is the voice of western alienation. He is a great Indigenous leader. All of these aspects can be critiqued in fact and in theory. All of them have been critiqued. They will likely continue to be part of Canada's ongoing dialogue. But insanity—that is the obsession of Canadians and it is what got Riel hanged. At Riel's trial the defence lawyers ran their insanity defence, and it was *their* insanity defence. It certainly wasn't Riel's chosen defence. The lawyers ignored Riel's objections.

The injustice of the trial, including how it was conducted and its result, has always been a major source of discomfort for the Métis, and indeed for the entire country. So much so that there are conferences about the defence of Riel, and several books and journal articles, one of which was written by the former chief justice of the Supreme Court of Canada, Beverley McLachlin.[7]

The essential elements of what is still considered unfair break down into four issues: (1) the charges; (2) the venue, judge and jury; (3) the denial of time for defence to prepare; and (4) the lawyers.

Macdonald and the justice minister, Sir Alexander Campbell, decided to charge Riel with high treason under the 1351 Statute of Treasons. Why did the Crown proceed under a statute that was over five hundred years old when there were other options?[8] The answer is simple: Macdonald wanted Riel to hang. He needed a statute that would guarantee a death sentence with no other option. If there was one thing Macdonald did not want, it was Riel alive and in prison. The only available statute with a mandatory death sentence was the 1351 Statute of Treasons. Both of the other statutes offered options of life imprisonment.[9]

Why did Macdonald want to hang Riel? There are several reasons. First, he needed to justify the massive public expenditure and the use of the army to put down what was really a small, localized incident that should have been dealt with by negotiation or political means. Second, Macdonald wanted a permanent solution to the problem of the Métis. They had been a thorn in his side for decades and he wanted them eliminated.

But there was great sympathy for the Métis generally, especially in Quebec, which left Macdonald without the option of a mass execution. The Liberal opposition was loudly blaming the government for causing the uprising in the first place.

Macdonald needed to distract public attention away from the government's role in instigating the war. He also needed to undermine the opposition claims that the Métis had legitimate complaints. For both Church and state, blaming everything on Riel was the perfect solution. Hang Riel and they would cut off the head, the voice and hopefully the heart of the Métis Nation. Macdonald thought it was the perfect and permanent solution to the Métis problem.

There remains a curious irony that Riel, a man who lived every moment of his life with fear and love of God, was charged with being "moved and seduced by the instigation of the devil" and not having "the fear of God in his heart."[10] He faced six counts of levying war against the queen—two charges for Duck Lake, two for Fish Creek (Tourond's Coulee) and two for Batoche. The duplicate charges for each battle reflect the uncertainty about Riel's citizenship. The first three charges presumed he was a Canadian citizen. The last three charges presumed he was an American. In fact, Riel had become an American citizen in 1883, making the duplicate charges inapplicable. The statute under which he was charged—and hence the fact he was facing a mandatory death penalty—became clear only partway through the proceeding.

The trial was initially going to be held in Manitoba. There, Riel would have been tried by a jury of twelve composed of six francophones and six anglophones. Other protections extended by law to defendants would have been available to Riel. But Macdonald changed the venue to Regina. In Regina Riel would have a lesser justice in the form of a jury not of his peers and a political appointee instead of an independent judge. His jury was composed of six white Protestant men and a judge who got his job by an appointment from Macdonald, and who could be fired if he didn't deliver the judgment Macdonald wanted.

Judge Hugh Richardson didn't speak French, which put Riel and all the francophones at a severe disadvantage. He denied all of Riel's lawyers' motions—seeking more time to prepare, to call witnesses and to obtain evidence. His conduct over the Métis trials showcased the patronage system that got him appointed. His decisions provide enduring evidence that he was not a highly skilled lawyer or judge.

Riel's lawyers were respected members of the bar and they worked conscientiously, but not on his behalf. Instead it appears they were working at the behest of the Quebec men who retained their services, and they reported to the priests. If they had worked for Riel, they would have respected his wishes as to how to conduct the defence. They would never have run an insanity defence over his objections, and they would have called to the stand at least some of the thirty Métis witnesses who were jailed next door. Instead they called no one and they resolutely resisted Riel's objections to the testimony put forward by the witnesses. This behaviour is highly problematic. It was 1885, but a lawyer was still obligated to represent the client's wishes, even if it would result in a guilty verdict. Every person has the right to determine his or her own defence, and no lawyer has the right to override that wish. But that is what happened to Riel.

There was a fundamental disconnect between Riel and his legal team as to how the trial should be conducted. Riel wanted a justification defence. His defence team viewed that as a legal non-starter. Riel's wish to run a justification defence was the only defence on the merits of the case. None of the other defences—insanity, questions about jurisdiction or breaches of his procedural rights—touched on what had actually happened to the Métis on the South Saskatchewan. Riel wanted nothing to do with any of the procedural defences. He wanted to defend himself based on the merits of the Métis cause. That, after all, was what the North-West Resistance had been all about.

Riel's mistake was to believe that justice in the Canadian system was available to him. He never wavered in his wish to present the Métis case to the court. But no one would allow the Métis case to be heard in the court—not the judge, not his lawyers and certainly not Macdonald. Riel was allowed to make his statement, but it was not evidence that could be considered by the jury. Perhaps Riel was insane—to believe he could get justice for the Métis in a Canadian court.

The jury found Riel guilty but recommended clemency. Richardson sentenced Riel to hang. The Manitoba Court of Queen's Bench dismissed the appeal. The Privy Council upheld the dismissal. The ball was then squarely in the court of Parliament. The prime minister, under pressure to at least appear neutral, appointed a medical commission to inquire into Riel's sanity. Dewdney confirmed Riel's sanity in a coded telegram to the prime minister. No one was surprised when Parliament confirmed Riel's sanity and rejected the jury's plea of clemency.

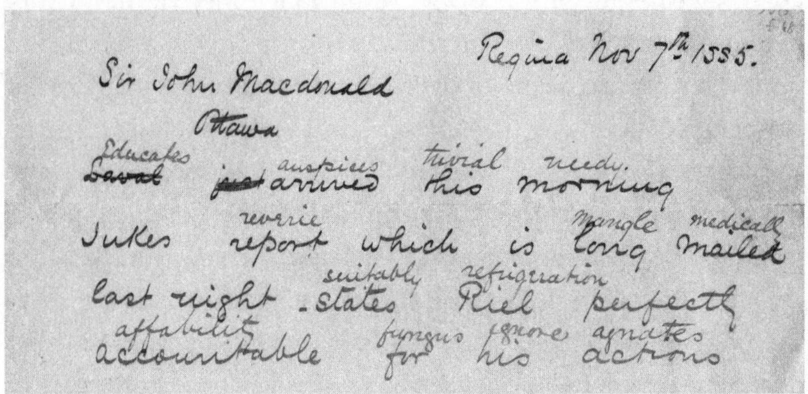

Regina Nov 7th 1885.

Sir John Macdonald

Ottawa

Educates auspices trivial needy.
~~Dewdney~~ ~~just~~ arrived this morning

reverie mangle medically
Jukes report which is long mailed

suitably refrigeration
last night. states Riel perfectly

affability fungus ignore agnates
accountable for his actions

Riel's code name is "refrigeration" in Dewdney's coded telegram to Macdonald confirming Riel's sanity (*Glenbow Archives M-320-1482*)

THE PETITIONS

Thousands petitioned the government about Riel.[11] The Orange Lodge immediately registered its demand that the sentence be carried out and clemency of any kind be refused: "[I]t is the sweetest savor of their nostrils to annihilate us [the English-speaking people in Canada] . . . but with the blessing of God we will yet conquer the blood-thirsty Indian and all his abettors . . . if this Riel, who is all of French and Indian instinct, will receive the gallows, then the English-speaking people might be more secure of their lives."[12] But most of the petitions sought clemency for Riel. There were fifty-seven petitions and telegrams from those who wished Riel's sentence to be commuted. They came from France, Great Britain, the United States, Quebec, Manitoba and Saskatchewan. They were signed by one person, or by hundreds, or by almost two thousand.[13]

The petitions raised various reasons for clemency. Some claimed that Riel's actions were the result of his aberration of mind, which raised a doubt as to his legal responsibility. One petition frankly called Riel a crank lacking the intellect necessary to be held responsible for his acts. Many of the petitions pointed to the lack of a fair trial.

Over eight hundred people from Chicago signed a petition saying that Riel's cause was that of all the Métis of the North-West, and his execution would be a refusal to do justice to a great portion of the population of Canada, with consequences. Some petitioners said the cause of the insurrection was the refusal of the Canadian government to grant to the French population of the Saskatchewan District their just rights and privileges that had been promised to them in 1874 by Lieutenant-Governor Morris. Petitioners from Quebec claimed:

> [T]he offence of which the said Louis Riel has been found guilty is purely political, and is shared in by a great number of Her Majesty's subjects and . . . the cause of Riel is that of all the . . . [Métis] of the North-West, of whom he was constituted the defender; that the rights of these people cannot be ignored without refusing them that justice which is due to every free citizen . . . and the execution of Riel . . . might become a cause, much to be regretted of dangerous conflicts and might drive to despair respectable and peace-loving people.[14]

Some of the petitions wanted the sentence to be delayed until a special commission had inquired into the nature of the troubles in the North-West and made a report. Two thousand people from Quebec drew attention to the many petitions sent by the Métis before they resorted to arms. Others argued the Métis had only taken up arms to defend their rights. The American under secretary of state urged clemency, noting that the causes that "provoked the revolt of the North-West, the extraordinary proceedings which characterized the trial . . . [and] the ill-feeling generated by these facts" were some of the many powerful reasons to commute the sentence.[15]

Americans pointed out that if their revolution had gone the other way, Washington, Franklin, Hamilton and Adams would have ended their days upon the scaffold. They quoted Burke's argument that "you cannot frame an indictment against a people."[16] Nor can you, they said, inflict capital punishment on one man for participation in public or quasi-political movements in which large bodies of people took part or sympathized.

The Métis from all over the North-West petitioned for Riel's life. The Métis of Red River sent fifteen petitions signed by Riel's relatives, supporters and friends, including his comrades in the Red River Resistance, André Nault, Elzéar Lagimodière and August Harrison.

And finally, from the only petition not signed by men: "A woman begs Canadian authorities pardon Riel."[17]

HIS SOUL GOES MARCHING ON

On the morning of November 16, 1885, the rising sun revealed a stunningly beautiful hoar frost coating the grasses, the trees and a brand-new gallows in Regina. It was the morning Louis Riel was to be hanged. By all accounts, Riel met death with great dignity. He made no final speech to justify his actions. He simply prayed and gave his soul, heart and body into the keeping of the God he had loved and served.

This quiet but profound gallows scene was not mirrored in the world outside. There the world was shrill with vitriol. Fifty thousand marched in the streets of Montreal, crying for Prime Minister Macdonald's head, while the newspaper headlines in English Canada crowed with victory at the death of the hated Riel. The excuse for hanging Riel was the North-West Resistance. But English Canada really hanged Riel as revenge for Thomas Scott.

Comparisons between Riel and John Brown arose immediately. John Brown and a small band of men had raided Harper's Ferry to rouse Americans against slavery. The opinion of the day was that John Brown was a crank. When Riel was hanged, Americans were quick to see the parallels between two men who were in the vanguard of what they called a "revolt against tyranny." Americans, no fans of the British, opined that it would be "difficult to find a place, no matter how inhospitable, where the blasting breath of British tyranny does not make itself felt."[18]

THOMSON & WILLIAMS,
UNDERTAKERS.

Winnipeg, Dec. 7th 188

Section

Plot At St Boniface

Name of deceased Louis Riel

Cause of Death Hung & Rebellion

Where Born St Boniface

Where Died Hung at Regina

Date of Death Nov

Religion R C

Married 28 yrs *Single*

Name of Attending Physician

Charges

Louis Riel's death certificate (*Teillet family papers*)

The Métis Nation did not die with Riel on that day in 1885. The Nation had suffered a blow, but within two years the Métis were already gathering their forces and forming a new organization. Riel was dead, but his soul became the spark that kept the flame of the Métis Nation alive. Like John Brown's movement, Riel's ideas would permeate the North-West and become a magnet around which Métis Nation rights and title would galvanize and begin to take more substantial form in the laws of Canada. Riel gave up his life for the Métis Nation and its rights. He has never been forgotten, and eventually, Canadians began to recognize the justice of the cause he fought for.

To this day Macdonald is remembered for slandering Riel and Quebec all in one ugly sentence when he said, "He shall hang though every dog in Québec bark in his favour."[19] But in hanging Riel, Macdonald ensured that Riel would live. On that fateful day in November 1885 when Riel was hanged, Macdonald created exactly what he sought to extinguish: a martyr and a movement. Both march on.

"*Riel—Martyr Politique!*" This handbill was printed, circa 1885, by l'Union, St. Hyacinthe, Quebec. (*Library and Archives Canada C-018084*)

PART SEVEN

SETTLEMENT

CHAPTER 26

SCRIP

Scrip is obsolete now and virtually unknown to most Canadians today. But it's still a household word in the Métis Nation. Scrip was a coupon that could be redeemed for money or land. Money scrip was usually issued in the amount of $80, $160 or $240. Land scrip was a coupon that, once cashed in, was supposed to issue to the bearer a plot of land in the amount of 80, 160 or 240 acres. Though a scrip coupon felt and looked like a large banknote, it did more than provide money or land. Scrip was a reward, a pacifier and an eraser. Both sides of the North-West Resistance received scrip. Soldiers were rewarded for their services with scrip. The government used scrip to pacify the Métis and to erase their claims to Aboriginal title. The Métis scrip process was a rotten deal. And everybody knew it.

SCRIP AND TREATY

If scrip was just a grant of land for the Métis, as it was for the soldiers, it would not have been such a rotten deal. But it was much more than that. It also purported to extinguish their individual identity as Métis and their collective Indigenous title to land. Since the Royal Proclamation of 1763, Britain, and then Canada, had operated on a policy that Indigenous lands could be purchased and title to their lands could be extinguished. For First Nations, treaties were the means by which this extinguishment was accomplished. One should not assume that the First Nations believed or have ever accepted that their treaties extinguished their title and rights. But the government always had control of the pen in drafting the treaties and control of what was explained to the First Nations during the treaty "negotiations." So the English versions of the treaties invariably contain cede, release, surrender provisions that purport to extinguish Indigenous title to those lands and transfer them to the Crown. Treaties were the wholesale transfer of large swaths of land to the Crown from one or more First Nation bands. Scrip was meant to accomplish the same thing, only it was done on an individual basis because the Crown did not accept the existence of a Métis collective with title and rights.

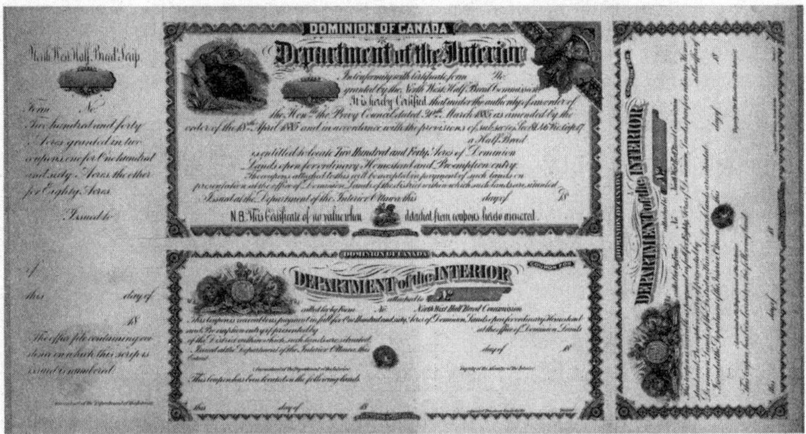

Métis scrip issued by the Department of the Interior (*Glenbow Archives NA-2839-3*)

There were several options on the table for Métis. If they were closely connected with a First Nation band, they were usually allowed, with the permission of the chief, to join the band and take treaty. Indeed, several chiefs pleaded with the Crown negotiators for Métis to be able to join them. When the Métis began to negotiate with the treaty commissioners, they requested their own bands and their own reserves. This is what happened in the Half-breed Adhesion to Treaty #3.

Many Métis took advantage of these opportunities, joined treaty and in so doing became "Indians." This happened often where treaty preceded scrip. When scrip was offered later, some Métis opted to transfer from treaty to scrip. There are also examples of Métis who took scrip and then switched to treaty. Some switched more than once. It was by no means a process with a clean divide between Métis and First Nations.

SCRIP PROCESS

The scrip application process was intimidating. Louis Morin described the scrip commission's visit to Île-à-la-Crosse. According to Morin, the scrip commissioners set up their office in a large tent and two Mounties stood on each side of the tent opening. The Métis had to enter the tent by walking through a police gate. The Mounties made an impression on the Métis, just as they were meant to. Police were used to put pressure on First Nations to sign treaties, and it was no accident that they were prominently placed at the entrance to the scrip commission tent. The Mounties were the gatekeepers of the process, a none-too-subtle display of Canadian force.

The application process was also an administrative nightmare in which fraudsters and impersonators, speculators, priests, lawyers and agents for the banks all took advantage of identity, language, geographic and literacy difficulties to obtain scrip. The speculators travelled with the scrip commission and were virtually part of the official party.

Interior of a scrip commission tent at Lesser Slave Lake, Alberta (*Glenbow Archives NA-949-22*)

In an attempt to maintain at least the appearance that the scrip commission was independent, most of the speculators were not allowed into the commission tent. The priest, however, had a place inside the tent and was in a privileged position to obtain scrip certificates of entitlement. "Obtain" is the appropriate word because, unlike the other speculators who at least paid something for the scrip certificate, the priests used their influence to have it passed over to them gratis. Once the commissioner issued a certificate, the Métis applicants had to walk by the table where the priest sat. The priest would hold out his hand and ask if they wanted him to care for their certificates. Many did. Asked if the priests ever returned the certificates,

Louis Morin shrugged and said he never knew the priests to give anything back.

If the Métis family declined to hand over their certificates to the care of the priest, they had to exit the tent through the Mountie gatekeepers and face the other speculators who offered a trade: paper cash for the certificate. Unable to read or write and having little or no experience with paper money, the Métis, particularly in the north, were at a severe disadvantage. The cash offered was much less than the value of the certificate, but many exchanged one piece of paper for the other.

SIGNED WITH AN *X*

Because most Métis at the time were illiterate, they signed their applications with an *X*, and the commissioner or his clerk wrote the applicant's name above and below the *X*. We have already noted that Joseph Riel was literate but his application was inexplicably signed with an *X*. For the illiterate, impersonators conveniently completed the process. One of the speculators fessed up about how it worked:

> [T]he buyers, when purchasing the scrip, would have the vendor sign a form of Quit Claim Deed. He would sign by making his mark, and this would be witnessed by two persons, presumably other dealers . . . the practice was for the holder of a scrip to pick out some local Indian or half-breed and take him to the Dominion Land Office and present him as the person named in the scrip. The holder of the scrip, pretending to be the agent of the half-breed, would designate the land.[1]

One of the impersonators was a man named L'Esperance. Monsieur L'Esperance attested to fifty conveyance instruments and forty-eight land scrip coupons or identified coupon holders in eight cities.[2] Since it is simply not possible for one man to have done all this, the creation of Monsieur L'Esperance provides a good idea of just how widespread the fraud was. An official with the federal Department of Justice described the process:

> It appears that the scrip was handed to the half-breeds by the agent of the Indian Department and it was then purchased, for small sums of course, by speculators. However the half-breed himself was required by the Department of the Interior to appear in person at the office of the land agent and select his land and hand over his scrip. In order to get over this difficulty the speculator would employ the half-breed to impersonate the breed entitled to the scrip. This practice appears to have been very widely indulged in at one time. The practice was winked at evidently at the time and the offences were very numerous.[3]

It was a system that could not have been implemented unless it was aided and abetted by land agents, lawyers, the Dominion Lands Office and perhaps the scrip commissioners themselves. Everybody knew about it.

The government certainly knew there were impersonations and forgeries and that these were criminal offences that should have been prosecuted under the law.[4] But in the opinion of Parliament, it was best just to change the law to make sure nothing interfered with the process of removing Métis title to the land and laundering their title into the market. The Criminal Code was amended to put a three-year limitation on all offences relating to "the location of land which was paid for in whole or in part by scrip or was granted upon certificates issued to half-breeds in connection with extinguishment of Indian title."[5]

In some cases a diligent Métis applicant would have had to travel over a thousand miles to locate scrip lands, and the trip would cost more than the land was worth. The entire process could take four years to complete, and the Métis applicants often had nothing to do with any of it after signing the application. The government proclaimed that no assignment of the right to scrip would be recognized in third parties. But it was third parties, not the Métis, who ended up in possession of the land scrip coupons. When it was all over, the Métis had virtually no land. The speculators, the banks and the Church ended up with the land and profited from the transactions along the way.

One problem was that a scrip coupon could not be converted to any land. Scrip had to be located on lands already open for homesteading on surveyed lands. There were no surveyed lands open for homesteading in the north. So Métis in the north who wanted to actually obtain land with their scrip had to move south. If you were already settled on lands in the south, you could not use your scrip to secure your homestead. This is why everybody knew the Métis would not end up with the land. Métis scrip was good for only one thing—selling.

SCRIP DOCUMENTS

For forty long years from 1885 to 1921, North-West scrip commissions travelled around Métis communities taking applications.[6] Scrip was a failure when it came to keeping land in the hands of the Métis, which was its stated purpose, but everybody knew that when it started. On the plus side, and only with the hindsight revealed by much academic work, the scrip documents have turned out to be a gold mine of information about the Métis Nation. The scrip application asked applicants for family information, including who their parents were and whether they were

Métis, where they lived now and in the past, if they were married, how many children they had, where their children were born and where they died.

The answers in the scrip documents show important events in the Métis collective memory. They all knew where they were during the "rebellions."

> I was in Montana in 1871. The year of the first rebellion I was between Cypress and Moose Mountain . . . The second rebellion I was in Montana Choteau County.[7]

> I saw Melanie [Deschamps] first at Judith's Basin . . . It was the year after the rebellion that she died.[8]

> I knew Pierre St Germain . . . and his brother Louis . . . before the Red River Rebellion.[9]

> I have known Louison Nipissing as long as I can remember . . . [His daughter] Madeleine is sixteen years of age . . . She was a year old when the rebellion was in progress.[10]

Despite the Old Wolves' objection to the use of the term "rebellion," the scrip records use it often. The documents always read as stiff English translations, so it is unclear whether "rebellion" is the actual word the Métis used, or whether it was the word the scrip commissioners wrote down.

In the responses to questions such as "Where have you lived?" and "Where do you reside?" each answer was usually a long list of locations. The Métis remembered where they were when their children were born, and since they tended to have a child every two years, the birth locations provide an extraordinary cache of evidence about their migratory patterns.

The documents show that thousands of Métis had no permanent place of residence.

> Most of my life has been spent with Louison Nipissing, hunting together in the days of the Buffalo and making a living since.[11]

> I was born in the North West . . . I was married to Gabrielle Leveille about thirty five years ago. We lived the life of hunters in the North Western Plains. Went every spring to Winnipeg to dispose of the result of the chase. We had our winter quarters in the territories, and we went to Winnipeg to trade our furs.[12]

> I knew Pierre St Germain . . . He followed the chase. He built a house at Cypress Hills to winter in. After living there a year he built another house at Wood Mountain. It is twenty five years or more since he became a resident of the territories . . . George St Germain [Pierre's son] was born on the trail as his parents were taking to Winnipeg the proceeds of their winter's hunt. That is nineteen years ago.[13]

Some applicants made simple statements such as "My parents were Plains hunters."[14] But when the application reads, "having no permanent domicile in either previous to the transfer," it seems to be the language of the commissioner.[15] It is difficult to imagine a Métis hunter using the word "domicile." The scrip applications and witness declarations contain valuable information, but they cannot be taken as the words of the Métis. They are the translations and interpretations written down by the commissioners.

While "domicile" was a commissioner's word, other words have a more authentic ring. Thousands of scrip records refer to the "Plains." It is a curious example of how the language has changed. Today most Canadians think of the Plains as American and call our flatland "the prairie." But back then Métis hunters always spoke of the Plains. Nancy Bird was born "on the Plains" and Marie Desjarlais was married "on the Plains."[16] Sometimes the location is more specific. Baptiste Cardinal's child "died of small pox on the road between Carlton and Lac La Biche."[17] On a happier note, Elizabeth Boucher's "mother married . . . in the Plains near Battle River."[18]

Nowhere on the scrip application does it say that scrip was a legal exchange for the extinguishment of Métis Aboriginal title. After all the chatty personal questions, there was only one question that gave any indication of the legal implications buried in the scrip application: whether the applicant had ever accepted commutation of their Indian title.

There is simply no Michif or Cree translation for "commutation." Most people today don't know what "commutation" means, so one can readily imagine the translation difficulties back in the late 1800s or early 1900s. For those who are not lawyers, "commutation" means substitution. In criminal law commutation is usually the substitution of a lesser punishment for the original sentence. In the context of scrip, the term appears to have been borrowed from the Indian Act, where it was used to extinguish the rights of First Nation women who married non-Indian men. So when the scrip commissioner asked a Métis applicant if he or she had ever accepted commutation, he was asking whether the Métis applicant had ever taken a payout for leaving treaty, or if the Métis applicant had taken a land grant under the Manitoba Act or scrip elsewhere.

It is doubtful that any of the Métis appreciated the legalities of scrip, especially that it would forever extinguish their

Métis Indigenous title. Most Métis believed the scrip process was not a one-time deal and would be repeated in the years to come. Indeed, it was common talk among the Métis throughout the Prairies that scrip would be reissued. This was a reasonable interpretation because the Métis knew First Nations received annual treaty payments. It suggests that the Métis thought the scrip process was more akin to lease than sale of their rights.

Another fact that everybody knew was that in the north, even as late as 1906, money was not commonly used. They were still using the "made beaver" system with the Hudson's Bay Company. Made beaver involved stacking pelts against a gun and the Company assessing how much purchase power they stacked up to. The stack would be valued differently according to the type of pelt and its condition. This was how the Métis in the north valued and purchased goods. While the Métis in the south had experience with money, the Métis in the north had no experience of how to value land and little knowledge of cash.

Scrip was issued only on an individual basis. Canada would not deal with the Métis Nation as an Indigenous collective. It would only—and even then grudgingly—agree to recognize Métis rights in individual parcels for the sole purpose of extinguishing those rights. It was a system of massive land speculation laundered through Métis scrip. By the end of the scrip process, which took decades, the government claimed Indigenous land rights for all Métis in the North-West had been extinguished and washed its hands of any further obligations to them. Virtually no Métis ended up with land but all Métis title was considered legally extinguished. The Supreme Court of Canada called it "a sorry chapter in our nation's history."[19]

SCRIP GEOGRAPHY

In order to access scrip, the Métis applicants had to be in the right place at the right time. But it was almost impossible to know what the right places and times were. They kept changing. Shifting borders always seemed to be called in to the effort to deny claims. The border between Manitoba and Ontario was one of the shifting borders.

Exactly where the border between Manitoba and Ontario was became the subject of a long legal dispute. Canada delayed approving Manitoba Act land grant and scrip applications for those who lived near that border pending a final determination on where it lay. In 1889, when the border was finally determined, the Métis who lived on the Ontario side of the new border on July 15, 1870, were denied. Métis who claimed they were in Manitoba on July 15, 1870, were theoretically eligible.

But not Old Nick Chatelain. He filed his claim in Winnipeg in 1878. Despite living most of his life in the Lake of the Woods/Rainy Lake area of Ontario, he claimed that he was in Red River on July 15, 1870, living with his daughter Marie Anne and her husband, Jean Baptist Ritchot. The evidence suggests that Chatelain was indeed in Red River on that date. Chatelain was deeply connected to the Métis participants in the Red River Resistance. His grandson Janvier Ritchot was the man who first stepped on the surveyor's chain and sat as a judge on the panel at the Thomas Scott trial. It was Chatelain who met with Riel and proposed dumping logs on Wolseley's army. That would have been in the summer of 1870.

Maybe the scrip bureaucrats knew about his diabolical suggestion. After all, it had been published in *La Minerve*. Perhaps they doubted his claim of residency in 1870. Perhaps they wanted to punish him for his participation in the Resistance.

Regardless, they denied his claim and most of the other Métis claims from that region. Very few were approved. It was a convenient way to deny Métis in northwestern Ontario any resolution of their rights.[20]

The other border that mattered was the American border. The United States had a history of including Métis in their treaty negotiations with First Nations. In many treaties American Indians insisted on including their Métis relatives.[21] In 1882 twenty-two townships along the Canadian border in Dakota Territory were set aside for treaty with the Chippewa. This was Turtle Mountain territory, and many Métis came home from Montana to take treaty. Over three-quarters of the Turtle Mountain Chippewa band were Métis.

The parties were split on what they wanted from the treaty. Chief Little Shell wanted to include the Métis who were related to the Turtle Mountain Chippewa, whether they were Canadian or American. The chief wanted the land to be held in common and he wanted the size increased to include the many Métis. The Métis wanted the land in severalty, meaning they wanted to own their parcels individually and not in common. Other Chippewa wanted to exclude the Canadian Métis. These discrepancies were never truly resolved, and Little Shell later repudiated the treaty originally signed in 1892. It took another twelve years to finalize a treaty.

Dividing the Métis into neat parcels of Canadian and American citizens missed the complexity of facts on the ground. Many Métis simply didn't know whether they were American or Canadian. During their hunts the Métis wandered back and forth across the invisible border. It was no easy matter for a nomadic group to say exactly where each child was born. Indeed, it seems that some Métis didn't understand the concept of state citizenship. Annie Jerome Branconnier remembered coming across the border from Walhalla (formerly St. Joseph), North Dakota, in the early 1900s. When her family were asked their nationality, they said they were Métis. They didn't see themselves as Canadians or Americans.

Choices about state citizenship were often made based on where the best offers were. Some Canadian Métis who were excluded from the 1892 Chippewa treaty began to return to Canada. When the Canadian government, in 1901, offered a new round of scrip to the Métis who had not received it between 1885 and 1886, more Métis crossed the border, thereby affirming their citizenship as Canadian. Another wave came to Canada after 1904.

But a significant number of Métis remained in North Dakota to take advantage of the land allotments offered by the treaty. Today, the Turtle Mountain Chippewa Band has a population of over thirty thousand. Despite its name, the Turtle Mountain Chippewa Band could be seen as an American Métis community. It continues to develop its Métis culture, and as with all Métis communities, it is heavily influenced by its familial ties and proximity with the Chippewa. The band has always maintained many ties to Canadian Métis, especially those who live on the Canadian side of the border at Turtle Mountain. It was at Turtle Mountain that the first Michif dictionary was published. It was at Turtle Mountain on the Canadian side in 2009 that Will Goodon shot the duck that eventually led to the resolution of Métis hunting and fishing rights in Manitoba.

Aside from the useful information we can now glean from the scrip documents, one must ask why the Métis wanted scrip. The Métis in Saskatchewan knew their cousins in Red River had been paid for their rights, but they also knew their relatives in

Manitoba didn't end up with land. According to Patrice Fleury, the Métis on the Saskatchewan first heard about scrip in 1883, when some of their relatives from Red River arrived and told them about the money they had received. The Métis in Batoche believed they had the same rights as their cousins in Red River. They didn't think it was fair that scrip went only to some children of the same family, merely because they resided in Red River on a particular date, while others who fled the reign of terror and now resided outside Manitoba got nothing.

The main cause of the North-West Resistance was the failure of the government to secure Métis landholdings. The mounting pressure on the government to resolve outstanding Métis land claims in the years and months leading up to the North-West Resistance pushed the government to set up a scrip commission to set aside land for the Métis heads of families and children. The government resisted until 1885, when it finally authorized an enumeration to implement the process that came to be known as North-West scrip. At first it was limited to those who would have received a land grant had they resided in Manitoba at the time of the transfer, so it was hardly a major concession. The offer didn't protect existing landholdings and it would only apply to a few. The commissioners were appointed just before the outbreak at Duck Lake. It was too little, too late. The Métis had seen this dance before in Manitoba. All the while the lands slipped away.

In 1885 Commissioner W. P. R. Street started negotiations with the Métis in Qu'Appelle. They wanted their *rangs* protected and they wanted land scrip for their children. They would agree to buy the *rangs* at a dollar an acre if they got a free grant of 160 acres from the nearest vacant lot. The deal was confirmed within a week. The Qu'Appelle arrangement shows the possibilities of quick settlement. But why did the Métis have to pay for land they were already on? It only makes sense if the Métis grant lands were converted into homesteader lands and thus fit within Canada's homestead policy.

The Métis community of Green Lake, Saskatchewan, provides a good example of how Canada's homestead policy worked to the disadvantage of Métis applicants. It started always with the surveys, which were every bit as problematic as they had been in Red River and on the South Saskatchewan. Two different surveys were required before the process could begin. It took years, and the cost of the land tripled and the patent fees rose by a third while the Métis waited for confirmation of their properties. Some were allowed to purchase their land over time, but would pay more in interest than the value of the lot.

This is a brief taste of the "sorry chapter" of scrip. Canadians pride themselves on a history of fairness and good governance available to all citizens. Nowhere is this taken more seriously than in property interests. But the Métis got no justice and no fairness in their land dealings. They were denied Crown protection granted to First Nations for their treaty lands and were defrauded of the legal protections provided to other Canadians. The sorry scrip chapter remains an outstanding issue for the Métis Nation.

CHAPTER 27

ST. PAUL DES MÉTIS

After Batoche the Métis entered their bitter years of hiding, *le grand silence.* They were scattered and their leaders were silenced. The buffalo were gone, and as the steamships, roads and railroads pushed west and north, the niche the Métis had filled as freighters came to an end. They began to live in large tent-camps on the fringes of the new Prairie towns, and they scared the living daylights out of the settlers. They were harassed by the Mounties, and while many tried to pick up work on farms or other labouring jobs, their reputation simply didn't recommend them as farm labourers.

The Métis in Red River had wanted to settle on reserves in 1870. Not all, but some still requested reserves into the 1880s. But when they asked for reserves, they were denied. Governments would grant Métis reserves only out of charity. It wasn't until the 1890s, at the urging of the priests, that the first Métis reserve (other than the Treaty #3 half-breed reserve) was finally established. Redemption was the plan. Indeed, the application to set up the reserve was entitled "A Philanthropic Plan to Redeem the Half-Breeds of Manitoba and the North-West Territories."[1]

Father Lacombe asked for land for the "amelioration of the *metis*" before they became a "source of danger for the settlers of the North-West." According to Lacombe, there were between seven and eight thousand French Métis in Manitoba and the North-West, of which about two-thirds were living "miserable and poor" in settlements, and the other third were scattered all over the country leading a "miserable life, camping near the new towns and settlements of the white people, where they are exposed to all kinds of demoralization."[2] He wanted a French Catholic enclave in what was becoming a sea of Protestants. At the time he proposed it, the Métis were virtually the only French Catholics available to create his enclave.

The Métis knew the place Lacombe chose for the reserve as St. Paul's Place. In 1896, Father Lacombe renamed it St. Paul des Métis. It became a gathering place for meetings, and when Gabriel Dumont visited in 1906, Métis came from miles around to listen to one of their great heroes. St. Paul des Métis was remarkably successful, with substantial homes and valuable improvements. Joe Dion, a non-treaty Cree, was impressed with life at St. Paul des Métis, saying that he had seen it at its best, with good homes, nice farms, and beautiful horses and carriages. Everybody had plenty to eat and good clothes to wear.[3]

But by 1908 the Church decided that St. Paul des Métis was no longer worthy of its efforts. The priests wanted a better and bigger class of French Catholics at St. Paul des Métis, which would not happen unless the colony was no longer a Métis-only reserve. So the priests proposed to the government that the reserve be disbanded. They kept their own portion of the townships and were reimbursed for the investments they had made ($68,000). The Métis were expendable. The withdrawal of the reservation was approved on August 13, 1908.

The Métis were outraged. They held a mass protest meeting and sent a petition to Ottawa signed by one hundred Métis. Having seen the deafening silence with which the government responded to previous Métis petitions, the reader will not be shocked to hear that only more silence greeted this latest one. On May 10, 1909, the St. Paul des Métis reserve was officially declared open to homesteaders.

It turned out that the Church had already been making deals with speculators who were using intimidation tactics to force the Métis off the lands. The Church defended its actions by claiming that the experiment had not "been of such a degree as to encourage them in continuance of effort in that direction."[4] This was despite the fact that the priests were making money off the Métis reserve. In 1902 Father Lacombe and Father Therien went on a fundraising tour of Quebec and the eastern United States and raised $21,000 by appealing to their benefactors to fund St. Paul des Métis. None of that money went to the Métis reserve. Instead it disappeared into the coffers of the diocese of St. Albert. When the crops failed in 1903, none of the money was made available.

An Edmonton syndicate handled the takeover. The syndicate included a former agent of the Catholic Church, a Dominion land agent and a local trader, all ably assisted by a law firm in Edmonton and by Father Therien, the priest who was in charge of St. Paul des Métis. The syndicate encouraged speculators who induced the Métis to sell out. But the Métis had nothing to sell. They didn't own their lands. Under the scheme set up by Father Lacombe, the Métis were occupiers, not owners. Father Therien wrote, "It must be supposed that Providence wanted the disappearance of our school and the ruin of our colony in order to establish in this region many

French-Canadian parishes . . . From the beginning we had to battle against two obstacles: the Métis and the English-speaking settlers."[5] He called it "providence," but it was likely no coincidence that the newly constructed nearby railway increased the value of the lands. The oblates would have made a tidy profit in selling to their new French-Canadian settlers.

Two men, Laurent Garneau and James Brady Sr., exposed the priests, the syndicate and its scheme. They raised enough of a stink that a royal commission was established to investigate. Technically, the lands were restored to the Métis. But it was too late. The clergy had initiated this attack on a working Métis settlement. That move let loose a vicious round of racial abuse, an echo of the reign of terror in Manitoba. Many of the Métis fled farther north where there were fewer antagonists. The only ones able to withstand the onslaught were the wealthier Métis who could purchase their lands.

Once again hundreds of Métis were forced off their lands. As more and more Métis were displaced, the places they could go were getting fewer and fewer. Now there was real law in the North-West, not just the distant law that had governed *in absentia* for the previous century. There were rules, policemen and judges. Specifically, there were new rules about vagrancy. The Métis now had new names applied to them: they were "squatters" if they built a home and tried to stay on the land in one place, and they were "vagrants" if they lived in camps or kept moving. Either way they were illegal.

All of Western society revolves around having an address. One must have a residence to obtain a driver's licence, or to get welfare or social assistance. Even access to education and medical care requires an address. Many Métis continued to live in tents and in family groupings. Tents were not considered an address.

The Métis were seen as diseased and dangerous vagrants. Some tried to stay in the south, but the refuge for many became the northern parts of the provinces.

The Métis Nation always had two branches. The southern branch was the Plains buffalo hunters and those who lived a more agrarian life and settled in the parishes in Red River, on the South Saskatchewan River and in other locations in the North-West. The northern branch was the woodland Métis who lived along the old voyageur highway. These Métis lived by hunting and fishing, trapping and freighting. The aftermath of the North-West Resistance, the end of the buffalo, the end of freighting and the violent hatred pushed many from the southern branch to join their relatives in the north.

CHAPTER 28

THE MÉTIS SETTLEMENTS IN ALBERTA

JIM BRADY AND MALCOLM NORRIS

The Métis Nation owes its continuing existence to a series of ardent nationalist leaders. Cuthbert Grant, James Sinclair, Jean-Louis Riel, Louis Riel and Gabriel Dumont were not the only nationalist Métis leaders; they are only the best known from the nineteenth century. In the twentieth century new leaders emerged for the Métis Nation. In Alberta in the 1930s, they were Jim Brady and Malcolm Norris.

The early part of the twentieth century brought a world of change to the Métis Nation. In Manitoba the Old Wolves were at work telling the stories, erecting monuments, publishing their letters and writing the history of the Métis Nation. But theirs was a focus in the rear-view mirror, an effort to remember, to not lose sight of their ancestors and their history. The Old Wolves were keeping the stories alive for all the Métis Nation. In northern Alberta Métis communities, something else was brewing, a new evolution of the Métis national struggle. These communities had welcomed waves of Métis from Red River after 1870 and another wave of Métis from Saskatchewan after 1885. The Métis took their nationalist politics with them wherever they went. Under new leaders, the Métis Nation was evolving.

The language changed. People no longer spoke of the Canadian Party and their agenda. Métis leaders had new words to describe what was happening to them. They began to speak of their long resistance as anti-colonialism. Brady and Norris brought something new to the battle: labour and socialist theory. Like Cuthbert Grant and Louis Riel, Brady and Norris were well educated. They were both committed to continuing the national struggle of the Métis Nation.

Norris grew up in Edmonton with stories of the Métis Nation, especially tales of Riel and Dumont. In his mother's stories, Riel was proudly remembered as a man who defended the weak. Brady grew up in St. Paul des Métis with the same stories. Brady's grandparents had both played a role in the North-West Resistance. His grandfather Laurent Garneau was part of the Red River Resistance and a spy for Riel during La Guerre Nationale. His grandmother was Eleanor Garneau, the woman who had saved her husband by washing Riel's incriminating letter into the family laundry. Brady's grandfather was saved from death, but his association with Riel and the Métis Nation had consequences for the rest of his life. In 1892 Garneau was elected to the North-West Territories Parliament in Regina but was never allowed to take his seat because of his previous involvement with Louis Riel. Brady and Norris were born and raised as Métis nationalists.

THE ALBERTA MÉTIS MOVEMENT

The Métis Nation was never a simple entity. There had always been northern and southern branches. There were the English

Métis and the French Métis. There were urban Métis and rural Métis. There were the buffalo hunters and the canoe brigades and the farmers. The Nation has always been a fluid mixing of these various languages, religions, geographies and economies. Now there were added complexities. By the 1930s the Métis Nation on the prairies was sharing its cultural space with a new group.

Since the late 1800s the government had been slimming down the numbers of Indians on its Indian Act registry. Many were forced out when they began to partake in the basic benefits of Canadian society—voting, education, joining a profession, marrying a non-treaty man, etc. They were called non-status Indians, referring to the removal of their "status" from the Indian Act registry. Non-status Indians found themselves in similar circumstances to the Métis Nation: they were landless and destitute. Together, the Métis and non-status Indians in the Prairies numbered some ten to twelve thousand, about a third of which were non-status Indians.

The non-status Indians didn't share the same Métis history, didn't see themselves as part of the Métis Nation and were not animated by the nationalism that defined the Métis Nation. The Métis referred to themselves as "Otipêyimisowak," which was not a term the non-status Indians ever adopted. The government crudely lumped all of them together into one box labelled "Métis and non-status Indians." But they were fundamentally different.

The Alberta Métis were still nomads. Most of them now lived in the northern parts of Alberta. They no longer followed the buffalo herds, freighted or traded. They lived in a seasonal round, moving to access resources that provided a subsistence living from hunting, fishing and trapping. The Métis, who had previously travelled thousands of miles in a year, now had a much-reduced territory in northern Alberta and Saskatchewan. Some Métis, mostly those from the southern parts, lived on small farms or worked for wages, living the life of itinerant labourers. There were Métis ranchers, some city dwellers and a few businessmen. But since 1885 the Métis had mostly put their heads down and practised avoidance.

It was another massive transfer of land jurisdiction that ignited the Alberta Métis. Until the late 1920s Crown lands in the Prairies were still federal lands and were still available to the Métis. But in 1928 the federal government began the process of transferring control of Crown lands to the three Prairie provincial governments. This transfer, like the transfer of Rupert's Land and the North Western Territory in 1870, threatened to undermine the Métis again. The provinces were going to open the lands up for homesteading.

The Alberta Métis movement began at Fishing Lake, a small Métis community in the forest just west of the Alberta-Saskatchewan border and about forty miles east of St. Paul des Métis. When the Métis at Fishing Lake learned about the plan to open up their area for homesteading, they understood that once again their occupation would not be recognized and they would lose their lands. By this time the Métis had had long experience with this particular show. There would be the government declaration about available land, then there would be surveys and, before they knew it, strangers would be claiming their lands. The government would do nothing to protect the Métis as prior occupants and they would be pushed out. It was an old story and everybody knew the plot.

Fishing Lake held meetings—lots of meetings. One of the ideas they discussed was an exclusive Métis reserve. They talked about a Métis reserve so much that word got out on the moccasin telegraph. There were rumours of families who wanted to come from Saskatchewan, southern Alberta and Montana. According to one Métis, Old Cardinal, it was all talk and no action. No one took the reins and pushed their protest forward. It was just like in Red River before Louis Riel gathered the forces. Needing some help, in 1930, the Métis of Fishing Lake approached Joe Dion, who was a schoolteacher at a nearby Indian reserve. Dion had lots to recommend him to the Métis. He was a nephew of Big Bear and he was a non-status Indian. Dion agreed to help. Over the next two years, more meetings were held and they began to attract more people.

They drafted several resolutions requesting land and a meeting with government. Then, in the summer of 1931, hundreds of Métis from communities all around Fishing Lake met on the shores of Cold Lake. At the meeting the Métis appointed a council, drafted a petition and collected over five hundred names. The petition set out their belief that they had some rights to the land. They would not interfere with anyone and were not asking for improvement from government. They wanted the right to occupy the land. A delegation was selected to meet with the Alberta provincial government. In response to the meeting, Alberta drafted a questionnaire it wanted the Métis organization to distribute. It was a tacit recognition of the Métis as a group with an issue that needed some attention. Dion worked at getting the questionnaire filled out by as many people as possible, and in this task he did not work only with the Métis; he also had non-status Indians fill it out.

More meetings throughout 1932 brought up other issues, such as hunting and fishing rights, health conditions, the lack of schools and jobs, and the denial of relief to destitute Métis. Dion travelled from community to community, encouraging discussion and holding meetings. They decided to hold a province-wide convention in December.

Dion was a kind, intelligent and helpful man, but he was as naive as Riel about politics. He believed facts would sway government. He believed that once government understood how many Métis and non-status Indians wanted and needed land, it would be granted. But government rarely acts on the basis of need, want, facts or logic. It was the brewing scandal of thousands of destitute provincial citizens and the frequency and size of the Métis meetings that caught the government's attention. Some say Alberta was shamed into action. But shame is a garment that government usually wears quite well. More likely they were getting votes by promising action on the Métis "problem."

Dion was no politician and he knew it. Enter Jim Brady, the Métis strategist, with his first advice to Dion: the Métis must be formally organized and they needed to build an organization in each community with strong leadership. Brady drafted a constitution for a new province-wide Métis organization "formed for the mutual benefit and the interest and the protection of the Métis of the Province of Alberta . . . a non-political and non-religious society, having as its sole purpose, the social interest and uplifting of the members of the Association and the Métis people of the said Province of Alberta."[1] There were self-government provisions that set up an executive council of the association as the governing body of all Métis on hoped-for land reserves. By this point they had organized with twenty-five elected councillors and a constitution. Meetings were held in other communities. Petitions were drafted.

By the time the December convention was held, the Métis had the trio of leaders they needed: Dion the community organizer, Brady the intellectual and political strategist, and

Norris the dynamic speaker and agitator. Norris was the man who revived flagging Métis spirits, reminded them of Métis nationalist history and linked the movement to its past. He gave the Métis hope.

By December 28, 1932, the Métis Nation had officially organized in Alberta as L'Association des Métis d'Alberta et des Territoires des Nord Ouest.[2] In English they were known as the Métis Association of Alberta. They had one simple goal: land. They believed it would give them the ability to provide for their homeless and destitute families, education for their children and better medical attention. They knew land was something the Alberta government had available to give them. Money during the Depression was hard to come by, but land was readily available, especially in the northern parts of the province, which were not best suited to farming. They sent a brief to the Alberta government setting out eleven areas they wanted for Métis settlements.[3]

The executive council of the Métis Association of Alberta, 1935. *Front row, left to right*: Malcolm Norris, Joseph Dion, James Brady. *Back row, left to right*: Peter Tomkins, Felix Callihoo. (*Glenbow Archives PA-2218-109*)

The new Métis organization also dealt with the identity and naming issue. Never again would they use the odious term "half-breed." Henceforth they would be known only as the Métis. Despite its name, the Métis Association of Alberta was not a Métis-only entity. To be eligible for membership a person had to be "Métis, or of Métis descent, who is a pioneer of Indian descent and their descendants, within the limitations of the Old North West Territories, the present North West Territories, the provinces of Alberta, Saskatchewan and Manitoba, or a non-treaty Indian having the above qualification or treaty Indians becoming enfranchised . . ."[4]

The identity issue was a wedge that the government exploited. When Dion stated that those in most need were treaty Indians who had been enticed to take scrip, he fed into the province's argument that the responsibility really lay with the federal government. Thus, he stirred up the issue of whether Métis were a federal or provincial responsibility, an issue that would plague the Métis until 2016 when the Supreme Court of Canada finally declared all Aboriginal peoples in Canada a federal responsibility.[5] But before that decision, for eighty-five years, the provinces and the federal government played what has often been described as a game of jurisdictional football with the Métis. Football is an entirely inappropriate description of what went on. In football, both sides want the ball. This was a game of jurisdictional hot potato. In the 1930s the hot potato game was in full swing. Alberta formally requested federal participation in the discussions about Métis land claims and was firmly rejected. The Métis, as far as the federal government was concerned, were a provincial problem.

In 1932 the new Alberta Métis organization declared itself a "non-religious society" and ended a century of domination by the Catholic Church when it removed the Church's control over Métis education. This would have a profound effect on Métis for the future. For a while the relationship with the Catholic Church remained strong, in large part influenced by the fact that Joe Dion was a staunch Catholic and defender of the Church. But a change had taken place. The priests recognized that the association had influence and they now sought its assistance.

The churches educated a few Métis children out of charity, but 80 per cent of the Métis children in Alberta were growing up without any education, a number Métis leaders believed was likely an underestimate. There were no public funds provided as there were for treaty Indians and white children in public schools. It was against the law for children not to be in school, but neither the federal nor the provincial government would accept responsibility for Métis children if they lived on Indian reserves. There simply were no schools in the remote areas where many Métis lived, and many Métis were still migrating seasonally. Their children rarely, if ever, went to school.

The Métis association began to press the Alberta government to authorize setting aside the lands they had selected. Amendments were made and new areas were added as Métis from other parts of Alberta began to participate, including some families evicted from their lands when Jasper National Park was established. The Métis continued to organize throughout the province. By 1935 there were forty-two local Métis associations. They had only rough data, but by their estimates there were some ten to thirteen thousand Métis in Alberta, although not all of them were members of the association. Five thousand Métis needed relief.[6]

Meetings—that's how they did it. They met repeatedly. They talked and talked again. Despite Old Cardinal's thought that talking was not doing, the meetings were what had always brought and kept the Métis Nation together. Meetings kept them focused and, as in all oral cultures, kept them knowing each other, knowing their history and knowing they needed to stay together to better their people. In this sense what was happening in Alberta was identical to the North-West Resistance and the Red River Resistance. It was the voice of the Métis Nation hauling itself meeting by meeting out of *le grand silence*.

Brady and Norris wanted to unite the Métis Nation. They looked beyond the Métis in Alberta and kept communications going with their brothers and sisters in other provinces. The Alberta Métis passed a resolution at their convention stating that it "fully supports and endorses the efforts of the Saskatchewan Métis Society to establish their Legal and Constitutional rights and our Secretary be instructed to convey fraternal greetings to their forthcoming Convention."

They didn't want the Métis to be seen merely as destitute people needing relief. They would use that label if they had to, but for Brady and Norris, their movement was always about the Métis Nation and its need for land and self-government. There was no battle for the political left or the right—nothing like that—just a struggle for land, resources and self-government. That's what Grant, the Riels and Dumont had fought for.

Brady set out a hierarchy of tactics to achieve their goals: organization, direct pressure on government (by way of petition and the courts), and voting power in mainstream politics—in that order. Brady believed that if petitioning failed, they could resort to the courts. But court is not a sure thing even in the twenty-first century. Back in the 1930s going to court would have resulted in a certain loss. Resorting to the use of political power was also chancy, because with the rapid immigration in the

Prairies, the Métis had become a minority group. They spent a lot of time petitioning, but it really accomplished very little. So, despite Brady's tactical hierarchy, he knew they really only had one tool—organizing.

Pete Tomkins joined Dion, Norris and Brady and they became affectionately known as the Big Four. The Church put great effort into dividing the Big Four. Bishop O'Leary issued dire warnings in the press about radicals and tried to use Dion's Catholicism to separate him from the other three. But the Big Four wanted to avoid an outright fight with the Church. It was simply too powerful. So, Brady, Norris and Tomkins decided to ask Dion to neutralize the Church's efforts. Norris wrote to Dion:

> An article appearing in the press a couple days ago emanating from Bishop O'Leary's palace warns all clergy + Catholic people to beware of organizations + individuals express[ing] radical ideals. Good God Joe, if it is radical to tell the truth about the conditions prevailing among our people and to advocate a rehabilitation of Métis then I am, you are, we are all Reds. If this is Christianity then I would prefer the beliefs + traditions of our Indian antecedants of a Happy Hunting Grounds in preference to the heaven + God as advocated by the clergy. I dread open opposition of the Clergy for they are too influential. Will you therefore write to Bishop O'Leary stating you have seen this article and are greatly concerned lest the Métis Association be considered as being Red.[7]

When Dion lamented their lack of Riel, Norris objected: "Joe we have plenty Riels and [it] only requires a little fanning of a spark that would become a flame." In urging Dion to throw himself more forcefully into the battle, Norris said, "We are behind you if it means a fight, throw your coat away, ours are already off and we are ready."[8]

THE EWING COMMISSION

By 1934 the Big Four had put so much pressure on the Alberta government that a royal commission was appointed to inquire into the conditions of the Métis. The Métis Nation had already been the subject of several commissions of inquiry. There was the Coltman Commission after 1816, and there were commissions after the Red River Resistance and another after the North-West Resistance. There were inquiries into scrip, Bremner's furs and into the children's land grants in Manitoba.

This new one was called the Ewing Commission, after its chief commissioner. The appointment of the commission was either the desperate last gasp of a party heading into a close election and needing Métis votes, an inquiry into just why the pesky Métis had not already been assimilated, or a way to pathologize the Métis as a disease that required a cure. Racism was the common factor. Either way, it would take time, and since all commissions only make recommendations, its findings could either be acted on fully, partially, or left to gather dust on a shelf. The political winds blowing when the report was released would determine its use.

But it was an opportunity for the Métis. Brady and Norris prepared written submissions but feared the commission would degenerate into a relief analysis. The only way they thought they could counter that was to present the history of the Métis Nation and to demonstrate the current state of the Métis economy as something that could be reversed. Since it seemed the Alberta government was prepared to set land aside for the Métis, the real issue for the Big Four was to get the commission to recommend that land be set aside under the control of the Métis Nation with the necessary political authority to govern their people. In their 1935 brief to the commission, they began by asserting that improvements to the economy and security of the Métis Nation required "the completion of our unification with the Canadian nation."[9] They went on to explain:

> The history of the Métis of Western Canada is really the history of their attempts to defend their constitutional rights . . . It is incorrect to place them as bewildered victims who did not know how to protect themselves against the vicious features which marked the penetration of the white man into the Western prairies.
>
> We are on much firmer ground when we refer to the glorious tradition of the Métis in fighting for a democratic opening of the West.

But Ewing did not want to hear about Métis nationalism and refused to let Norris present his case fully. There would be no discussion about Métis nationalism, rights, unity or history, and no discussion about the Métis who were successful. Métis, in the commission's eyes, were poor individuals and their destitute state was their own fault. They were a pathological problem, an illness that needed fixing. The commission wanted to hear about disease, lack of access to education, and poverty. Nothing more. Containment, oversight and assimilation were the cure for the disease of being Métis. It was exactly what the Big Four had hoped to avoid. The Métis idea of self-government over its own land base died before it was born.

In 1938 the Metis Population Betterment Act passed in Alberta. It gave effect to the recommendations of the commission. The lands set aside were for those Métis who were unable to support themselves. The Métis Association of Alberta tried to include at least one settlement in central or southern Alberta and a settlement at Grand Cache for the Métis families who had been evicted from what was now Jasper National Park. Both requests were rejected. It was not that there were no Métis in the south, but the government wanted to keep the Métis reserves away from the settlers. The Métis were encouraged to move north. In the end twelve Métis settlements were created: Fishing Lake, Elizabeth, Kikino, Buffalo Lake, East Prairie, Gift Lake, Peavine, Paddle Prairie, Marlboro, Touchwood, Cold Lake and Wolf Lake.

Although councils were set up on the settlements, the government moved quickly to increase its own control and diminish the size of the grant of land and powers. It redefined "Métis" by adding a blood quotient requirement. Henceforth Métis were persons with not less than a quarter of "Indian" blood. The minister granted himself many administrative powers and the administration was placed into the hands of a provincial government department. In 1952 the government granted itself the power to appoint the majority of councillors on each settlement council. Two settlements, Marlboro and Touchwood, never really got off the ground. Then in 1960, as part of its plans to establish the Primrose Lake Air Weapons Range, the province unilaterally took back two of the settlements, Cold Lake and Wolf Lake.

Alberta set up the Métis settlements to owe their jurisdiction, authority and power to the province. Funding was the tool Alberta used to undermine Métis self-government. It controlled the direction of the settlement governments when it funded its preferred objectives, and cut or denied funding when a proposed initiative didn't suit its purposes. Despite the problems, there were eight Métis settlements in Alberta. To this day they are the only Métis land base in the Métis Nation.

The Big Four succeeded in getting land, but in the process the Métis Association of Alberta was sidelined. Norris and Brady withdrew and both signed up to go overseas. The Second World War was about to engulf them all.

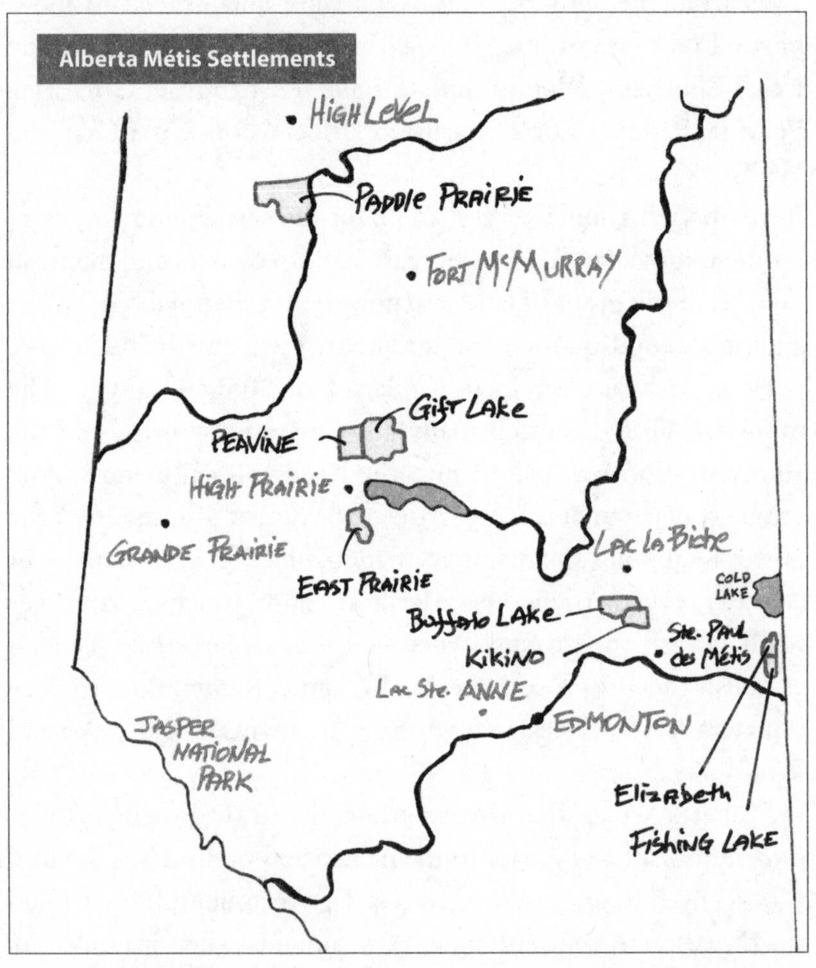

Alberta Métis Settlements

CHAPTER 29

ROCK BOTTOM

THE SECOND WORLD WAR

Métis Nation men played a prominent role in the Second World War. The South Saskatchewan Regiment, the Regina Rifles and the Royal Winnipeg Rifles had large numbers of Métis soldiers. Métis soldiers enlisted in the navy and in the air force. They took part in many of the main engagements in the Second World War.[1] Some, like Vital Morin, Frank Goodon and Roger Teillet, were prisoners of war.

In many Métis communities, virtually the entire population of healthy young men signed up. Why did they sign up? When the Second World War began in September 1939, the Métis were living on the margins of society, subjugated economically and culturally. Their history of resistance had not endeared them to their new neighbours. They were landless and many were still migratory. It was this grinding poverty and alienation that motivated Métis men to sign up in such large numbers. Even the poor army pay was more than twice what they could make by other means. Many hungered for acceptance, for the camaraderie and for the chance to show people that they had some worth. During the war they proved themselves to be loyal warriors.

They did not completely lose sight of Métis Nation issues in the long years of the war. Jim Brady took the opportunity to visit Marcel Giraud in Paris in 1946. Giraud was an anthropologist working on a massive anthropological study of the Métis Nation, *Le Métis Canadien*. When Brady was on leave, he spent five days reading the proofs of Giraud's thesis, which to this day is still the most complete anthropological study of the Métis Nation. For the most part during the war, however, the energy that had been building in Métis Nation organizations dissipated. Too many of the young men were gone, and those left were simply struggling to survive.

The boys who went overseas came back with a new set of eyes. They had seen Europe and they had taken part in the brutal carnage of the war. They came home with new ideas and a greater understanding of politics and power. The arrival of the men back from overseas was the catalyst for a new wave of Métis activism and nationalism. The Old Wolves were gone now, and it was their grandsons, veterans of the war, who took up the battle of their fathers and grandfathers.

It wasn't a new starting point for the Métis. They had never lost sight of the Métis Nation. But it was a new starting point for Canada's transformation. In the aftermath of the Second World War, a massive experiment in humanity began, one that is still happening. This is the human rights wave born in the horrors of the Second World War. It came from a profound belief shared by men and women all over the world after the war—the new understanding that all people deserve to be treated with dignity, that we are all human, and that there is no honour and never an excuse for oppression based on race, religion, culture or colour.

The sense then was: Never again! We won't let this happen again. We will not stand by. We will create universal norms, customs and laws to ensure human dignity is protected. We will work together as United Nations, and the world will change for the better. Canadians wholeheartedly embraced this new world view. It was a profound shift from the beliefs and attitudes that had been used for so long against the Métis Nation.

On an individual level, the Second World War changed our Canadian soldiers. Indigenous men signed up for service in unprecedented numbers. And non-Indigenous Canadian boys, most for the first time, actually met First Nation and Métis boys. They fought together and they were forced to depend on each other. They learned that they had the same fears, the same courage and the same loves, and they learned to engage in a common cause. After that, it was difficult for those non-Indigenous Canadian boys to come home and pick up their old prejudices.

This is when the modern Métis rights movement started. The seeds were sown in the soil of horror—when Canadians looked at what happened, knew it was wrong and knew it must change. Thus began, among many other things, the United Nations, the American civil rights movement, the American Indian Movement and, as part of that wave, the Indigenous rights movement in Canada. It took a while to get going. Such fundamental change doesn't happen overnight.

THE ROAD ALLOWANCE PEOPLE

Since at least the 1930s, governments in the Prairies had believed they had a "Métis problem."[2] As the press repeatedly reported, the Métis were a "hard people with whom to deal. They are wanderers . . . and the big trouble is that there are so many of them."[3] In 1949 government officials from Manitoba, Alberta and Saskatchewan met to discuss the Métis "problem." The problem, as they saw it, was the economic and cultural situation of the Métis, who were plagued by a high level of illiteracy, destitution, infant mortality, and poor diet and health. They saw two foundations for the problem: the nomadic life of the parents, and the discrimination by local officials. Rights and nationalism never entered the discussion. In short, the Métis needed "improvement."[4]

One of the big problems was the lack of land recognition. As the immigrants had moved in and taken over the land, the Métis were called "squatters." Land they had long called their own was now "owned" by people with pieces of paper. Possession and occupation, long the standard for common law ownership in English law, was not the law of Canada. Ownership was proven solely by official paper. Having lost their lands to the speculators through the survey, homestead and scrip processes, the Métis lived wherever they could as long as they could, and then, when pushed off their lands, they moved to the public lands available along railroads, roads and Crown lands. There, they built cabins and took on yet another name: the "road allowance people."

The route to life on the road allowances varied. Rita Vivier Cullen was born in 1936. Rita's grandparents arrived on the road allowance on the run from the authorities in North Dakota. The men were gone on a hunting trip when the authorities took all the children away to residential school in Walhalla (formerly St. Joseph). When the men returned home to find their children gone, they headed to the school. Holding the nuns at gunpoint, the Vivier men reclaimed their children and ran with their families over the border toward

St. François Xavier. They settled on the road allowance beside the Assiniboine River. Rita lived with her family in a one-room log house. The floor was mud with braided rag rugs. The exterior was whitewashed every summer. Her grandparents lived across the river in their own log cabin. Rita remembers it as a nice, cozy little place.[5]

Maria Campbell (*Women of the Métis Nation*)

Maria Campbell, a respected Métis Elder, author and another road allowance child, painted a completely different picture:

> So began a miserable life of poverty which held no hope for the future. That generation of my people was completely

> beaten. Their fathers had failed during the Rebellion to make a dream come true; they failed as farmers; now there was nothing left. Their way of life was a part of Canada's past and they saw no place in the world around them, for they believed they had nothing to offer. They felt shame, and with shame the loss of pride and the strength to live each day. I hurt inside when I think of those people. You sometimes see that generation today; the crippled, bent old grandfathers and grandmothers on town and city skid rows; you find them in the bush waiting to die; or baby-sitting grandchildren while the parents are drunk. And there are some who even after a hundred years continue to struggle for equality and justice for their people. The road for them is never-ending and full of frustrations and heart-break.[6]

One of the Métis Nation leaders of the 1970s and 80s, Jim Sinclair, was born on a road allowance in Saskatchewan in 1933. He grew up in a slum shack, and when the authorities evicted his family from the shack, they moved to a tent city farther away from the town. In 1950 Jim's parents moved to the "nuisance grounds" on the outskirts of Regina. The nuisance grounds constantly shifted as Regina expanded. "Nuisance" was how Regina thought of the slum. In fact, it was a Métis tent city in a garbage dump.

There were many Métis shantytowns and road allowance communities in Saskatchewan and Manitoba. In the 1950s there were twenty-six such settlements in Manitoba, identified by the government as fringe settlements with a slum mentality. They were typically unserviced areas on urban edges, with colourful names like The Big Eddy, Tin Town, Little Chicago, Dog Patch, The Corner and Rooster Town.

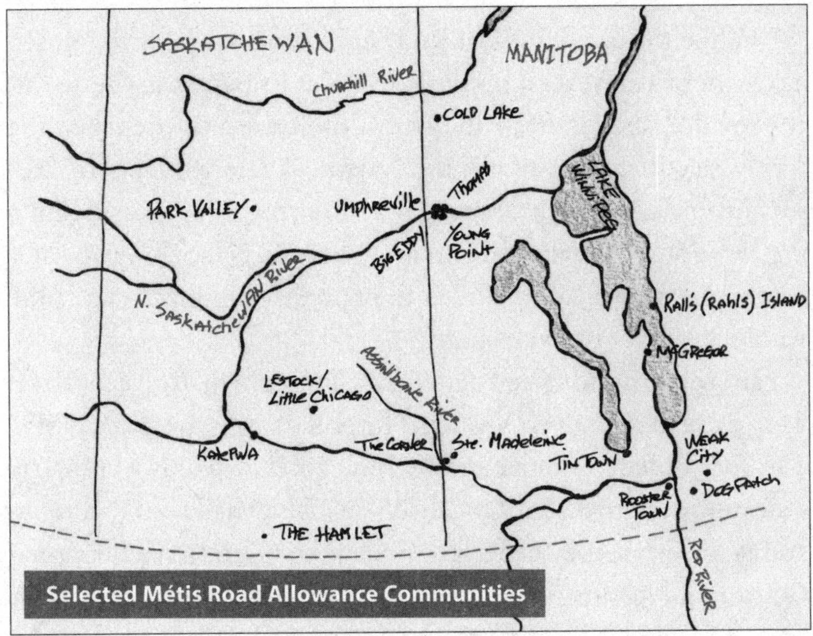

Selected Métis Road Allowance Communities

ROOSTER TOWN

As far as the good (non-Indigenous) people of Winnipeg were concerned, Rooster Town was nothing more than squalor and filth. Its Métis residents had no morals and they were all shiftless and lazy. Rooster Town's Métis were Winnipeg's untouchables. Parents warned their children never to touch Métis children from Rooster Town. You might get a disease if you did.

Winnipeg of the 1950s wanted to present itself as a city that was not plagued by disease-ridden, poor Métis. Certainly, they didn't want what amounted to a village of them so close to the centre of town. It was much too close for comfort. The urban land they were occupying was far too valuable to be used for a Métis shantytown. The Métis were not Indian enough to be acknowledged as having land rights, and they were too Indian to benefit from any policy other than slum clearance. One thing was certain: they were not wanted in the city.

While the conditions of Rooster Town were poor, it housed a community of several hundred Métis at its height in the 1930s. It provided shelter from the storm of abuse and prejudice the Métis faced when they left their town. Their attempts to preserve their community meant that Rooster Town was a shifting location. They moved and they moved again, always farther south and west until finally, in the 1950s, Winnipeg turned the whole area over to developers.

In 1959 the fourteen families still living in Rooster Town were evicted and given seventy-five dollars to move out by May 1 or fifty dollars to move out by June 30. The Métis were fairly quiet and resigned about the evictions. They had seen it coming and it was what they expected. Today the Grant Park Shopping Centre and Grant Avenue run over Rooster Town. Ironically, both are named after Cuthbert Grant, the first leader of the Métis Nation.

Rooster Town, 1959 (*Gerry Cairns/Winnipeg Free Press*)

STE. MADELEINE

Ste. Madeleine was a Métis settlement located just southwest of Russell, Manitoba. It was a logical place to settle because it was well known to the Métis. It was on the route the Métis travelled to get to the buffalo herds, and it later became part of the Carlton Trail. It was also near important Hudson's Bay Company trading posts at St. Lazare and Fort Ellice. Ste. Madeleine was one of the refuge places where Métis landed when they fled from the reign of terror during the 1870s. Many of the families who settled in Ste. Madeleine were originally from Baie St. Paul, St. François Xavier and St. Norbert. Another wave of Métis arrived after the North-West Resistance. By 1935 there were about 250 Métis in Ste. Madeleine.

Many were itinerant labourers working for the nearby white farmers. As we have seen elsewhere, the Métis were not commercial farmers. Every family had a vegetable garden, but they mostly used their lands as scrub pasture for their few cows and horses. It's just as well that they didn't try to commercially farm the land, because it was sandy soil and would have made for very poor grain crops. Over the years the lands were subdivided as fathers handed over parcels to their grown children. The effect was that a uniquely Métis settlement was created. Because of the family connections in Red River and Saskatchewan, it was well known throughout the Métis motherland. Despite the fact that many had been there since the 1870s, the Métis in Ste. Madeleine didn't own their lands. The few who had acquired homestead lands were never able to pay their taxes.

The 1930s, the Dirty Thirties, were a terrible time on the prairies. There were serious droughts, and soil drifted for hundreds of miles. The winds and the drifting soil created blinding storms that obliterated the skies. The force of the wind was such that the impact on skin left scars. The problem was the farming practices. Farmers left the bare soil of their plowed fields open to the wind. Much of the land should never have been plowed at all because the soil was simply too poor and there was not enough water. This was the bald prairie that nobody wanted as homestead lands in the 1870s. But the introduction of new wheat species had led the government and homesteaders to believe that any land on the prairie would do. It was a huge mistake.

In 1935 Ottawa passed the Prairie Farm Rehabilitation Act (PFRA). It was Ottawa's attempt to deal with the drought and the drift of soil. The idea was to seed the bare soil with grass for grazing. In a story we are brutally familiar with by now, they began with a survey. Three years later the survey was complete and community pastures were designated. Ste. Madeleine was to be one of the community pastures.

The basic theory of British and Canadian common law is that no person can be deprived of his or her land without compensation, and this was the theory adopted under the new act. Homesteaders whose land would become community pastures were offered full compensation or good farming land in exchange for their sandy soil. They were also offered assistance to relocate. But everything depended on whether they had paid their taxes.

In Ste. Madeleine, a community where Métis had been living since the 1870s, few people had ever been able to pay their taxes, and by the 1930s those taxes would have been more than the property was worth. It didn't really matter how much the taxes were; the Métis in Ste. Madeleine had no possible way to pay them. That meant the government could order the destruction of their homes and community with no compensation and no thought for what the people would do or where they would go.

That is exactly what happened. The government paid the locals $60,000 to do the dirty deed, and the locals did it for the money and the jobs. One of the locals provided his perspective: "Everybody wanted jobs. They wanted the PFRA to bring jobs in . . . Lets get them bloody Breeds out of there and have some work. Let's give them a few bucks and chase them out of there . . . Everybody was for that."[7] Métis houses were burned and their dogs were shot while they watched. Ironically, because the Métis were not engaged in commercial farming, they didn't leave their land with exposed soil and were not contributing to the soil erosion problem on the prairie. Their small farms didn't need rehabilitation, and the $60,000 paid to the locals was probably more than what the Métis properties and back taxes were worth.

Ste. Madeleine lives in the memories of the Manitoba Métis, another story in the long dispossession of the Métis Nation from their lands. One of the consequences of this long dispossession is that the Métis have maintained their mobility. Canada went to great trouble and expense to stop First Nations from pursuing their mobile lifestyle. They were settled on reserves. Today First Nations move less than any other people in Canada. But all actions taken by the state—the scrip process, the dismantlement of the communities the Métis created, the refusal to recognize their collective identity—all contributed to the Métis' ongoing mobility. Today the Métis on the Prairies are still mobile. We know poor and young populations are highly mobile, but even taking those factors into account, the data show that Métis on the Prairies are significantly more mobile than the non-Indigenous population.[8]

SASKATCHEWAN

Like the Métis in Alberta, the Saskatchewan Métis became divided into northern and southern branches. The Métis in southern Saskatchewan reorganized, and by 1929 l'Union Métisse du Local #1 de Batoche resolved "*de s'organiser suivant plus au moins la constitution Métis du Manitoba.*"[9] In July they held a conference of the Union Métisse Nationale. In attendance were delegates from the *métisse de Manitoba*. Also at the assembly were the Union Métisse de la Saskatchewan and *les gens* Métisse. They resolved to form a Union Métisse Nationale l'Ouest and to adopt the flag of the Manitoba Métis "*comme drapeau de l'union Métisse de l'Ouest.*"[10] By 1930 the Métis women in Saskatchewan were organizing as well. But the national organization never got off the ground, and the southern Saskatchewan organizational machine held a few meetings and then slumbered.

Green Lake was an exception. Alex Bishop was the local president. He kept the local in Green Lake alive. And it was Bishop who awoke the Métis national consciousness in the north. During the fight to establish the Métis settlements in Alberta, Bishop had kept in touch with Jim Brady and Malcolm Norris. The links were there but they were fragile. Then, after the Second World War, Brady and Norris arrived and set about trying to revive the spirits of the Saskatchewan Métis.[11] It was not an easy thing to do.

The Métis in northern Saskatchewan were quite different from their relations in northern Alberta. The Métis in northern Alberta had never lost their national consciousness. But the Métis in northern Saskatchewan had little to connect them to their southern Métis family. The freighters and boatmen who had provided the links were now trappers, hunters and fishermen who didn't travel back south. They had grown isolated in the north. They followed a seasonal round, and the communities were a temporary rendezvous before the families went back out on the round again. Any vestiges of the Saskatchewan Métis Society were in the south.

In the 1940s Saskatchewan set up an experimental farm project for the Métis. The Saskatchewan government, following Alberta's lead, stressed that it was working to relieve present conditions, not addressing past injuries or rights. One of the experimental farms was set up at Green Lake, where each Métis family received forty acres of land with a ninety-nine-year lease.

Most of the Métis who ended up on the Green Lake farm came from the south. Many came from the area just north of Qu'Appelle. Métis families were bundled onto trains, and as the train departed for Green Lake, the people watched as men set fire to their homes. They were supposed to be going to a new home. But there was no housing when they arrived, and the land was heavily wooded and would take ages to clear. The lots were too small for commercial farming. The Green Lake farm was supposed to be a relief measure, but there was no relief. There was nothing to support them while they got on their feet. The southern Métis had simply been shipped north and left to fend for themselves in a land they didn't know. They were ill-equipped, had little by way of farming skills and they had no equity in the land. Most of them left.

The 1950s saw little action on the Métis political front in Saskatchewan. But things started to change in the 1960s. In 1961 the Métis organized a commemorative service at Batoche. Both Norris and Brady attended. It was a small service with about thirty or forty attendees. The next year, 1962, the government invited Norris to speak at another commemorative service at Batoche. It was sponsored by the Royal Regiment of Canada and was supposed to be a step toward reconciliation. Norris was expected to be grateful for the opportunity and to make nice. Instead he gave them a history lesson, and it was not the history they knew.

The event was called a service "To Honour Those Who Fell in the Saskatchewan Rebellion of 1885." If the Old Wolves had still been around, they would have objected to the use of the term "rebellion." Norris did not hesitate to set the record straight. He called Riel a patriot who waged a battle similar to the battles fought by William Lyon Mackenzie and Louis-Joseph Papineau. He objected to the monument at Fish Creek that misstated the facts. It called the Métis rebels and said they had been defeated when in fact they had held off the army against overwhelming odds. Norris blasted them all and finished by telling them that the conditions of the Métis Nation were "a blot on our country." Then he led them to Gabriel Dumont's grave and unveiled a new monument. It was a classic Métis speech. He made them uncomfortable. He told them they were wrong, told them what they should be thinking and doing, and then staged his own event.

Métis leaders all learned from Norris how to stage these kinds of events. Another Saskatchewan leader, Jim Sinclair, also had a flair for staging events that grabbed attention. When Central Mortgage and Housing Corporation (CMHC) gave the Saskatchewan Métis Society a meagre $5,000 for a housing program, Sinclair had the entire amount converted into nickels and dimes and carted in wheelbarrows into the CMHC offices in Regina. He dumped the huge pile of coins on the floor. The Métis, he told reporters, were fed up with nickel-and-dime programs.

Sinclair's nickel-and-dime stunt has become a well-known story among Métis activists. Tony Belcourt, the president of the Métis Nation of Ontario in the early 1990s, knew Sinclair well and loved the nickel-and-dime story. He told that story when he was considering liberating the noose that was used to hang Riel. At the time it was on display at Casa Loma in Toronto. Belcourt was disturbed that the RCMP were displaying the noose in Ontario. It was a nasty reminder of the way John Schultz and Charlie Mair had displayed rope they claimed had been used to bind Thomas Scott. They had used such props in Ontario to stir up the Orange Lodge. What did the RCMP intend by displaying in Ontario the noose that hanged Riel?

Belcourt thought that liberating the noose from Casa Loma could be used to generate a grand discussion about Métis rights. He would welcome a debate, maybe even a trial over whether the Mounties had any right to keep and display the noose that hanged Riel. Belcourt never did move forward with that plan, but it was the kind of stunt Sinclair and Norris would have admired. Decades after the nickel-and-dime stunt, another Saskatchewan Métis leader, Clément Chartier, was so frustrated at being limited to observer status in a meeting that he went to it with a black piece of fabric tied like a gag over his mouth.

Imagine the pile of nickels and dimes that cascaded onto the floor, the look on the housing officials faces and the noise of the metal coins. What a scene it must have been! And when Chartier sat through a meeting with a black cloth over his mouth, the message was clear. It is often difficult to get attention for Métis issues, and these leaders taught the Métis Nation that the government and press respond to dramatic gestures—the government with embarrassment, and the press with glee. The Métis

Nation has never been above turning up the volume on the government embarrassment knob.

MANITOBA

By the 1950s the term "Métis" was a dirty word in the Prairies. Some shied away from the identity because of the prejudice they experienced. There was little advantage to claiming Métis heritage and much to be lost—housing, jobs and even love. Meanwhile Prairie governments continued to seek solutions to the Métis "problem." The ideas adopted by the Ewing Commission and the Saskatchewan government now took on a new name: community development. This movement purported to both decolonize and fight poverty. Essentially, the idea was to help people help themselves.

The government of Manitoba eventually commissioned a study of the Métis problem.[12] The 1959 Lagassé report enumerated 23,579 Manitoba Métis and called for integration. By this, Jean Lagassé said, he did not mean assimilation. Lagassé claimed that he was not looking to blend the Métis into Canadian society to the point where their culture disappeared. Lagassé thought it was possible to integrate to a point where there would be a "harmonious interaction of social or cultural entities that retain their identity."[13] The role of the state was to promote that movement through self-help but based on a respect for the Métis as an ethnic group having civil and human rights. The distinction between integration and assimilation was the kind of subtlety that academics appreciate, but it proved to be virtually impossible to incorporate into government programs.

Lagassé's report was a product of its time and reflected his Catholic leanings and morality. His attitudes toward Métis history (rather romantic), Métis women (too promiscuous) and the

Métis way of life (unremitting poverty) came through loud and clear. The Métis were immoral, according to Lagassé, because Métis women actually liked sex. Some reports reveal more about their author than about the subject of the study.

His proposed solutions were impractical. He believed that relocation to urban centres was the best long-term solution to Métis poverty. We should be clear about what he was proposing here: mass relocation of all Métis and non-status Indians to the city. This idea would have horrified most Winnipeggers, who in the 1950s thought that all Aboriginal people should be rooted *out* of the city. The upheaval his proposal would cause to the Métis culture was never considered. Casual labour, traditional hunting and fishing, and seasonal work were all seen as inadequate means of obtaining a proper standard of living. So, despite some statements that gave lip service to protecting Métis culture, the conclusions and recommendations of the report worked to undermine it. In fact, one of Lagassé's conclusions was that Métis culture and Canadian culture were incompatible. One wonders how he thought he could integrate an incompatible Métis Nation culture into Canadian culture without assimilation.

Lagassé had particular trouble defining the Métis. He simply could not come to grips with the complexities of such a people. He didn't know where to start, and in the end he printed a list of things Canadians said about the Métis. He mixed up ideas of culture, class, race and self-identification. He used outside recognition as a way of defining the Métis. His definition also contained a buried concept that the Métis were a dwindling people destined for extinction. According to Lagassé, a Métis was a person with some Indian ancestry who could still be recognized as Métis because of their way of life, or to take it one step further, because of the way of life of their immediate blood relations.

The idea of integration was problematic in the implementation of the community development projects the study spawned. Remember, this was supposed to be the people helping themselves. The ideas from the Lagassé report filtered down into the Manitoba bureaucracy and influenced decision-making, particularly when Manitoba began the era of mega projects in its northern reaches. The failure to appreciate who the Métis were and the clumsy definition put forward by Lagassé would come back to haunt the Métis Nation in Manitoba for generations. It laid the foundation for their exclusion from consideration when Manitoba Hydro began the Churchill River Diversion, a project that decimated Métis communities such as Grand Rapids. The influx of new mining towns and the relocations and disruptions caused by the mega projects all ignored the Métis Nation as a collective entity.

It was a convenient position for the Manitoba government, and one that even in the twenty-first century has not changed. In 2018 the Manitoba government cancelled two multi-million-dollar agreements between Manitoba Hydro and the Manitoba Metis Federation. The agreements were an attempt by Manitoba Hydro to establish a new relationship with the Métis. When the premier cancelled the first agreement, calling it "persuasion money," nine out of ten of the Hydro board directors resigned. When the second agreement was cancelled, the president of the Manitoba Metis Federation, David Chartrand, harkened back to the bitter history between the province and the Métis Nation. He said, "Why in the hell would you make that decision? What guided you? Is it vindictiveness? Do you want to get revenge on the Métis people because they stood up against you?"[14] *Plus ça change.*

PART EIGHT

RENAISSANCE

CHAPTER 30

THE FIFTH NATIONAL RESISTANCE

REORGANIZING THE MÉTIS NATION

In the 1960s the Métis Nation reorganized in the Prairies. The catalyst for the reorganization was the same threat the Métis had always faced: displacement. But this time the Métis were not being displaced because of settlement. For most Métis, especially in the northern parts of the provinces, the reorganization began in response to natural resources development—oil and gas in Alberta, uranium mining in Saskatchewan and hydro in Manitoba.

New leaders took over the reins. Stan Daniels was the Métis Association of Alberta's president. Howard Adams, Rod Bishop and Jim Sinclair were working in Saskatchewan, and when the Manitoba Metis Federation officially organized in 1967, its new president was Adam Cuthand.

By the 1970s the search was on for something more than provincial organizations. The three Prairie Métis organizations formed the Native Council of Canada. Within a few years they invited the non-status Indians and Métis from other provinces into the organization. Thus began a period when the Métis Nation was represented by a pan-Indigenous organization. The Native Council of Canada lobbied the government and at the same time became delivery agents for government programs and services to Métis and non-status Indians.

After 1973, when the courts began to recognize the legal existence of Indigenous title and land rights, the federal government was forced to deal with the land claims of First Nations.[1] But Canada refused to extend this recognition to the Métis Nation, claiming it had fully extinguished all Métis land rights. As far as Ottawa was concerned, that satisfied any obligations it may have had to the Métis as individuals. It had never recognized the Métis Nation. Case closed.

The Native Council of Canada and the provincial organizations began to have annual assemblies as well as local and regional meetings. Métis scholars began to research their history and the law. They started to tell the old stories to the assemblies, and this new generation of Métis became better educated about the law and Indigenous rights. The Métis Nation's history formed the basis for a developing legal theory of Métis rights. Métis nationalism, a theme that had never been far from the surface in the Prairies, once again resonated loudly. But that national pride clashed with the aspirations of non-status Indians. The two groups, the Métis and non-status Indians, may have shared an organization but they shared little else. Their histories and trajectories were entirely different. Non-status Indians invariably tied their identity and culture to the First Nations they were connected to. The Native Council of Canada, the only national voice for the Métis, was thus compromised in its goals and aspirations. In 1977 Saskatchewan and Manitoba withdrew.

HARRY DANIELS

In the late 1960s Canada began three decades of constitutional debates. The 1960s also saw the rise of another dynamic Métis Nation leader: Harry Daniels. Harry was handsome and dapper, a dancer, an actor, smart and politically savvy. He was an inspiring speaker, passionate about Métis rights, and he was a scrappy fighter. He became the first voice of the Métis Nation in the constitutional debates.

Harry Daniels, 1998 (*The Canadian Press/Fred Chartrand*)

Riel had absorbed the ideas of Papineau and the thinking behind the American and French revolutions. Colonial theory, the labour movement and socialism inspired Norris and Brady. Daniels absorbed the revolutionary ideas and zeal of the American civil rights movement, the Black Panthers, the American Indian Movement, Frantz Fanon's writings from Africa, and the human rights revolution that was sweeping the world. It was a powerful mix.

Prime Minister Pierre Elliot Trudeau's move to patriate

the Constitution became the target for Daniels. Trudeau was greatly attached to his "two founding nations" idea, the theory that Canada was founded by the English and French nations. Daniels attacked the idea. There were not two founding nations. In fact the Métis Nation was a politically independent nation when it joined Canada. The Manitoba Act was a contract of Confederation, a promise. Canada had broken that contract and turned the Manitoba Act into an empty broken promise.

Daniels argued that the Métis Nation's identity was "suppressed and denied by the federal government in Ottawa, which looked only to England and France for its notions of culture."[2] When "multiculturalism" became the new buzzword, Daniels wanted Canada to know that Riel was the father of this idea. Multiculturalism? Bah! That was just repackaging the "two founding nations myth with some Ukrainian Easter eggs, Italian grapes and Métis bannock for extra flavour."[3]

Daniels saw the constitutional debates as an opportunity to gain recognition for the Métis Nation with a distinct status within Confederation. He wanted participation and feared the Métis Nation's voice and rights would be drowned out in the fierce federal-provincial horse-trading. When his fears proved true, Daniels staged an eight-hour sit-in in the House of Commons. He maintained that the sit-in was just a continuation of the meeting, albeit without the justice minister and other federal committee members. The point was to force the issue of the participatory status of the Native Council of Canada and through them, the participation of the Métis Nation. As Daniels put it, "We represent a whole nation of people who have been alienated. We have been trying for more than a century to get into Confederation." The Métis Nation wanted what they had always wanted: they wanted in, but on their own terms.

On January 30 Justice Minister Jean Chrétien confirmed that the clause "The aboriginal and treaty rights of the aboriginal peoples of Canada are hereby recognized and affirmed" would be included in the Constitution. This was not nearly enough for Daniels. He demanded specific reference to the Métis in the clause. Chrétien tried to foist Daniels off with an assurance that the phrase "aboriginal peoples" would be generously interpreted. Daniels was often charming and he had a great sense of humour, but he could be Métis blunt too. With Chrétien he was . . . well, let's put it this way: he wasn't exactly polite. No deal, is what he said. No deal unless the Métis are specifically recognized. Daniels lobbied everyone. Committee members were harangued in hallways and corridors. And they listened. The deal was disintegrating under Chrétien's fingers. With minutes to go before the cameras rolled, Chrétien announced an amendment to the Aboriginal rights clause, a new sub-clause. The new drafting was "The aboriginal and treaty rights of the aboriginal peoples of Canada are hereby recognized and affirmed. In this Act, 'aboriginal peoples of Canada' includes the Indian, Inuit and Métis peoples of Canada."

The wording did not specifically reference the Métis Nation, but the provision uses the word "peoples" three times. The new constitutional protection was not designed to protect individual Aboriginal rights. It was designed to give protection to the rights of Aboriginal collectives. Daniels's insistence on the specific inclusion of the Métis peoples of Canada left the door open for other Métis peoples to claim constitutional protection if they could prove they were ever a people. He never had any doubt the Métis Nation would meet this standard.

There was a significant group of Métis lawyers and advisers around Daniels, and they all deserve credit for their work. But in the end it was Harry Daniels's tenacity that got the Métis included in the Constitution Act, 1982. Louis Riel put the Métis into the Canadian Constitution with their inclusion in the Manitoba Act, 1870. Harry Daniels got the Métis included in section 35 of the Constitution Act, 1982.

Was Daniels right to put so much pressure on the federal government and insist that the Constitution of Canada specifically recognize the Métis Nation as "one of the aboriginal peoples of Canada"? Today the Métis Nation celebrates him for what he accomplished in 1981. But in 1982 it was not clear that Daniel's achievement could be considered a victory.

The Manitoba Metis Federation was particularly concerned. They had been preparing to launch a lawsuit that took aim at the failure to properly implement the Métis treaty that Riel had negotiated in sections 31 and 32 of the Manitoba Act, 1870. The president of the Manitoba Metis Federation, John Morrisseau, wanted to focus on the first Métis constitutional provisions that had not been fulfilled. He worried that the absence of Aboriginal consent on an amendment clause would permit the removal of sections 31 and 32 of the Manitoba Act, 1870. The Manitoba and Saskatchewan Métis organizations forced Daniels to make the Native Council of Canada's support for patriation of the Constitution conditional on Aboriginal consent for constitutional amendments.[4]

Canada felt stung by the now conditional Métis support. Then on April 15, 1981, the Manitoba Metis Federation launched its lawsuit. On April 24, 1981, in perhaps the fastest government response the Métis Nation has ever experienced, Justice Minister Jean Chrétien sent a letter categorically rejecting the idea that Canada had any outstanding obligations with respect to Métis land claims.

Why put your efforts into a new constitutional clause when Canada would not fulfill its obligations under its first constitutional promise? There was little reason to expect things would change. To the Métis Nation it appeared that individual rights would be guaranteed, but their collective rights would not. Daniels had been the bold face of Métis support for patriation of the Constitution and the new Aboriginal rights clause. With the Chrétien rejection of Métis rights from the first Constitution and mounting disapproval from the Métis Nation, Daniels stepped down as president of the Native Council of Canada.

In September 1981 the Supreme Court of Canada forced Prime Minister Trudeau to abandon his plan for unilateral federal patriation, and with this judgment, the provinces gained considerable bargaining leverage. The Western premiers didn't like the Aboriginal rights clause. They didn't much like the Charter either, and in the horse-trading that ensued, the Aboriginal rights clause was sacrificed for Charter support. The provinces were afraid of the broad nature of the clause.

In the summer of 1980 the Native Council of Canada had established its own Constitutional Review Commission. It was Daniels's way of involving Aboriginal people in the constitutional discussions. Daniels was the commissioner. The deputy commissioners were Margaret Joe (Commodore), Rheal Boudrias, Duke Redbird, Viola Robinson and Elmer Ghostkeeper.[5] The commission went on the road and held meetings across Canada. It got an earful from the Métis in Manitoba about the constitutional promises already made and broken. Daniels wouldn't even call a meeting in Saskatchewan. In July 1981 Daniels stepped down, and Jim Sinclair became the commissioner of the Constitutional Review Commission.

DIVORCE

It became the task of Elmer Ghostkeeper and Jim Sinclair to pick up where Daniels had left off. Ghostkeeper was the president of the Alberta Federation of Métis Settlements. Under his leadership the Alberta Métis settlements were regaining their own voice. Manitoba might be fighting for fulfilment of the promises made in the Manitoba Act, but the settlements had land and they had a form of self-government. They were already in court against Alberta to stop the province from taking their resource money and further encroaching on their self-government powers. Ghostkeeper was maintaining the lawsuit, was encouraging the settlements to flex their jurisdictional muscle and was also on the Constitutional Review Commission. He wanted constitutional protection for Métis settlement lands. Alberta had shut down some settlements already, and Ghostkeeper wanted to make sure that would never happen again.

Elmer Ghostkeeper, 1981 (*The Canadian Press/Gordon Karam*)

Would the Aboriginal rights clause protect the Alberta Métis settlement lands? Ghostkeeper thought so and he wanted the clause back in. He joined a crowd of five thousand protesters in Edmonton to put pressure on Premier Peter Lougheed to put the clause back into the Constitution. But it was not Ghostkeeper and the settlements who broke the provincial deadlock on the Aboriginal protection clause. When Clément Chartier, a Métis lawyer, explained that Indigenous rights were not new rights and that they already existed, Premier Lougheed latched on to the idea and proposed inserting the word "existing" into the clause, thereby ensuring that the rights protected were those that existed as of the effective date of the patriated Constitution. The provinces accepted the proposal and Parliament adopted it in December 1981. Defining the existing rights was deferred to the First Ministers' conferences that were to follow.

The new Constitution recognized three distinct Aboriginal peoples in Canada—Indians, Inuit and Métis. But non-status Indians were not a distinct group. They were individuals from First Nations all across the country whose only common issue was that they had lost their status under the Indian Act. They had serious legal issues but not constitutional ones, and the upcoming constitutional conferences were specifically about constitutional rights.

By 1982 the Native Council of Canada's president and vice-president were both non-status Indians. The Métis Nation had initially created the organization, but it was now fully captured by non-status Indians who wanted to press on their issues, not Métis Nation issues. Who then would represent the Métis Nation at the upcoming constitutional conference to determine the content of Métis Nation rights in the new Constitution?

The issue of representation at the 1983 First Ministers'

conference collided with the issue of Métis Nation representation on its only national organization. Ghostkeeper wanted a Métis national voice, which would never be achieved, he was convinced, if the Métis Nation stayed under the umbrella of the Native Council of Canada. A committed group of Métis nationalists began to gather, inspired by Ghostkeeper. A divorce was in the making.

There would be two available seats at the table for the Native Council of Canada during the conferences. Since First Nations were already well represented with two seats, Sinclair wanted the two Native Council of Canada seats for the Métis Nation. The Native Council of Canada vehemently disagreed. The Métis walked out. Actually, describing their exit as "walking" is a bit of an understatement. They were angry and defiant. Sinclair resigned as commissioner of the Constitutional Review Commission. The marriage of convenience between the Métis Nation and non-status Indians was over. It was January 14, 1983.

CREATING THE MÉTIS NATIONAL COUNCIL

On January 22, 1983, over one hundred Métis from all over the Métis Nation met in Edmonton to form their own national organization. Representatives came from northwest Ontario, Manitoba, Saskatchewan, Alberta, the Métis settlements and northeast British Columbia. The meeting established a Métis Constitutional Council to participate in the constitutional conference. The members were the three Prairie provincial organizations and the Federation of Métis Settlements.[6] Ghostkeeper opened the meeting by quoting Louis Riel, who had said that the Métis Nation would rise again a century after his death. It was almost exactly a century since Canada hanged Riel in 1885. The symbolism struck a chord with everyone there.

The First Ministers' conference was scheduled for March 15

and 16, 1983. Everything about the conference pointed to the exclusion of the Métis Nation. But the conference was crucial. All the other Indigenous peoples had processes to deal with the government, plus the conference. The Métis Nation had no processes and everyone denied they had rights. They only had one chance and it was the First Ministers' conference. But they had no seat at the table.

Ghostkeeper put the Métis Nation case forward at a meeting with federal and provincial government representatives. He referred again to Louis Riel and reminded them that Riel had been denied his seat in Parliament. Ghostkeeper accused the chair of repeating history. He blasted Canada for excluding them from the conference. Then the Métis walked out. They wrote a letter to Trudeau informing him that they were forming their own national organization and that they wanted two seats at the table. And then they went to court.

On March 8, 1983, members of the boards of the Prairie Métis organizations established a new national governing body, the Métis National Council. There were immediate casualties in the establishment of the Métis National Council, and Elmer Ghostkeeper was one of them. The Métis Association of Alberta agreed to come on board, but only if it was the sole organization representing the Métis in Alberta. The decision to run the Métis National Council as a federation of provincial organizations left the Federation of Métis Settlements, the body that represented the only Métis with a land base, out of the national body. The Métis settlements would have to be represented by the Métis Association of Alberta, the province-wide body, or not be part of the Métis National Council at all. The Métis settlements opted to stay out, and to this day this particular political rift within the Métis Nation has not been healed.

Clément Chartier was elected to represent the Métis Nation at the upcoming First Ministers' conference. The Métis National Council filed an injunction to stop the conference unless they were invited to the table. The judge urged the parties to try settlement discussions. But the lawyers were getting nowhere. Then, just minutes before they were to reconvene court in the afternoon, Chartier got word that Canada had agreed to their demand for separate representation.

Clément Chartier, president of the Métis National Council, circa 2017 (*Métis National Council*)

The offer from Canada was contingent on the Métis National Council dropping its lawsuit. Chartier was also promised that a Métis Nation land base could be inserted into the agenda. The catch was that Canada only offered one seat. It wasn't fair, and Sinclair and Chartier were not happy about the inequity, but they accepted. Everyone held press conferences. The Métis claimed victory. The Native Council of Canada cried foul and railed against the heresy of Métis nationalist claims. All this took place just five days before the First Ministers' conference began.

CONSTITUTIONAL CONFERENCES OF THE 1980s

With hindsight it is easy to see how overblown expectations were for the conferences. The first conference was a two-day affair. Defining the content of Aboriginal rights could never be accomplished in two days—but that's 20/20 hindsight. At the time there was hope. Chartier and Sinclair spoke passionately about the history of the Métis Nation and their desire for a land base and self-government—a place, as Chartier put it, that the Métis Nation could call its own. Sinclair argued for the need for constitutional protection to keep Métis Nation rights out of the reach of the political winds of fortune. The reason the Métis Nation was still fighting a hundred years after Riel was because the Canadian democracy had failed them. This was an opportunity to change that history, to walk down a better road. Some amendments were made to the Aboriginal protection clause, but there was no progress on rights definition in the 1983 First Ministers' conference or in the 1984 conference.

The 1985 conference involved different players. Brian Mulroney's Conservatives were in power in Ottawa, and there was only one topic: self-government. Canada's approach required the provinces to commit to the negotiation of self-government. British Columbia, Alberta and Saskatchewan were not prepared to make such a constitutional commitment, and the agreement was watered down to a non-binding political accord. The Métis

National Council reluctantly agreed, but the First Nations and Inuit would not agree. Thus ended the third First Ministers' conference.

The final round was in 1987. Self-government dominated the conference as it had in 1985. The three Western provinces reiterated their previous position. They would not agree to a commitment to negotiate self-government. British Columbia stepped back even further when it said there was no room in the Constitution for Aboriginal self-government. None of the Western provinces wanted to enshrine an undefined inherent Aboriginal right to self-government in the Constitution.

Jim Sinclair, 1987 (*The Canadian Press/Chuck Mitchell*)

Jim Sinclair had the last word. He used it to blast the premiers. He started with British Columbia's premier, an immigrant who claimed the right to refuse to even negotiate self-government rights with the original inhabitants. Quebec was next for not coming to the aid of the Métis Nation. He saved most of his wrath for Saskatchewan. This was a province that subsidized alcohol so it was the same price in the north as in Regina, but would not give a subsidy for milk for children. This was a province that had recently given a blank cheque and land to an American pulp and paper company—more land than all the reserves in Canada—and this it did with an open-ended agreement. No definitions were asked of them. Sinclair went on to say:

> We have struggled hard to make a deal. We have kept our end of the bargain . . . One thing I want to say, as we leave this meeting: I am glad that we stuck together on a right that is truly right for our people, right for all of Canada, and right within international law throughout the world . . . We have the right to self-government, to self-determination and land . . . This is not an end. It is only the beginning . . . Do not worry, Mr. Prime Minister and Premiers of the provinces . . . our people will be back.[7]

When he was done all the Aboriginal people in attendance burst into applause. And it was all done on live TV. The First Ministers' Conferences were a failure from the Métis Nation's perspective, but it had gained its national voice in the Métis National Council.

NO PARDON FOR RIEL

The next round of constitutional negotiations headed down the same road the First Ministers' Conferences had already walked. When the Meech Lake Accord was up for ratification, the question was whether the offer of "distinct society" status for Quebec provided an opening for the Métis Nation. Yvon Dumont, president of the Manitoba Metis Federation, in defiance of all the other Indigenous organizations, thought there was a possibility for the Métis Nation to also be recognized as a distinct society. He was the only Indigenous leader to support the Meech Lake Accord. Ultimately it didn't matter. The Meech Lake Accord was doomed, and Canadian attention was galvanized by two events: the Oka crisis in the summer of 1990, and the threat of a Quebec sovereignty referendum in 1992.

As unlikely as it seems, these two issues brought Louis Riel back into Canadian consciousness. What did Riel have to do with a Mohawk uprising at Oka and the Quebec sovereignty referendum? It seems an unlikely triad, but it can be explained by the historical relationship between the federal government and Indigenous peoples, and the historical relationship between Quebec and the rest of Canada.

For centuries Canada has denied, stalled or stifled the legitimate rights and grievances of Indigenous peoples. There is a predictable cycle of peaceful protest and government denial that eventually erupts in violence. Names like Batoche, Ipperwash and Oka each contain a story of Indigenous resistance.

Oka became a household word when the Mohawks set up barricades to prevent the expansion of a golf course onto their ancestral lands. Most of the press ignored the real issue: Canada's failure to resolve Mohawk land claims. After decades of peaceful agitation by the Mohawks to stop the continual erosion of their lands, Canada still refused to even consider negotiation or a peaceful resolution to the issue. In closing off legitimate avenues of resolution, the federal government created the perfect setting for the eruption in the summer of 1990.

Only after Oka did the government begin to address the long-outstanding land issues of the Mohawks. In response to the events at Oka, the government did what we have seen many times in this history—they set up a royal commission. This one was called the Royal Commission on Aboriginal Peoples.

In 1987 Canada's first ministers negotiated the Meech Lake Accord. The process of the Meech Lake Accord negotiations fuelled the anger and resistance of Indigenous peoples because the issue of their rights had not been addressed. Because the Meech Lake Accord would have recognized Quebec as a distinct society, its defeat fuelled the anger and resistance of Quebec. Quebec felt rejected by English Canada, and the creation of the Bloc Québécois—a party devoted to Quebec nationalism and separatism—was one of the results.

Ottawa was being pressured on all sides to respond to the two outstanding and troubling issues of Canadian unity, Quebec and Indigenous peoples. The narrow defeat of the Quebec referendum on sovereignty in 1995 shook the government's complacency about the enduring commitment of Canadians to maintaining Canada. The violence that was building in Indigenous communities also needed to be addressed.

Finally, in January 1998 the government released its response to the report of the Royal Commission on Aboriginal Peoples. The response was in the form of a new government policy, *Gathering Strength*. The policy was described as an "action plan designed to renew the relationship with Aboriginal peoples of Canada." The policy stated that the commission's report had acted as a catalyst and an inspiration for the federal government's decision to set a new course in its policies for Indigenous peoples. But when the draft policy was shared with Indigenous leaders prior to its announcement, there was nothing in it for the Métis Nation.

Métis Nation leaders were outraged that there was no new course in Canada's policies or any meaningful action plan for the Métis Nation. Virtually overnight, Canada redrafted a statement of reconciliation. All Métis Nation issues that required reconciliation were reduced to the issue of a pardon for Riel. It was preposterous. In 1992 the Manitoba Legislative Assembly had already passed a unanimous resolution to honour the role of Louis Riel in the founding of Manitoba. That same year, the House of Commons and the Senate passed unanimous resolutions to recognize and honour the role of Louis Riel: "[T]hat this House recognize the unique and historic role of Louis Riel as a founder of Manitoba and his contribution in the development of Confederation; and that this House support by its actions the true attainment, both in principle and practice, of the constitutional rights of the Métis people."[8] With all the wrongs that needed to be dealt with, it was outrageous for Canada to suggest that once again affirming the contributions of the Métis and reflecting Riel's place in history would even begin to address the issues. Métis Nation leaders could hear Riel turning over in his grave.

It was in this dynamic context, where the issues of Quebec and Indigenous peoples were so intertwined, that the movement to exonerate Riel was reinvigorated. It is no surprise that Quebec influenced the exoneration movement. Quebec has always played a role in the Riel debate. After the initial uprising began in 1885, the French-language press in Quebec slowly came to the support of the Métis Nation. When Riel's death sentence was pronounced, support in Quebec turned to outrage. After the hanging in November 1885, the relationship between francophones and anglophones in Canada was forever changed. French Canadians believed Riel died because he was French and Catholic; they saw the loss of Riel as the loss of French access to the West. In the immediate aftermath of Riel's death, the Conservative government in Quebec, seen as Protestant and English, was roundly defeated. The new Quebec government was nationalistic and devoted to Quebec autonomy. In this way, the hanging of Louis Riel fertilized the nascent movement we call Quebec separatism.

Quebec has never let go of its attachment to Riel, and Quebec nationalism continues to play a role in the Riel exoneration dialogue. To that end, private member's bills to exonerate Riel have been sponsored by members of the Bloc Québécois, and the motivating force behind the Bloc-sponsored bills is exoneration of a francophone leader, not a Métis leader. If Riel were to be exonerated, it would set a precedent that would make it harder to accuse Quebec's separatist leaders of treason. In 1996 and again in 1997, Riel exoneration bills were introduced into Parliament. The debate in the House of Commons tied together the issues of reconciliation for Quebecers and francophones, and exoneration of Riel. On October 21, 1996, Jean-Paul Marchand, a Bloc Québécois member, spoke during the second reading of An Act to Revoke the Conviction of Riel:

> Louis Riel was led before a jury of six Anglophones and tried by an anglophone judge in Regina . . . In that same year, French was banned in Manitoba. Louis Riel was, in fact, the victim of a miscarriage of justice that reflected the attitude to francophones at the time. People in Quebec knew that Louis Riel's cause was just . . . and Quebecers and francophones across the country were outraged by the decision made by a jury of six anglophones, negating the rights of Louis Riel. Despite the uproar this caused in Quebec, even John A. Macdonald,

> the Prime Minister of Canada at the time, said: "All the dogs in Quebec can bark, but Louis Riel shall hang." John A. Macdonald said that. It was a way to punish the French fact in the west, although the rights of francophones were supposedly guaranteed. I may also point out to my dear colleagues from western Canada that subsequently the rights of francophones in Manitoba were abolished for one hundred years.
>
> The conviction of Louis Riel was unjust, unacceptable and unpardonable. If people want to reconcile Canada with its francophones, let them adopt, fairly and squarely, a formula to absolve or pardon Louis Riel.[9]

The Riel exoneration movement is part and parcel of the fabric of Canada.[10] Exoneration for a francophone leader is intimately connected with the place of francophones and Quebec within our society. For many Quebec proponents, exoneration has little to do with the man—Riel—and even less to do with his people—the Métis Nation.

Whether called exoneration or a pardon, such an act is one of extrajudicial clemency. It is a government grant of political expediency. It is never about justice or mercy. Clemency is never a statement of the accused's innocence and always implies guilt and forgiveness. The government would be exonerating itself, not Riel. That is why the Métis Nation has rejected all calls for a pardon or exoneration. In their opinion it was Canada that committed the crime of hanging Riel. It would be more logical for the Métis Nation to pardon Canada. As one of the Métis Nation's legal scholars, Paul Chartrand, put it, "the hanging of Louis Riel is a stain on the honour of Canada. Let the stain remain."[11]

A NEW MÉTIS NATION TREATY—THE MÉTIS NATION ACCORD

Over a decade of Métis Nation constitutional negotiations culminated in May 1992 with the Métis Nation Accord. In the Charlottetown round, there was no confusion about who negotiated for the Métis Nation. The main issue for them was the jurisdictional question. Under the Canadian division of powers, "Indians, and Lands reserved for the Indians" was a jurisdiction allocated to the federal government. For the purposes of this provision, s. 91 (24), the term "Indians" is a purely legal term. It is not a cultural identification. First Nations and Inuit, vastly different Indigenous cultures, were known to be included. But the Métis Nation was ignored, which was a problem because it allowed the jurisdictional hot potato to continue to be juggled between the provinces and the federal government. It always left the Métis Nation with nothing and no one to talk to in government. Yvon Dumont, the president of the Métis National Council, staged a filibuster in Edmonton to press on this issue.

Constitutional provisions are supposed to be given a large and liberal interpretation, which would logically mean that all Indigenous people were included in the clause that gave jurisdiction to the federal government. But logic was not what guided the federal government's refusal to include the Métis Nation. It was money. They were afraid that the provinces, which currently covered Métis programs and services, would off-load them onto the federal government. First Nations didn't want Métis in "their" provision. They worried that the financial pie, already sliced too thin, would be cut into many more pieces.

These positions infuriated the Métis Nation. It was a question of constitutional law, not a financial decision. Opening up federal jurisdiction to include the Métis Nation didn't have to mean First Nations would get less. After much negotiation, the Métis Nation secured an agreement to amend federal jurisdiction to include the Métis and a further agreement not to reduce services. Negotiations would begin for a Métis land base, and governments would fund and participate in an enumeration and registration of the Métis.

With those important agreements under their belt, the Métis proceeded to draft the treaty they named the Métis Nation Accord. When the Métis Nation draft treaty was put on the table, the First Ministers agreed to the content. They balked at making it a constitutionally protected treaty, but they did agree to make it legally binding. Constitutional protection would have been better, but the Métis Nation Accord stood as the gold star agreement for the Métis.

It was a politically negotiated agreement that gave the Métis Nation the foundation they sought. There was recognition of the Métis Nation, a definition of Métis Nation citizens, a commitment to resources for an enumeration, the development of a registry, negotiations for lands and resources, an agreement by the provinces to provide lands, devolution of programs and services, self-government negotiations, an amendment to s. 91 (24) to include Métis, and funding for Métis institutions. The Métis settlements in Alberta would be protected and the Métis Nation Accord would be binding on the provinces and the federal government. All parties—the Métis Nation, the federal government and the provinces—agreed to the Métis Nation Accord.

It was a remarkable achievement and if it had been implemented, the course of Métis Nation–government relations would have changed forever. Unfortunately, the Canadian public voted the Charlottetown Accord down in a referendum and the Métis Nation Accord went down with it.

CHAPTER 31

THE HUNT FOR JUSTICE

HISTORY ON TRIAL

Canadians rejected the Charlottetown Accord, but not because of the Indigenous provisions. The Canadian public supported a reset of the relationship between the state and Indigenous peoples. But government fled from any further constitutional debates, and in its flight it retreated from a relationship with the Métis Nation. It was depressing to start over, and decades have been lost because the federal government lacked the political will to work positively with the Métis Nation.

The Métis kept the Métis Nation Accord alive through the 1990s, particularly in the drafting of the Métis chapter in the report of the Royal Commission on Aboriginal Peoples. But the government reverted to its entrenched position. It again claimed it had no jurisdiction for the Métis Nation and it would not include them in its processes to resolve lands and resource issues. With no other option, the Métis Nation took to the courts.

Not that they were ever out of the courts. For two hundred years the Métis have been caught in the currents and riptides of law. Every major event in the history of the Métis Nation has, with one exception (the Battle of the Grand Coteau), been the subject of litigation. That's two hundred years of court and commissions of inquiry.

So, in the 1990s the Métis Nation began litigation that eventually took in every province of the North-West as it fought for recognition of Métis rights inch by inch, mile by mile, and province by province.[1] In the course of this battle, a new generation of Métis Nation warriors arose—Métis lawyers.[2] They led the court battles throughout the Métis Nation. Métis men and women were fed up with government rules and laws keeping them off the land and undermining their ability to access animals and fish for food. Where previously the Métis hid their food harvesting practices, they now took a stand. They would not hide and they would let the courts decide. The Métis Nation called it "the hunt for justice."

Métis lawyers took on literally hundreds of hunting and fishing cases across the Métis Nation. The incidents that gave rise to the cases occurred in close proximity to several historic Métis Nation settlements, rendezvous and wintering sites and trade routes—near the Methy Portage, at Qu'Appelle Lakes and Green Lake, and at Rainy Lake, Cypress Hills and Turtle Mountain. Each time the Métis Nation went to court, Métis legal warriors put Canada's history on trial. Litigating Métis rights became a continuation of the Métis Nation's ongoing resistance in the North-West Resistance, the Red River Resistance and at the Frog Plain. The court was simply another forum to continue what is now a two-hundred-year war.

The history of the Métis is a prolonged "battle" for two things: First, recognition, a place in this country for the Métis as a nation, not just as individuals with some mixed Euro-Canadian heritage, but as a collective entity, a people, an Indigenous nation. Second, as a nation, the Métis believe they have at least some rights to the lands and resources. Why? It's a gut-level belief for Métis. For them it's simple: it's fair because they were here; they existed as a nation in the North-West before Canada arrived. They believe that fact gives the Métis Nation some rights, and they have never backed down from this belief.

While the common law has a long history of litigating land and resource disputes, the scale of the Indigenous history trials in Canada is staggering. Since 1982 over sixty Indigenous rights cases have been litigated before the Supreme Court of Canada. No other constitutional clause has been the subject of so much litigation in such a short period of time. Hundreds of millions of dollars have been spent. As of early 2017 the federal Department of Justice had more than three thousand Indigenous cases before it. That was 10 per cent of its litigation load. But the liability was 84 per cent of an estimated one trillion dollars. This is a staggering set of figures that should give all Canadians pause to question why we are pursuing litigation against Indigenous peoples and at what cost.

The lines in this David and Goliath battle are clearly drawn. The government dresses itself in the role of Captain Canada defending the rights of Canadians against Indigenous people, who are seen as a domestic problem that must be solved, always with a view to a permanent and final solution. The idea that there is a final solution to any people should give us all pause.

In these Indigenous rights trials Canada argues: (1) that it owns all the lands and resources in Canada, (2) that it can make all the decisions about how the lands and resources are used, and (3) that it gets the benefits of the lands and resources. Indigenous rights litigation, including the many Métis Nation cases, challenges each of those beliefs. The Métis Nation has always claimed its right to a say and a share. Since 1982 the courts have increasingly recognized and supported that right.

THE MANITOBA METIS FEDERATION CASE

Red River has always been the heartland of the Métis Nation. When so many Métis were forced out of Red River because of the lack of an amnesty for their leaders, because of the violence during the reign of terror, and because of the deliberate undermining of the promises in the Manitoba Act, a sense of betrayal and outrage arose in the Métis Nation. That outrage has never died. Because of it, the Métis Nation lost its land base in its heartland. This loss has always been an ocean of injustice for the Métis. They have never let it go. Why? Perhaps because of that meeting at Joseph Riel's house in 1909. The Old Wolves were stubborn and they refused to let the loss of their lands go unanswered. They were the ones who reorganized, started gathering documents, and started protesting and writing.

The Métis Nation is full of stories about how the Métis lost their land in Red River. They are all variations on being forced out of Red River, about the reign of terror and about how the Manitoba Act had been administered. The Manitoba Métis leaders all knew the story the Old Wolves published. It was the Manitoba Metis Federation's publishing arm, Pemmican Publications, that published the English translation of the Old Wolves' book. But the Old Wolves had not gone to Ottawa to look at the archival documents there. The new researchers did. The Manitoba Métis worked on the research for years before they finally filed the claim.

The children of the Old Wolves set up new political organizations. The Union Nationale had never ceased its representation of the Métis Nation, but it had a strict requirement that Métis members be Catholic and fluent in French. By the 1960s most Métis in Manitoba didn't speak French anymore. The French was lost in the diaspora after 1870, in the world wars and in the gradual anglicization of the entire country outside Quebec.

With the loss of the French language, many central and cherished values were also anglicized. The English language does not assign a gender to the land, and this resulted in the loss of the concept that the North-West was the Métis Nation's motherland. The Métis began to call the North-West their homeland. The Manitoba Metis Federation, seeking to reassure its members that it was not solely a French organization, even dropped the accented *é* from "Métis" in its name.

One value that did not get anglicized was the Métis Nation's culture of honour and its aspiration to justice, which continues to stand in stark contrast to the British values that have generally guided English Canada—a well-ordered society captured in the phrase "peace, order and good government." The Métis Nation has always regarded Canada's claim to be a well-ordered society as a myth based on complacency, habit, exclusion and denial.

The Manitoba Metis Federation started in 1967. It provided an organization for all Manitoba Métis, including those who didn't speak French, weren't Catholic or just weren't too fussed about language or religion. Their gig was politics, but they were also moving on social issues like housing. They were especially interested in rights issues. They were in a new position to carry on the fight for rights in federal and provincial law and politics, something the Old Wolves in the early 1900s had shied away from.

Their sons and daughters were not shy about it. They had grown up hearing the resistance stories. They knew about the language and religious rights too, but those were not their concern. This new generation of Métis activists wanted to do something about the land. After years of research they finally filed their lawsuit in 1981. Their claim was basically this:

- *The Facts:* The Métis had negotiated a treaty with Canada. The terms were in ss. 31 and 32 of the Manitoba Act. It promised to protect the Métis existing land holdings (s. 32) and to provide 1.4 million acres to their children (s. 31). The process ensured that the children didn't get the land and most of the Métis who had existing land holdings lost them.
- *The Law:* The Manitoba Act was part of the Constitution of Canada. The constitutional promise meant ensuring the Métis actually got the land (as opposed to an empty promise or a piece of paper). The constitutional promise in the Manitoba Act was breached. That was supposed to mean something in law.
- *The Order Sought*: The Manitoba Metis Federation wanted a declaration from the court that the constitutional promises had been broken. They wanted to use the declarations to force Canada back to the negotiation table. They wanted to re-negotiate their treaty.

The case was parked while the Métis Nation focused on the First Ministers' conferences from 1983 to 1987, and again through the Meech Lake and Charlottetown rounds of constitutional negotiations. There was always a hope that a negotiated political accord would make litigation unnecessary. They almost did it in the Charlottetown round when they negotiated the Métis Nation Accord. But when the referendum defeated the proposed constitutional changes, the Métis Nation Accord was defeated as well.

The case was reinvigorated in 1997 when David Chartrand emerged as the new leader of the Manitoba Metis Federation. Chartrand said he was prepared to go to the wall financially and politically to see the case through. And he did just that. It cost millions to take the case through trial, to the Court of Appeal and finally to the Supreme Court of Canada. And it was a tough slog. They lost at trial and at the Court of Appeal.

The lower court judges all found reasons to dismiss the case. They said the Métis were too late bringing the case to court and that too much time had passed. The events had taken place in the nineteenth century, and the lower court judges sided with the Manitoba and federal governments, who objected to being sued over the actions of their great-grandparents. The land grants and scrip had been issued, at least on paper, and that, claimed both governments, met the promises in the Constitution. All the laws, regulations and orders may have defeated the purpose of the promises, but they were lawfully done. And anyway, the Manitoba Metis Federation was just a not-for-profit corporation. It could not claim to be a government or to hold any rights. According to the lower courts, the Manitoba Metis Federation could not even bring the case to the court and they certainly could not obtain a remedy from the court.

But Chartrand is a stubborn man. He had already changed the name of the case. He wanted it to be named after the people, so he had it renamed as the Manitoba Metis Federation case. He dug in his heels, found more money to pay the lawyers and told them to appeal it to the Supreme Court of Canada.

The Supreme Court of Canada was not sympathetic to the issues that had so decided the lower court judges. They focused on one main issue: the systematic defeat of the constitutional promise. The treaty-like promise to the Métis was one of the compacts of Confederation. It had persuaded the Métis to lay down their arms. The promise should have been kept. So, the justices said it remained an outstanding obligation. There was unfinished business with the Métis, and the Manitoba Metis Federation had every right to bring the case to the courts and to obtain a remedy.

David Chartrand, president of the Manitoba Metis Federation, circa 2018 (*Courtesy of the Manitoba Metis Federation*)

It was complete vindication for Chartrand and the Manitoba Métis who had stood behind him for all those years. Louis Riel and the Old Wolves would have been proud. The victory in the Supreme Court of Canada gave Chartrand and the Manitoba Metis Federation the leverage they needed to finally bring Canada to a negotiation table.

The negotiations are beginning to bear fruit. On September 22, 2018, Canada and the Manitoba Metis Federation entered into a reconciliation agreement that will support the creation of their own government. It took a century and a half to correct the law, to begin to fix the system that had purposefully dispossessed the Métis of their lands, and repair the damage caused by the reign of terror, all of which had taken such a huge toll on the Métis Nation. But as Chartrand said, "It is bringing us back into Confederation."[3]

CINDY GLADUE

If the Manitoba Metis Federation case was one step forward in the courts on Métis Nation land and self-government, the Cindy Gladue case was five thousand steps back for the women of the Métis Nation.[4] We saw an early indication of how the justice system abused Métis women in the 1881 trial of Marie Trottier. Marie had been a witness in that trial, not the accused. But she was the one on trial. She was so ill she had to be carried in on a stretcher, but the full force of the law was inflicted on her. Unfortunately, nothing much appears to have changed in our courts when it comes to Métis women. Indeed, it seems to be far worse.

The statistics about violence against Indigenous women in Canada are only just coming to light. Statistics Canada reported in 2014 that the rate of homicides for Indigenous women and girls was six times higher than for non-Indigenous females. Indigenous females had an overall rate of violent victimization that was close to triple that of non-Indigenous females, and visible Indigenous identity in and of itself was a risk factor for violent victimization of Indigenous females.[5] No one has teased out the numbers of Métis women victims from this bundle of pan-Indigenous statistics. But Canadian institutions, particularly the justice system, play a role in the steady, violent abuse and murder of Métis women and girls.

In 2015 an Edmonton court facilitated a shockingly violent act against a Métis woman. Under the gloss of Canadian law, the trial was called *R. v. Barton*.[6] But this was no trial of a white man. It was the trial of Cindy Gladue, the victim. Ms. Gladue was found dead in a bloody bathtub. The Crown's case was that she died from a large wound in her vaginal wall caused by a sharp object. Bradley Barton, a man who admitted to having violent sex with her the night before, was charged with first-degree murder, but at trial he was found not guilty.

How Cindy Gladue died is shocking enough. The court made it much worse. During the trial, the forensic pathologist, Crown counsel and the judge all thought it necessary for the jury to see the actual wound that caused Cindy's death. To that end the pathologist cut out her pelvis and brought "the tissue" into court. At the trial the judge commented that it was "novel" to bring body parts into court and that indeed it seemed that this was a case of first instance. But he allowed it. Cindy's dismembered body was brought into court as evidence and was displayed before her mother's eyes and before the jury.

Métis women marched in the streets. Everyone in the country was shocked.

Cindy Gladue was a Métis woman from Alberta. She was a mother of three children. She is one of the thousand-plus murdered and missing Indigenous women in Canada who have been subjected to the system that passes for justice for Indigenous people in Canada. The fact that a pathologist would cut her into pieces and even conceive of bringing her body into court as evidence is unthinkable. It seems inconceivable that this would happen to anyone other than an Indigenous woman—to a white woman, unlikely; to a man, never. That Crown counsel would even consider this travesty brings a horrific new meaning to the "honour of the Crown," something the Métis have long claimed to know only in its absence. How could any judge, the keeper of our procedural law, even consider sanctioning such a travesty? It was the ultimate dehumanization of a woman who was already the victim of gender-based violence, and it sent a brutal message to Indigenous women across Canada. The courts will quite literally allow Indigenous women to be cut into pieces, by the state, and served up on a platter the state calls justice.

The dismemberment and public display of Cindy Gladue's body also violated Métis cultural practices with their dead. While many Métis Nation citizens are now Christians, their culture has always been a unique blend of practices taken from both Western and Indigenous peoples. Many Metis who are practising Christians also participate in Indigenous ceremonies. They see no inherent conflict in incorporating both belief systems into their lives. Christian practices do not preclude the important Métis cultural value of maintaining an ongoing relationship with their dead.

All cultures have their own ways of dealing with the dead. For the Métis Nation the body, even after death, remains an integral part of *wahkootowin*. The reciprocal relationship of that kinship connection does not die. After death there are rituals and ceremonies that have long been part of the Métis Nation's mourning and spiritual practices. How they dispose of bodies and how they are cared for and remembered is important to them.

It is important for Métis to be buried intact with their families. There are stories that the buffalo hunters would travel with their dead for hundreds of miles to return a body to Red River. One can only imagine what it was like for a buffalo hunter family in the 1860s to carry a deceased relative in a Red River cart for hundreds of miles on a journey that would have taken months. It speaks to how important it was to them. No one would undertake such a challenging journey under such circumstances if it were not a significant part of their culture. But that was part of the Métis Nation tradition.

Like all cultures, the Métis Nation has adapted over the centuries. It came to be influenced by Christian churches. It came under the influence of Canadian law. The people no longer travel in Red River carts. They no longer hunt buffalo. But the value they accord their women, their cultural traditions for the dead, the importance of family, and the dignity and care they give to bodies, the careful maintenance of *wahkootowin*, have not changed. Those beliefs were formed long ago and have not disappeared.

In one of the many Métis Nation court cases, the Métis Nation of Alberta tried to have the court recognize and respect their burial customs and traditions. In 2007 they went to court to stop the disinterment of one of their sons and the removal of his body to the RCMP cemetery in Regina.[7] They were unsuccessful because statutory law in Canada has no place for Métis Nation burial customs and traditions. It also provides no recognition of their spiritual beliefs about the dignity and honour they give to the bodies of their dead. Canadian law roughly and without consideration overrides the Métis Nation custom of respecting the bodily integrity of the dead and of keeping Métis families together in life and in death.

The Métis Nation also has its own values about justice and due process. Like the British common law, the Métis value precedent and cite it when resolving disputes. It was their practice to have a dispute heard by those with particular expertise in the issue at hand. There was always more than one person to hear a dispute. Most importantly, in Métis Nation culture, they allowed the victims, the injured and their families to be heard and their wishes to be considered in determining the appropriate process, during the process and when considering the remedy. This is not to say that the victims were permitted to claim that their vengeance would override the collective values of justice and due process. But due consideration was given to victims. Otherwise justice does not restore harmony to the community, and that is one of the goals of Métis Nation justice. Family, the Métis Nation culture, and the dignity they afford to men, women and children are not something lost in the quest for justice. Métis Nation Laws of the Prairie do not discard humanity and the dignity accorded to individuals in the name of justice.

The Canadian justice system seems to be doing just the opposite. The Métis trial of Thomas Scott has been heavily criticized as "morally repugnant because of the procedures followed."[8] The implication is that in the Canadian justice system, no such morally repugnant procedures would ever take place. But as the Marie Trottier and Cindy Gladue cases show only too clearly, the Canadian justice system can be morally repugnant and violent, savage and cruel toward Indigenous women.

In the 1960s the Métis Women's Association of Manitoba wrote a manifesto called "It Needs to Be Said."[9] It decried the abuse and inequity suffered by Métis women. Part of the cry of the Métis women in the 1960s was against their own men and leadership who ignored the violence. At that time the leadership of the Métis Nation was entirely male. Things have changed. Now the presidents of three of the five provincial Métis Nation organizations are women and more than 50 percent of their leaders are women.[10] Women exercise a strong voice in the governance of the Métis Nation. But it still needs to be said that Canadians have no right to claim the moral high ground with respect to the issue of justice or violence against women.

Melanie Omeniho, president of the Women of the Métis Nation, circa 2018 (*Ke Ning/Women of the Métis Nation*)

Led by Melanie Omeniho, the Women of the Métis Nation/ Les Femmes Michif Otipemisiwak went to court to fight for the dignity of Métis women. They intervened at the Supreme Court of Canada to press the highest court in the land for justice for Cindy Gladue, to ensure that Métis women are respected and that women who are the victims of gender-based violence are accorded due dignity whether they survive the violence or not. Demanding that the Canadian state cease dismembering Métis women and displaying their body parts in court is not something the Métis Nation ever thought it would have to fight for. When the Supreme Court of Canada issued its judgment in the Cindy Gladue case in May of 2019, it sent the case back for retrial but only on manslaughter, not murder. This is the latest in a string of cases where white men have admitted to killing Indigenous people and been acquitted of murder. The message to Indigenous people is that they can be killed with impunity. The court was also, shamefully, silent on the issue of dismemberment.

CHAPTER 32

MÉTIS IDENTITY

WHO ARE THE MÉTIS?

Another battle that is not over is the fight over Métis identity. It is a subject that confuses everyone. Some of the confusion stems from the fact that "Métis" is a European word. The use of a term like "Métis" to describe an Indigenous people follows in the tradition of the naming of many Indigenous peoples. *Dene* and *Inuit* both can be translated as "the people." But because they are words in an Indigenous language, outsiders don't feel readily able to include themselves. "Métis," however, is a French word that describes an Indigenous people. Many feel justified in defining it to suit their purposes.

It's a problem—a big problem. *Lii vyeu*, "the old ones," didn't pronounce "Métis" as it is commonly pronounced today (Maytee). They would have pronounced it as "Michif," which is also the name of the Métis Nation's language. It would be better if the Métis Nation spelled its name as the old ones pronounced it—Michif Nation. Some of the confusion—not all—would abate. But naming is an organic thing and not readily susceptible to command.

The Métis Nation has always been a people of many names. Individual citizens of the Métis Nation usually describe themselves as Bois-Brûlés, Métis, Michifs or Otipêyimisowak. Outsiders have named them in their own languages or according to their own understandings. The French called them Bois-Brûlés and Métis. The English mostly called them half-breeds. The Sioux described the Métis as the flower beadwork people. There is even a Plains Indian sign-language term for the Métis that combines the sign for cart and man. Most names reflect one of four concepts: (1) skin colour, (2) the Métis as a subset of First Nations or Euro-Canadians, (3) mixed ancestry, or (4) their independence.[1]

In the first category, names that reflect skin colour, the early records contain many references to the Métis as "Bois Brûlé," meaning "burnt wood," likely stemming originally from observations that the Métis are of lighter complexion than First Nations or darker than whites.[2] Sometimes individual Métis were called simply "Brûlés." Bois-Brûlés and Brûlés were the names originally used by Métis to describe their collective.[3] Bois-Brûlés, as a collective descriptor, gradually fell out of use, and by the 1830s the people were usually known as Métis.

In the second category, First Nations often claim the Métis as part of their collective and deny the Métis Nation's existence as a distinct people. The Cree term for the Métis was "Âpihtawikosisân." *Âpihtaw* means "half" and *kosisân* means "of the people."[4] This sense, that Métis are not a distinct people, is not merely a historical attitude. It is quite common today for Métis to be told by First Nations that their identity as a member of the Métis Nation is shallow, lacking in understanding and insufficient. There is a sense that if one is Métis, one is not the real deal. As Métis poet Marilyn Dumont so aptly put it, it is a built-in prejudice "that says he's leather and I'm naugahyde."[5]

From the other side of the divide, the Euro-Canadians, comes an attitude that is also pejorative but of a different kind. The English have long called the Métis "half-breeds." Although the term was mostly applied to those with some British heritage, it also is used as a translation of "Métis." The term "half-breed" did not come into general usage until after 1821 and did not take on pejorative connotations until after 1860, which coincides with the importation of a virulent form of racist ideology into the North-West.

As Frantz Fanon has pointed out, we don't breed humans, so all references to "half-breeds" carry the ugly insinuation that one is only half human. It takes little imagination to understand which half is an animal. The term, and the habitual practice of historians, anthropologists, social scientists and now the courts of referring to the mixed ancestry of the Métis, places an unfortunate emphasis on what Chris Anderson calls "hybridity," the denial that a Métis individual is a whole being, which also presumes that the members of the other two hegemonies (First Nations and Euro-Canadians) are somehow pure.[6]

The word "half-breed" also conjures up individuals, not collectives. It reduces the individual to a mere genealogical fact. It implicitly denies a collective existence, culture and heritage. Half-breeds are historical eunuchs, cultural mules. The term is odious in every respect. The Métis Nation has long objected to its use. Unfortunately, its constant appearance in the historical records makes it difficult to entirely avoid.

Sometimes in the historical records, "half-breed" and "English Métis" are used in the same sentence to refer to the same people. Sometimes "Métis" is used to include both English- and French-speaking individuals. Some records use "Métis" only for the

French-speaking Métis. The only consistency in the record is that there is no consistency.

The fourth category of Métis names notes the several terms that emphasize their independence—"*gens libres*," "*hommes libres*" and "Freemen"—although these terms could also include non-Métis. The Cree coined another term for the Métis—"Otipêyimisowak," meaning "the people who command themselves" or "the independent people."[7] The term may have originated as a translation of "Freemen." But if that was its origin, "Otipêyimisowak" soon took on new meaning for the Métis. To the Cree, the Métis were known as Otipêyimisowak because their settlements and lifestyles were distinct from both settlers and First Nations, and because the Métis made it known to the Cree that they did not agree with the idea of being confined to a reserve. This, the Métis believed, would result in the loss of independence and of their highly prized mobility. The Métis still proudly assert that they are Otipêyimisowak.

Modern historians note that whichever term is used to describe the Métis Nation of the Canadian North-West, the collective of people is essentially the same. The preference of the people themselves is to use "Métis." Louis Riel himself described his preference for the term "Métis."[8] The fact that we have a record indicating exactly what a well-known historical Métis leader thought about the name lends significant authenticity to the self-ascription.

Several historians and commentators have sought to divide the Métis into subgroups based on their language (French or English), religion (Catholic or Protestant) or economy (hunting or farming). The Métis Nation has never paid much attention to these attempts to divide them. The English Métis and the French Métis, regardless of their religion, whether they were settled in a community and farming, or chasing the buffalo and living on the Plains, took political action together in 1816, throughout the 1820s to 1860s, in 1869 to 1870, and again in 1885. They joined together to create the Métis settlements in Alberta in the early 1930s and later formed the modern-day Métis organizations. Their two-hundred-year history of collective political action shows that these differences existed but were not divisive.

THE MÉTIS NATION'S DEFINITION OF "MÉTIS"

Until the constitutional negotiations in the 1980s and early 1990s, the Métis Nation had never attempted a national definition. There were early definitions of Métis Nation citizens, but these definitions were regional, not national. During the 1992 Charlottetown constitutional negotiations, the Métis National Council put forward a definition of "Métis" and "Métis Nation" for inclusion in the Métis Nation Accord. It was not determined by or negotiated with outsiders. The "Métis Nation" was defined as the collective of the individuals and those they accepted. The definition created a core group that would determine whether and on what terms it would accept others.

The Métis rights cases in the courts in the early 2000s forced further definitional changes. The Métis Nation of Ontario was successful in pushing the first Métis rights case through to the Supreme Court of Canada. It confirmed the existence of a regional Métis community in Sault Ste. Marie, Ontario. As the *Powley* case moved up the chain of courts, the Métis Nation grew concerned that the courts would take the definition out if its hands, thus undermining their right of self-determination. They began to hold assemblies across the Métis Nation where they debated a definition.

In 2002 the Métis Nation arrived at a new definition. "Métis" means a person who self-identifies as Métis, is distinct from other Aboriginal peoples, is of historic Métis Nation ancestry and who is accepted by the Métis Nation. The definition is *national* in the sense of the Métis Nation's boundaries, not in the sense that it corresponds to the national boundaries of the Canadian state. This remains the Métis Nation's definition of its citizens.

The first part of the definition requires an individual to voluntarily self-identify as Métis and not as a subset of some other Indigenous group. The second requirement is that the applicant be of historic Métis Nation ancestry. This means that it is not enough to have some ever-so-great Indian grandmother. One must prove, with documentary evidence, a direct ancestral connection to a member of the historic Métis Nation. Since the Métis Nation only came into existence in 1816, references to ever-so-great Indian grandmothers prior to this date and outside of the geographic territory of the Métis Nation are insufficient. Only when accepted by the Métis Nation can that individual say he or she is a citizen of the Métis Nation.

Registration of Métis Nation citizens is taking place in each province. The registries are only to include individuals who provide documentary evidence proving that the applicants meet the Métis National Council's definition.

DEFINING THE BOUNDARIES OF THE MÉTIS NATION

The boundaries of the Métis Nation have always been more social than geographic. For two centuries hundreds of thousands of Métis have believed they are part of the Métis Nation. They have imagined the Nation in their hearts and minds and souls. Many have fought and died for that nationalist vision. For ten generations, thousands have spent their entire lives constructing and maintaining the Métis Nation. They trace their identity through their historical story, and they rely on that story to justify their historic and modern presence. The stories of the Métis Nation are the essence of its identity.

This is the social boundary of the Métis Nation. It is filled with the Métis Nation's history, music, art, stories, dances, language, laws, customs and traditions. The Métis have passed this social context and space from one generation to the next for two hundred years. It is this social boundary that separates the Métis Nation from other Indigenous peoples and other Canadians. Although other Indigenous peoples and other Canadians live on the same land and share the same state, none of these "others" share the Métis Nation's social boundaries—its culture, social and political histories, kinship ties and cultural geography.

The historic geographic boundaries of an Indigenous people were generally based on natural geographic features such as watersheds, mountains, lakes, deserts and forests. Such historic Indigenous geographic boundaries were never solid walls; rather, they were porous and allowed for overlapping and shared lands and resources between different groups. As access to resources and political power shifted, the historic geographic boundaries of a people could also shift. Disease and war could diminish one group's territory and allow another to expand.

The historic boundaries of the Métis Nation extended from its most eastern community in Rainy Lake/Lake of the Woods to the Rockies in the West, from the Plains in what is now the United States to the boreal forests of northern Saskatchewan, Manitoba and Alberta. It was never defined and the people over the centuries used the various parts of their motherland in concentrations that shifted with time, the economy, politics and weather.

The assertion of sovereignty by Canada and the United States has affected the boundaries of all Indigenous nations. State boundaries have bisected peoples and created new political barriers. In the 1980s the Métis Nation articulated political boundaries based on the provincial political boundaries. These new boundaries were not based on historic social or geographic boundaries. They were born out of the need for the Métis Nation to deal with the realities of the Canadian political geography. The new Métis Nation provincial boundaries are not organic in the sense that defined its historic motherland. They are not derived from the natural landscape and are instead more or less straight lines arbitrarily imposed on the historic social and geographic boundaries of the Métis Nation. The Métis Nation accepts these provincial political boundaries for its three Prairie organizations but rejects them for Ontario and British Columbia. Thus the modern Métis Nation geographic boundaries are a unique combination determined by modern political realities and by historic use and occupation.

In November 2018, the Métis National Council adopted a draft map that sets out the boundaries of the Métis Nation. The core of the draft map is not contentious. It is the boundaries that people argue about. Does the Métis Nation really go so far into the Northwest Territories and British Columbia? How far down into the United States does it go? How far into Ontario? Further work on the boundaries will be undertaken in future with the intention of confirming the boundaries and removing "draft" from the Métis Nation map.

THE "RACE-SHIFTERS"

In 2003 the Supreme Court of Canada, in a case called *R. v. Powley*, held that there was a Métis rights-bearing community in Sault Ste. Marie, Ontario. The case was successful at all levels of court and ushered in a new era of recognition for the Métis. Unfortunately, the case also instigated a new phenomenon: people in Quebec and eastern Canada began to claim to be Métis.[9] The "new Métis" represent a disturbing new trend in white settler communities that are now "indigenizing" themselves. Historians Adam Gaudry and Darryl Leroux have been closely monitoring this development.[10]

For the Métis Nation the very idea that anyone, let alone tens of thousands of people, would claim to be Métis swiftly progressed from a curiosity post-*Powley* to an infuriating reality by 2015. Some of these "new Métis" were even claiming to be part of the Métis Nation, adopting their symbols and flying the Métis Nation infinity flag. Their appropriation of Métis Nation symbols, as if they are in the public domain, forced the Métis Nation in 2015 to trademark its name "Métis Nation" and its infinity flag. The "new Métis" claim, though they were thousands of miles away from the fighting and no army was sent to have them "put down," that they suffered the racist fallout from the Red River Resistance and the North-West Resistance.

The common denominator for all of these new claimants is that their identity as Métis relies on a long-dead Indian ancestor. They claim there is a three-century void they are now filling based solely on the revival of lost identities with no connection to a modern, living Métis culture in eastern Canada. As Gaudry points out, these "new Métis necro-communities" are communing solely with the dead. The "new Métis" can demonstrate no historical Métis community and their dead ancestor is an "unmoored Métis," tethered to no historic or living Métis community.[11]

This is a new form of colonialism whereby the settlers appropriate Métis identity based solely on claims of having an ever-so-great Indian grandmother. For these groups "Métis" is based on one fact—a genealogical claim—that is bolstered by mystical claims that after discovering their genealogical connection, they always knew and always felt like Métis. They are *race-shifting*.

The "new Métis" cast their newly acquired identity as a journey of personal self-discovery. Gaudry likens the trend to the beliefs of New Agers who create their own personal reality and where identity is purely a personal choice. Because it is seen as a personal journey of self-discovery, no one is permitted to critique it.[12] The journey is often accompanied by a claim that justifies their recent identification on the basis of hiding. They claim their ancestors hid for centuries because of racism. Now they are coming out of hiding.

One of the "new Métis" groups in Quebec, which began as a group of white hunters, recast themselves as Métis in order to lobby against a Mi'kmaw land agreement. This group has grown to over twenty thousand members. There are now at least twenty such organizations in Quebec, all created since 2004. Ten of these organizations accounted for at least forty-two thousand members by the end of 2017.

Leroux notes that over twenty-five thousand people in Nova Scotia identified as Métis in the 2016 Canadian census. Less than a thousand identified as Métis in the 1996 census. There are now eight "Acadian-Métis" organizations, which have appropriated the expulsion of Acadians and are recasting Acadians as Métis.[13] The expulsion of the Acadians is an important Canadian historical event, but it was never an Indigenous story. The Acadians were always part of the settler society and they were not expelled because they were Métis.

The recent readily available access to DNA testing for ancestry further bolsters these "new Métis." The smallest drop of Indigenous ancestry will suffice to justify a new identity as

Métis. Indeed, recent court cases show that their claims can reach back twelve generations for an Indigenous ancestor.[14] They repurpose any historical figure with mixed ancestry (and some who are purely French) as Métis and claim that their culture remained hidden for *three hundred years*. As Darryl Leroux notes,

> Of the 2,011 individual genealogies the CMAM [Communauté Métis Autochtone de Maniwaki] submitted for its case (from their six thousand members), an incredible 75 percent registered a root ancestor born in the 1600s . . . about 25 percent listed an "Indigenous" root ancestor who, by scholarly consensus, wasn't even Indigenous. At least five hundred members without any actual Indigenous ancestry have been granted membership.[15]

The courts have been justifiably incredulous. One judge in Quebec wrote, "What emerges from this defence . . . is its remarkable creativity." The judge went on to say, "It would be easier to nail Jell-O to a wall than to locate the ins and outs of the remarkably vague and elusive allegations that one finds about the existence of a Métis community."[16] Despite all courts (fifty-two as of early 2019) denying their claims outright, membership in these organizations continues to grow at astonishing rates.[17]

These organizations are lobbying provincial and federal governments for recognition and are using their new cards to gain access for their members to university programs and other benefits for Indigenous peoples. Universities and colleges, some with dozens of social scientists on faculty, seem unable to grapple with the identity claims.

The "new Métis" are also often openly dismissive of the Métis Nation. If they can normalize their genealogical communing with the dead as legitimate Métis claims, they will undermine the long history and legitimate claims of the Métis Nation. So, in an awkward turn of events, the Métis Nation, at least for the time being on a fairly friendly footing with the federal government, is being forced to fight a rear-guard action against these new eastern groups.

The Métis Nation is adamant that these "new Métis" are not part of the Métis Nation. To date, the Métis Nation has repeatedly stated that its boundaries have never included Quebec and eastern Canada, that these eastern groups are not part of the Métis Nation, and that they should not be appropriating the symbols of the Métis Nation.

The eastern groups are now litigating their claims, and the Métis Nation is being drawn into the litigation. The Métis Nation put its history on trial to defend its rights to lands and resources. Now it will put its history on trial to defend against the race-shifters who are trying to appropriate its name, history, identity and symbols.

CHAPTER 33

FREEDOM AND INFINITY

Freedom is the core value of the Métis Nation. The Nation was born and forged in a fight for freedom. That core value is expressed in the infinity symbol on the flag of the Métis Nation.

There have been many theories about why the infinity symbol was chosen. Some say the two joined circles are two Red River cartwheels placed together. Others say it is the joining of two peoples, Canadians and First Nations. Some say it is based on the Scottish flag of St. Andrew. These are all interesting and fanciful theories that have no historical foundation. In fact, no one knows whose idea it was to put the infinity symbol on the flag in 1815 or why the infinity symbol was chosen.[1]

Though the reason for choosing the infinity symbol is lost to history, it has always been a good symbol for the Métis Nation. The symbol suggests that the future and the past are inescapably bound together, ever circling and feeding each other. The symbol also suggests the idea of infinite freedom from boundaries and arbitrary limitations. These ideas—freedom and the relationship of the past to the future—lie at the heart of the Métis Nation's raison d'être.

The Métis Nation's ancestors sought freedom, and with that freedom they chose to become a separate people. It was a grand imagining and the Nation has spent two hundred years fighting for the freedom to continue that dream. In the course of that long battle, they have had to convince others of their existence as a collective. The Métis Nation has been forged in this battle for freedom, recognition, land, resources and rights.

During that time, it has suffered losses, but it has also moved forward. Today it is in a new era in Indigenous-Crown relations. Canada has generally accepted the need for reconciliation with its Indigenous peoples, including the Métis Nation. On April 13, 2017, Canada and the Métis National Council signed a new Métis Nation Accord. In the new accord, Canada agrees that it is in everyone's best interest to work with the Métis Nation on a nation-to-nation, government-to-government relationship, to end the legacy of colonialism in federal legislation, policies and practices, and to uphold the special constitutional relationship between the Métis Nation and the Crown as "partners in Confederation." This is what the Métis Nation has always sought. They have fought for the right to be just such a partner.

The Métis Nation is an Indigenous nation of the Canadian North-West with a storied history. It is a case history of powerful imagination made real. The people stand firmly on their history, secure in their belief that their past battles, celebrated in their stories and songs, will eventually enable a future where they will be free to be the nation of their dreams, the one they first sang into being in 1816.

Acknowledgements

This book has benefited greatly from the work of historians such as Auguste de Trémaudan, Guillaume Charette, L.-A. Prudhomme, Phillipe Mailhot, Allen Ronaghan, Doug Sprague, Gwynneth C. D. Jones, Arthur Ray, Frank Tough, Brenda Macdougall, Nicole St-Onge, Carolyn Podrushny, Diane Payment, Bernard Boquel, Lawrence Barkwell, Raymond Huel, Norma Jean Hall, Dale and Lee Gibson, Fred Shore, Adam Gaudry, Darryl Leroux and many more.

I thank the Métis writers who provided the words and thoughts of the people: Cuthbert Grant, Peter Garrioch, Louis Goulet, Louis Riel, Joseph Riel, Gabriel Dumont, Peter Erasmus, Marie Rose Smith, Marguerite Caron, Jim Brady, Malcolm Norris, Howard Adams, Harry Daniels, Elmer Ghostkeeper, Maria Campbell and many more.

I must also thank many people for their support and assistance during the writing of this history: Sakej Henderson, Leroy Little Bear, Clément Chartier, Jason Madden, Paul Chartrand, Guadalupe Jolicoeur, John Teillet and Dan Teillet for much needed review and comment; Dominique Louer and Louise Scatliff for the French translations; Norman Fleury for the

Michif translations; Louise Scatliff for her unflagging encouragement and assistance, archival detective work, responding to endless queries and providing access to our grandfather's documents; Mike Teillet, Ed Henderson and Dave Henderson for map and image assistance; Danielle Teillet for document retrieval in Ottawa; Kathy Teillet for editorial assistance and lifelong inspiration; Rick Salter and the late Arthur Pape for years of mentorship; Samantha Haywood, my agent; Patrick Crean, my editor, for his encouragement and keen insight; and HarperCollins for the opportunity to write this book. Special thanks go to my family and especially to my husband, Ed Henderson, for his much needed and appreciated love and support; and to all my friends, colleagues and family who patiently listened to me talk too much about this book in the making.

Finally, I raise my hands to my Métis Nation ancestors for blessing me with this rich heritage, impressing me with an obligation to continue it, and for listening and speaking to me during the long hours of writing. This book could not have been written without all of you.

NOTES

Introduction

1. This has changed quite dramatically. Several Métis artists have become well known in the late twentieth and early twenty-first centuries, including Christi Belcourt, David Garneau and many others.
2. Taché, *Sketch of the North-West of America*, 206.
3. Clément Chartier, QC, Paul Chartrand, IPC, Jason Madden, Marc LeClair, Kathy Hodgson-Smith, Michelle LeClair-Harding and Lionel Chartrand.
4. Dobbin, *The One and a Half Men*, attributing the quote to James Dreaver.
5. Begg, *History of the North-West*, 1:161–62.
6. Giraud, *The Métis in the Canadian West*, 1:477.
7. Stanley, *The Birth of Western Canada*, 8.
8. Flanagan, *Louis "David" Riel: Prophet of the New World*, 30.
9. Trémaudan, *Histoire de la nation métisse.*
10. Gaudry, "Communing with the Dead," 170; Gaudry and Leroux, "White Settler Revisionism," 116–42.
11. In October 2018 the Assembly of Nova Scotia Mi'kmaq Chiefs and the Métis National Council signed a Memorandum of Understanding, agreeing to work collaboratively on the issue of individuals claiming Métis ancestry in Nova Scotia. Both the Métis Nation and the Mi'kmaq are concerned that these claims undermine their respective nations' right to determine their own citizens and protect their rights and title.

Chapter 1: The Old Wolves

1. *Lii vyeu* is the name for elders in the Métis language, Michif. There is a photo in the Teillet Family Papers called "*Les anciens de l'Union Nationale Metisse.*" Bernard Bocquel entitled his book about these men and their descendants *Les Fidèles à Riel.*

2. At the same time in Batoche, Saskatchewan, a group of Métis was also organizing as l'Association Saint Joseph. Louis Riel had founded the first Métis association in Batoche in 1884. He named it l'Union Métisse Saint-Joseph.
3. Over the years the Métis had several flags. This one had a white background with a Union Jack in the top left-hand corner and three gold fleurs-de-lis in the other corners. The flag at the 1887 Batoche meeting had an image of Saint Joseph, a buffalo and a rifle crossed with an arrow.
4. Joseph Riel, *Bulletin Winnipeg*, 4 August 1913, and *Le Devoir*, 10 July 1913.
5. The Métis objected to the words "rebels" and "rebellion" again in 1925, when the word was used on a cairn commemorating the "North-West Rebellion." The Historic Sites and Monuments Board of Canada erected the cairn.
6. Guillaume Charette (1884–1952) graduated from University of Manitoba Law School in 1910. He was a long-time president of Union Nationale Métisse Saint-Joseph du Manitoba, and he made it their mission to correct the historical record of the Métis Nation in the public consciousness.
7. McArthur to Goulet, 12 May 1930, SHMF.
8. Trémaudan, *Hold High Your Heads*, 59.
9. *Winnipeg Free Press*, 9 July 1935. The Old Wolves published a greatly reduced version. It was the Great Depression and they could not afford to publish the entire manuscript.
10. Samuel A. Nault, president, Société historiques et Union Nationale, as quoted in Bocquel, *Les Fidèles à Riel*, 366.

Chapter 2: The Voyageurs

1. Nute, *The Voyageur*, 100.
2. Lord Selkirk personally invited Louis Nolin to settle in Red River in 1816 as a reward for his interpretation services. In 1820 his brothers Jean Baptiste and Augustin joined him. They received three grants of land in Assiniboia.
3. Irving, *Astoria*, 23–24.
4. Ballantyne, *Hudson Bay*, 236–37.
5. Bigsby, *Shoe and Canoe*, 119.
6. Moore, *Thomas Moore's Complete Poetical Works*, 153.
7. Irving, *Astoria*, 23–24.
8. McKenney, "Sketches of a Tour to the Lakes," 288–89.
9. Ross, interview with an old engagé in 1825, *Fur Hunters of the Far West*, Vol. 2, 236–37.

Chapter 3: The Mothers of the Métis Nation

1. There is an Andrew Kirkness (b. 1770 in the NWT) married to a Marguerite Mowat (Indian, b. 1772) listed in the "Genealogies of Red River Households, 1818–1870" in Sprague and Frye, *The Genealogy of the First Métis Nation*, Table 1.

Chapter 4: Going Free

1. Red River was not the only "retirement" settlement. Former employees also settled outside the Métis Nation in Mattawa, Sault Ste. Marie and other locations.
2. Henry, *New Light on the Early History of the Greater Northwest*; see entries for *Fort Dauphin*, *Upper Red River* and *Lower Red River* in table "Report of Northwest Population, 1805," 282.
3. Leacock, "The Montagnais," 57.
4. Kennicott, in *Transactions of the Chicago Academy of Sciences*, Vol. 1, 177.
5. Finlayson to Hargrave, 29 February 1836.
6. George Croghan to the Lords of Trade, 8 June 1764, quoted in White, *The Middle Ground*, 269.
7. Nute, *Caesars of the Wilderness*, 61.

Chapter 5: The First National Resistance

1. Lord Selkirk's first colony in Prince Edward Island was a success. His second in Ontario failed.
2. The colonists were not all Scots or Highlanders. Some were from Ireland, the Orkney Islands and Glasgow.
3. McGillivray to Harvey, 24 June 1815.
4. *Inverness Journal*, 21 June 1811.
5. Notice sent by Governor Macdonell to Hudson's Bay Company posts. Begg, *History of the North-West*, 1:174.
6. Macdonell later claimed that he was surprised that the "free Canadians and half-breeds" considered this order to be an infringement of their liberty. Coltman described Macdonell's claim as the "pretensions of Miles McDonnell," in *W. B. Coltman Report Transcription*, 158.
7. Grant was born in 1793 at Fort Tremblante, Saskatchewan. When his Nor'Wester father died in 1799, young Cuthbert and his sisters went to live with his mother's Cree relations. In 1801 he was sent to Montreal for his education.
8. They also named William Shaw, Bonhomme Montour and Alexander Fraser as captains under the leadership of Grant.
9. The flag had already been raised in the fall of 1815, where it is described in the Narrative of James Sutherland, Selkirk Papers (SP), 1946–47, as "red with a figure of 8 placed horizontally in the middle"; "A Narrative Out—Outrages" SP, 1950; Peter Fidler's Brandon House post journal entry for 1 June 1816, HBCA, B.22/a/19–20, 36, where he describes the flag as "blue about 4 feet square & a figure of 8 horizontally in the middle"; Narrative of Peter Fidler, SP, 2.515.
10. Edmonton House post journal, 30 May 1816, HBCA B.60/a/15, 41.
11. Bostonais Pangman, one of the appointed Brûlés captains, was hunting for the colonists at this time.

Chapter 6: Victory at the Frog Plain

1. Giraud, *The Métis in the Canadian West*, 1:460.
2. *Grenouillière* is a marshy area with many frogs. Michif translation is by Norman Fleury.
3. Peter Fidler wrote, "I believe & what I learn from Mr. Pambrun that the 1/2 breeds are nearly master of McDonell—or at least he is obliged to wink at their proceedings not to make them leave him till his intended plans are put into execution or done but the person who assembles them is surely accountable for their conduct." Brandon House post journal, 3 June 1816, HBCA B.22/a/19.
4. McGillivray to Harvey, 24 June 1815.
5. *W. B. Coltman Report Transcription*, 188.
6. Martin, *Lord Selkirk's Work in Canada*, 136.
7. Coltman to Sherbrooke, 16 May 1818.
8. The "middle ground" is a term used by Richard White, by which he means a space where parties can seek compromise and which is only possible if both parties cannot achieve their goals by means of force. White, *The Middle Ground.*
9. Coltman to Sherbrooke, 16 May 1818.
10. *W. B. Coltman Report Transcription*, 186 and 193. The depositions taken after the battle suggest that after being initially shot in the thigh, Governor Semple was shot fatally by an Indian.
11. *Narratives of John Pritchard, Pierre Chrysologue Pambrun and Frederick Damien Heurter, 29.*
12. The governor-general's proclamation, 16 July 1816.
13. "No representations of farce or folly that was ever enacted on any stage, could come near to the real life that is exhibited here." Gale to Lady Selkirk, 23 June 1817, as quoted in Martin, *Lord Selkirk's Work in Canada*, 135.
14. Martin, *Lord Selkirk's Work in Canada*, 153.

Chapter 7: After the Merger

1. Grant to J. D. Cameron, 13 March 1816. "[I]n fact the Traders shall pack off with themselves also, for having disregarded our orders last spring."
2. "*L'Italia è fatta, ma chi farà ora gl'Italiani?*" The quote is from the first meeting of the newly united Italian Parliament at Turin in 1860. Latham, *Famous Sayings and Their Authors*, 234.
3. I am indebted for these thoughts on Métis family and relationships to Brenda Macdougall's insights in her book *One of the Family*, 7–10; and to Norman Fleury for his thoughts on Métis family relationships and Michif during an interview with him on 16 June 2016 in Winnipeg.
4. Brenda Macdougall and Nicole St. Onge, "Rooted in Mobility: Metis Buffalo Hunting Brigades."

5. Slobodin, *Metis of the Mackenzie District*, 73, referring to Red River Métis, as distinct from the northern Métis living in the Mackenzie District.

CHAPTER 8: THE BUFFALO HUNTERS

1. Ross, *Red River Settlement*, 273.
2. Simpson to Colville, 31 May 1824.
3. "Métis Laws of the Hunt (circa 1840): (1) No buffalo to be run on the Sabbath-day; (2) No party to fork off, lag behind or go before without permission; (3) No person or party to run buffalo before the general order; (4) Every Captain with his men, in turn, to patrol the camp, and keep guard; (5) For the first trespass against these laws, the offender to have his saddle and bridle cut up; (6) For the second offence, the coat to be taken off the offender's back, and be cut up; (7) For the third offence, the offender to be flogged; and (8) Any person convicted of theft, even to the value of a sinew, to be brought to the middle of the camp, and the crier to call out his or her name three times, adding the word 'thief' at each time." Ross, *Red River Settlement*, 249–50.
4. Howard, *Strange Empire*, 52.
5. Parkman, *The Oregon Trail*, 328.
6. Ross, *Red River Settlement*, 243.
7. Keating, *Narrative of an Expedition to the Source of St. Peter's River*, 39.
8. Milton and Cheadle, *The North-West Passage by Land*, 44–45.
9. Taché, *Sketch of the North-West*, 106.
10. Fleury, "Reminiscences," Saskatchewan Archives Board.
11. Nicollet, *Joseph N. Nicollet on the Plains and Prairies*, 187.

CHAPTER 9: THE IRON ALLIANCE

1. Provencher to Halkett, 10 August 1822, in Nute, *Documents*, 358.
2. Provencher to Bishop Plessis, 11 August 1822, in Nute, *Documents*, 364.
3. Howard, *Strange Empire*, 49, quoting Major Lawrence Taliaffero, an American Indian agent.

CHAPTER 10: THE MÉTIS NATION ARMY

1. Morton, *A History of the Canadian West*, 808.
2. Joseph McGillivray, as recounted in Cox, *Adventures on the Columbia River*, 338–40.
3. Morton, *A History of the Canadian West*, 809. Simpson to Governor Pelly, October 1845.
4. Simpson to the Committee, 28 October 1835, and Simpson to Lord Metcalf, 6 November 1845.

Chapter 11: The Battle of the Grand Coteau

1. Jean-Baptiste Falcon is the son of the Métis bard Pierre Falcon.
2. Account by François Falcon, son of Jean-Baptiste Falcon, Ste. Anne des Chênes, 23 May 1938, in Barkwell, "Dakota-Métis Battle on the Grand Coteau: 1851," 7.
3. *Nor'Wester*, 9 October 1862, Assiniboine Chief Red Stone.

Chapter 12: The Second National Resistance

1. Journal of Peter Garrioch, 237, *AM.*
2. Ross, *Red River Settlement*, 223–24.
3. Journal of Peter Garrioch, 236, *AM.*
4. Ray, "Diffusion of Diseases," 150. There were influenza epidemics in 1834, 1837, 1843, 1845, 1847 and 1850.
5. Ross, *Red River Settlement*, 363. Ross identified cholera as "the bloody flux" and says its ravages were more deadly than the influenza and measles.
6. Ibid., 365.
7. Erasmus, *Buffalo Days and Nights*, 86.
8. Begg, *History of the North-West*, 236.
9. Gibson, *Law, Life and Government at Red River*, 1:16.
10. Ibid., 22 and n12.
11. Lambton, *Report on the Affairs of British North America*, 41.
12. Simpson to Shepherd, 8 August 1857.
13. 1856 Memorial of Bishop Anderson, in Oliver, *The Canadian North-West*, 1310–14.
14. Simpson to H. H. Berens, 18 July 1856.
15. Journal of Peter Garrioch, 241, *AM.*
16. Petition, 29 August 1845. J. Sinclair and others to A. Christie, Governor, Red River Settlement. Signatories are James Sinclair, Baptiste Laroque, Thomas Lagan, Pierre Liverduré, Joseph Monkman, Baptiste Wilkey, Baptist Fanian, Alexi Goulet, Antoine Morrin, William MacMillan, Louis Letendre, Robert Montour, Edward Harmon, John Dease, Henry Cook, William Bird, John Vincent, Peter Garrioch, Jack Spence, Jack Anderson, James Monkman, Antoine Dejarlais and Thomas McDermott.
17. Another petition in French was dated 17 February 1847.
18. Ross, *Red River Settlement*, 84.

Chapter 13: Taking the Fight to the Court

1. *The Public Interest vs. Peter Hayden*, General Quarterly Court of Assiniboia [Case 10], 1846, in Gibson, *Law, Life, and Government at Red River*, 2:36–40.
2. Ibid., 37.
3. *Andrew McDermot v. Bapt. Fanyant, Pierre Poitras, Louison Morin, & Pascal Berland* [*sic*], General Quarterly Court of Assiniboia [Case 25], 1847, in Gibson, *Law, Life, and Government at Red River*, 2:52–54.

4. For a record of the trial and analysis, see Gibson, *Law, Life, and Government at Red River*, 2:114–18.
5. Anonymous letter, *Morning Chronicle* (London), published 3 October 1849. Likely written by Peter Garrioch.
6. *Hudson's Bay Company v. Sayer et al.*, in Gibson, *Law, Life, and Government at Red River*, 2:114. The final jury was Donald Gunn, William Thomas, James Tait, Narcisse Marion, Philip Kennedy, James Monkman, John Vincent, Robert Sandison, Prospère Ducharme, Françoise Bruneau, Martin Lavallé and Dominique Ducharme.

CHAPTER 14: THE THIRD NATIONAL RESISTANCE

1. The Canada First movement renamed itself the Canadian National Association and became an official political party in 1874.
2. Schultz's first fraud was his identity. When Schultz arrived in Red River, he was twenty-one years old. After he arrived he began to claim he was a medical doctor. He claimed to have obtained his medical degree at a very prestigious college, Oberlin in Ohio. He also claimed to be a graduate of Queen's College in Kingston and of Victoria University in Cobourg. Oberlin has no record of him. Queen's College recorded his attendance for two terms, and Victoria University recorded his attendance for one term. None of these colleges granted Schultz a degree. Schultz was an imposter, a fake doctor.
3. Clark, "Schultz, Sir John Christian," quoting Sheriff Colin Inkster.
4. Charette, *Vanishing Spaces*, 59.
5. The parish of Sainte-Anne-des-Chênes was also known as Oak Point in English or Pointe-des-Chênes in French. It was a wintering site for Métis families as early as 1820. It is on the Seine River southeast of St. Boniface. In 1852 Ojibwa Chief Nashakepenais asked the Métis (mostly the large Nolin family) to enter into a formal purchase agreement for land at Pointe-des-Chênes. The chief was interested in expanding the village. The Métis-Ojibwa joint venture thrived and within five years had a store, hotel and trading post. The Oblate missionaries established a chapel there in 1862, and in 1867 the parish was renamed Sainte-Anne-des-Chênes.
6. Morrison, "The Robinson Treaties of 1850: A Case Study," 7.
7. The full text of Mair's letter is in Morton, *Alexander Begg's Red River Journal*, 395–99.
8. Mair was the author of *Tecumseh* and considered a "rising poet." To be fair, the letter in which Mair disparaged Métis women in Red River was a private one to his brother, who subsequently had it published without Mair's knowledge. Morton, *A History of the Canadian West*, 866. Begg, *History of the North-West*, 1:366.
9. Mary Sarah and Annie were the daughters of Andrew McDermot and Sarah McNab. Bannatyne was married to Annie. Governor McTavish was married to Annie's older sister Mary Sarah.

10. The full text of this letter in the original French is in Huel and Stanley, *The Collected Writings of Louis Riel*, 1:13–16; full text in English is in Morton, *Alexander Begg's Red River Journal*, 399–402.
11. e. e. cummings, "[anyone lived in a pretty how town]."
12. *New Nation*, 16 March 1870.
13. Macdonald to Tupper, in Morton, *A History of the Canadian West*, 874.
14. Deposition of Taché, in *Report of the Select Committee on the Causes of Difficulties in the North-West Territory in 1869–70*, 12.
15. McDougall to Macdonald, 31 October 1869.

CHAPTER 15: THE RESISTANCE BEGINS

1. Ritchot to Cartier, 30 May 1870. Ritchot described the land claimed as marked by a line that ran on the west from Turtle Mountain to St. Ann/Poplar Point on the Assiniboine River; on the east, from the American border to Lake Winnipeg and included Sainte-Anne-des-Chênes; on the south, by the American border; and on the north, following the Assiniboine River as far as Fort Garry and then along the Red River to just above the mouth of the Seine River.
2. Dugast to Taché, 24 July 1869.
3. McDougall to Gibbard, *The Globe*, 6 August 1863, reprint of a letter originally published in full in the *Quebec Mercury*. "It is essentially necessary that the rights of our lessees and the majesty of the law should be vindicated in the Algoma district."
4. Macdonald, quoted in Morton, *A History of the Canadian West*, 872.
5. "Report—1874," Dennis's deposition, 186.
6. J. S. Dennis, "Memorandum of Facts and Circumstances connected with the active Opposition by the French Half-breeds in this Settlement to the prosecution of the government Surveys," 11 October 1869, *Correspondence Relevant to the Recent Disturbances in the Red River Settlement*, 5: "No arms were seen with the party." The names of the Métis were given as "Louis Riel, leader, De Saugré and Son, Baptiste Nona [Nault], Baptiste Treuau [Tourond] and three Sons, François Charest, Bideau Non [Nault], Edward Morin [Edouard Marion], Mannin Non [Nault], Janvive Richot, Benjamin Non [Nault]; three others names not known."
7. Major Webb, the surveyor, was "ordered by the leader of the party at once to desist from further running the line, and in fact notified that he must leave the country on the south side of the Assiniboine, which country the party claimed as the property of the French Half-breeds, and which they would not allow to be surveyed by the Canadian Government." Ibid.
8. McDougall's memorandum requesting the rifles was signed 15 September 1869. Cabinet approved it on 22 September 1869. The rifles and ammunition

left Kingston on 1 October 1869, two weeks before the Métis stepped on the surveyors' chain.

9. Benjamin Nault and twenty men were sent as lookouts to Pointe à Saline (Aubigny). Baptiste Nault led more lookouts to Marion's Lake, just above St. Jean Baptiste. Declaration of André Neault [*sic*], Teillet Family Papers.
10. Ibid.
11. "*Monsieur, Le Comité national des Métis de la Rivière Rouge, intime à Monsieur W. McDougall l'ordre de ne pas entrer sur le Territoire du Nord-Ouest sans un permission special de ce comité*," in Oliver, *The Canadian North-West*, Vol. 1, 880.
12. Attributed to U.S. senator S. I. Hayakawa.
13. Begg, *History of the North-West*, 1:376–77.
14. Minutes of the Council of Assiniboia, 25 October 1869.
15. The Métis did not name their codified laws the Red River Code. Ritchot's notes call the Métis laws codified in Red River in 1869 "*Code Fondamentale*," (Fundamental Code). See Ritchot, *Cahier Historique* 2, 5–6.
16. McDougall to Secretary of State for the Provinces, 4 November 1869.
17. *St. Paul Press*, 4 November 1869, "Spectator."
18. Morton, *Alexander Begg's Red River Journal*, 162.

CHAPTER 16: BRINGING IN THE ENGLISH MÉTIS

1. Macdonald to Rose, 23 February 1870.
2. The delegates at the November convention were André Beauchemin, John Bruce (president), François Dauphinais, Louis LaSerte, Pierre Lavieller, Charles Nolin, W. B. O'Donoghue, Pierre Paranteau Sr., Jean Baptiste Perrault, Pierre Poitras, Louis Riel (secretary), Baptiste Touron, Dr. Bird, Thomas Bunn, John Garrioch, Donald Gunn, Geo. Gunn, Maurice Lowman, Henry McKenney, H. F. O'Lone, Chief Henry Prince, James Ross, Robert Tait, William Tait.
3. Louis Riel's Notes of the Convention of Twenty-Four, November 16–December 1, 1869.
4. Proclamation of Governor McTavish, 16 November 1869; full text of the proclamation can be found in Begg, *History of the North-West*, 1: 394–96, 395.
5. Louis Riel's Notes of the Convention of Twenty-Four, November 16–December 1, 1869, 426.
6. Three women were also included in the group, although the Métis made it clear that they were not under arrest and could leave any time.

CHAPTER 17: CANADA SNEAKS INTO RED RIVER

1. Morton, *History of the Canadian West*, 895; "Report—1874," Smith's deposition, 94.
2. Macdonald to Geo. Stephen, 13 December 1869.

3. Gay was rumoured to be a spy, but no one knew which country he might be spying for. He claimed to be a correspondent for a Paris newspaper. If so, there is no record of any reporting and there is also no record of how he became a "captain." His small red journal containing provisioning notes is in the Teillet Family Papers.
4. Morton, *A History of the Canadian North-West*, 898.
5. Letter of Pierre Léveillé, *New Nation*, 27 May 1870.
6. Louis Schmidt, "Memoires de Louis Schmidt," 22 February 1912.
7. Morton, *Alexander Begg's Red River Journal*, 270.
8. Ibid., 272.
9. Remarks of Louis Riel, as reported in *New Nation*, 21 January 1870.
10. The committee was composed of Louis Riel, Louis Schmidt and Charles Nolin for the French party, and James Ross, Dr. Bird and Thomas Bunn for the English party.
11. List of Rights (2ND), 29 January 1870; full text is in Begg, *History of the North-West*, Vol. 1, 452–54, 454.

CHAPTER 18: FATEFUL DECISIONS

1. 5 July 1869–24 August 1870. On 5 July 1870 the French Métis marked out their territory and began to send out mounted patrols, evict claim-stakers and fill in wells. On 24 August 1870 Wolseley's troops arrived.
2. *New Nation*, 8 April 1870.
3. *New Nation*, 4 March 1870.
4. The firing squad was Pierre Champagne, Marcel Roi, Cap Deschamp, François Thibault, Augustin or Alexander Parisien and François Guillemette.
5. The delegates had discretion with respect to Articles 1, 2, 3, 4, 6, 7, 15, 17, 19 and 20.
6. Wolseley to his brother Dick, 6 April 1870.
7. Macdonald to Rose, 23 February 1870.
8. Cartier to Young, 30 June 1870.
9. Dumont, *Gabriel Dumont Speaks*, 31. "Before leaving Winnipeg I told Riel, if it comes to war send for me and I will come with the Indians."
10. Simpson to Howe, 19 August 1870. "The Half Breeds & Indians of Red River had been tampering with them telling them that the Troops were going to the settlement to take their lands from them by force & advising the Rainy Lake Indians not to assist the soldiers make any treaty or receive any presents this year."
11. Trémaudan, *Histoire de la Nation Métisse*, 242–43.
12. *Toronto Telegraph*, 8 September 1870.
13. *Montreal Gazette*, 16 September 1870.

14. *La Minerve*, 11 August 1870 (Fort Garry, 19 July). Dubuc, the author of the article in *La Minerve*, identified Chatelain as an Indian. Newly arrived in Red River, Dubuc did not know that the people Chatelain represented identified as half-breeds. According to Dubuc, Riel told Chatelain that "if advantageous treaties were proposed, they should accept them." They took Riel's advice and in 1875 signed the Half-breed Adhesion to Treaty #3.
15. Wolseley's proclamation, in Morton, *Alexander Begg's Red River Journal*, 392.

Chapter 19: The Reign of Terror

In April 2018 the author appeared on a CBC *Ideas* radio show called "The Trial of Sir John A. Macdonald: Would he be guilty of war crimes today?" Some of the material on the reign of terror that was originally written for this chapter can also be heard on that show. The show is available as a podcast at https://www.cbc.ca/radio/ideas/the-trial-of-sir-john-a-macdonald-would-he-be-guilty-of-war-crimes-today-1.4614303.

1. *New Nation*, 13 May 1870; Denison, *The Struggle for Imperial Unity*, 26.
2. Houston and Smyth, *The Sash Canada Wore.*
3. Waite, *Canada 1874–1896*, 111–12.
4. Resolution from a Toronto Orange Lodge, *The Globe*, 13 April 1870.
5. Stanley, *The Birth of Western Canada*, 155.
6. "The Storm in Upper Canada," *New Nation*, 6 May 1870.
7. "Memorandum connected with Fenian Invasion of Manitoba in October, 1871," Lieutenant-Governor Archibald, November 1871, in *Report of the Select Committee on the Causes of Difficulties in the North-West Territory in 1869–70*, 140.
8. Macdonald, quoted in Morton, *A History of the Canadian West*, 872.
9. Macdonald to Rose, 23 February 1870.
10. Macdonald to George Stephen, 13 December 1869.
11. Testimony of Lieutenant-Governor Archibald, in *Report of the Select Committee on the Causes of Difficulties in the North-West Territory in 1869–70*, 137. See also at 137 an extract of a letter from Cartier to Archibald, 3 September 1870, confirming that warrants had been issued and were in the hands of constables.
12. Archibald to Macdonald, 13 December 1871.
13. Morton, *Alexander Begg's Red River Journal*, 549.
14. *The Telegraph* (Fort Garry, 6 September), 22 September 1870. "They [the French Métis] are said to be moving off, and some have it that they are concentrating in various localities. Fear, I think, is the chief cause of their moving . . ." Three days later the paper reported that "they are going off by the hundred . . ."
15. *St. Paul Daily Pioneer*, 14 March 1871.

16. *The Telegraph* (Fort Garry, 3 September) 16 September 1870.
17. Cunningham, *The Telegraph*, 7 October 1870. The article reported a conversation between Cunningham and Elzéar Goulet in St. Boniface the day before he was murdered. According to Cunningham, Goulet was anxious about the lack of amnesty and, though he had business in Winnipeg, was afraid to "cross the river" for fear that the volunteers would insult and assault him.
18. *Le Métis*, 4 September 1872, reported that Moise Normand and Joseph St. Germain were beaten and threatened by soldiers with knives while trying to cross the bridge over the Assiniboine River.
19. *Telegraph*, 4 October 1870.
20. *Volunteer Review*, 27 March 1871.
21. *Telegraph*, 6 September 1870.
22. *Telegraph*, 22 September 1870; *The Globe*, 22 September 1870.
23. *La Minerve*, 10 September (Fort Garry, 27 August), 1870.
24. It is difficult to get an exact number of prisoners captured by the Métis during the Red River Resistance. Fifty-three men were captured on 10 December 1869 after the standoff at Schultz's residence. After that, another twelve men from Snow's party were captured. Forty-eight men of the Portage party were captured on 17 February 1870. The difficulty in getting a total arises from the fact that many men escaped and were recaptured. On 15 February 1870 twenty-four men were discharged and some of them were also recaptured. Woodington, "Diary of a Prisoner in Red River Rebellion"; MacArthur, "The Red River Rebellion"; Begg, *The Creation of Manitoba*, 289; and Barkwell, "Riel's Prisoners (1869–70)."
25. I am indebted to Lawrence Barkwell, coordinator of Métis Heritage and History Research, Louis Riel Institute, for his compiled list of the reported violent incidents that took place during the reign of terror, *The Reign of Terror against the Métis of Red River*. Barkwell compiled his list from newspaper accounts, diaries and reports of the day.
26. *The Globe*, 6 September 1870. *Telegraph*, 27 September 1870. *Manitoban*, 14 January 1871.
27. His family was married into the Rolettes, the Lagimodières and the McDermots. His brother Roger was a member of the Council of Assiniboia.
28. 27 January 1871, British Colonial Office minute paper/42/702722, p. 160.
29. Lord Kimberly, 9 March 1871.
30. *St. Paul Daily Pioneer*, 16 September 1870.
31. *La Minerve*, 18 July 1871.
32. *St. Paul Daily Pioneer*, 6 October 1870.
33. *Report of the Select Committee on the Causes of Difficulties in the North-West Territory in 1869–70*, 162 and 205. The petitioners were Pierre Parenteau (*père*), Jos. St. Germain, Louis Desrivières, Matthia Norman, Charles

Neault, Paul Proulx, Benj. Neault, François Marion, Pierre St. Germain, Pierre Parenteau (*fils*), François Frébucher, Bapt. Boudreau, Bapt. Laderoute, Louis Dumas, Matthias Sansregret, Jos. Neault, Amable Gaudry (*fils*), Godefroy Neault, Maxime Lépine, André Nault, J. B. Ritchot, Pierre Sauvé, Joseph Sauvé, Louis Carrière, Damase Carrière and François Poitras.

34. Waite, *Canada 1874–1896*, 111–12.
35. *Le Métis*, 12 October 1872.
36. *St. Paul Daily Pioneer*, 14 March 1871.
37. *St. Paul Daily Pioneer*, 4 January 1871.
38. *St. Paul Press*, 15 March 1871
39. *Le Métis*, 14 August 1872.
40. *St. Paul Daily Pioneer*, 9 June 1871
41. *La Minerve*, 18 July 1871.
42. *Le Métis*, 1 May 1872.
43. *Le Métis*, 2 March 1872, 14 August 1872, and 12 October 1872.
44. *The New York Times*, 12 June 1871.
45. Barkwell, *Reign of Terror against the Métis of Red River*, 8–9.
46. Riel and Lépine to Lieutenant-Governor Morris, 3 January 1873.
47. Catherine McKenna, quoted in Parks Canada News Release, 12 January 2018.
48. Bolt, "The Crown Prerogative as Applied to Military Operations," 13. The men in attendance were Ambroise Lépine, Pierre Léveillé, Elzéar de la Gimodière, J. R. Ritchot, Pierre Parenteau, Joseph St. Germain, André Nault, Baptiste Touron, Baptiste Lépine, Baptiste Beauchemin, Maxime Lépine and Louis Riel. As was their custom they elected a president and two secretaries for each meeting. That day Pierre Parenteau was president and Baptiste Touron and Louis Riel were secretaries.
49. Teillet Family Papers, and see English translation of the meeting minutes in Trémaudan, "Louis Riel and the Fenian Raid of 1871."
50. Ibid., 138.
51. The Fenians took the fort at Pembina at 7:30 on the morning of Thursday, October 5, 1871.
52. Trémaudan, "Louis Riel and the Fenian Raid of 1871," 140.
53. Ibid., 141.
54. *Report of the Select Committee on the Causes of Difficulties in the North-West Territory in 1869–70*, 153.
55. Archibald to Macdonald, 9 October 1871.
56. Archibald to Macdonald, 8 March 1871.
57. Taché to Howe, 9 June 1870. "[T]hat all irregularities of the past will be totally overlooked or forgiven; that nobody will be annoyed for having been either leader or member of the Provisional Government, or for having acted under its guidance. In a word, that a complete and entire amnesty (if not

already bestowed), will surely be granted before the arrival of the troops, so that every one may remain quiet, and induce others to do the same."

58. Ritchot and Scott, Petition to the Queen, 8 February 1872. *Ritchot's Journal*, 156, states that the document was prepared at the insistence of Sir George Cartier.
59. *Ritchot's Journal*, 154. "Her Majesty was going to proclaim a general amnesty immediately, that we could set out for Manitoba, that the amnesty would arrive before us . . . in any event it would arrive before the lieutenant governor. That meantime he [Governor-General Young] was going to give me assurance in writing the assurance that no one would be molested while awaiting the proclamation of the amnesty . . ."
60. *The Globe*, 20 May 1870.
61. *The Globe*, 17 November 1869.
62. Ontario premier Blake's $5,000 bounty was split between ten men: $2,000 went to William Farmer (he swore the information on which Lépine was arrested, served the warrant on Lépine, sat on the grand jury and was a witness at Lépine's trial); $400 went to Francis Cornish (the Crown prosecutor, and later Winnipeg's first mayor); $400 went to C. B. Thibaudeau (Cornish's partner); $330 went to Edward Armstrong (sherriff); $330 went to Léon Dupont; $330 went to John S. Ingram (convicted of severely beating Joseph Dubuc, he arrested Lépine and became the first chief of Winnipeg Police in 1874); $330 went to John A. Kerr; $300 went to Rev. George M. Young (author of the memo in the judge's trial book and witness at Lépine's trial); $290 went to Thomas Hughes, and $290 went to H. W. Smith.
63. Chief Justice Wood and Schultz ended up suing each other in a case that went all the way to the Supreme Court of Canada, but they began as a cozy friendship. In short order after his arrival, Wood cleared Schultz on a perjury charge and a charge that he had falsely sworn.

Chapter 20: Canada Takes the Land

1. The system of long rectangular river lots was originally developed in Normandy, later adopted in Quebec and then used by the Métis in the North-West.
2. Archibald to Howe, 27 December 1870.
3. Cartier to Ritchot, 23 May 1870.
4. Chartrand, *Manitoba's Métis Settlement Scheme of 1870*, 3.
5. *Manitoba Metis Federation v. Attorney General of Canada and Attorney General of Manitoba*, Amended Statement of Claim, Manitoba Court of Queen's Bench, filed 12 November 2004, para. 57.
6. Ibid., para. 58(d).

7. *Manitoba Metis Federation v. Attorney General of Canada and Attorney General of Manitoba*, 2013 SCC 14, [2013] 1 SCR 623, paras. 92 and 99.
8. Manitoba Act, 1870, s. 32. "For the quieting of titles, and assuring to the settlers in the Province the peaceable possession of the lands now held by them, it is enacted as follows:
   1. All grants of land in freehold made by the Hudson's Bay Company up to the eighth day of March, in the year 1869, shall, if required by the owner, be confirmed by grant from the Crown.
   2. All grants of estates less than freehold in land made by the Hudson's Bay Company up to the eighth day of March aforesaid, shall, if required by the owner, be converted into an estate in freehold by grant from the Crown.
   3. All titles by occupancy with the sanction and under the licence and authority of the Hudson's Bay Company up to the eighth day of March aforesaid, of land in that part of the Province in which the Indian Title has been extinguished, shall if required by the owner, be converted into an estate in freehold by grant from the Crown.
   4. All persons in peaceable possession of tracts of land at the time of the transfer to Canada, in those parts of the Province in which the Indian title has not been extinguished, shall have the right of pre-emption of the same, on such terms and conditions as may be determined by the Governor in Council.
   5. The Lieutenant Governor is hereby authorized, under regulations to be made from time to time by the Governor General in Council, to make all such provisions for ascertaining and adjusting on fair and equitable terms, the rights of Common, and rights of cutting Hay held and enjoyed by the settlers in the Province, and for the commutation of the same by grants of land from the Crown."
9. Dr. Frank Tough and Doug Sprague are two of the scholars who have investigated the chain of scrip documents.
10. *Commission of Inquiry into Infant Lands, AM*; and the *Lang Conspiracy* cited in Sprague, *Canada and the Métis*, 137–38.
11. Sprague, *Canada and the Métis*, 125.
12. Howe to McDougall, 7 December 1869.
13. Macdonald to Smith, 3 January 1870.
14. McMicken to Macdonald, 12 November 1871.
15. Trémaudan, *Histoire de la Nation Métisse*, 447; translation in *Hold High Your Heads*, 209.
16. Heber Archibald quoted in Ens, "Métis Lands in Manitoba," 9. And see *MMF v. Canada*, Trial Transcripts, vol. 13, 108, cross-examination of T. Flanagan. Quoting Archibald, "Public opinion here at the time, was, I

suppose, the opinion of 9 out of 10 members of the profession—vis: that it was an improvident grant to the Halfbreeds . . ."

17. Wood to Mackenzie, 25 May 1875.
18. *Le Métis*, "Resignation de l'Honorable M. Archibald," 8 May 1872; *The Globe*, 13 April 1870.
19. Mailhot, "Ritchot's Resistance," 225–27, n1 *and* n2. Mailhot cites two sources. The first is a manuscript history of St. Jean Baptiste prepared by Father Sylvio Caron. The second source is L. A. Prud'homme, "Monsieur l'abbé Joseph David Fillion," Mémoires de la Société du Canada, Section I, 1927. According to Mailhot, Father Ritchot led a group of Métis men to the Rivière-aux-Rats southeast of St. Norbert. This area was the woodlot for the Métis of St. Norbert, Ste. Agathe and St. Vital and it was where they had been wintering their livestock. Under Ritchot's supervision nearly sixty Métis staked their standard twelve-chain (eight-hundred-foot) frontages and planted gardens along the Rivière-aux-Rats. Thirty-eight of these claims were staked by St. Norbert families on lands that later became the communities of St. Pierre-Jolys and St. Malo. More Métis families relocated from St. Norbert to an area near what would become St. Jean Baptiste. Some of these families sold their old claims for the price of the improvements and then moved to the new claimed land believing they would be secured.
20. *Le Métis*, 8 June 1871; Bourke to McMicken, "In accordance with this consent and advice we reckoned up the number of persons in our parish entitled to receive the said grant estimated the quantity of Land required and then (proceeded to) mark off the Blocks."
21. *Le Métis*, 8 June 1871.
22. "Reserves des Métis Français Situés sur la Rivière-Rouge et Autres," *Le Métis*, 8 June 1871.
23. *Le Métis*, 27 March 1872, "Reserve des Métis." One such meeting was held on 24 March 1872 in St. Norbert. It included Métis from St. Norbert, St. Vital, St. Boniface and Ste. Agathe.
24. *Le Métis*, 20 March 1871.
25. *Le Métis*, 15 June 1871, " . . . *ce que le Métis ont choisi comme leurs reserves sera confirmé, M. Archibald voulant bien regarder leur choix comme le sien proper.*"
26. The actual process of granting the 1.4 million acres of Section 31 land required Métis individuals to make an application, in the form of an affidavit, before government appointed commissioners. The drawings and allotment of the lands began on 30 October 1876. All but seven of the parish allotments were completed in 1877, and 1,115 patents were issued in that year. Allotments were made during 1879 and the early months of 1880 in the five remaining parishes. Patent issue was practically completed in 1880.

27. *New Nation*, 16 March 1870, "Our Situation."
28. *Le Métis*, 22 June 1871, "*C'est ni à tel hôtel, ni à tel restaurant, ni à tel bureau de sédition qu'ils doivent se renseigner.*"
29. The term "armed emigration" comes from Denison. Denison, *Soldiering*, 179; Denison, *The Struggle for Imperial Unity*, 43.
30. *Commission of Inquiry into Infant Lands, AM*, 6.
31. Ibid., 9. In the commission's examination of the Parenteau case, the parents received $600 for the land, and the next day the land sold to the solicitor whose firm made the application for $1,200. The same land sold a short time later for $1,900.
32. Ibid., 2 and 6.
33. Ibid., 10.
34. *Le Métis*, "Reserve des Métis," 27 March 2017, 2. They protested that the government in Ottawa was not respecting their rights and was not honouring the land agreement it made with them in 1870. They resolved to energetically oppose these measures and to take every fair and effective means of enforcing their resolutions. They formed a surveillance committee to do it.
35. Ritchot to Macdonald, 15 January 1881. Ritchot reminded Macdonald of his promise that "all lands thus taken were and would be the property of those who were in possession thereof."
36. In 1881 Ritchot called on Macdonald to remember and to keep his promise. Ritchot took Macdonald to task for the deception being practised solely to dispossess the Métis. The sequence of events is as follows: During the Manitoba Act negotiations, Macdonald and Cartier proposed that "The lands will be chosen throughout the province by each lot and in several lots and in various places, if it is judged to be proper by the local legislature which ought itself to distribute these parcels of land to heads of families in proportion to the number of children existing the time of the distribution." The delegates wanted local control. Cartier and Macdonald argued that their language had to stay in the legislation but they would issue an order in council guaranteeing local control. Ritchot wrote to Cartier, "*Nous étions convenus . . . de laisser le choix et la division des terrains devant être divisés entre enfants des Métis à la Législature Locale.*" Instead of an order in council, Cartier promised local control. *Ritchot's Journal* entries for 2, 5 and 18 May 1870; letter, Cartier to Ritchot, 23 May 1870.
37. "Addendum to Treaty Three by the Half Breeds of Rainy Lake and Rainy River," *Indian Treaties and Surrenders*, Vol. 1 (Saskatoon: Fifth House), 1992: 308–9.
38. Ibid.
39. Graham to Pither, 2 July 1878.
40. Reserves 16A, 16D and 18B.

41. Morris, *Treaties of Canada with the Indians*, 69.
42. McColl Report to the Superintendent General of Indian Affairs, 1883.
43. *Le Métis*, "Resignation de l'Honorable M. Archibald," 8 May 1872.
44. Codd to Dennis, 19 November 1873.
45. An Act to amend "An Act respecting the appropriation of certain Lands in Manitoba," RSC, Ch. 52, 1875.
46. Order in Council, 26 April 1875.
47. Order in Council, 20 April 1876.
48. Dennis to Codd, 24 October 1877.
49. Two years later a policy amendment permitted scrip to be applied to staked claims, but by then most of these lands had already been lost. Partial "Memorandum on the subject of the so-called Staked Claims in Manitoba."
50. Petition of eighteen claimants, that the survey ill reflects their previous agreed-upon boundaries, 4 November 1873; Whitcher to Deputy Minister of the Interior, 13 November 1873. A map of the lands claimed by the petitioners is in Library and Archives Canada, National Map Collection, 54106.
51. *The Globe*, 4 August 1870.

CHAPTER 21: THE DIASPORA

1. McMicken to Macdonald, 13 January 1873.
2. *Le Métis*, 20 March 1872, 2. Thirty-two families left with Father Moulin to relocate to St. Pierre Mission at Reindeer Lake in northern Manitoba.
3. There is a plaque in Fort Frances that commemorates a Métis family, the Calders, who moved there "after the Louis Riel uprising."
4. Macfarlane, "Unfortunate Women of My Class," 40–44.
5. The Saskatchewan wintering camp at Prairie Ronde was near the town of Dundurn; Grosse-Butte was near Humboldt; Petite-Ville was near Fish Creek.
6. Payment, *The Free People*, 302, provides a list of the Métis wintering at St. Laurent on 31 December 1871 at Appendix 1, Table 1.1. According to Payment, there were 321 people: 63 men, 58 women, 198 children and 567 horses. All except three (two priests and Marguerite Ouellette, who was a farmer and domestic servant) were identified as hunters.
7. "Condensed Report of a Meeting of the Métis Winterers at the Mission of St. Lawrence on the South Saskatchewan near Carlton, 31 December 1871," Glenbow Archives, Richard C. Hardisty fonds, series 9, M-477-144.
8. Fisher et al., "Address to the Lieutenant Governor, Alexander Morris," 5 May 1873, Sessional Papers, No. 116, 48 Victoria, 1885: 1–2.
9. Clarke to Smith, 15 January 1872.
10. Smith to the governor and committee, 1 August 1870.
11. The North-West Council was established in Winnipeg on 8 March 1873.

12. Father Belcourt and Alexander Ross both wrote about the Laws of the Hunt. "They had a code of laws and were governed by a council of twelve, under their chosen chief Gabriel Husier [Lussier?]," "Samuel O'Connell reminiscence, 1875," 1–7 Montana Historical Society.
13. Ritchot's notes call the Métis laws codified in 1869 the "Fundamental Code." Father Ritchot made a point of noting that the Métis were making the effort to codify their laws and pass them in assembly. Similar processes seem to have been adopted in Qu'Appelle and St. Laurent. See Fisher et al., "Address to the Lieutenant Governor, Alexander Morris," 1. The Laws of St. Laurent were first adopted on 10 February 1873. Additional laws were added on 10 December 1873. The Laws of St. Laurent were updated at assemblies between 1873 and 1875.
14. Fisher et al., "Address to the Lieutenant Governor, Alexander Morris."
15. Woodcock, *Gabriel Dumont*, 95–97.
16. *Copy of the Laws and Regulations Established for the Colony of St. Laurent on the Saskatchewan.*
17. Chambers, *Royal North-West Mounted Police*, 35.
18. "Petition of the Half-breeds of St. Laurent to the Lieutenant Governor," 1 February 1878. Signed by Gabriel, his *X* mark, Dumont, chairman, and Alex Fisher, secretary.
19. Smith, "The Adventures of the Wild West of 1870," 1–6 Glenbow Archives.
20. Personal communication with George Fleury, 11 March 2017, Winnipeg.

Chapter 22: The Fourth National Resistance

1. The alliances listed are the ones that operated in the Canadian North-West, largely around the Canadian-American border. The Blackfoot Confederacy was composed of the T'suu T'ina (Sarcee), Pikani, Siksika, Kainai and Aaniih (Gros Ventre). The Dakota Confederacy was composed of the Mdewakanton, Wahpetons, Wahpekutes, Sissetons, Yanktons, Yanktonais and Tetons. The Nehiyaw Pwat, also known as the Iron Alliance, was composed of the Cree, Assiniboine, Ojibwa and Métis Nation.
2. *The Globe*, 15 September 1885.
3. Riel, "Les Métis: Dernier Mémoire de Louis Riel," in Trémaudan, *Histoire de la Nation Métisse*, 445.
4. Lalonde, "Colonization Companies and the North-West Rebellion," 54–65. A list of directors and their connections to the Conservatives is set out in McLean, *1885: Métis Rebellion or Government Conspiracy?*, 47.
5. Dewdney to Macdonald, 23 July 1884.
6. Combet, *Gabriel Dumont: Memoirs*, 49–50.
7. "Petition of Edmonton Half-breeds to Sir John A. Macdonald, May 1880," for example, asked that the Métis be put "on an equal footing with our relatives and friends in Manitoba." They wanted scrip (a government-

issued coupon that could be redeemed for money or land) to satisfy their claims, and they wanted confirmation of title to lands already occupied. They also wanted to be able to select railway lands with their scrip allocations.

8. Petition to the Right Honourable Sir John A. Macdonald from St. Antoine de Padoue, South Saskatchewan River [Batoche] signed by Gabriel Dumont, Jean Caron, Emmanuel Champagne, Louis Batoche and forty-two others, 4 September 1882.
9. Barkwell, *Cypress Hills Métis Hunting Brigade Petition of 1878 for a Métis Reserve*. The men who signed both the 1878 Cypress Hills petition and an 1880 Montana petition are: Jean Charette, Joseph Charette, Michel Davis, William Davis, François Xavier Fagnant, Theophile Fagnant, William "Kee-tar-kiss" Fagnant, Baptiste Gariépy, Elie Gariépy, Leonide Gariépy, Sever Hamelin, Antoine Lafontaine dit Faillant, William Laframboise, Pierre "Ah-show-e-ge-shig" Laverdure, Pierre Léveillé, Norman Marion, Antoine "Ratte" Ouellette, Joseph Ouellette and Edouard Wells.

Chapter 23: La Guerre Nationale

1. Barkwell, *Cypress Hills Métis Hunting Brigade Petition of 1878 for a Métis Reserve*, 5–6. The Métis signatories to the Cypress Hills petition who were also at the Battle of the Grand Coteau included Pascal Breland, Patrice Breland, Thomas Breland, Isidore Dumont Sr. dit Ecapow [Aicawpow], Jean Baptiste "Che-ma-ma" Falcon, Louis "Mar-yarm-mons" Laframboise and August Laframboise, Gabriel Léveillé, Pierre Léveillé, Louis Malaterre, Alex Malaterre, André Trottier, Antoine Trottier, Charles DeMontigny, Toby David Poitras, Theodore Poitras, Edward Donald Wells, Eduard "Neddy" Wells and James François Whitford.
2. "Petition of the Half-breeds during the 'Black Winter' to Privy Council of the North-West Territories, 1878." Signed by 276 men. They asked for land "[c]ommencing at a point upon the international line, where crossed by the Pembina River; thence running west along said line, 150 miles; thence at right angles, north 50 miles; thence due east, 150 miles; thence due south, 50 miles, to point of beginning."
3. Barkwell, *Cypress Hills Métis Hunting Brigade Petition of 1878 for a Métis Reserve*, 6. The men who signed both are: Jean Charette, Alex Gardy (Gaddy), Bonaventure Gariepy, François Lafontaine, Daniel Ledoux, Joseph Lemire, Joseph Léveillé, Peter (Pierre) Léveillé, Louis Militaire (Malaterre), Joseph Parisien, Baptiste Pelletier, Alex Pelletier and John Wells.
4. W. L. Orde to Minister of Interior, 3 April 1880.

5. Richardson to Dennis, 13 January 1880.
6. Gabriel Dumont, as quoted by Amédée Forget in his report to Lieutenant-Governor Dewdney, 18 September 1884, in Reid, *Louis Riel and the Creation of Modern Canada*, 144.
7. "Report from Dr. Kittson," *LAC*, Kittson to Macleod, 1 July 1880, 2.
8. Ibid.
9. Macdonald to Dewdney, 17 September 1883; *House of Commons Debates*, 9 May 1883, 1107.
10. Macdonald to Dewdney, 2 September 1884. The Mounties had arrived in the North-West Territories in 1873. By 1876 there were about one hundred police just at Fort Carlton and Battleford. Officially called the North-West Mounted Police, the force was sent into the North-West after the "Cypress Hills Massacre" to bring the wild West and particularly the whisky trade under control. Morris, *Treaties of Canada with the Indians*, 202. The police buildup was not solely attributable to the Indians and Métis. A near riot at Prince Albert over the location of the telegraph line brought another rush of police in November 1883.
11. Chambers, *The Royal North West Mounted Police*, 16, quoting Colonel P. Robertson-Ross, Commanding Officer of the Militia of Canada and Adjutant General, who wrote a report in 1872 entitled *A Reconnaissance of the North-West Provinces and Indian Territories of the Dominion of Canada*.
12. "Fleury, Patrice," Saskatchewan Archives Board, 27413, A-515, 5–6.
13. Clarke to Dewdney, 11 May 1884.
14. Moïse Ouellette was Gabriel Dumont's brother-in-law. Two additional companions, Calixte Lafontaine and Philippe Gariépy, who were travelling to Montana to see relatives, later joined them.
15. Trémaudan, *Histoire de la Nation Métisse*, 291.
16. Langevin to Macdonald, 6 November 1884.
17. Order in Council, P.C. 135, 28 January 1885.
18. In September 1884 Riel was called to a meeting at the rectory in St. Laurent, where he found five priests, a representative of Lieutenant-Governor Dewdney and Joseph Forget, who was on the board of directors of the Canadian Pacific Railway. This is the group that offered Riel a seat on the North-West Council and, when he declined that, a seat in the Senate.
19. On 18 August 1884, the size of the Mountie detachment at Prince Albert was increased. At Fort Carlton a police post oversaw two hundred men distributed between Battleford, Carlton, Prince Albert and Fort Pitt.
20. Dewdney to Macdonald, 11 March 1885.
21. "Riel's Proposal," *Regina Leader* (Evening Edition), 21 April 1885.
22. Fleury, "Reminiscences," 6, Saskatchewan Archives Board. "It was in the early part of March that parties passing through told us that our petition

would be answered by powder and bullet, and it was this that started the rebellious action."

23. Reports as to the number of police vary. Dumont said eighty. Other reports say five hundred.
24. Riel, *The Diaries of Louis Riel*, 54–55. Joseph Ouellette, Gabriel Dumont, Pierre Gariépy, Isidore Dumont, John Ross, Philippe Gariépy, August Laframboise, Moïse Ouelette, Calixte Lafontaine and Napoléon Nault were the signatories.
25. Fleury, "Reminiscences," Saskatchewan Archives Board, 6.
26. Moïse Ouellette's Account, 62, *SHMF*, Boîte 1346, Chemise 066. [English transcripts. French handwritten accounts in Chemise 065.]
27. Dumont, *Gabriel Dumont Speaks*, 47.
28. Ibid., 48.
29. Bishop Bourget, *Lettres pastorals*, 31 May 1858.
30. M. Lussier, curé of Boucherville, Quebec, as cited in Lindsey, "The Ultramontane Movement in Canada," 570.
31. Ibid., 561.
32. *The Globe*, 23 March 1885.
33. *The Globe*, 28 March 1885.
34. Radforth, "Celebrating the Suppression of the North-West Resistance of 1885," 602.
35. *World*, 29 March 1885.
36. Radforth, "Celebrating the Suppression of the North-West Resistance of 1885," 619.
37. Governor-General Lansdowne to Macdonald, 31 August 1885.
38. Ibid.; Macdonald to Governor-General Lansdowne, 3 September 1885.
39. Macdonald to Governor-General Lansdowne, 3 September 1885.
40. The Mounties reported ten deaths and had thirteen wounded. Two of their wounded later died.
41. Caron's Account, 5, *SHMF*, Boîte 1346, Chemise 066.
42. Moïse Ouellette's Account, *SHMF*, Boîte 1346, Chemise 066, 11.
43. The site was designated a national historic site in 1923. At that time it was named the Fish Creek National Historic Site. On 17 November 2007 the site was renamed the Battle of Tourond's Coulee/Fish Creek National Historic Site.
44. Isidore Dumas's Account, *SHMF*, Boîte 1346, Chemise 066, 30.
45. Middleton reported ten deaths and had forty-six wounded.
46. In 1892 Garneau was elected to the North West Territories Parliament in Regina, but he was refused entry due to his previous involvement with Louis Riel.
47. Cassels, *Diary*, 14.

48. All numbers of Middleton's men are from Hildebrand, *The Battle of Batoche*, 30–31.
49. Middleton reported eight deaths and had forty-six wounded.

Chapter 24: After Batoche

1. *Port Hope Evening Guide*, 13 July 1888.
2. Langford, "One of the Biggest Mysteries in Métis History Gets Even More Puzzling," *Maclean's*, 21 June 2017, https://www.macleans.ca/news/canada/the-enduring-mystery-of-the-bell-of-batoche.
3. The full story of the bell can be found at https://www.cbc.ca/doczone/episodes/the-mystery-of-the-bell.
4. Stobie, *The Other Side of Rebellion*, 3. Bremner was proud of his mixed-race heritage but rejected the term "Métis," which he understood to apply only to the French Métis.
5. *The Queen vs. Charles Bremner et al*, in Canada, *Epitome of Parliamentary Documents*, 347.
6. Patrice Tourond's Account, *SHMF*, Boîte 1346, Chemise 066, 74.
7. V. Grandier et al., to the Hon. Sir A. Campbell, 10 July 1885, PAA OMI, St. Albert 8, Codex Historicus, 25 juillet 1885.
8. Dumont, *Gabriel Dumont Speaks*, 23.

Chapter 25: The Trial of Louis Riel

1. The twenty-four men charged with treason felony were Joseph Arcand, Pierre Parenteau, Moïse Parenteau, Emmanuel Champagne, Maxime Lépine, Pierre Gariépie, Albert Monkman, Philip Gariépie, Alexis Lombarde, Philip Garnot, Alexander P. Fisher, Pierre Henri, Moïse Ouellette, Ignace Poitras, Baptiste Vandal, Baptiste Rocheleau, Joseph Delorme, Maxime Dubois, Pierre Vandal, Alexander Cadieux (Kitwayo), Francis Tourond, Patrice Tourond, Joseph Pilon and James Short.
2. Joseph wrote, "I hear that you are writing of your life. Do not give this book to anyone. Keep it for me. I feel very much attached to it. Regarding your wife, I will be seeing her soon. Answer immediately. Return cost paid." Translation by the author of the telegram reproduced on p. 365.
3. Personal conversation with Lucienne Vouriot (grandniece of Louis Riel), 28 May 2017, St. Boniface, Manitoba.
4. Knox, "The Question of Louis Riel's Insanity."
5. The three doctors are F. X. Perrault, Dr. Brunelle and Dr. A. Jukes. The quote is from Dr. Juke's report, CSP, "Epitome of Parliamentary Documents in Connection with the North-West Rebellion, 1885," A. Jukes to Lieutenant Governor Dewdney, 6 November 1885. See coded telegram, p. 372.
6. Louis Riel to Edmond Mallet, 2 July 1875, as quoted in Knox, "The Question of Louis Riel's Insanity."

7. McLachlin, "Louis Riel: Patriot Rebel."
8. In 1838 Upper Canada passed An Act to protect the Inhabitants of this Province against Lawless Aggressions from Subjects of Foreign Countries, at peace with Her Majesty, 1 Vic. Chap. 3. This was subsequently amended by 3 Vic. Chap. 12 (1840). The statute was so heavily relied on in the 1860s to prosecute the Fenians that it became known as the "Fenian Act." Under the Fenian Act, it was treason for a citizen of another country, an alien, to levy war against Canada. This would have been an appropriate statute under which charges could have been laid against Louis Riel because he had become an American citizen on 16 March 1883. The Canadian Treason-Felony Statute, 1868, 31 Victoria c. 69, was formerly titled An Act for the Better Security of the Crown and of the Government. Under s. 5 it was treason-felony to levy war against the Crown or the government.
9. This same statute was used to hang eight men for high treason during the War of 1812.
10. *The Queen vs. Louis Riel*, [1885] NWT, 1 (Magistrates Court), 3–7; [1885] Man. Q.B. appeal, 302 (aff'd); 10 HL 675 (Privy Council) (aff'd), reprinted in *The Queen v. Louis Riel* (New York: Gryphon Editions), 1992.
11. All petitions can be found at Canada, Sessional Papers, No. 43(e), 49 Victoria, Petitions.
12. Petition of Charles O'Hara, labourer.
13. Petition signed by the Mayor of St. Sauveur and 1,851 others.
14. Canada, Sessional Papers, No. 43(e), 49 Victoria, Petitions, 256–64.
15. Petition of G. Powell, U.S. Under Secretary of State, 265.
16. Petitions, 259–60.
17. Ibid., Telegram to Marquis of Lansdowne from Juliette Adam.
18. "The Death of Riel," *Bloomington Daily Leader*, 17 November 1885.
19. Quoted in Parkin, *Sir John A. Macdonald*, 244.

Chapter 26: Scrip

1. Tough and McGregor, "The Rights to the Land May Be Transferred," 53, quoting William Parker Fillmore, a scrip buyer during the Treaty Ten Commission in 1906.
2. Battleford, Saskatoon, Humboldt, Regina, Estevan, Moose Jaw, Medicine Hat and Calgary. Ibid., 52.
3. Memorandum for Mr. Newcombe, 14 October 1921.
4. Senator Sir James Lougheed read a letter from the Parliamentary counsel Francis R. Gisborne, 21 June 1922 in the Senate, as cited in Tough and McGregor, "The Rights to the Land May Be Transferred," 54.
5. Criminal Code, 1910, Revised Statutes of Canada, 1906, c. 146, 5.408 and see also 5.469.

6. The first Half-breed Scrip Commission occurred in 1885 and dealt with the claims of Métis people who, on or before 15 July 1870, were living in territory that had since been ceded to the government by treaties with First Nations. Ten other scrip commissions followed: 1886 (continuation of 1885 work); 1887 (completion of 1885 work); 1889 (claims within the territory of the Treaty 6 adhesion); 1899 (claims within the territory of Treaty 8); 1900 (claims of Métis born in the North-West Territories between 15 July 1870 and 31 December 1885); 1901 (claims of Métis resident in the portion of Manitoba outside its original boundaries, and the remaining claims in the North-West); 1906–07 (claims within the territory of Treaty 10); 1908–10 (claims within the territory of the Treaty 5 adhesion); and 1921 (claims within the territory of Treaty 11).
7. Scrip Application of Baptiste Gariepy.
8. Witness Declaration of Antoine Ouellette.
9. Witness Declaration of Samson Breland.
10. Witness Declaration of Timothy Dumont.
11. Ibid.
12. Scrip Application of Eliza Cyr.
13. Scrip Application of George St. Germain.
14. Scrip Application of Réné Pagé.
15. Ibid.
16. Scrip Application of Nancy Bird; Scrip Application of Marie Desjarlais.
17. Scrip Application of Baptiste Cardinal.
18. Scrip Application of Elizabeth Boucher.
19. *R. v. Blais*, [2003] 2 SCR 236, para. 34.
20. It appears that very few people from the Rainy Lake area applied for Manitoba Act land grants. Four were Chatelain's family members (Narcisse, Marie, Nicolas and Louis). The others include Nancy Loutit and John Linklater.
21. Treaty with the Chippewa–Red Lake and Pembina Bands, 1863, known as "The Old Crossing Treaty," 38 Congress, 1 session, *Confidential Executive Documents*, P. Collections (Minnesota Historical Society, http://collections.mnhs.org/MNHistoryMagazine/articles/15/v15i03p282-300.pdf). Over half of those in attendance at the treaty negotiations were Métis. One year later the treaty was amended. Instead of a land grant, the Métis received a one-time buyout of scrip for 160 acres. Acceptance of scrip meant that person was no longer eligible for future annuities.

Chapter 27: St. Paul des Métis

1. Lacombe Memorial, 27 March 1895, Annex "B" to P.C. 3723, 28 December 1895, Glenbow Archives, James Brady Fonds, Series 3, M-125-31.
2. Ibid., 7.

3. Dion, "An Account by J. F. Dion of His Activities in the Métis Association of Alberta," 10 September 1940, in Hatt, "The Response to Directed Social Change on an Alberta Métis Colony," 244–47.
4. Maber to Oliver, 22 January 1909, 2.
5. Sawchuk, Sawchuk and Ferguson, *Métis Land Rights in Alberta*, 172 n53.

CHAPTER 28: THE MÉTIS SETTLEMENTS IN ALBERTA

1. "Constitution of (Provisional) Organization—Métis Association of Alberta," 18 December 1932, on motion moved by F. Callihoo, seconded by J. McLean, carried. Glenbow Archives, James Brady Fonds, Series 3, M-125-32, 21–26.
2. The first elected executive council was Joe Dion, president; Malcolm Norris, vice-president; Felix Callihoo, second vice-president; Henry Cunningham, third vice-president; and James Brady, secretary-treasurer. The name was changed in 1934 to the English version: the Métis Association of Alberta. The name change also reflected the fact that the organization did not represent the Métis of the Northwest Territories.
3. Fishing Lake, Green Jackfish Lake, Wolf Lake, Muskeg Prairie, Grouard, Fort Vermilion, Big Horn, North West of White Court, Primrose, Conklin and White Fish Lake. Undated Report by Joseph Dion to R. G. Reid, Minister of Lands and Mines, 3–5.
4. "Constitution of (Provisional) Organization—Métis Association of Alberta," s. II(b), 18 December 1932, on motion moved by F. Callihoo, seconded by J. McLean, carried. Glenbow Archives, James Brady Fonds, Series 3, M-125-32, 21–26.
5. *Daniels v. Canada (Indian Affairs and Northern Development)*, [2016] 1 SCR 99, 2016 SCC 12.
6. Evidence and Proceedings Half-Breed Commission, Edmonton, Alberta, 25 February 1935, 20.
7. Norris to Dion, 16 December 1933 Glenbow Archives, Joseph Dion Fonds, M-331-2, 3–4.
8. Ibid., 3–4.
9. "Alberta Métis Association Brief—1935 (preamble)," Glenbow Archives, James Brady Fonds.

CHAPTER 29: ROCK BOTTOM

1. These included defence of Hong Kong (7–25 December 1941), the Dieppe Raid (19 August 1942), the Battle of Ortona (23–31 May 1944), D-Day (6 June 1944), the Falaise Campaign (7–16 August 1944), the Battle of the Scheldt (31 October–8 November 1944), the Rhineland Campaign (February 1945) and the Liberation of the Netherlands (March 1945). Prefontaine, "War and the Métis," 3.

2. Unanimous resolution of the Saskatchewan Ninth Legislature, 28 March 1939.
3. *Yorkton Enterprise*, 21 January 1943.
4. Notes from a meeting of government officials "for the purposes of discussion the Métis problem in the Provinces of Manitoba, Saskatchewan and Alberta," 13 July 1949.
5. Sworn testimony of Rita Cullen (née Vivier), trial transcripts, *R. v. Goodon*, Vol. 4, 106.
6. Campbell, *Halfbreed*, 8.
7. Zeilig and Zeilig, *St. Madeleine*, interview with Lazare Fouillard, 191–92.
8. According to Statistics Canada's 2001 census, 23 per cent of the population that identified themselves as Métis changed residences in the year prior to the census, compared with only 14 per cent of the non-Aboriginal population. According to the 2006 census, Métis mobility rates within large urban centres were 35 to 40 per cent higher than the non-Aboriginal population. In the Alberta five-year migration data, Métis were 11 per cent more mobile than the non-Aboriginal population and 16 per cent more than registered Indians. Also, in Alberta the one-year migration rate for Métis was 24 per cent higher than for the non-Aboriginal population.
9. Minutes of meeting of l'Union Métisse du Local #1 de Batoche, 30 June 1929.
10. Minutes of meeting of l'Union Métisse du Local #1 de Batoche, 24 July 1929. Samuel Nault was nominated president general; Eugene Caron was nominated vice president general; Edmond Boyer was assistant secretary.
11. Norris became a member of the Green Lake local in 1947.
12. The subsequent report was not limited to Métis. It dealt with Métis and non-status Indians—in other words, all Aboriginal people who were not considered a federal responsibility at that time.
13. Lagassé, *The People of Indian Ancestry*, 77–78.
14. "Pallister Comes under Fire after Province Cancels 2nd Agreement with Manitoba Metis Federation," 31 October 2018, cbc.ca/news/canada/manitoba/metis-mmf-government-agreement-hydro-manitoba-1.4885479.

Chapter 30: The Fifth National Resistance

1. *Calder et al. v. Attorney General of British Columbia*, [1973] SCR 313.
2. Daniels, 21 August 1978.
3. "The Métis and Multiculturalism," brief presented to the Third Canadian Conference on Multiculturalism, 27–29 October 1978, Ottawa, in Daniels, *We Are the New Nation*, 51.
4. There was also concern about the lack of an entrenchment clause. By "entrenchment," they meant a clause similar to s. 1 of the draft Charter of Rights and Freedoms, which stated that "The Canadian Charter of

Rights and Freedoms guarantees the rights and freedoms, subject only to such reasonable limits prescribed by law as can be demonstrably justified in a free and democratic society." The Aboriginal rights clause was not in the Charter and contained no such guarantee. Legal advice provided to the Native Council of Canada raised the possibility that Aboriginal rights might be unenforceable without such entrenchment. In the opinion of the author, this advice was unfortunate and wrong. No Canadian constitutional provision can be legally unenforceable.

5. Barkwell, "Métis and Non-Status Indian Constitutional Review Commission, 1981," 2.
6. There was a provision to bring in BC and northwestern Ontario Métis in the future.
7. Weinstein, *Quiet Revolution West*, 114–16.
8. Resolution to Recognize the Historic Role of Louis Riel, House of Commons and Senate of Canada, 10 March 1992, by Joe Clark, then Minister of Constitutional Affairs. The Manitoba Legislative Assembly unanimously passed a Resolution to Recognize the Historic role of Louis Riel as Founder of Manitoba in May 1992.
9. Hansard, House of Commons, 21 October 1996, Jean-Paul Marchand, Bloc Québécois member for Québec East, speaking to Bill C-297, second reading of An Act to Revoke the Conviction of Louis David Riel.
10. From 1983 to 2001, twelve bills were proposed in Parliament to exonerate Louis Riel. None has passed. There has never been a government-sponsored bill to exonerate Louis Riel.
11. Paul Chartrand, remarks at a Métis conference, Saskatoon, Saskatchewan, June 2003.

Chapter 31: The Hunt for Justice

1. A complete record of Métis litigation can be found in Teillet, *Métis Law in Canada*.
2. Clément Chartier, QC, Jean Teillet, IPC, Jason Madden, Michelle LeClair-Harding, Lionel Chartrand and Kathy Hodgson-Smith were the Métis lawyers who represented Métis hunters and fishers in court.
3. "Ottawa Signs Self-Government Deal with Métis in Manitoba," *The Globe and Mail*, 22 September 2018.
4. The author was the lawyer for the Women of the Métis Nation in their intervention at the Supreme Court of Canada in *R. v. Barton*. The case was argued on 11 October 2018. Much of the discussion in this section also appears in the written submissions of the Women of the Métis Nation in that case. The oral argument before the court can be viewed online at https://scc-csc.ca/case-dossier/info/webcastview-webdiffusionvue-eng.aspx?cas=37769&id=2018/2018-10-11--37769&date=2018-10-11. The Women

of the Métis Nation oral submissions start at three hours and twenty-three minutes into the webcast.

5. Boyce, "Victimization of Aboriginal People in Canada, 2014," 3, 9, 18.
6. *R. v. Barton*, 2015 ABQB 159, para. 1. The reasons for judgment in the *voir dire* determined the admissibility of the "preserved pelvic region of the deceased in this case, Ms. Cindy Gladue."
7. *Johnston v. Alberta (Director of Vital Statistics)*, 2007 ABQB 597 (CanLII).
8. Flanagan, *Louis "David" Riel: Prophet of the New World*, 30.
9. "It Needs to Be Said" is reproduced in Doxtater, "The Métis Women's Association of Manitoba," 177–78.
10. As of February 2019, the president of the Métis Nation of Ontario is Margaret Froh, the president of the Métis Nation of Alberta is Audrey Poitras, and the president of the Métis Nation British Columbia is Clara Morin Dal Col.

Chapter 32: Métis Identity

1. Bakker, *A Language of Our Own*, 65.
2. Ibid., 64, where he notes that "Bois-Brûlé" may be a translation of an Ojibwa term, *wi:ssakkote:w'inini*, meaning "half-burnt woodmen."
3. Jones, "The Métis of Southern Manitoba in the Nineteenth Century," 24; Falcon, "The Battle of Seven Oaks," 5–9.
4. Bakker, *A Language of Our Own*, 65.
5. Dumont, "Leather and Naughahyde," 58.
6. Anderson, *Métis.*
7. *Report of the Royal Commission on Aboriginal Peoples*, vol. 4, ch. 5, 500.
8. Riel, "The Métis, Louis Riel's Last Memoir," in Trémaudan, *Hold High Your Heads*, 200.
9. *R. v. Powley*, [2003] 2 SCR 207.
10. Gaudry and Leroux, "White Settler Revisionism and Making Métis Everywhere."
11. Gaudry, "Communing with the Dead."
12. Ibid., 171.
13. Leroux, "Self Made Métis," 37.
14. *R. v. Jean-Denis Castonguay*, 2002 CanLII 49690.
15. Leroux, "Self Made Métis," 36.
16. *Quebec (Procureure generale) c. Sequin*, 2017 QCCS 1881 at para. 158.
17. The information on these eastern groups comes from a series of court cases that can be found in Teillet, *Métis Law in Canada.*

Chapter 33: Freedom and Infinity

1. The Métis Nation has adopted at least five flags over its two-hundred-year history, including the infinity flag in 1815 and the Papineau flag in the

1840s. A flag was raised in the Red River Resistance in 1869, another in the North-West Resistance in 1885, and still another by the Old Wolves and in Batoche in the first part of the twentieth century. Toward the end of the twentieth century, the Métis Nation went back to its first flag, the infinity flag with a red or blue background, which continues to be used as its national flag. The infinity symbol is also used as a stand-alone symbol to represent the Métis Nation. It has become standard Canadian practice to use an eagle feather as the symbol to represent First Nations, an inukshuk to represent the Inuit, and the infinity symbol to represent the Métis Nation.

Bibliography

Amos, Andrew, ed. *Report of Trials in the Courts of Canada, Relative to the Destruction of the Earl of Selkirk's Settlement on the Red River*. London: John Murray, 1820.

Anderson, Benedict. *Imagined Communities: Reflections on the Origin and Spread of Nationalism*. London: Verso Books, 2006.

Anderson, Chris. *"Métis": Race, Recognition, and the Struggle for Indigenous Peoplehood*. Vancouver: UBC Press, 2014.

Anderson, Mark Cronlund, and Carmen L. Robertson. *Seeing Red: A History of Natives in Canadian Newspapers*. Winnipeg: University of Manitoba Press, 2011.

Arthur, Elizabeth. "Dickson, James: Self-Styled 'Liberator of the Indian Nations.'" *Dictionary of Canadian Biography*, http://biographi.ca/en/bio/dickson_james_7E.html.

Atwood, Mae, ed. *In Rupert's Land: Memoirs of Walter Traill*. Toronto: McClelland and Stewart, 1970.

Bakker, Peter. *A Language of Our Own: The Genesis of Michif, the Mixed Cree-French Language of the Canadian Métis*. New York and Oxford: Oxford University Press, 1997.

Ballantyne, Robert Michael. *Hudson Bay: Everyday Life in the Wilds of North America*. London: T. Nelson and Sons, 1879.

Barkwell, Lawrence. *The Reign of Terror against the Métis of Red River*. Gabriel Dumont Institute, 2018, http://www.metismuseum.ca/resource php/149078.

———. "Métis and Non-Status Indian Constitutional Review Commission, 1981." SCRIBD, 2012, https://www.scribd.com/document/83202667/Metis-and-Non-Status-Indian-Constitutional-Review-Commission.

———. "Riel's Prisoners (1869–70)." Gabriel Dumont Institute, 2015, http://www.metismuseum.ca/resource.php/15063.

———. *Cypress Hills Métis Hunting Brigade Petition of 1878 for a Métis Reserve*. Winnipeg: Louis Riel Institute, 2015.

Barkwell, Lawrence, Leah M. Dorion and Audreen Hourie. *Metis Legacy II: Michif Culture, Heritage and Folkways*. Saskatoon: Gabriel Dumont Institute, 2006.

Barkwell, Lawrence, Leah Dorion and Darren R. Préfontaine. *Metis Legacy: A Metis Historiography and Annotated Bibliography*. Winnipeg and Saskatoon: Louis Riel Institute and Gabriel Dumont Institute, 2001.

Beal, Bob, and Rod Macleod. *Prairie Fire: The 1885 North-West Rebellion*. Edmonton: Hurtig Publishers, 1984.

Begg, Alexander. *The Creation of Manitoba*. Toronto: Hunter, Rose, 1871.

———. *History of the North-West*. 3 vols. Toronto: Hunter, Rose, 1894.

Beltrami, J. C. *A Pilgrimage in Europe and America*. London: Hunt and Clarke, 1828.

Berger, Thomas. "Guth Lecture 2013: The Manitoba Métis Decision and the Uses of History." *Manitoba Law Journal* 38, no. 1 (2013): 1–27.

Bigsby, John J. *The Shoe and Canoe*. London: Chapman and Hall, 1850.

Bocquel, Bernard. *Les Fidèles à Riel*. St. Vital: Les Éditions de la Fourche, 2012.

Bolt, Major Alexander. "The Crown Prerogative as Applied to Military Operations." Office of the Judge Advocate General Strategic Legal Paper Series. Ottawa: National Defence, 2, 2008.

Boulton, Major Charles. *Reminiscences of the North-West Rebellions*. Toronto: Grip Printing and Publishing, 1886.

Bourget, Bishop. *Instruction pastorale de Mgr. l'évêque de Montreal sur l'indépendance et l'inviolabilité des États pontificaux. Montréal: Catholic Church, Diocese of Montréal, 1860, 1–40.*

Boyce, Jillian. "Victimization of Aboriginal People in Canada, 2014." *Juristat* 36, no. 1 (2016) Statistics Canada Catalogue no. 85-002-X.

Brown, Jennifer S. H. "A Closer Look at Fur Trade Marriage." In *From Rupert's Land to Canada: Essays in Honour of John E. Foster*, edited by Theodore Binnema, Gerhard J. Ens and R. C. MacLeod, 59–80. Edmonton: University of Alberta Press, 2001.

———. "The Métis: Genesis and Rebirth." In *Native People, Native Lands: Canadian Indians, Inuit and Métis*, edited by Bruce Alden Cox, 136–45. Montreal and Kingston: McGill-Queen's University Press, 2002.

———. *Strangers in Blood: Fur Trade Company Families in Indian Country*. Vancouver: UBC Press, 1980.

Bryce, George. *The Remarkable History of the Hudson's Bay Company Including That of the French Traders of North-Western Canada and of the North-West, XY, and Astor Fur Companies*. Toronto: William Briggs, 1900.

Bumsted, J. M., ed. *The Collected Writings of Lord Selkirk*. 2 vols. Winnipeg: Manitoba Record Society, 1984 and 1987.

———. *Fur Trade Wars: The Founding of Western Canada*. Winnipeg: Great Plains Publications, 1999.

———. *Reporting the Resistance: Alexander Begg and Joseph Hargrave on the Red River Resistance*. Winnipeg: University of Manitoba Press, 2003.

———. *Trials and Tribulations: The Red River Settlement and the Emergence of Manitoba, 1811–1870*. Winnipeg: Great Plains Publications, 2003.

Burley, David G. "'Rooster Town': Winnipeg's Lost Métis Suburb, 1900–1960." *Urban History Review* 42, no. 1 (2013): 3–25, https://id.erudit.org/iderudit/1022056ar.

Callihoo, Victoria. "Early life in Lac Ste. Anne and St. Albert in the Eighteen Seventies." *Alberta Historical Review* 1, no. 3 (November 1953): 21–26.

———. "Our Buffalo Hunts." *Alberta Historical Review* 8, no. 1 (Winter 1960): 24–25.

Camp, G. S. "The Turtle Mountain Plains-Chippewas and Metis, 1797–1935." Ph.D. diss., University of New Mexico, 1987.

Campbell, Maria. *Halfbreed*. Toronto: McClelland and Stewart, 1973.

Canada. *Correspondence Relative to the Recent Disturbances in the Red River Settlement*. London: William Clowes & Sons, 1870. https://archive.org/details/cihm_30620/page/n5.

Canada, Department of the Secretary of State. *Epitome of Parliamentary Documents in Connection with the North-West Rebellion, 1885*. Ottawa: Maclean, Roger, 1886.

Canada. *Sessional Papers*. Papers and Correspondence, Petitions. 48 Victoria, 1885, Vol. 13.

Carr, Edward Hallett. *What Is History?: The George Macaulay Trevelyan Lectures Delivered in the University of Cambridge, January–March 1961*. New York: Alfred A. Knopf, 1963.

Carter, Sarah. *Aboriginal People and Colonizers of Western Canada to 1900*. Toronto: University of Toronto Press, 1999.

Cassels, R. S. *Diary of Lieut. R. S. Cassels, North-West Field Force, 1885*. https://qormuseum.files.wordpress.com/2012/12/1885-cassels-nw-field-force-diary.pdf.

Chambers, Captain Ernest. *The Royal North-West Mounted Police: A Corps History*. Montreal: Mortimer Press, 1906.

Charette, Guillaume. *Vanishing Spaces: Memoirs of Louis Goulet*. Translated by Ray Ellenwood. Winnipeg: Éditions Bois-Brulés, 1980.

Chartrand, Paul L. A. H. "Aboriginal Rights: The Dispossession of the Métis." *Osgoode Hall Law Journal* 29, no. 3 (1991): 457–82, http://digitalcommons.osgoode.yorku.ca/ohlj/vol29/iss3/2.

———. *Manitoba's Métis Settlement Scheme of 1870*. Saskatoon: Native Law Centre, University of Saskatchewan, 1991.

Clark, Lovell. "Schultz, Sir John Christian." In *Dictionary of Canadian Biography*. University of Toronto/Université Laval, 2003. http://biographi.ca/en/bio/schultz_john_christian_12E.html.

Combet, Denis, ed. *Gabriel Dumont: Memoirs*. Translated by Lise Gaboury-Diallo. St. Boniface: Les Éditions du Blé, 2006.

Copy of the Laws and Regulations Established for the Colony of St. Laurent on the Saskatchewan. Gabriel Dumont Institute, 2008. http://www.metismuseum.ca/resource.php/12631.

Coues, Elliott, ed. *Forty Years a Fur Trader on the Upper Missouri: The Personal Narrative of Charles Larpenteur, 1833–1872*. New York: Francis P. Harper, 1898.

Coutts, Robert, and Richard Stuart, eds. *The Forks and the Battle of Seven Oaks in Manitoba History*. Winnipeg: Manitoba Historical Society, 1994.

Cowie, Isaac. *The Company of Adventurers: A Narrative of Seven Years in the Service of the Hudson's Bay Company*. Lincoln and London: University of Nebraska Press, 1993.

Cox, Ross. *Adventures on the Columbia River, Including the Narrative of a Residence of Six Years on the Western Side of the Rocky Mountains, among Various Tribes of Indians Hitherto Unknown, Together with a Journey across the American Continent*. Vol. 2. New York: J. & J. Harper, 1832.

Dales, J. H. "'National Policy' Myths, Past and Present." *Journal of Canadian Studies* 14, no. 3 (Fall 1979): 92–94.

Daniels, Harry. *We Are the New Nation*. Ottawa: Native Council of Canada, 1979.

Denison, George T. *The Struggle for Imperial Unity: Recollections and Experiences*. London: MacMillan, 1909.

Devine, Heather, and Margaret Clarke. "A History of the Métis at Buffalo Lake: A Historical Report." The Métis Nation of Alberta—Region Three, June 2009.

Dobbin, Murray. *The One-and-a-Half Men: The Story of Jim Brady and Malcolm Norris, Metis Patriots of the 20th Century*. Regina: Gabriel Dumont Institute, 1981.

Dorge, Lionel. "The Metis and the Canadian Councillors of Assiniboia." *The Beaver*, Summer 1974, 39–45.

Doxtater, Marlene M. "The Métis Women's Association of Manitoba." In *The Other Natives: The-Les Métis, 1885–1978*, vol. 2, edited by Antoine S. Lussier and D. Bruce Sealey, 171–186. Winnipeg: Manitoba Metis Federation Press and Éditions Bois-Brulés, 1978.

Dugas, Georges. *The First Canadian Woman in the Northwest, or the Story of Marie Anne Gaboury, Wife of John Baptiste Lajimonière, Who Arrived in the*

Northwest in 1807, and Died at St. Boniface at the Age of 96 Years. Translated by J. M. Morice. Winnipeg: Manitoba Free Press, 1902.
———. *Histoire de l'ouest Canadien*. Montreal: Librairie Beauchemin, 1906.
———. *Histoire Véridique des faits qui ont Préparé Le Mouvement Des Métis à la Rivière Rouge en* 1869. Montreal: Librairie Beauchemin, 1905.
———. *Un Voyageur des pays d'En-Haut*. St. Boniface: Éditions des Plaines, 1981.
Dumont, Gabriel. *Gabriel Dumont Speaks*. Translated by Michael Barnholden. Vancouver: Talon Books, 1993.
Elliott, Jack. *Hivernant Archaeology in the Cypress Hills*. M.A. thesis, University of Calgary, 1971.
Ens, Gerhard. *Homeland to Hinterland: The Changing Worlds of the Red River Métis in the Nineteenth Century*. Toronto: University of Toronto Press, 1996.
———. "Métis Agriculture in Red River during the Transition from Peasant Society to Industrial Capitalism: The Example of St. François Xavier, 1835–70." In *Swords and Ploughshares: War and Agriculture in Western Canada*, edited by R. C. McLeod, 239–62. Edmonton: University of Alberta Press, 1993.
———. "Métis Ethnicity, Personal Identity and the Development of Capitalism in the Western Interior: The Case of Johnny Brown." In *From Rupert's Land to Canada: Essays in Honour of John E. Foster*, edited by Theodore Binnema, Gerhard J. Ens and R. C. MacLeod, 161–77. Edmonton: University of Alberta Press, 2001.
———. "Métis Lands in Manitoba." *Manitoba History* 5 (Spring 1983): 2. http://www.mhs.mb.ca/docs/mb_history/05/metislands.shtml.
———. "Prologue to the Red River Resistance: Pre-liminal Politics and the Triumph of Riel." *Journal of the Canadian Historical Association* 5, no. 1 (1994): 111–23.
Erasmus, Peter. *Buffalo Days and Nights*. Calgary: Fifth House, 1999.
Falcon, Pierre. "The Battle of Seven Oaks." In *Songs of Old Manitoba*, edited by Margaret Arnett MacLeod, 1–9. Toronto: Ryerson Press, 1959.
Ferland, Marcien. *Au temps de la Prairie: L'histoire des Métis de l'Ouest canadien racontée par Auguste Vermette, neveu de Louis Riel*. Saint-Boniface, Manitoba: Les Éditions du Blé, 2000.
Fisher, John, et. al. "Address to the Lieutenant Governor, Alexander Morris." Public Meeting at Fort Qu'Appelle, 5 May 1873. In Canada, Sessional Papers No. 116, *Papers and Correspondence in Connection with Half-Breed Claims and Other Matters Relating to the North-West Territories*. 48 Victoria, 1885.
Flanagan, Thomas. *Louis "David" Riel: Prophet of the New World*. Toronto: University of Toronto Press, 1979.

Foran, Timothy Paul. "'Les Gens de Cette Place': Oblates and the Evolving Concept of Métis at Île-à-la-Crosse, 1845–1898." Ph.D. diss., University of Ottawa, 2011.

———. "Marrying Well: Catholic Matrimony and the Construction of Métis Kinship Networks, 1850–1885." Paper presented at the International Council for Canadian Studies, Ottawa, 2012.

Foster, John E. "Some Questions and Perspectives on the Problem of Métis Roots." In *The New Peoples: Being and Becoming Métis in North America*, edited by Jacqueline Peterson and Jennifer S. H. Brown, 73–91. Winnipeg: University of Manitoba Press, 1985.

———. "Wintering, the Outsider Adult Male and the Ethnogenesis of the Western Plains Métis." In *From Rupert's Land to Canada: Essays in Honour of John E. Foster*, edited by Theodore Binnema, Gerhard J. Ens and R. C. MacLeod, 179–92. Edmonton: University of Alberta Press, 2001.

Frémont, John Charles. *Memoir of My Life*. Chicago and New York: Belford, Clarke, 1887.

Galbraith, John S. "British-American Competition in the Border Fur Trade of the 1820s." *Minnesota History* (September 1959): 241–49.

Gat, Azar, and Alexander Yakobson. *Nations: The Long History and Deep Roots of Political Ethnicity and Nationalism.* Cambridge: Cambridge University Press, 2013.

Gates, Charles M., ed. *Five Fur Traders of the Northwest: Being the Narrative of Peter Pond and the Diaries of John Macdonell, Archibald N. McLeod, Hugh Faries, and Thomas Connor.* Minneapolis: University of Minnesota Press, 1933.

Gaudry, Adam. "Communing with the Dead: The 'New Métis,' Métis Identity Appropriation, and the Displacement of Living Métis Culture." *American Indian Quarterly* 42, no. 2 (Spring 2018): 162–90.

Gaudry, Adam, and Darryl Leroux. "White Settler Revisionism and Making Métis Everywhere: The Evocation of Métissage in Quebec and Nova Scotia." *Critical Ethnic Studies* 3, no. 1 (Spring 2017): 116–42.

Gellner, Ernest. *Nations and Nationalism*. Ithaca, New York: Cornell University Press, 2006.

Gibson, Dale. *Law, Life and Government at Red River.* 2 vols. Montreal and Kingston: McGill-Queen's University Press, 2015.

Gibson, Dale, and Lee Gibson. *Attorney for the Frontier: Enos Stutsman*. Winnipeg: University of Manitoba Press, 1983.

———. *Substantial Justice: Law and Lawyers in Manitoba, 1670–1970*. Winnipeg: Peguis Publishers, 1972.

Giraud, Marcel. *The Métis in the Canadian West*. Translated by George Woodcock. Edmonton: University of Alberta Press, 1986.

Glazebrook, G. P. de T., ed. *The Hargrave Correspondence, 1821–1843*. Toronto: Champlain Society, 1938; reprinted New York: Greenwood Press, 1968.

Gosman, Robert. *The Riel and Lagimodière Families in Métis Society, 1840–1860*. Manuscript Report no. 171. Ottawa: Parks Canada, 1975, 1977.

Gottfred, Angela. "What the Voyageurs Wore: Voyageur Clothing from Head to Toe, 1774–1821," *Northwest Journal* online. http://www.northwestjournal.ca/XVII1.htm.

Grant, John Francis. *A Son of the Fur Trade: The Memoirs of Johnny Grant*. Edited by Gerhard J. Ens. Edmonton: University of Alberta Press, 2008.

Greenland, Cyril. "The Life and Death of Louis Riel Part II: Surrender, Trial, Appeal and Execution." *Canadian Psychiatric Association Journal* 10, no. 4 (August 1965): 253–65.

Halkett, John. *Statement Respecting the Earl of Selkirk's Settlement upon the Red River in North America: Its Destruction in 1815 and 1816; and the Massacre of Governor Semple and His Party with Observations upon a Recent Publication Entitled "A Narrative of Occurrences in the Indian Countries, &c."* London: John Murray, 1817.

Hall, Norma Jean. "A 'Perfect Freedom': Red River as a Settler Society, 1810–1870." M.A. thesis, University of Manitoba, 2003.

———. Provisional Government of Assiniboia website, https://hallnjean2.wordpress.com.

Harmon, Daniel W. *Journal of Voyages and Travels in the Interior of North America*. Toronto: George N. Morang, 1904.

Hatt, Ken. "The North-West Scrip Commissions as Federal Policy." *Canadian Journal of Native Studies* 3, no. 1 (1983): 117–29.

———. "The Response to Directed Social Change on an Alberta Métis Colony." Ph.D. diss., University of Alberta, 1969.

Healey, W. J. *Women of Red River*. Winnipeg: Hignell Printing, 1967.

Henry, Alexander the Younger. "Henry's Journal." In *New Light on the Early History of the Greater Northwest: The Manuscript Journals of Alexander Henry, Fur Trader of the Northwest Company, and of David Thompson, Official Geographer and Explorer of the Same Company, 1799–1814*, vol. I., edited by E. Coues. New York: Francis P. Harper, 1897.

Heriot, George. *Travels through the Canadas, Containing a Description of the Picturesque Scenery on Some of the Rivers and Lakes; with an Account of the Productions, Commerce, and Inhabitants of Those Provinces*. Philadelphia: M. Carey, 1813.

Hickey, Bernard. "The Voyageurs: Images of Canada's Archetypal Frontiersmen." In *A Talent(ed) Digger, Creations, Cameos, and Essays in Honour of Anna Rutherford*, edited by Geoffrey V. Davis, et al. Amsterdam: Brill Rodopi, 1996.

Hildebrand, Walter. *The Battle of Batoche: British Small Warfare and the Entrenched Métis*. Vancouver: Talon Books, 2014.

Hind, Henry Youle. *Narrative of the Canadian Red River Exploring Expedition of 1857, and of the Assiniboine and Saskatchewan Exploring Expedition of 1858*. 2 vols. London: Spottiswoode, 1860.

Hobsbawm, E. J. *Nations and Nationalism since 1780*. Cambridge: Cambridge University Press, 1992.

Hogue, Michel. *Metis and the Medicine Line: Creating a Border and Dividing a People*. Regina: University of Regina Press, 2015.

Houston, Cecil J., and William J. Smyth. *The Sash Canada Wore: A Historical Geography of the Orange Order in Canada*. Toronto: University of Toronto Press, 1980.

Howard, Joseph Kinsey. *Strange Empire: A Narrative of the Northwest*. New York: William Morrow, 1952.

Huel, Raymond J. A., *Archbishop A.-A. Taché of St. Boniface: The "Good Fight" and the Illusive Vision."* Edmonton: University of Alberta Press, 2003.

———. "The Clergyman as Historian: The Rev. A.-G. Morice, O.M.I., and Riel Historiography." *CCHA Historical Studies* 52 (1985): 83–96.

———. "Living in the Shadow of Greatness: Louis Schmidt, Riel's Secretary." N.d., https://www.scribd.com/document/192324731/Schmidt-Louis-Riel-s-Secretary.

———. "The Oblates of Mary Immaculate in the Canadian North West: Reflections on 150 Years of Service, 1845–1995." *Western Oblate Studies* 4 (1996): 15–45.

———. "The Oblates, the Métis, and 1885: The Breakdown of Traditional Relationships." *CCHA Historical Studies* 56 (1989): 9–29.

———. *Proclaiming the Gospel to the Indians and the Métis*. Edmonton: University of Alberta Press, 1996.

Huel, Raymond J. A., and George F. G. Stanley, eds. *The Collected Writings of Louis Riel*. Edmonton: University of Alberta Press, 1985.

Hutchinson, Dave. "Métis Veterans: Remembrances." Draft. November 28, 1993. http://www.metismuseum.ca/resource.php/07190.

Innis, Harold A. *The Fur Trade in Canada*. Toronto: University of Toronto Press, reprinted 2001.

Irving, Washington. *Astoria; or Enterprise beyond the Rocky Mountains*. Paris: Beaudry's European Library, 1836.

Jamieson, Col. Frederick C. "The Edmonton Hunt." *Alberta Historical Review* 1, no. 1 (April 1953): 21–33.

Jones, Gwynneth C. D. "The Historic Métis in Southern and Central Alberta." Unpublished report, 2009.

———. *Historical Profile of the Great Slave Lake Area's Mixed European-Indian Ancestry Community*. Ottawa: Department of Justice Canada, Research and Statistics Division, 2005.

———. "The Métis of the South Slave Area of the Northwest Territories." Unpublished report, 2000.

———. "The Métis of Southern Manitoba in the Nineteenth Century: A Historical Report." Unpublished report, 2005.

Jones, Gwynneth C. D., and Public History Inc. "Characteristics of pre-1850 and Métis Families in the Vicinity of Sault Ste. Marie, 1860–1925." Unpublished report, 1998.

Keating, William H. *Narrative of an Expedition to the Source of St. Peter's River, Lake Winnepeek, Lake of the Woods, &c, Performed in the Year 1823*. Vol. 2. London: Geo. B. Whittaker, 1825.

Kennicott, Robert. "A Rubbabo Journal for Friends at Home." In *Transactions of the Chicago Academy of Sciences*, Vol. 1. Ann Arbour: The Academy, 1869.

Knafla, Louis A., and Jonathan Swainger, eds. *Laws and Societies: In the Canadian Prairie West, 1670–1940*. Vancouver: UBC Press, 2005.

Knox, Olive. "The Question of Louis Riel's Insanity." *Manitoba Historical Society* 3, no. 6 (1949–50). http://www.mhs.mb.ca/docs/transactions/3/rielinsanity.shtml.

LaFleche, François Richer. "Letter dated September 4, 1851." In *Rapport sur les Missions du Diocèse de Québec*, Mars, 1853, No. 10. Quebec: Des Presses a Vapeur D'Augustin Côté, 1853, 44–70.

Lagassé, Jean H. *The People of Indian Ancestry*. Ottawa: Dept. of the Secretary of State, 1968.

Lalonde, André N. "Colonization Companies and the North-West Rebellion." In *1885 and After: Native Society in Transition*, edited by Barron, F. Laurie and James B. Waldram, 54–65. Regina: University of Regina, 1986.

Lamb, R. E. "Friction between Ontario and Quebec Caused by the Risings of Louis Riel." Ph.D. diss., University of Ottawa, 1953.

———. "Troops to Red River." *Mid America: An Historical Quarterly*, Volume XXXIX, New Series, Vol. XXVIII, (1957): 21–38.

Lamb, W. Kaye, ed. *Journal of a Voyage on the North West Coast of North America during the Years 1811, 1812, 1813 and 1814*, by Gabriel Franchère. Translated by Wessie T. Lamb. Toronto: Champlain Society, 1969.

———, ed. *Sixteen Years in Indian Country: The Journal of Daniel Williams Harmon 1800–1816*. Toronto: Macmillan, 1957.

Lambton, John George, Earl of Durham. *Report on the Affairs of British North America*. London: House of Commons, 1839.

Latham, E. *Famous Sayings and Their Authors*. London: Swan Sonnenschein, 1906.

Leroux, Darryl. "Self-Made Métis." *Maisonneuve*, 69 (Fall 2018): 31–39.

Lytwyn, Victor P. "In the Shadows of the Honourable Company: Nicholas Chatelain and the Métis of Fort Frances." In *Contours of a People: Metis Family, Mobility, and History*, edited by Nicole St-Onge, Carolyn

Podruchny and Brenda Macdougall, 194–229. Norman: University of Oklahoma Press, 2012.

MacArthur, Peter. "The Red River Rebellion," *Manitoba Pageant* 18, no. 3 (Spring 1973). http://www.mhs.mb.ca/docs/pageant/18/redriverrebellion.shtml.

Macdougall, Brenda. "'The Comforts of Married Life': Métis Family Life, Labour, and the Hudson's Bay Company." *Labour/Le Travail*, 61 (Spring 2008): 9–39.

———. *One of the Family: Metis Culture in Nineteenth-Century Northwestern Saskatchewan.* Vancouver: UBC Press, 2010.

Macdougall, Brenda, and Nicole St. Onge. "Rooted in Mobility: Metis Buffalo Hunting Brigades." *Manitoba Historical Society* 71. (Winter 2013). http://www.mhs.mb.ca/docs/mb_history/71/metisbrigades.shtml.

MacEwan, Grant. "Victoria Callihoo: Granny." In *Mighty Women: Stories of Western Canadian Pioneers.* Vancouver/Toronto: Greystone, 1995.

Macfarlane, Christine. "'Unfortunate Women of My Class': Prostitution in Winnipeg, 1870–1910." M.A. thesis, University of Manitoba/University of Winnipeg, 2002.

Mackenzie, Alexander. *Voyages from Montreal through the Continent of North America to the Frozen and Pacific Oceans in 1789 and 1793 with an Account of the Rise and State of the Fur Trade*. Vol. 1. New York: A.S. Barnes, 1903.

MacLeod, Margaret Arnett, ed. *Songs of Old Manitoba*. Toronto: Ryerson Press, 1959.

MacLeod, Margaret Arnett, and W. L. Morton. *Cuthbert Grant of Grantown: Warden of the Plains of Red River.* Toronto: McClelland and Stewart, 1963.

Mailhot, Philippe R. "Ritchot's Resistance: Abbe Noel Joseph Ritchot and the Creation and Transformation of Manitoba." Ph.D. diss., University of Manitoba, 1986.

Martin, Chester. *Lord Selkirk's Work in Canada*. Toronto: Oxford University Press, 1916.

McGuigan, Peter. "1816: A Year without Summer." *The Beaver*, June/July 2003, https://www.canadashistory.ca/explore/environment/1816-the-year-without-summer.

McLachlin, Beverley. "Louis Riel: Patriot Rebel." *Manitoba Law Journal* 35, no. 1 (2011): 1–13.

McLean, Don. *1885: Métis Rebellion or Government Conspiracy?* Winnipeg: Pemmican Publications, 1985.

McLean, John. *Notes of a Twenty-Five Years' Service in the Hudson's Bay Territory*. 2 vols. London: Richard Bentley, 1849.

Milton, Viscount, and W. B. Cheadle. *The North-West Passage by Land.* London: Cassell, Petter and Galpin, 1865. Reprinted Toronto: Coles Publishing Company, 1970.

Moore, Thomas. *Thomas Moore's Complete Poetical Works*. Princeton: T. Y. Crowell and Company, 1895.

Morice, A.-G., O.M.I. *A Critical History of the Red River Insurrection after Official Documents and Non-Catholic Sources*. Winnipeg: Canadian Publishers, 1935.

———. *Dictionnaire Historique Des Canadiens et Des Métis Français de l'Ouest*. Montreal: Granger Frères, 1980.

———. *History of the Catholic Church in Western Canada: From Lake Superior to the Pacific 1659–1895*. Toronto: Musson Book, 1910.

———. *La Race Métisse: Étude critique en marge d'un livre recent*. Winnipeg: Chez l'Auteur, 1938.

Morton, Arthur S. "Forrest Oakes, Charles Boyer, Joseph Fulton, and Peter Pangman in the North-West, 1765–1793." *Proceedings and Transactions of the Royal Society of Canada*, 3d ser., sec. II, 31 (1937): 91–95.

———. *A History of the Canadian West to 1870–71*. Toronto: University of Toronto Press, 1973.

Morton, W. L., ed. *Alexander Begg's Red River Journal*. New York: Greenwood Press, 1969.

———. *Manitoba: The Birth of a Province*. Vol. 1. Manitoba Record Society Publications: 1965.

Narratives of John Pritchard, Pierre Chrysologue Pambrun and Frederick Damien Heurter Respecting the Aggressions of the North-West Company against the Earl of Selkirk's Settlement upon Red River. London: John Murray, 1819.

Nelson, George. *My First Years in the Fur Trade: The Journals of 1802–1804*. Edited by Laura Peers and Theresa Schenck. Montreal: McGill-Queen's University Press, 2002.

Nicollet, Joseph N. *Joseph N. Nicollet on the Plains and Prairies: The Expeditions of 1838–39, with Journals, Letters, and Notes on the Dakota Indians*. Edited and translated by Edmund C. Bray and Martha Coleman Bray. Saint Paul: Minnesota Historical Society, 1976.

Nute, Grace Lee. *Documents Relating to Northwest Missions 1815–1827*. Saint Paul: Minnesota Historical Society, 1942.

———. *The Voyageur*. Minneapolis: Minnesota Historical Society Press, 1987.

———. *The Voyageur's Highway: Minnesota's Border Lake Land*. St. Paul: Minnesota Historical Society Press, 1941, 2002.

O'Byrne, Nicole C. "'No other weapon except organization': The Métis Association of Alberta and the 1938 Metis Population Betterment Act." *Journal of the CHA*, New Series 24, no. 2 (2013): 311–52.

Oliver, E. H. *The Canadian North-West: Its Early Development and Legislative Records*. Vol. 1. Ottawa: Government Printing Bureau, 1915.

Oppen, William A. "The Riel Rebellions: A Cartographic History." *Cartographica*, Monograph no. 21–22, supplement no. 1–2 to *Canadian Cartographer* 15 (1978).

Ouimet, Adolphe. *La Verité sur la Question Métisse au Nord-Ouest*. Montreal: 1889. http://peel.library.ualberta.ca/bibliography/1517.html.

Parkin, George R. *Sir John A. Macdonald*. Toronto: Morang, 1910.

Parkman, Francis. *The Oregon Trail: Sketches of Prairie Rocky Mountain Life*. http://www.gutenberg.org/files/1015/1015-h/1015-h.htm.

Payment, Diane. *The Free People–Li Gens Libres: A History of the Métis Community of Batoche, Saskatchewan*. Calgary: University of Calgary Press, 2009.

———. "Native Society and Economy in Transition at the Forks, 1850–1900." Environment Canada, Microfiche Report Series 383.

Peterson, Jacqueline. "Many Roads to Red River: Métis Genesis in the Great Lakes Region, 1680–1815." In *The New Peoples: Being and Becoming Métis in North America*, edited by Jacqueline Peterson and Jennifer S. H. Brown, 37–71. Winnipeg: University of Manitoba Press, 1985.

Piper, Liza. "Colloquial Meteorology." In *Method and Meaning in Canadian Environmental History*, edited by Alan MacEachern and William J. Turkel, 102–123. Toronto: Nelson, 2009.

Podruchny, Carolyn. *Making the Voyageur World: Travelers and Traders in the North American Fur Trade*. Toronto: University of Toronto Press, 2006.

Pope, Sir Joseph, ed. *Correspondence of Sir John A. Macdonald*. Toronto: Oxford University Press, 1921.

Praxis Research Associates. "Historic Métis in the Rainy River and Kenora Districts of Ontario: Fishing Practices and Off-Reserve Residence." Ontario Ministry of Natural Resources, 2002.

Racette, Calvin. *Métis Development and the Canadian West*. Saskatoon: Gabriel Dumont Institute, 1985.

Radforth, Ian. "Celebrating the Suppression of the North-West Resistance of 1885: The Toronto Press and the Militia Volunteers." *Social History* 47, no. 95 (November 2014): 601–39.

Radisson, Pierre Esprit. *Voyages of Peter Esprit Radisson, Being an Account of His Travels and Experiences among the North American Indians, from 1652–1684*. Boston: Prince Society, 1885.

Ray, Arthur J. "Diffusion of Diseases in the Western Interior of Canada, 1830–1850." *Geographical Review* 66, no. 2 (April 1976): 139–57.

———. "An Economic History of the Robinson Treaties Area before 1860." Unpublished report, 1998.

———. *Indians in the Fur Trade: Their Roles as Trappers, Hunters, and Middlemen in the Lands Southwest of Hudson Bay*, 1660–1870. Toronto: University of Toronto Press, 1974.

———. "Métis Economic Communities and Settlements in the 19th Century." Unpublished report, 2005.

Reid, Jennifer I. M. "Faire Place à une Race Métisse: Colonial Crisis and the Vision of Louis Riel." In *Religion and Global Culture: New Terrain in the Study of Religion and the Work of Charles H. Long*, edited by Jennifer I. M. Reid. Lanham: Lexington Books, 2003.

———. *Louis Riel and the Creation of Modern Canada: Mythic Discourse and the Postcolonial State*. Albuquerque: University of New Mexico Press, 2008.

Report of the Royal Commission on Aboriginal Peoples. Ottawa: Canada Communication Group, 1996.

Report of the Select Committee on the Causes of the Difficulties in the North-West Territory in 1869–70. Ottawa: I.B. Taylor, 1874.

Riel, Louis. *The Diaries of Louis Riel*, edited by Thomas Flanagan. Edmonton: Hurtig Publishers, 1976.

Rivard, Ron, and Catherine Littlejohn. *The History of the Métis of Willow Bunch*. Saskatoon: Rivard & Littlejohn, 2003.

Roberts, A. C. "The Surveys in the Red River Settlement in 1869." Supplement to *Canadian Surveyor* 24 (June 1970): 238–48.

Robertson, James Tyler. "The 'Long Knives,' the 'Sons of Nature,' and 'Our Province': Rev. John Strachan's Views on the Indigenous People and the Motives for the American Invasion of Upper Canada, 1812–1814." In *Historical Papers*, edited by Brian Gobbett, Bruce L. Guenther and Robynne Rogers Healey, 41–58. Canadian Society of Church History, 2009. https://csch-sche.ca/historical-papers/historical-papers-canadian-society-of-church-history/2009-historical-papers.

Robinson, H. M. *The Great Fur Land, or, Sketches of Life in the Hudson's Bay Territory*. New York: G.P. Putnam's Sons, 1879.

Ronaghan, Allen. "The Archibald Administration in Manitoba, 1870–1872." Ph.D. diss., University of Manitoba, 1987.

———. "Charles Mair and the North-West Emigration Aid Society." *Manitoba History* 14 (Autumn 1987), http://www.mhs.mb.ca/docs/mb_history/14/emigrationaidsociety.shtml.

———. "James Farquharson—Agent and Agitator." *Manitoba History* 17 (Spring 1989). http://www.mhs.mb.ca/docs/mb_history/17/farquharson_j.shtml.

———. "The Confrontation at Rivière aux Îlets de Bois." *Prairie Forum* 14, no. 1 (Spring 1989): 1–10.

Ross, Alexander. *The Fur Hunters of the Far West: A Narrative of Adventures in the Oregon and Rocky Mountains*. Vol. 2. London: Smith, Elder, 1855.

———. *The Red River Settlement: Its Rise, Progress, and Present State with Some Account of the Native Races and Its General History, to the Present Day*. London: Smith, Elder, 1856.

Sawchuk, Joe. *The Metis of Manitoba: Reformulation of an Ethnic Identity*. Toronto: Peter Martin Associates, 1978.

Sawchuck, Joe, Patricia Sawchuck and Theresa Ferguson. *Metis Land Rights in Alberta: A Political History*. Edmonton: Metis Association of Alberta, 1981.

Schmidt, Louis. "Memoires de Louis Schmidt." *Le Patriote de L'Ouest* (Duck Lake, Saskatchewan), January 25, February 1, 8, 15, 22 and 27, 1912. http://peel.library.ualberta.ca/newspapers/PDW/.

Sealey, Bruce, and Antoine S. Lussier. *The Métis: Canada's Forgotten People*. Winnipeg: Pemmican Publications, 1975.

Shulman, Martin, and Don McLean. "Lawrence Clarke: Architect of Revolt." *Canadian Journal of Native Studies* 3, no. 1 (1983): 57–68.

Siggins, Maggie. *Riel: A Life of Revolution*. Toronto: HarperCollins, 1994.

Slobodin, Richard. *Metis of the Mackenzie District*. Ottawa: Canadian Research Centre for Anthropology, 1966.

Smith, Anthony D. *The Ethnic Origins of Nations*. Oxford: Blackwell Publishers, 1986.

Smits, David D. "The Frontier Army and the Destruction of the Buffalo: 1865–1883." *Western Historical Quarterly* 25, no. 3 (Autumn, 1994): 312–38.

Sprague, D. N. "Dispossession vs. Accommodation in Plaintiff vs. Defendant Accounts of Métis Dispersal from Manitoba, 1870–1881." In *The Western Métis: Profile of a People*, edited by Patrick Douaud, 125–44. Regina: University of Regina Press, 2007.

———. *Canada and the Métis, 1869–1885*. Waterloo: Wilfred Laurier University Press, 1988.

Sprague, D. N., and R. P. Frye. *The Genealogy of the First Métis Nation: The Development and Dispersal of the Red River Settlement, 1820–1900*. Winnipeg: Pemmican Publications, 1983.

Sprenger, Herman. "The Métis Nation: Buffalo Hunting versus Agriculture in the Red River Settlement, 1810–1870." In *Native People, Native Lands: Canadian Indians, Inuit and Métis*, edited by Bruce Alden Cox, 120–35. Montreal and Kingston: McGill-Queen's University Press, 2002.

Spry, Irene M. "The Ethnic Voice: The Memoirs of G. W. Sanderson 1846–1936." *Canadian Ethnic Studies* 17, no. 2 (1985): 115–34.

———. "The Metis and Mixed-Bloods of Rupert's Land before 1879." In *The New Peoples: Being and Becoming Métis in North America*, edited by Jacqueline Peterson and Jennifer S. H. Brown, 95–118. Winnipeg: University of Manitoba Press, 1985.

———. "The Transition from a Nomadic to a Settled Economy in Western Canada, 1856–96." Ottawa: Royal Society of Canada, 1968.

St-Onge, Nicole. "The Dissolution of a Métis Community: Pointe à Grouette, 1860–1885." *Studies in Political Economy* 18, no. 1 (1985): 149–72, DOI: 10.1080/19187033.1985.11675607.

———. *Saint-Laurent, Manitoba: Evolving Métis Identities, 1850–1914*. Regina: University of Regina, 2004.

St-Onge, Nicole, Carolyn Podruchny and Brenda Macdougall, eds. *Contours of a People: Metis Family, Mobility, and History*. Norman: University of Oklahoma Press, 2012.

Stanley, George F. G. *The Birth of Western Canada: A History of the Riel Rebellions*. Toronto: University of Toronto Press, 1963.

Stobie, Margaret R. *The Other Side of Rebellion: The Remarkable Story of Charles Bremner and His Furs*. Edmonton: NeWest Press, 1986.

Stonechild, Blair. "The Iron Alliance and Dominion of the Northern Plains, 1690 to 1885: Implications for the Concept of Iskunican." Unpublished report, 2003.

Taché, Monsignor. *Sketch of the North-West of America*. Translated by Captain D. R. Cameron. Montreal: John Lovell, 1870; French publication, 1868.

Teillet, Jean. *Métis Law in Canada*. Looseleaf, annually updated. Vancouver and Toronto: Pape Salter Teillet, LLP, 2nd edition, 2017.

Thompson, David. *Narrative 1784–1812*. Edited by Richard Glover. Toronto: Champlain Society, 1962.

Thompson, Napoleon. *The Gibbet of Regina: The Truth about Riel: Sir John A. Macdonald and His Cabinet before Public Opinion by One Who Knows*. New York: Thompson & Moreau, 1886.

Thornton, John P. "The National Policy, the Department of the Interior and Original Settlers: Land Claims of the Métis, Green Lake, Saskatchewan, 1909–1930." M.A. thesis, University of Saskatchewan, 1997.

Tough, Frank. "Aboriginal Rights versus the Deed of Surrender: The Legal Rights of Native Peoples and Canada's Acquisition of the Hudson's Bay Company Territory." *Prairie Forum* 17, no. 2 (Fall 1992): 225–50.

———. *As Their Natural Resources Fail: Native Peoples and the Economic History of Northern Manitoba, 1870–1930*. Vancouver: UBC Press, 1996.

Tough, Frank, and Erin McGregor. "'The Rights to the Land May Be Transferred': Archival Records as Colonial Text—A Narrative of Métis Scrip." *Canadian Review of Comparative Literature* 34, no. 1 (2007). https://journals.library.ualberta.ca/crcl/index.php/crcl/issue/view/687.

Trémaudan, A. H. de. "The Execution of Thomas Scott." *Canadian Historical Review* 6 (1925): 225–35.

———. *Histoire de la nation métisse dans l'ouest Canadien*. Montreal: Éditions Albert Lévesque, 1935. Translated by Elizabeth Maguet as *Hold High Your Heads: History of the Métis Nation of Canada*. Pemmican Publications, Winnipeg: 1982.

———. "Louis Riel and the Fenian Raid of 1871." *Canadian Historical Review* 4, no. 2 (1923): 132–44.

———. "Notes and Comments: Louis Riel's Account of the Capture of Fort Garry, 1870." *Canadian Historical Review* 5, no. 1 (1924): 146–59.

Van Kirk, Sylvia. *Many Tender Ties: Women in Fur-Trade Society, 1670–1870*. Norman: University of Oklahoma Press, 1980.

Vrooman, Nicholas. "Cree, Assiniboine, Ojibwa, and Michif: The Nehiyaw Pwat Confederacy/Iron Alliance in Montana." Paper presented at the Montana Historical Society Annual Meeting, September 19, 2014. https://www.scribd.com/document/369568302/Nehiyaw-Pwat-The-Iron-Alliance-Cree-Assiniboine-Ojibwa-Michif.

Waite, P. B. *Canada 1874–1896: Arduous Destiny*. Toronto: McClelland and Stewart, 1971.

Wallace, William Stewart. *Documents Relating to the North West Company*. Toronto: Champlain Society, 1934.

Warren, William W. "History of the Ojibway People." Saint Paul: Minnesota Historical Society, 1885; 2nd edition, 2009.

W. B. Coltman Report Transcription. Library and Archives Canada. http://data2.archives.ca/e/e447/e011163878-t.pdf.

Weinstein, John. *Quiet Revolution West: The Rebirth of Métis Nationalism*. Calgary: Fifth House, 2008.

White, Bruce M. "Cadotte, Joseph." In *Dictionary of Canadian Biography*. University of Toronto/Université Laval, 2003. http://www.biographi.ca/en/bio/cadotte_joseph_6E.html.

White, Richard. *The Middle Ground: Indians, Empires, and Republics in the Great Lakes Region, 1650–1815*. Cambridge: Cambridge University Press, 2010.

Widder, Keith. *Battle for the Soul: Métis Children Encounter Evangelical Protestants at Mackinaw Mission, 1823–1837*. East Lansing: Michigan State University Press, 1999.

Wilcocke, Samuel Hull, ed. *Report of the proceedings connected with the disputes between the Earl of Selkirk, and the North-West Company, at the assizes held at York in Upper Canada, October 1818: From minutes taken in court*. Montreal: James Lane & Nahum Mower, 1819.

Witgen, Michael. *An Infinity of Nations: How the Native New World Shaped Early North America*. Philadelphia: University of Pennsylvania Press, 2012.

Woodcock, George. *Gabriel Dumont: The Métis Chief and His Lost World*. Edmonton: Hurtig Publishers, 1975.

———. "Grant, Cuthbert." In *Dictionary of Canadian Biography*. University of Toronto/Université Laval, 2003. http://www.biographi.ca/en/bio/grant_cuthbert_1854_8E.html.

Woodington, Henry. "Diary of a Prisoner in Red River Rebellion." *Niagara Historical Society Publications* 25 (1913): 32–56.

Wright, Barry, and Susan Binnie, eds. *Canadian State Trials*. Vol. 3: *Political Trials and Security Measures, 1840–1914*. Toronto: University of Toronto Press, 2009.

Zeilig, Ken, and Victoria Zeilig. *St. Madeleine: Community without a Town, Métis Elders in Interview*. Winnipeg: Pemmican Publications, 1987.

Archival Sources

AM	Archives of Manitoba, Winnipeg
GA	Glenbow Archives, Calgary
HBCA	Hudson's Bay Company Archives, Archives of Manitoba, Winnipeg
LAC	Library and Archives Canada, Ottawa
OMI	Fonds oblat de la province Alberta-Saskatchewan
PAA	Provincial Archives of Alberta
SHMF	Société historique métisse fonds, Centre du Patrimoine, Société Historique de Saint-Boniface, St. Boniface, Manitoba
SP	Selkirk Papers

Archibald, Adams G. (Lieutenant-Governor), Correspondence and Papers 1869–1873, Despatch Books 1871–1872 and Register of Letters Patent 1870–1872, M1-3, M781, AM.

Brady, James, Fonds, GA.

Commission of Inquiry into the Administration of Justice as to Infant Lands and Estates, 20 December 1881. Records of the Legislative Assembly, RG 7, B1, Sessional Papers, Box 12, File 3, AM.

Dewdney, Edgar, Fonds, GA.

Dion, Joseph, Fonds, GA.

Early Canadiana Online, http://eco.canadiana.ca/

Evidence and Proceedings Half-Breed Commission, Edmonton, Alberta, February 25, 1935. James Brady Fonds, M-125-38a, GA. https://www.glenbow.org/collections/search/findingAids/archhtm/brady.cf.

Fleury, Patrice. Reminiscences, 1924. A-515, Saskatchewan Archives Board, http://digital.scaa.sk.ca/ourlegacy/permalink/27413.

Hardisty, Richard C., Fonds, GA.

Internet Archive. https://archive.org/

Journal of Peter Garrioch, Red River, 1843–47. MG9, A78-3, AM.

Laurie, P. G., Diary, 1869, 1870, E. L. Storer Papers, Saskatchewan Archives Board.

Macdonald, Sir John A., Papers, MG 26 A, LAC.

Morris Papers, AM.

Nor'Wester, https://digitalcollections.lib.umanitoba.ca.

"Samuel O'Connell Reminiscence, 1875." SC547, Montana Historical Society, Helena.

Peel's Prairie Provinces, http://peel.library.ualberta.ca/index.html, University of Alberta.

RCMP Records, LAC.

"Report from Dr. Kittson of the North-West Mounted Police Stationed at Fort Macleod, Concerning the Insufficiency of Rations Issued to the Indians of the Northwest Territories, 1880–1915." RG 10, reel C-10126, vol. 3726, file 24811, LAC.

Riel Rebellion Telegram, GA.

Selkirk Papers, AM.

Smith, Marie Rose. "The Adventures of the Wild West of 1870." Undated manuscript. M1154, file 3, GA.

Smith, Marie Rose. "Eighty Years on the Plains." M-1154-4, GA. https://www.glenbow.org/collections/search/findingAids/archhtm/smithmr.cfm.

Teillet Family Papers, private collection.

Virtual Museum of Métis History and Culture, Gabriel Dumont Institute, www.metismuseum.ca.

Index

Note: *Page references in italics indicate maps and illustrations.*

Homeland of the Métis Nation